NEW
MATHS
IN ACTION

S3³

Members of the
Mathematics in Action Group
associated with this book:

D. Brown
R.D. Howat
G. Meikle
E.C.K. Mullan
R. Murray
K. Nisbet

Published in 2004 by:
Nelson Thornes Ltd
Delta Place
27 Bath Road
CHELTENHAM
GL53 7TH
United Kingdom

07 08 / 10 9 8 7 6 5

A catalogue record of this book is available from the British Library

ISBN 978 0 7487 8540 7

Illustrations by Oxford Designers and Illustrators
Page make-up by Tech-Set Ltd

Printed and bound in Croatia by Zrinski

Acknowledgements

Ben Curtis/Press Association: 125; Corel 5 (NT): 272; Corel 17 (NT): 11; Corel 28 (NT): 20 bottom; Corel 417: 136; Corel 423: 268; Corel 445 (NT): 137; Corel 584: 175; Corel 608 (NT): 73; Digital Vision 1 (NT): 169; Digital Vision 7 (NT): 8, 9; Digital Vision 9 (NT): 27; Digital Vision 12 (NT): 163; Kazuyoshi Nomachi/Science Photo Library: 19; NASA: 160; Photodisc 22 (NT): 34; Photodisc 45 (NT): 3; Photodisc 51 (NT): 77, 245; Photodisc 55 (NT): 140, 223; Science and Society Picture Library/Claire Richardson: 20 top; Science Photo Library: 41, 145.

The publishers have made every effort to contact copyright holders but apologise if any have been overlooked.

Contents

Introduction

This book has been specifically written to address the needs of the candidate attempting the Standard Grade Mathematics course at Credit Level. It is a two-year course and Book S4[3] will be required to complete the syllabus.

The content has been organised to ensure that the running order of the topics is consistent with companion volume S3[2], aimed at General Level candidates. This will permit the flexibility of dual use, and facilitate changing sections during the course if required.

Throughout the book, chapters follow a similar structure.

- A review section at the start of each chapter ensures that knowledge required for the rest of the chapter has been revised.
- Necessary learning outcomes are demonstrated and exercises are provided to consolidate the new knowledge and skills. The ideas are developed and further exercises provide an opportunity to integrate knowledge and skills in various problem solving contexts.
- Challenges, brainstormers and investigations are peppered throughout the chapters to provide an opportunity for some investigative work for the more curious.
- Each chapter ends with a recap of the learning outcomes and a revision exercise which tests whether or not the required knowledge and skills addressed by the chapter have been picked up.

The final chapter of the book contains revision exercises, one for each of the 13 preceding chapters.

A teacher's resource pack provides additional material such as further practice and homework exercises and a preparation for assessment exercise for each chapter.

1 Calculations and the calculator

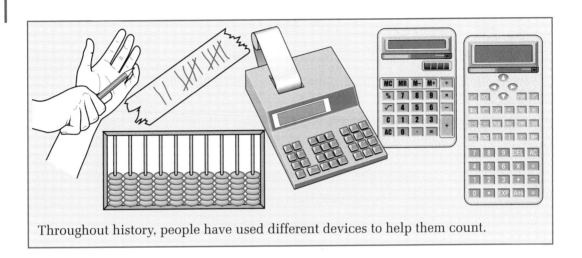

Throughout history, people have used different devices to help them count.

1 REVIEW

◀◀ Exercise 1.1

Calculate:

1 **a** $7·47 + 11·8$ **b** $4·31 − 1·72$ **c** $31·8 × 7$ **d** $61·2 ÷ 9$
   e $35 − 18·93$ **f** $26 + 1·46$ **g** $7·08 × 6$ **h** $37 ÷ 5$
   i $9·4 × 11$ **j** $49·08 ÷ 12$

2 Find the value of:
   a $130 × 60$ **b** $1040 × 20$ **c** $550 × 900$ **d** $18\,000 ÷ 900$
   e $5600 ÷ 140$ **f** $4\text{ million} ÷ 200$ **g** $120\,000 ÷ 150$ **h** $3300 ÷ 165$
   i $990 × 110$ **j** $4920 ÷ 120$

3 Calculate the value of:
   a $8·54 × 10$ **b** $4·68 × 100$ **c** $0·03 × 1000$
   d $23·51 ÷ 100$ **e** $0·2 ÷ 100$ **f** $3·86 × 20$
   g $0·97 × 500$ **h** $14·8 × 800$ **i** $60·5 × 6000$
   j $0·049 × 70$ **k** $9·6 ÷ 600$ **l** $1·12 ÷ 70$
   m $17 ÷ 400$ **n** $15 ÷ 3000$ **o** $2·45 × 0·1$

4 Work out the value of:
   a $7 + 3 × 9$ **b** $14 − 2 × 5$ **c** $4 × (3 + 2)$ **d** $9 × 2 + 3 × 5$
   e $3 × 4^2$ **f** $(3 × 4)^2$ **g** $8 + 12 ÷ 4$ **h** $10 − 4 ÷ 2$
   i $13 − 4 + 6$ **j** $\frac{1}{2}$ of $20 − 3$

5 Write down the value of:

a 9^2	**b** 1^2	**c** 13^2	**d** 40^2
e $\sqrt{16}$	**f** $\sqrt{121}$	**g** $\sqrt{\frac{1}{4}}$	**h** $\sqrt{900}$

6 $\pi = 3\cdot141\,592\,654$ (to 9 decimal places). Round π to:

a 3 decimal places   **b** 2 decimal places   **c** 1 decimal place.

7

Fly to the USA

Exchange rate: £1 = \$1·5964

Change the following amounts to dollars (to 2 decimal places):

a £10   **b** £100   **c** £1000

8 a In 1989 the population of the UK was fifty-seven million, two hundred and eighteen thousand (to the nearest thousand). Write this number in figures.

b The area of the UK is 244 755 km². Calculate the average number of people per km², to the nearest whole number.

9 Estimate, then calculate, correct to 2 decimal places:

a $\dfrac{530 \times 64}{213}$ **b** $4\cdot612 + 9\cdot452$

c $14\cdot3 \times 7\cdot66 \times 2\cdot02$ **d** $\frac{19}{3} + \frac{25}{6}$

Investigations

1 In the following puzzle you have to press the 'equals' button after each digit. Can you link the digits 1 to 9 in order by the operations '+' or '×' so that, after each 'equals', the calculator displays an odd number?

Examples of early failures: $1 = \times 2 = \dots$ fails because the result is 2 (even)

$1 = + 2 = + 3 = \dots$ fails because the result is 6 (even)

a Comment on the winning strategy.

b What number is displayed after you key in '9 ='?

2 Explore these sums with your calculator.

a i $1 =$

$1 + 2 + 1 =$

$1 + 2 + 3 + 2 + 1 =$

ii From the pattern of answers, can you now work these out?

$1 + 2 + 3 + \dots + 99 + 100 + 99 + \dots + 3 + 2 + 1$

b i $1 =$

$1 + 3 =$

$1 + 3 + 5 =$

ii What is the sum of the first 500 odd numbers?

iii What, then, is the sum of the first 500 even numbers, starting with 2?

c sum i $1 - 3 + 5 - \dots$ for 100 terms

ii $1 - 2 + 3 - 4 + \dots$ for 100 terms

2 Significant figures

The significant figures in a number are those that give us an idea of
i the value of a number or   **ii** the accuracy to which it was made.

This picture shows people queuing for concert tickets.
Organisers said that 963 people queued altogether.
There are 3 significant figures here.
The 9 adds the most value (900).
It is the most significant digit.

Rounded to the nearest ten there are 960 people.
Now there are only 2 significant figures.

Rounded to the nearest thousand there are 1000 people.
Now there is only 1 significant figure.

Note: it appears that the trailing zeros are not significant,
    but in some contexts they are.

For example, the 10 on a 10 pence coin has 2 significant figures,
as there are exactly 10 pence, not 9 or 11!
There are exactly 360° in a revolution.
There are 3 significant figures here.

When working with whole numbers you usually need to know the context before
you can state how many significant figures there are in a number which has trailing
zeros.

When working with decimals, every digit after the most significant is also
significant. (In this case only leading zeros are not significant.)

Examples: To 1 significant figure:
          $27 = 30$ (1 s.f.) $685 = 700$ (1 s.f.)
          $0.733 = 0.7$ (1 s.f.) $0.000\ 429\ 6 = 0.0004$ (1 s.f.)
          To 2 significant figures:
          $2451 = 2500$ (2 s.f.) $0.0148 = 0.015$ (2 s.f.)
          $0.504 = 0.50$ (2 s.f.) $8.0123 = 8.0$ (2 s.f.)

Exercise 2.1

1 Round each of the following to 1 significant figure:
  a 2345   **b** 4760   **c** 149   **d** 37 228   **e** 53
  f 2·88   **g** 39·02   **h** 0·621   **i** 0·009 07   **j** 0·098 76

2 Round each of the following to 2 significant figures:
  a 5273   **b** 189   **c** 484·5   **d** 22 176   **e** 3·141 59
  f 0·832   **g** 0·001 75   **h** 7·015   **i** 0·8977   **j** 0·054 32

3 Estimate, then calculate, correct to 2 significant figures:
  a $24 \div 7$ **b** 1.5×0.97 **c** $2 \div 9$ **d** $(4.6)^2$

4 Estimate, then calculate, correct to 3 significant figures:

    a $1{\cdot}47 \times 6{\cdot}85$ **b** $\frac{292}{3}$ **c** $(13{\cdot}8)^2$ **d** $773 \times 15{\cdot}2 \div 3{\cdot}14$

5 Cian measured the diameter of his Frisbee and found it was 23·4 cm.

    On his calculator he worked out that the area of the Frisbee was 422·732 707 5 cm².

    a How many significant figures are in the data?

    b To what number of significant figures should the answer be given?

    c Write down the area, rounded appropriately.

6 i Estimate the area of these shapes by rounding the data to 1 significant figure.

  ii Calculate the area of each shape, rounding to an appropriate number of
     significant figures.

    a
    b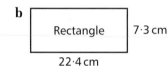
    c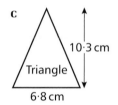

7 Estimate, then calculate:

    a the number of minutes in 16 hours

    b the number of days in 39 weeks

    c the cost of one book if 56 books cost £462

    d the average of 17·7 kg, 18·4 kg and 20·3 kg.

---

3 Calculator practice

Scientific calculators are programmed with algebraic logic. This means they follow
the rules of **priority** of calculation.

Given a chain of calculations the machine will perform the steps in the following
order:

Brackets, Of, Division/Multiplication, Addition/Subtraction. (Remember BODMAS.)

Other operations fit within this structure.

For example, **squaring** and finding the **square root** would normally be performed
after 'Of' and before Division/Multiplication.

Take care when doing any calculation. A calculator will only perform the task
requested.

Sometimes the brackets are 'understood' to be there.

Example 1 $\dfrac{6 + 14}{5} = \dfrac{(6 + 14)}{5} = (6 + 14) \div 5 = 4$ What would happen if you just
                                                                  typed $6 + 14 \div 5$?

Example 2 $\dfrac{30}{2 \times 5} = \dfrac{30}{(2 \times 5)} = 30 \div (2 \times 5) = 3$ What would happen if you just
                                                                  typed $30 \div 2 \times 5$?

Exercise 3.1

For each expression:
i check that the first set of data produces the given value (to 3 s.f.)
ii evaluate it for the other sets of data, to 3 s.f. where appropriate.

1 $\dfrac{x}{y}$

    a When $x = 5$ and $y = 7$ answer = 0·714
    b When $x = 11$ and $y = 3$
    c When $x = 8·4$ and $y = 1·6$

2 $p + \dfrac{q}{r}$

    a When $p = 4$, $q = 3$ and $r = 5$ answer = 4·6
    b When $p = 6$, $q = 1$ and $r = 4$
    c When $p = 11$, $q = 12$ and $r = 13$

3 $\dfrac{a + b}{c}$

    a When $a = 7$, $b = 4$ and $c = 9$ answer = 1·22
    b When $a = 3·5$, $b = 2·9$ and $c = 4·5$
    c When $a = 136$, $b = 85$ and $c = 107$

4 $\dfrac{de}{f}$

    a When $d = 19$, $e = 8$ and $f = 7$ answer = 21·7
    b When $d = 8·2$, $e = 5·6$ and $f = 14·1$
    c When $d = 144$, $e = 103$ and $f = 1436$

5 $g - \dfrac{h}{i}$

    a When $g = 7·4$, $h = 1·2$ and $i = 0·8$ answer = 5·9
    b When $g = 16$, $h = 24$ and $i = 5$
    c When $g = 100$, $h = 135$ and $i = 227$

6 $j(k + l)$

    a When $j = 5$, $k = 7$ and $l = 2$ answer = 45
    b When $j = 1$, $k = 5$ and $l = 9$
    c When $j = 3$, $k = 4$ and $l = 2$

7 $\dfrac{m}{n + p}$

    a When $m = 25$, $n = 3$ and $p = 8$ answer = 2·27
    b When $m = 186$, $n = 75$ and $p = 39$
    c When $m = 5·4$, $n = 4·3$ and $p = 2·8$

8 $\dfrac{x}{yz}$

    a When $x = 17$, $y = 3·2$ and $z = 1·1$ answer = 4·83
    b When $x = 0·3$, $y = 19$ and $z = 2·5$
    c When $x = 3200$, $y = 47$ and $z = 82$

9 $(r+s)^2$

    a When $r=5$ and $s=3$ answer = 64

    b When $r=9{\cdot}9$ and $s=3{\cdot}6$

    c When $r=305$ and $s=123$

10 $\sqrt{t^2+w^2}$

    a When $t=6$ and $w=9$ answer = 10·8

    b When $t=17$ and $w=11$

    c When $t=8{\cdot}5$ and $w=10{\cdot}4$

---

4 Powers and roots

Reminders $7^2 = 7 \times 7 = 49$ On a calculator: [7] [x^2] [=]   **49**

            $\sqrt{49} = 7$ (because $7 \times 7 = 49$)   [$\sqrt{\ }$] [49] [=]   **7**

Similarly $2^4 = 2 \times 2 \times 2 \times 2 = 16$ [2] [y^x] [4] [=]   **16**

We say '2 raised to the power of 4 is 16' or 'the fourth power of 2 is 16'.

We can reverse this process by taking the fourth root of 16 to get 2.

This would be written $\sqrt[4]{16} = 2$.   [4] [$\sqrt[x]{y}$] [16] [=]   **2**

Example 1   What number when raised to the power 4 gives 81?

           We must find the fourth root of 81.

           $\sqrt[4]{81} = 3$

Example 2   **a** Find the third root of 125 (the cube root).

           b Say what it means.

           a $\sqrt[3]{125} = 5$

           b It tells us that $5^3 = 125$.

Exercise 4.1

1 State the value of:

    a 2^5 **b** 4^3 **c** 1^7 **d** 10^4 **e** 12^2 **f** $\left(\frac{1}{2}\right)^2$

2 State the value of:

    a $\sqrt[3]{8}$ **b** $\sqrt[4]{16}$ **c** $\sqrt{100}$ **d** $\sqrt[3]{27}$ **e** $\sqrt[5]{1}$ **f** $\sqrt[3]{343}$

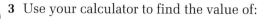

3 Use your calculator to find the value of:

    a 6^4 **b** 11^5 **c** $1{\cdot}4^3$ **d** $0{\cdot}6^4$ **e** $8{\cdot}3^3$

4 Find the value of each of the following, to 3 s.f.

    a $\sqrt[3]{11}$ **b** $\sqrt[4]{75}$ **c** $\sqrt[7]{1404}$ **d** $\sqrt{9{\cdot}9}$ **e** $\sqrt[3]{1{\cdot}71}$

5 Use the appropriate buttons to help you calculate each of the following to 3 s.f.

    a $4 \times 9 \cdot 7^2$ **b** $5 \times 6 \cdot 6^3$ **c** $5^2 \times 3^4$ **d** $6^2 + 4^2$

    e $\sqrt{(3^2 + 4^2)}$ **f** $\dfrac{1 \times \sqrt{5}}{2}$ **g** $1 \cdot 09^3 \times \sqrt[3]{34}$ **h** $\sqrt[4]{\dfrac{19 \cdot 2}{3 \cdot 14}}$

6 Calculate the volume of each cube, correct to 3 s.f.
   (Use the power button on your calculator.)

1·6 cm

23 mm

3·5 m

19·4 m

7 Find the length of the sides of cubes with the following volumes (by finding the cube
root of each volume). Round your answer to 2 s.f. where necessary.

    a 729 cm³   **b** 83 m³   **c** 1992 mm³   **d** 1·54 m³

---

5 Repeated calculation

The calculator is very useful when repeated calculations have to be made.

The method used (memory or constant facility) will vary depending on
the type of calculator.

Check out how to do this on your calculator. It will save you time and effort.

Example   To convert British pounds to Swedish kronor we multiply
           each amount by 12·613.
           To make things easier we could store this number in the calculator's
           memory.

Exercise 5.1

1 Use the memory on your calculator to calculate, correct to 2 decimal places:

    a $16 \times 31 \cdot 55$ **b** $137 \times 31 \cdot 55$ **c** $426 \div 31 \cdot 55$

    d $1000 \div 31 \cdot 55$ **e** $144 - 31 \cdot 55$ **f** $27 + 31 \cdot 55$

2 Mrs Shiel gave her maths class a test out of 80.
   To change the scores to percentages she multiplies each mark by 1·25.
   Change each of the following marks out of 80 to the nearest whole percentage:

    a 43   **b** 59   **c** 36   **d** 77   **e** 14

3
> 1 nautical mile = 1·852 kilometres

    a Change these distances from nautical miles to kilometres:

      i 12 nautical miles   **ii** 56 nautical miles   **iii** 190 nautical miles

    b Change these distances from kilometres to nautical miles (to 3 s.f.):

      i 13 km   **ii** 76·5 km   **iii** 424 km

4 Sorcha did her shopping at the Cash 'n' Carry.
The prices did not include VAT, so she had to multiply each price by 1·175 to find out how much in total she had to pay.
Find the total cost, to the nearest penny, of items marked:

a £90   **b** £50·50   **c** £150   **d** £870   **e** £1070

5 A travel agent advertised an exchange rate for American dollars of £1 = \$1·5915.

  a Use this rate to convert the following to dollars, correct to 2 decimal places:

    i £53   **ii** £627   **iii** £9030   **iv** £1 000 000

  b Using the same rate, convert these amounts to pounds, correct to the nearest penny:

    i \$30   **ii** \$175·50   **iii** \$4444·44   **iv** \$1 000 000

Challenge

1 By using trial and error and trial and improvement and the x^y button, calculate the value of x where $x^3 = 32$. Give your answer correct to 2 d.p.

2 By a similar method calculate:
  a the length of the side of a square whose area is 44 cm²
  b the edge of a cube of volume 60 cm³
  c the value of x if $x^2 + x = 8$
  d the value of x if $x^3 - x = 11$.

6 Large and small numbers

The Earth is 93 000 000 miles from the Sun.
Pluto is 40 times as far.
Most calculators will allow you to enter 93 000 000 into their display.
If we try to calculate the distance from Pluto to the Sun, however, the result is likely to be too large for the display and one of the following will appear:

$$3.72^9 \quad \text{or} \quad 3.72^{\varepsilon 9} \quad \text{or} \quad 3.72^{\times 10^9}$$

Now $40 \times 93\ 000\ 000 = 3\ 720\ 000\ 000$

So 3 720 000 000 is represented by $3·72 \times 10^9$, i.e. $3·72 \times 1\ 000\ 000\ 000$

This way of representing a number is called **standard form** or **scientific notation**.

Every number can be expressed in the form $a \times 10^n$ where $1 \leqslant a < 10$ and n is a positive or negative whole number.

- a will be a number with the decimal point coming after the first digit.
  The number of digits in a is the number of significant figures in the number.
- We can treat n as an instruction of how far to move that point to get the number we want to represent.
- A negative in the power is used to move the point to the left.

Examples

$5{\cdot}61 \times 10^4 = 56\ 100$	...	The point has moved 4 places to the right.
$5{\cdot}61 \times 10^3 = 5610$	...	The point has moved 3 places to the right.
$5{\cdot}61 \times 10^2 = 561$	...	The point has moved 2 places to the right.
$5{\cdot}61 \times 10^1 = 56{\cdot}1$	...	The point has moved 1 place to the right.
$5{\cdot}61 \times 10^0 = 5{\cdot}61$	...	The point has moved 0 places to the right.
$5{\cdot}61 \times 10^{-1} = 0{\cdot}561$	...	The point has moved 1 place to the left.
$5{\cdot}61 \times 10^{-2} = 0{\cdot}0561$	...	The point has moved 2 places to the left.
$5{\cdot}61 \times 10^{-3} = 0{\cdot}005\ 61$	...	The point has moved 3 places to the left.

Exercise 6.1

1 Express each number in standard form.
  a 500 **b** 60 **c** 1700 **d** 23 000
  e 56 000 000 **f** 98 700 **g** 1 750 000 **h** 83

2 Write each number in scientific notation using negative powers.
  a 0·7 **b** 0·07 **c** 0·007 **d** 0·081
  e 0·42 **f** 0·000 039 **g** 0·152 **h** 0·000 6

3 Write each number in the form $a \times 10^n$ where $1 \leqslant a < 10$ and n is a positive or negative whole number.
  a 670 **b** 0·05 **c** 20 600 **d** 0·000 88
  e 18 000 000 **f** 0·2 **g** 0·0213 **h** 1·9

4 Rewrite the numbers in these sentences in standard form.
  a The speed of light is 300 000 000 metres per second.
  b The population of Britain is roughly 55 000 000.
  c An acre is 4046 square metres.
  d The distance from Neptune to the Sun is 4 497 000 000 km.
  e The radius of the orbit of an electron is 0·000 000 05 mm.
  f A lottery winner won $18 200 000.
  g The thickness of a thread is 0·0006 m.

5 **a** It is estimated that the weight of the Earth is about
    6 600 000 000 000 000 000 000 tonnes.
    Write this weight in scientific notation.
  b A drawing pin weighs 0·000 001 2 tonne.
    Write this in scientific notation.

6 Write these numbers in *normal*, or floating point, form.

a 7×10^4	**b** $3 \cdot 2 \times 10^3$	**c** 6×10^{-2}	**d** $1 \cdot 5 \times 10^{-3}$
e $7 \cdot 4 \times 10^7$	**f** $2 \cdot 8 \times 10^{-4}$	**g** $9 \cdot 66 \times 10^{-3}$	**h** $7 \cdot 215 \times 10^{-1}$
i $1 \cdot 14 \times 10^{-3}$	**j** $2 \cdot 35 \times 10^0$	**k** $7 \cdot 03 \times 10^1$	**l** 8×10^{-10}

7 Rewrite the numbers in these sentences in *normal* form.

a The population of midges in a swarm was estimated as $3 \cdot 2 \times 10^5$.

b The area of the Sahara desert is $8 \cdot 6 \times 10^6 \, \text{km}^2$.

c Pluto's mass is $2 \cdot 5 \times 10^{-3}$ times the Earth's mass.

d The number of letters handled by one sorting office was $8 \cdot 37 \times 10^6$.

e The mass of a neutron is $1 \cdot 675 \times 10^{-27} \, \text{kg}$.

8 a A centillion is 10^{600}. How many zeros does it have?

b The mass of a photon is $3 \times 10^{-53} \, \text{kg}$.
How many zeros are there after the decimal point?

---

7 Standard form on a calculator

Numbers can be entered into a calculator using the $\boxed{\text{EXP}}$ key (or $\boxed{\text{EE}}$ key on some calculators).

For example, $5 \cdot 6 \times 10^{-2}$ can be entered by typing $5 \cdot 6$ $\boxed{\text{EXP}}$ -2.

Calculations can then be performed.

Example   Light can travel 3×10^8 metres in one second.
There are $3 \cdot 15 \times 10^7$ seconds in a year.
How far does light travel in a year?

$(3 \times 10^8) \times (3 \cdot 15 \times 10^7)$ ... Key in 3 $\boxed{\text{EXP}}$ $8 \times 3 \cdot 15$ $\boxed{\text{EXP}}$ 7
to get the answer $9 \cdot 45 \times 10^{15}$.

Exercise 7.1

1 Perform the following calculations, then write your answer in
    i standard form   **ii** *normal* (floating point) form.

a $4 \times (5 \times 10^7)$	**b** $3 \times (4 \cdot 1 \times 10^6)$	**c** $3 \cdot 5 \times (3 \cdot 82 \times 10^{-3})$
d $(9 \times 10^4) \div 5$	**e** $(6 \cdot 4 \times 10^{-3}) \div 8$	**f** $3 \cdot 2 \div (4 \times 10^{-4})$
g $(5 \times 10^3) \times (8 \times 10^6)$	**h** $(3 \cdot 5 \times 10^5) \times (2 \cdot 1 \times 10^{-2})$	**i** $(9 \cdot 6 \times 10^2) \times (3 \times 10^{-4})$
j $(2 \cdot 1 \times 10^6) \div (7 \times 10^2)$	**k** $(2 \cdot 4 \times 10^0) \div (1 \times 10^{-3})$	**l** $(8 \cdot 4 \times 10^3) \div (1 \cdot 2 \times 10^{-1})$

2 $P = 7 \cdot 3 \times 10^5$, $Q = 9 \cdot 8 \times 10^{-2}$, $R = 1 \cdot 85 \times 10^7$, $S = 2 \cdot 04 \times 10^{-5}$, $T = 7 \cdot 6 \times 10^4$.

a Which of these numbers is the greatest?

b Which is the lowest number?

c One number in the list is roughly ten times greater than one of the others.
Which two numbers are they?

3 $A = 4 \cdot 2 \times 10^3$, $B = 1 \cdot 9 \times 10^6$ and $C = 5 \cdot 0 \times 10^{-4}$.

Calculate the value of each expression, giving your answer in standard form.

    a AB **b** BC **c** $\dfrac{B}{A}$ **d** $\dfrac{A}{C}$

4 An aircraft flying at Mach 1 has a speed of $3{\cdot}315 \times 10^2$ m/s. Multiply this speed by $2{\cdot}4$ to convert Mach $2{\cdot}4$ to metres per second.

5 Light travels $9{\cdot}46 \times 10^{12}$ km in one year. Calculate the distance it travels in $1{\cdot}2 \times 10^3$ years.

6 There are 5×10^9 red blood cells in 1 ml of blood. Calculate, in scientific notation, the number of red blood cells in:
  a 1 litre of blood   **b** $6{\cdot}25$ litres of blood.

7 The mass of the Earth can be calculated in kilograms by using the formula
$$m = \frac{gR^2}{G}$$
where $g = 9{\cdot}8$, $R = 6{\cdot}37 \times 10^6$ and $G = 6{\cdot}67 \times 10^{-11}$.
Calculate the mass of the Earth, to 3 significant figures.
Express your answer in the form $a \times 10^n$ where a is rounded to 3 s.f.

8 You should have found the mass of the Earth is $5{\cdot}96 \times 10^{24}$ kg.
The table below shows the mass of other planets in relation to the mass of Earth.
For example, Neptune is $17{\cdot}2$ times as big as the Earth.

	Planet	Times mass of Earth
a	Neptune	17.2
b	Mars	0.11
c	Saturn	95
d	Venus	0·8

Calculate the mass of each planet in scientific notation, to 3 significant figures.

9 The galaxy we live in has a diameter of 10^5 light years.
1 light year $= 9{\cdot}5 \times 10^{12}$ km.
  a Calculate the diameter of the galaxy in kilometres.
  b The distance round the galaxy is about three times its diameter. Calculate the distance round the galaxy in kilometres.

10 The distances of Neptune and Venus from the Sun are $4{\cdot}497 \times 10^9$ km and $1{\cdot}082 \times 10^8$ km respectively. Calculate:
  a the difference in these distances in standard form
  b the ratio of the distances, to the nearest whole number.
    [Hint: (Neptune ÷ Venus) : 1]

Exercise 7.2

1 Calculate, giving your answer in standard form:
  a $(7{\cdot}2 \times 10^5) \times (1{\cdot}3 \times 10^6)$ **b** $(2{\cdot}2 \times 10^{-4}) \times (4{\cdot}7 \times 10^{-8})$
  c $(6 \times 10^5) \times (9{\cdot}5 \times 10^{-2})$ **d** $(3{\cdot}03 \times 10^{11}) \div (1{\cdot}01 \times 10^{-6})$
  e $\dfrac{3{\cdot}6 \times 10^{-10}}{2{\cdot}4 \times 10^{-5}}$

2 a Evaluate $(7{\cdot}92 \times 10^5) \times (8{\cdot}5 \times 10^{-2})$, giving your answer in scientific notation, rounded to 3 significant figures.

  b Similarly evaluate:

    i $(6{\cdot}7 \times 10^3) \times (9{\cdot}13 \times 10^4)$

    ii $(7{\cdot}4 \times 10^4) \div (1{\cdot}9 \times 10^{-1})$

    iii $\dfrac{4{\cdot}1 \times 10^{-6}}{5{\cdot}6 \times 10^9}$

3 Given that $A = 8{\cdot}8 \times 10^3$, $B = 1{\cdot}54 \times 10^{-6}$ and $C = 2{\cdot}07 \times 10^{-10}$, calculate the following, correct to 2 significant figures:

  a AB **b** C^2 **c** $\dfrac{B}{C}$ **d** $\dfrac{(AC)^2}{B}$

4 The surface area of an asteroid can be calculated using the formula $A = 12{\cdot}56\, r^2$, where r is the radius of the asteroid. Calculate, to 3 significant figures, the surface area of an asteroid of radius $7{\cdot}6 \times 10^6$ metres.

5 A popular visitor attraction is open seven days a week in the summer season. On average $1{\cdot}53 \times 10^4$ visitors attend each day.

  a Calculate, to 3 significant figures, the total number of people who attended the attraction during June, July and August.
    Leave your answer in standard form.

  b Each visitor spent, on average, £27 at the attraction.
    How much money did they take?

Investigation

a Look for a pattern as you calculate:
  i 9999×2 **ii** 9999×3 **iii** 9999×4
b Now write down the answers for multiplying 9999×5 up to 9999×9.

8 Common fractions

Reminders
- A **common** fraction has a numerator and a denominator.
- The **value** of the fraction can be calculated by dividing the numerator by the denominator.
- A **proper** fraction is one whose value is less than 1.
- An **improper** fraction is of the form $\dfrac{a}{b}$ where $a > b$.
- A **mixed number** is made up of a whole number and a proper fraction.

We can handle fractions on the calculator by using the button $a^{b}/_{c}$

Example 1 Express $\frac{9}{12}$ as a decimal fraction.

9 $\boxed{a^{b/c}}$ 12 $\boxed{=}$ gives a display of $\boxed{3\text{r}4}$ then $\boxed{a^{b/c}}$

gives $0{\cdot}75$.

Note: $\frac{9}{12}$ expressed in its simplest form is $\frac{3}{4}$.

Example 2 Express $\frac{7}{4}$ as a mixed number.

7 $\boxed{a^{b/c}}$ 4 $\boxed{=}$ gives $\boxed{1\text{r}3\text{r}4}$ which means $1\frac{3}{4}$

Example 3 Express $4\frac{3}{5}$ as an improper fraction.

4 $\boxed{a^{b/c}}$ 3 $\boxed{a^{b/c}}$ 5 $\boxed{=}$ then $\boxed{2\text{nd}}$ $\boxed{a^{b/c}}$ gives $\boxed{23\text{r}5}$ … $\frac{23}{5}$

Example 4 Add $4\frac{3}{5}$ and $\frac{2}{3}$.

4 $\boxed{a^{b/c}}$ 3 $\boxed{a^{b/c}}$ 5 $\boxed{+}$ 2 $\boxed{a^{b/c}}$ 3 $\boxed{=}$ $\boxed{5\text{r}4\text{r}15}$ … $5\frac{4}{15}$

Exercise 8.1

1 Express each fraction in its simplest form.

  a $\frac{2}{4}$ **b** $\frac{6}{10}$ **c** $\frac{24}{96}$ **d** $\frac{33}{77}$ **e** $\frac{21}{7}$

2 Express each fraction as a mixed number.

  a $\frac{5}{4}$ **b** $\frac{11}{3}$ **c** $\frac{24}{7}$ **d** $\frac{47}{9}$ **e** $\frac{52}{12}$

3 Write each mixed number as an improper fraction.

  a $3\frac{1}{2}$ **b** $4\frac{2}{3}$ **c** $1\frac{9}{10}$ **d** $11\frac{2}{7}$ **e** $22\frac{1}{8}$

4 A vinyl record made $33\frac{1}{3}$ revolutions per minute as it spun on a turntable. Express $33\frac{1}{3}$ as an improper fraction.

5 Calculate:

  a $\frac{1}{7} + \frac{2}{7}$ **b** $\frac{2}{5} - \frac{1}{10}$ **c** $\frac{4}{9} + \frac{5}{18}$ **d** $\frac{7}{10} - \frac{3}{5}$

  e $4\frac{1}{3} + 1\frac{2}{9}$ **f** $1\frac{1}{8} - \frac{1}{2}$ **g** $\frac{1}{4} \times \frac{3}{5}$ **h** $\frac{3}{7} \div \frac{1}{2}$

  i $\frac{3}{8} \times \frac{2}{9}$ **j** $2\frac{1}{2} \times 1\frac{3}{4}$ **k** $\frac{4}{5}$ of $\frac{1}{2}$ **l** $4\frac{9}{10} \div 1\frac{2}{5}$

Exercise 8.2

1 Use your calculator to help you find four pairs of equivalent fractions.

  a $\frac{6}{9}$ **b** $\frac{48}{64}$ **c** $\frac{6}{10}$ **d** $\frac{30}{45}$ **e** $\frac{3}{4}$ **f** $\frac{14}{18}$ **g** $\frac{39}{65}$ **h** $\frac{49}{63}$

2 Express each fraction as a mixed number.

  a $\frac{7}{3}$ **b** $\frac{15}{7}$ **c** $\frac{31}{6}$ **d** $\frac{104}{11}$

3 Write each mixed number as an improper fraction.

  a $4\frac{3}{5}$ **b** $1\frac{9}{11}$ **c** $15\frac{7}{8}$ **d** $133\frac{1}{3}$

4 How far is it from:
  a the church to the stables
  b the town to the farm
  c the farm to the stables
  d the town to the church?

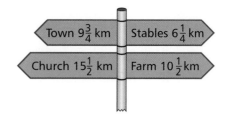

5 How many programmes each lasting $\frac{3}{4}$ of an hour could be recorded on a 3 hour tape?

6 One morning half the students at Jack's school arrived before 8.55 am.
  Three-eighths of the students arrived between 8.55 and 9 am when the bell rang.
  What fraction of the students arrived:
  a before the bell rang   **b** after the bell rang?

7 Niamh counted 93 black sheep in a flock. This was three-eighths of the whole flock.
  How many sheep were in the flock?

8 Nails $1\frac{1}{4}$ inches and $2\frac{3}{8}$ inches long are driven into a piece of wood $3\frac{1}{16}$ inches thick.

  How far is the point of each nail from the other side of the wood?

9 a Calculate the perimeter of
    i the rectangle   **ii** the square.
    All lengths are in centimetres.
  b Calculate the area of
    i the rectangle   **ii** the square.
  c Find the difference in the area of the
    rectangle and the square.

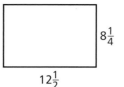

10 A fully loaded truck can carry $6\frac{3}{4}$ tonnes of sand.
  a Calculate the least number of loads needed to move 26 tonnes of sand.
  b What weight of sand is in the final load if the lorry is fully laden for all the
    other trips?

11 A picture is enlarged $2\frac{1}{2}$ times. The original was $5\frac{1}{3}$ inches high and $15\frac{5}{8}$ inches wide.
  a Calculate   **i** the height   **ii** the width of the enlargement.
  b Calculate the area of   **i** the original   **ii** the enlargement.

12 The board shows some *rough* conversions.
  Calculate the approximate number of:
  a pounds in 7 kg
  b kilograms in 23 pounds
  c litres in 3 gallons
  d miles in 40 km
  e inches in 2 metres
  f inches in 18 cm.

Rough History
1 inch = $2\frac{1}{2}$ cm
1 gallon = $4\frac{1}{2}$ litres
1 kilogram = $2\frac{1}{4}$ pounds
1 kilometre = $\frac{5}{8}$ mile

Challenge

Rule 1   Everyone at a table shares the cakes on that table equally.

Rule 2   Each person arriving has to go to the table where he or she will get the most cake, after sharing.

Rule 3   If there is a choice of 'equal' tables, go to the one with fewest people.

Three tables are set up as shown.

Table 1   Table 2   Table 3

Alice arrives first and goes to Table 1. She would have 4 cakes if no one else arrived.
Bernie is next. If he goes to Table 1 he would get 2 cakes, so he goes to Table 2.
Investigate the choice of table and share of cakes as Carl, Dave, Eileen, Finlay, Grace, Hannah, Imogen and Josh arrive one by one, in that order.
When the nineteenth person arrives they start eating.
What fraction of cake does the nineteenth person get?

9 Ratio

Ratios are used for comparing, sharing or mixing quantities.
The parts of a ratio should be reduced to the same units.
Once this has been accomplished we can:

● drop the units
● simplify the ratio in a manner similar to that used for common fractions.

Example 1   Ally has £3·50. Toni has 95p.
Write the ratio of Ally's to Toni's money in its simplest form.
Ally : Toni = £3·50 : 95p
$$= 350p : 95p \quad \textbf{... reduce to same units (p)}$$
$$= 350 : 95 \quad \textbf{... drop units}$$
$$= 70 : 19 \quad \textbf{... simplify by dividing parts by 5}$$

Generally, the simplest form will have no decimal fractions.

Example 2   Express the ratio 1·5 : 40 in its simplest form.
$$1·5 : 40 = 15 : 400 \quad \textbf{... multiply parts by 10 to eliminate decimals}$$
$$= 3 : 80 \quad \textbf{... divide by 5 to simplify}$$

Exercise 9.1

1 Write each of these ratios in its simplest form:

   a 33 : 44   **b** 45 : 135   **c** 144 : 128   **d** 95 : 133   **e** 550 : 1000

   f 3·5 : 14   **g** 17·5 : 24·5   **h** 3·2 : 4·8   **i** 9·8 : 7

2 For each ratio   **i** reduce the parts to the same units   **ii** simplify:

   a 25 p : £2·75   **b** 450 g : 1·5 kg   **c** 650 kg : 2 tonnes   **d** 12 mm : 3 cm

   e 1 km : 50 cm   **f** 3 litres : 750 ml   **g** $2·80 : $0·56   **h** 2·2 m : 77 cm

3 **i** Reduce each mixed number to an improper fraction.

   ii Multiply each side by a suitable number to get rid of the fractions.

   iii Simplify each ratio.

   a $\frac{3}{7} : \frac{7}{8}$ **b** $\frac{3}{4} : 1\frac{1}{4}$ **c** $\frac{7}{8} : 2\frac{3}{8}$

Splitting quantities

Example 3   Rachel and Steve share a paper round. Rachel works 3 days.
Steve works 2. They are given £60 in wages to share out.
Divide £60 in the ratio 3 : 2 to share the money fairly.

Rachel has to get 3 parts and Steve 2 parts ... **5 parts altogether.**
£60 ÷ 5 = £12 ... **each part is worth £12.**

So Rachel gets 3 × 12 = £36 and Steve gets 2 × 12 = £24.

Example 4   When a piggy bank was broken open it was
discovered there was a mix of ten pence coins,
five pence coins and two pence coins in the
ratio 5 : 3 : 2.
There were 150 coins in total.
a How many of each type of coin were there?
b How much money had been in the bank?

   a 5 + 3 + 2 = 10 parts.
      150 ÷ 10 = 15 coins in one part.
      So there are 5 × 15 = 75 ten pence coins;
      3 × 15 = 45 five pence coins; 2 × 15 = 30 two pence coins
   b 75 × 10 + 45 × 5 + 30 × 2 = 750 + 225 + 60 = 1035 pence = £10·35

Exercise 9.2

1 Split:

   a £500 in the ratio 3 : 7   **b** £77 in the ratio 1 : 6

   c £1000 in the ratio 3 : 2   **d** 240 g in the ratio 5 : 3

   e 56 metres in the ratio 4 : 3   **f** 850 ml in the ratio 1 : 4

   g 832 mm in the ratio 5 : 8   **h** 6 kg in the ratio 7 : 5

   i 4·5 km in the ratio 4 : 5

2 a Share £550 between Jo and Chuck in the ratio Jo : Chuck =
    i 7 : 4   **ii** 2 : 3   **iii** 3 : 7.
  b i   Which ratio favours Jo?
    ii   Compare Chuck's best and worst share-outs.

3 Red and yellow paint are mixed in the ratio 2 : 5 to make orange paint.
How much of each colour would be needed to make 161 litres of orange paint?

4 Crumble mix is made by mixing flour, butter and sugar in the ratio 4 : 2 : 1.
How much of each would be needed to make 140 grams of crumble mix?

5 Concrete is made by mixing cement, sand and gravel in the ratio 1 : 2 : 3.
How much of each would be needed to make 150 kg of concrete?

6 Eric and Doug work together doing gardening for
their neighbours. In one week Eric worked 4 hours
30 minutes and Doug worked 6 hours.
  a Work out the ratio of Eric to Doug's hours in its
    simplest form.
  b The boys are paid £63 for their week's work.
    How much should each get?

7 In a school of 1122 pupils, the ratio of pupils with blonde, brunette and auburn hair
was 11 : 9 : 2. Calculate how many pupils had each hair colour.

8 Ian wants to make green paint by mixing blue and yellow paint.
To get the shade he requires he must mix blue and yellow in the ratio 3 : 5.
Ian has 42 litres of blue paint and 55 litres of yellow.
  a Ian makes as much green paint as he can. How much is that?
  b He has some paint left over.
    i   What colour is it?   **ii**   How many litres of it are left over?

9 A lottery company uses the money raised to make donations to charity, provide
prize money, give profit to investors and pay tax.
The company decides to split the money raised in the ratio 4 : 7 : 2 : 1.
In one week the lottery raised £$5 \cdot 11 \times 10^6$.
How much money would go to each cause this week?

10 Emily makes herbal tea to sell to her friends.
She mixes tea and herbs in the ratio 22 : 3.
  a How much of each would she need to make 5 kg of herbal tea?
  b She buys the tea for £1 per 100 g and the herbs 75p for 100 g.
    She sold all her herbal tea for £$1 \cdot 20$ per 100 g.
    How much profit did she make?

11 Coffee was blended using three different types of beans.
The ratio of Colombian to Kenyan to Brazilian was 2 : 3 : 2.
  a How much of each was needed to make 245 kg of coffee?
  b Colombian coffee costs the merchant £$4 \cdot 50$ per kilogram, Kenyan costs £5.25
    per kilogram and Brazilian £$3 \cdot 80$ per kilogram.
    If the merchant sells the blend at £$6 \cdot 30$ per kilogram, how much profit does he make?

◄◄ **RECAP**

Significant figures

The significant figures in a number are those that give us an idea of
i   the value of a number or   **ii**   the accuracy to which it was made.
For example, 963 has 3 significant figures.
The 9 adds the most value (900). It is the **most significant** digit.
963 = 960 to 2 significant figures

When a number contains a decimal point, then all the digits after the most
significant digit are also significant. For example, 0·040 50 has 4 significant figures.

Order of operations

Given a chain of calculations, each part should be carried out in a special order:
Brackets, Of, Division/Multiplication, Addition/Subtraction. (Remember BODMAS.)
Squaring and finding the **square root** are performed after 'Of' and before **Division/
Multiplication.**

Calculator keys

Squares and roots can be found as follows:

square, e.g. $7^2 = 49$ ...
$\boxed{7}$ $\boxed{x^2}$ $\boxed{=}$ $\boxed{49}$

square root, e.g. $\sqrt{49} = 7$ ...
$\boxed{\sqrt{}}$ $\boxed{49}$ $\boxed{=}$ $\boxed{7}$

powers, e.g. $2^4 = 16$ ...
$\boxed{2}$ $\boxed{y^x}$ $\boxed{4}$ $\boxed{=}$ $\boxed{16}$

other roots, e.g. $\sqrt[4]{16} = 2$ ...
$\boxed{4}$ $\boxed{^xy}$ $\boxed{16}$ $\boxed{=}$ $\boxed{2}$

Brackets can be used to force parts to be done first.
Memory can be used to increase efficient use.
Fractions can be entered by using the fraction button, e.g. enter $4\frac{3}{5}$ by keying
4 $\boxed{a^{b}/_{c}}$ 3 $\boxed{a^{b}/_{c}}$ 5

Numbers in standard form can be entered, e.g. to enter 3×10^4 key 3 $\boxed{\text{EXP}}$ 4.

Standard form

Any number can be expressed in the form $a \times 10^n$ where $1 \leq a < 10$ and n is a
positive or negative whole number, e.g. $341\ 220 = 3·4122 \times 10^5$;
$0·001\ 02 = 1·02 \times 10^{-3}$.
The number of digits in a gives the number of significant figures.

Ratio

A ratio can be simplified in a similar way to a fraction.
A quantity can be split up into any given ratio.

1 Calculate, correct to 3 significant figures:

   a $\dfrac{145 + 79}{61}$ **b** $61 + \dfrac{79}{145}$ **c** $79(145 - 61)$

   d $\sqrt{(145^2 + 61^2)}$ **e** $(79 - 61)^4$ **f** $\dfrac{1}{2 \times 79 + 61 - 145}$

2 Evaluate, correct to 3 significant figures:

   a $5 \cdot 2^3$ **b** $\sqrt[3]{3 \cdot 75}$ **c** 8×6^4 **d** $\sqrt[5]{57 \cdot 5 + 32 \cdot 6}$

3 Which of the following is the best estimate for $3 \cdot 2 \times 18 \cdot 3$?

   a $580 \cdot 6$ **b** $45 \cdot 6$ **c** $58 \cdot 56$ **d** $21 \cdot 5$

4 Eva earns £31 284 per annum.

   a How much does she earn in a month?

   b What is her weekly wage? Give your answer to the nearest penny.

5 Write each number in standard form.

   a The number of trees in an Amazonian forest was estimated as 1 560 000.

   b In electronics, the unit the microfarad is 0·000 001 farad.

6 The British government spends fifty million pounds per hour.

   a Express what they spend per day in scientific notation.

   b How much is this per year?

7 Use your calculator to work these out in scientific notation, to 3 significant figures:

   a $(4 \cdot 21 \times 10^7) \times (3 \cdot 95 \times 10^8)$

   b $(6 \cdot 6 \times 10^3) \div (1 \cdot 8 \times 10^9)$

   c $(1 \cdot 1 \times 10^{-5}) \times (5 \cdot 4 \times 10^{-8})$

8 In 1889 a swarm of locusts weighing 550 000 tonnes, and containing 250 000 000 000 insects, crossed the Red Sea. Calculate the weight of one locust in tonnes, writing your answer in standard form.

9 Calculate, giving your answers in their simplest form:

   a $\frac{2}{5} \times \frac{3}{4}$ **b** $\frac{7}{8} + \frac{1}{4}$ **c** $\frac{5}{6} - \frac{2}{3}$ **d** $\frac{5}{8} \div \frac{1}{2}$

   e $1\frac{3}{8} + 3\frac{1}{4}$ **f** $1\frac{1}{6} \times 2\frac{1}{4}$ **g** $4\frac{1}{3} - 2\frac{5}{6}$ **h** $1\frac{2}{7} \div 1\frac{3}{4}$

10 Spanners increase in regular steps.

   What size is halfway between $\frac{3}{4}$ inch and $\frac{7}{8}$ inch?

11 $\frac{2}{5}$ of a group are male. $\frac{2}{3}$ of the remainder are under 21.

   a What fraction of the group are females aged 21 or over?

   b There are 300 people in the group. How many are female and under 21?

12 **a** Split £35 in the ratio 4 : 3.

   b In April the ratio of dry days : rainy days : snowy days was 3 : 2 : 1. How many of each type of day were there in April?

2 Integers

For centuries mathematicians argued about whether or not negative numbers were necessary. As late as the sixteenth century, numbers less than zero were sometimes called 'absurd' numbers. In the seventeenth century, John Napier, a famous Scottish mathematician, referred to them as 'defective' numbers. It was the end of the seventeenth century before they were widely called 'negative' numbers.

Integers are positive and negative whole numbers.

'Napier's Bones', invented by John Napier in the early 1600s, were multiplication tables inscribed on strips of wood or bone.

1 REVIEW

a Temperature

A negative sign (−) is taken to mean '**below zero**'.
We read −2 °C as '2 degrees Celsius below zero' or 'negative 2 degrees Celsius'. On a weather report you may hear it read as 'minus 2 degrees Celsius'.

b Coordinates

The position of any point in two dimensions can be described using a coordinate diagram and positive and negative coordinates.
The negative sign means 'to the left of the origin' on the x axis and 'below the origin' on the y axis.
Point A is $(-2, 1)$, B is $(2, -2)$ and C is $(-3, -2)$.

c Sea level

The maximum depth of Loch Ness is −230 m.
The negative sign means 'below sea level'.

d Profit and loss

A loss of £3000 can be recorded as a negative profit.
The negative sign means 'a loss of'.

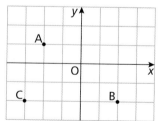

◀◀ **Exercise 1.1**

1 Here are some temperatures around the world one day:

Anchorage	$-17\,°C$	London	$1\,°C$
Belfast	$0\,°C$	Moscow	$-7\,°C$
Edinburgh	$-2\,°C$	New York	$-1\,°C$
Helsinki	$-12\,°C$	Sydney	$36\,°C$
Lanzarote	$18\,°C$	Toronto	$-9\,°C$

  a Rewrite this list in order of temperature. Start with the coldest.
  b How many degrees colder was
    i New York than London
    ii Toronto than Edinburgh?
  c How many degrees warmer was
    i Lanzarote than Toronto
    ii Moscow than Helsinki?
  d What was the range in temperature?

2 The temperature change in Aberdeen was noted every three hours over a 24-hour period. The table gives the details. The temperature at midnight was $-5\,°C$.

Time	3 am	6 am	9 am	noon	3 pm	6 pm	9 pm	midnight
Temp. change	fell 2 °C	fell 3 °C	rose 1 °C	rose 2 °C	rose 4 °C	rose 1 °C	fell 3 °C	fell 2 °C

Write down the temperature in Aberdeen at:

a 3 am	**b** 6 am	**c** 9 am	**d** noon
e 3 pm	**f** 6 pm	**g** 9 pm	**h** midnight.

3 This map of Eve's Isle has its origin at Bren, its capital city.

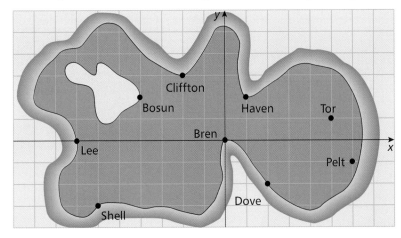

  a Make a list of the places on the map and write their coordinates beside them.
  b The islanders have decided to change the capital to Cliffton.
    The new map of Eve's Isle will have Cliffton as its origin.
    Write down the coordinates of the places on the new map when the origin is at Cliffton.

c There is a motorway on Eve's Island. Between $(-6, -3)$ and $(-2, 0)$ the motorway is straight. At the midpoint of this straight stretch of motorway there is a village called Midway. What are the coordinates of Midway?

4 a How far below the top of the mountain is the cloud?

b How far from the bottom of the sea is the diver?

c How far above the diver is the submarine?

d How far is it from the plane to the bottom of the sea?

e How far is the cloud above the diver?

f If the mountain (from sea level to the peak) were to sit on the sea bed, how far below sea level would its peak be?

g If the sea level rose 5 m, what would be the depth of the sea bed?

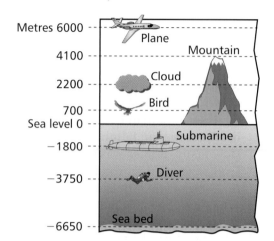

5 Beryl the Baker sometimes makes a profit and sometimes makes a loss. The bar graph shows the 'profit' made each month last year.

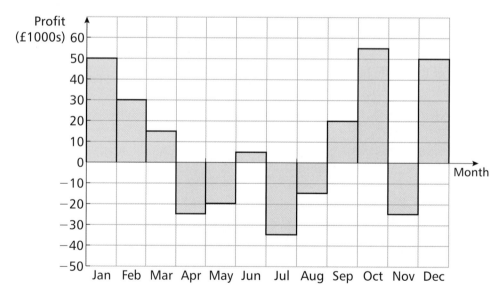

a For how many months did Beryl make
  i a profit
  ii a loss?

b How much more of a 'profit' did Beryl make in October than in July?

c How much more of a loss was made in July than in May?

d What profit was made over the year?

2 Ordering integers

Integers can be represented on a number line.
The further to the right a number is on the number line, the bigger it is.

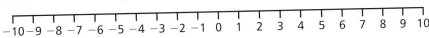

Example 1   5 is to the right of 2 on the number line, so 5 is bigger than 2.
We write: $5 > 2$.
'$>$' means 'is greater than' or 'is bigger than'.

Example 2 -2 is to the right of -3 on the number line, so -2 is bigger than -3.
We write: $-2 > -3$.

Example 3 -4 is to the left of -1, so -4 is smaller than -1.
We write: $-4 < -1$.
'$<$' means 'is less than' or 'is smaller than'.

The number line can also be drawn vertically.
Then bigger numbers are above smaller numbers.

Exercise 2.1

1 Rewrite each pair of numbers with $>$ or $<$ between them to make a true statement.
   a 2 ■ 7   **b** 3 ■ 0   **c** -2 ■ 0   **d** -5 ■ 4
   e -1 ■ -7 **f** -4 ■ -3 **g** 9 ■ -12 **h** -14 ■ 11
   i -99 ■ -101 **j** $-2{\cdot}4$ ■ -2

2 Write these numbers in order of size, smallest first.
   a 4, -7, -1, -6 **b** -3, -8, 1, -1
   c 0, -2, 1, -3 **d** 6, -4, 2, -5

3 Write down the number that is:
   a 1 greater than -2 **b** 1 less than -4
   c 2 bigger than -15 **d** 3 less than -10
   e 3 greater than -20 **f** 5 bigger than -3
   g 4 less than 3   **h** 6 less than 2

4 Use a number line to help you find the smallest integer larger than:
   a 3·5   **b** 5·2   **c** $-2{\cdot}1$
   d $-2{\cdot}8$ **e** $-8{\cdot}5$ **f** $-12{\cdot}9$

5 Write down the largest integer smaller than:
   a 6·3   **b** 3·7   **c** $-1{\cdot}6$
   d $-4{\cdot}9$ **e** $-2{\cdot}5$ **f** $-21{\cdot}3$

6 Copy and complete the 'Balance' column in the bank statement. Pay-ins are marked '+' and pay-outs are marked '−'.

Date	Pay in/out (£)	Balance (£)
3 May	+35·00	35·00
5 May	−20·00	
9 May	+10·00	
12 May	−30·00	
14 May	−7·00	
14 May	+10·00	

7 A(−1, 1), B(−4, 1) and C(−2, −5) are three vertices of parallelogram ABCD.

   a Find the coordinates of D, the fourth vertex.

   b The x coordinate of each vertex is increased by 2.
     The y coordinate of each vertex is decreased by 3.
     Find the new coordinates of A, B, C and D.

   c The original parallelogram is reflected in the x axis.
     Find the coordinates of the images of A, B, C and D.

Challenge

When working with spreadsheets it is sometimes useful to turn a decimal number into the nearest integer that is smaller than it. For example, 3·7 would turn into 3. To get this to happen we type =INT(3·7) and 3 appears in the cell. The illustration shows that =INT(2·1) gives 2 and =INT(5·3) gives 5.

What does =INT(−4·3) give?

	SUM	▼	× √	▦	=	=INT(−4.3)

	A	B	C	D
1	3	INT(3.7)		
2	2	INT(2.1)		CI
3	5	INT(5.3)		
4	=INT(−4.3)	INT−4.3)		

If you have access to a computer, try different positive and negative decimals. Explore what is happening when you type in =INT(N+0·5) where N is some decimal number.

---

3 Adding integers

Treat the addition of two numbers as a set of instructions.
Start at the first number and do what the second number tells you (where 3 means 3 steps to the right, and −3 means 3 steps to the left).

Example 1   2 + 3 means '2 add 3'.
           Start at 2 and go 3 to the right.
           2 + 3 = 5

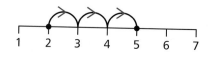

Example 2 $-3 + 5$ means '-3 add 5'.
Start at -3 and go 5 to the right.
$-3 + 5 = 2$

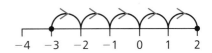

Example 3 $4 + (-6)$ means '4 add (-6)'.
Start at 4 and go 6 to the left.
$4 + (-6) = -2$

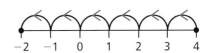

Example 4 $-1 + (-3)$ means '-1 add (-3)'.
Start at -1 and go 3 to the left.
$-1 + (-3) = -4$

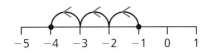

Exercise 3.1

1 A number line may be useful to help you calculate the following:
a $-2 + 3$ **b** $-4 + 7$ **c** $-5 + 3$ **d** $-4 + 1$ **e** $3 + (-7)$
f $6 + (-2)$ **g** $3 + (-8)$ **h** $2 + (-5)$ **i** $4 + (-7)$ **j** $-2 + (-3)$
k $-4 + (-1)$ **l** $-3 + 3$ **m** $-5 + (-5)$ **n** $1 + (-1)$ **o** $0 + (-4)$

2 Evaluate the following:
a $9 + (-4)$ **b** $-15 + 12$ **c** $-18 + 21$ **d** $36 + (-9)$ **e** $23 + (-15)$
f $-1 + (-35)$ **g** $-32 + (-5)$ **h** $29 + (-29)$ **i** $87 + (-100)$ **j** $-37 + (-37)$

3 Copy and complete the addition table.

+	−5	−2	4	−3
−5				
−2				
4				
−3				

4 What is the **OUT** number for each of these number machines?

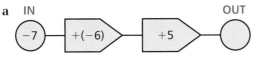 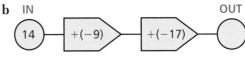

5 Here are some number patterns formed by adding the same amount each time.
   i   Continue each pattern for three more terms
   ii   What number is being *added* each time?

   a $3, 11, 19, 27, \ldots$ **b** $50, 47, 44, 41, \ldots$ **c** $-10, -8, -6, -4, \ldots$
   d $-21, -17, -13, -9, \ldots$ **e** $-5, -12, -19, -26, \ldots$ **f** $34, 25, 16, 7, \ldots$

6 Calculate each of these pairs.
   a i $8 + (-5)$ **ii** $8 - 5$ **b i** $7 + (-1)$ **ii** $7 - 1$
   c i $13 + (-6)$ **ii** $13 - 6$ **d i** $9 + (-9)$ **ii** $9 - 9$
   What do you notice about each pair of answers?

4 Subtracting integers

This subtraction table is partially complete.

We know that a number subtracted from itself gives zero, e.g. $3 - 3 = 0$, $-1 - (-1) = 0$, etc., and so we have a diagonal of zeros.

We know that zero subtracted from a number doesn't alter the number, e.g. $5 - 0 = 5$, so we can fill in the column headed '0'.

Some of the subtractions do not involve negative numbers, so we can fill these in.

Second number

−	−5	−4	−3	−2	−1	0	1	2	3	4	5
5						5	4	3	2	1	0
4						4	3	2	1	0	
3						3	2	1	0		
2						2	1	0			
1						1	0				
0						0					
−1					0	−1					
−2				0		−2					
−3			0			−3					
−4		0				−4					
−5	0					−5					

First number (label for rows)

Exercise 4.1

1 Copy the above table.
   a Notice that as we move to the left, each number is 1 bigger than the one before it. Use that pattern to complete the top six rows.
   b Notice that as we go down the table, each number is 1 less than the number above it. Use the pattern to help you complete the table.

2 Use your completed table to help you write down the answers to these:
   a $5 - (-4)$ **b** $4 - (-3)$ **c** $3 - (-1)$ **d** $1 - (-5)$ **e** $0 - (-2)$
   f $-1 - (-3)$ **g** $-2 - (-4)$ **h** $-5 - (-1)$ **i** $-1 - 2$ **j** $-4 - (-5)$

3 Perform each pair of calculations.
   a i $9 - 2$ **ii** $9 + (-2)$ **b i** $2 - 5$ **ii** $2 + (-5)$
   c i $1 - 4$ **ii** $1 + (-4)$ **d i** $0 - 1$ **ii** $0 + (-1)$
   e i $-1 - 2$ **ii** $-1 + (-2)$ **f i** $-4 - 3$ **ii** $-4 + (-3)$
   g i $-2 - (-3)$ **ii** $-2 + 3$ **h i** $-3 - (-1)$ **ii** $-3 + 1$

The **negative** of 2 is -2. The **negative** of -3 is 3.
In Exercise 4.1 we saw that:

> **subtracting a number is the same as adding its negative.**

Example 1 $2 - 3 = 2 + (-3) = -1$ *Example 2* $1 - (-4) = 1 + 4 = 5$

To subtract:
express the subtraction as an addition, then use the number line.

Exercise 4.2

1 If necessary, use a number line to help you with these calculations.

   a $7 - 8$ **b** $6 - 12$ **c** $0 - 8$ **d** $-1 - 3$

   e $-4 - 5$ **f** $-6 - 7$ **g** $-5 - (-8)$ **h** $-9 - (-6)$

   i $-7 - (-12)$ **j** $-8 - (-8)$

2 Find the value of:

   a $36 - 100$ **b** $52 - (-39)$ **c** $-27 - 18$ **d** $-14 - (-3)$

   e $-16 - (-25)$ **f** $12 - (-13)$ **g** $-28 - (-17)$ **h** $-18 - (-35)$

3 Evaluate:

   a $10 - (-6)$ **b** $8 + (-9)$ **c** $-6 + (-11)$

   d $7 - 15$ **e** $-5 + 11$ **f** $-9 - (-12)$

   g $14 + (-14)$ **h** $-14 - (-14)$ **i** $-7 - 21$

   j $-1 - (-10)$ **k** $-3 + (-23)$ **l** $-8 + 7$

4 Calculate the total profit or loss made by Gary's Garage over the year.
($+1$ stands for a profit of £1000. -1 stands for a loss of £1000.)

	Jan	Feb	Mar	Apr	May	Jun	Jul	Aug	Sep	Oct	Nov	Dec
Profit/Loss	-4	1	8	6	-2	-5	-1	3	9	-4	1	-3

5 The table gives some information about the average surface temperatures on the planets of the solar system.

	Mercury	Venus	Earth	Mars	Jupiter	Saturn	Uranus	Neptune	Pluto
Temp. (°C)	179	453	8	4	-153	-185	-214	-225	-236

   a What is the difference in the average temperature between

      i Venus and Mercury

      ii the Earth and Jupiter

      iii Saturn and Pluto?

   b How many degrees warmer, on average, is

      i Mercury than Jupiter

      ii the Earth than Saturn

      iii Jupiter than Neptune?

   c The maximum temperature recorded on Mercury is 427 °C.
The minimum temperature is -92 °C.
The difference between the maximum and the minimum is called the **range**.
What is the range in temperature on Mercury?

   d The maximum temperature recorded on Earth one day was 47 °C.
The range in temperatures that day was 65 degrees.
What was the minimum temperature on Earth that day?

6 The diagram shows the highest point
and the lowest point on Earth.
It also gives the average height of land
and the average depth of the sea bed.
a What is the difference in height
between the bottom of the
Mariana Trench and the top
of Everest?
b What is the difference between the
average height of the land and the
average depth of the sea bed?
c If Everest were put in the Mariana
Trench, how far below sea level
would its peak be?

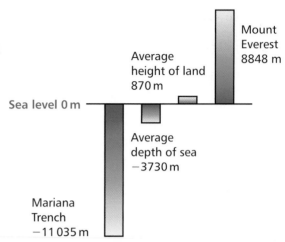

Mount Everest 8848 m

Average height of land 870 m

Sea level 0 m

Average depth of sea −3730 m

Mariana Trench −11 035 m

---

5 Letters and numbers

Examples

1 What is $x + 2$ when $x = -3$?
$x + 2 = -3 + 2 = -1$

2 Evaluate $4 - y$ when $y = -5$.
$4 - y = 4 - (-5) = 9$

3 Simplify $2a^2 - (-a^2)$.
$2a^2 - (-a^2) = 2a^2 + a^2 = 3a^2$

4 Simplify $5p - 3q + 2p - q$.
$$5p - 3q + 2p - q = 5p + 2p - 3q - q$$
$$= 7p - 4q$$

Exercise 5.1

1 Find the value of each expression using the given values of x, y, ...
  a $1 - x$; $x = -2$
  b $3 + y$; $y = -5$
  c $a + 10$; $a = -3$
  d $u - 7$; $u = 2$
  e $t - 4$; $t = -3$
  f $6 - s$; $s = -7$
  g $x + 8$; $x = -11$
  h $9 + y$; $y = -3$
  i $-2 + a$; $a = 5$
  j $-8 + w$; $w = -4$
  k $2 - x$; $x = 7$
  l $-10 + y$; $y = 6$
  m $x + y$; $x = 3$, $y = -4$
  n $a - b$; $a = 7$, $b = 9$
  o $y - x$; $x = -3$, $y = -2$
  p $m - n$; $m = -8$, $n = -7$
  q $-x - y$; $x = 1$, $y = -4$
  r $-b + a$; $b = -12$, $a = -5$

2 The height, h metres, of a hang-glider above the top of a cliff edge after t seconds is
$h = t - 20$.
  a Find the height after:
    i 30 seconds
    ii 20 seconds
    iii 5 seconds.
  b Explain what each answer in **a** means.

3 The Hi-fly Airline calculates its profit (£*P*) per flight by using the formula
$P = 100n - 12\,000$, where *n* is the number of passengers.

  a Calculate the profit when the number of passengers is:

    i   50   **ii**   100

    iii 150   **iv** 200.

  b What is the 'break-even' number?

4 A ball is thrown up from the edge of a cliff
12 metres above the sea.
The height of the ball above the cliff, *h* metres,
after *t* seconds, is given by the formula $h = 4t - t^2$.

  a Copy and complete the table.

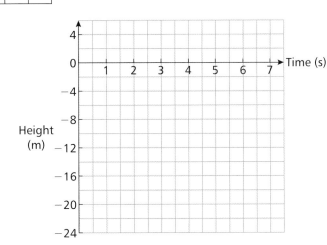

t	0	1	2	3	4	5	6	7
h	0	3				-5		

  b Using axes and scales as
shown, draw a graph
on squared paper of the
flight of the ball.

  c How long does it take the
ball to reach the sea?

5 $2a + a = 3a$ $7x - (-4x) = 7x + 4x = 11x$ $-3m + m = -2m$

In a similar way, simplify:

  a $6x - x$ **b** $3y + (-2y)$ **c** $-4a - 3a$

  d $t - 5t$ **e** $m - (-2m)$ **f** $-2d + (-4d)$

  g $-3x - 6x$ **h** $-c - (-3c)$ **i** $x^2 - (-x^2)$

  j $3y^2 + (-4y^2)$ **k** $-a - (-a)$ **l** $-7p^2 + 2p^2$

6 Simplify:

  a $6m - 4m + 3m$ **b** $5k - 3k - 2k$ **c** $3a + (-a) + (-a)$

  d $2e - 3e + e$ **e** $-2x - (-7x) + (-3x)$ **f** $6p - (-5p) + (-4p)$

  g $-y^2 - 3y^2 + 9y^2$ **h** $b^3 - 4b^3 - 2b^3$ **i** $-x^2 + 7x^2 - 11x^2$

7 Simplify:

  a $2a + a + b - 3b$ **b** $5m - m - 3n - n$ **c** $3x + 2y + 5x - 3y$

  d $4p - 3q - p - q$ **e** $c - d - 5c + d$ **f** $-2a + b - 6b - a$

  g $3a^2 - 2b^2 - 5a^2 + 4b^2$ **h** $4xy - 3x^2 - 5xy + 4x^2$ **i** $ab - bc - ac - bc - ac - ab$

Investigation

Calculate the possible differences between pairs of cards in each set. How many different values can you find for each set?

Set 1 [1] [2]

Set 2 [1] [2] [3]

Set 3 [1] [2] [3] [4]

Can you find a formula for set *n*?   **Set n** [1] [2] [3] [4] ... [n + 1]

Challenges

1 *Rule:* The sum of the numbers in any two circles goes in the square between them.

Example   (−2) → [3] ← (5)

Copy and complete: **a** (3) → [−4] ← ( )

b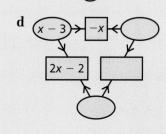

c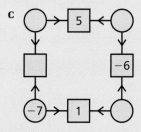

d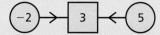

2 Copy and complete this obstacle course.

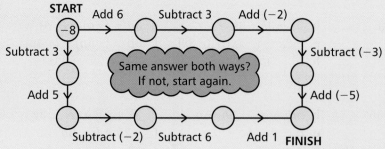

6 Multiplying integers

Here is a partially completed multiplication table.

The following facts have been used to help make the entries:

- Any number times zero equals 0.
- Zero times any number equals 0.
- Any number multiplied by 1 remains the same.
- 1 times any number equals that number.

Second number

First number

×	−5	−4	−3	−2	−1	0	1	2	3	4	5
5						0	5	10	15	20	25
4						0	4	8	12	16	20
3						0	3	6	9	12	15
2						0	2	4	6	8	10
1	−5	−4	−3	−2	−1	0	1	2	3	4	5
0	0	0	0	0	0	0	0	0	0	0	0
−1						0					
−2						0					
−3						0					
−4						0					
−5						0					

Exercise 6.1

1 a Copy the table.

 b $5 \times (-5)$ means five *negative fives*

$\Rightarrow 5 \times (-5) = (-5) + (-5) + (-5) + (-5) + (-5) = -25$

Use this idea to fill in the top section of the table.

 c $2 \times 3 = 3 \times 2 = 6$. Similarly, $(-2) \times 3 = 3 \times (-2) = -6$.

Use this idea to fill in the lower right-hand section of the table.

 d Look at the number patterns in the rows and columns of the table. Use these patterns to complete the table.

2 From your completed table find the value of:

a $2 \times (-4)$	**b** $1 \times (-3)$	**c** -5×2
d -2×1	**e** $3 \times (-5)$	**f** -4×4

> You should notice that:
> - a positive number × a negative number = a negative number
> - a negative number × a positive number = a negative number

3 From your table find the value of:

a $-3 \times (-4)$	**b** $-5 \times (-1)$	**c** 4×2
d $-2 \times (-3)$	**e** 1×3	**f** $-4 \times (-4)$

> You should notice that:
> - a positive number × a positive number = a positive number
> - a negative number × a negative number = a positive number

4 Calculate:

  a i 6×3 **ii** $6 \times (-3)$ **iii** -6×3 **iv** $-6 \times (-3)$

  b i 8×9 **ii** $8 \times (-9)$ **iii** -8×9 **iv** $-8 \times (-9)$

  c i -7×3 **ii** $-7 \times (-3)$ **iii** 7×3 **iv** $7 \times (-3)$

  d i $-10 \times (-1)$ **ii** $10 \times (-1)$ **iii** -10×1 **iv** 10×1

5 Find the value of:

  a -3×8 **b** -7×1 **c** $6 \times (-5)$ **d** $-9 \times (-2)$

  e $4 \times (-10)$ **f** 12×6 **g** -1×9 **h** -17×1

  i $0 \times (-6)$ **j** 7×7 **k** $1 \times (-1)$ **l** -15×0

  m $-13 \times (-2)$ **n** $(-3)^2$ **o** $(-10)^2$ **p** $(-1)^2$

  q $75 \times (-1)$ **r** -12×1 **s** 16×3 **t** $10 \times (-100)$

6 Using the numbers 2, 3 and -4 we can form three products, namely:

$2 \times 3 = 6$; $2 \times (-4) = -8$; $3 \times (-4) = -12$

In a similar way, use each set of three numbers to form three products.

  a $2, -3, -6$ **b** $-4, -1, 3$ **c** $-7, 2, 6$ **d** $-2, -5, -8$ **e** $-3, 10, -9$

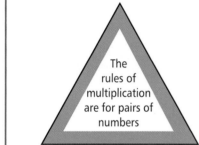

If there are more than two numbers take them two at a time.

Remember: BODMAS

Example 1 $4 \times (-3) \times 5$

$$= -12 \times 5$$
$$= -60$$

Example 2 $4 + 3 \times (-2)$

$$= 4 + (-6)$$
$$= -2$$

Exercise 6.2

1 Calculate:

  a $-3 \times 2 \times (-1)$ **b** $-5 \times (-4) \times 6$ **c** $7 \times (-3) \times 2$ **d** $4 \times (-4) \times (-5)$

  e $-1 \times (-7) \times 4$ **f** $15 \times 73 \times 0$ **g** $-9 \times (-2) \times (-3)$ **h** $(-4)^2 \times (-3)$

  i $72 \times (-2)$ **j** $(-1)^3$ **k** $(-5)^3$ **l** $(-10)^3$

  m $(-2)^2 \times (-6)$ **n** $(-3)^2 \times (-1)^2$ **o** $-3 \times (-6)^2$ **p** $-1 \times (-7)^2$

  q $(-4)^3 \times 3$ **r** $6 \times (-10)^3$ **s** $24 \times (-1)^4$ **t** $(-2)^3 \times (-3)^2$

2 Calculate:

  a $3 \times 5 - (-6)$ **b** $-7 \times (-3) + (-3)$ **c** $5 + 3 \times (-4)$ **d** $-4 + 6 \times (-1)$

  e $8 - 2 \times (-6)$ **f** $1 - (-2) \times (-3)$ **g** $-6 + (-1) \times 3$ **h** $5 - (-3) \times 2$

  i $-1 - (-1) \times (-1)$ **j** $1 + (-1) \times 1$ **k** $3 + (-2)^2$ **l** $6 - (-3)^3$

3 Calculate:

  a $2(3 - 4)$ **b** $-6(4 - 5)$ **c** $5(-2 - 3)$ **d** $-1(8 - 11)$

  e $(-2 + 5)^2$ **f** $(-3 - 4)^2$ **g** $-6(2 - 7)$ **h** $-2(-1 - 12)$

Challenge

Choose any three numbers in order, in a row, column or diagonal. Multiply the first two, then add or subtract the third. This gives you a **target number**. For example, here are the three ways of getting the target number -1:

−2	3	−1	2
1	0	5	−7
−7	−6	4	−5
−4	6	−3	7

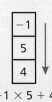

−2	3	−1

$-1 \times 3 - (-2)$

$-1 \times 5 + 4$ $-7 \times 0 + (-1)$

a Find one solution for each of these target numbers:

  i 7   **ii** -9 **iii** -3 **iv** 19

b Find **i** the highest possible target number

         ii the lowest target number.

---

7 More letters and numbers

Example 1   Given $x = -3$, calculate the value of: **a** $1 - 4x$ **b** $2x^2 - 5x$

$$
\begin{aligned}
\textbf{a} \quad 1 - 4x &= 1 - 4 \times (-3) \\
&= 1 - (-12) \\
&= 1 + 12 = 13
\end{aligned}
\qquad
\begin{aligned}
\textbf{b} \quad 2x^2 - 5x &= 2 \times (-3)^2 - 5 \times (-3) \\
&= 2 \times 9 - (-15) \\
&= 18 + 15 = 33
\end{aligned}
$$

Example 2   Simplify: **a** $5a \times (-4a)$ **b** $(-y)^2$

        a $5a \times (-4a) = -20a^2$ **b** $(-y)^2 = -y \times (-y) = y^2$

Exercise 7.1

1 Given $x = -2$, calculate the values of:

  a $x + 2$ **b** $3x - 5$ **c** $4 + 2x$ **d** $7 - x^2$ **e** $6x^2$ **f** $5(x - 2)$

2 Given $p = -4$, calculate the values of:

  a $2 - p$ **b** $p^2 - p$ **c** $3p + 5$ **d** $(p + 1)^2$ **e** $1 - 2p^2$ **f** $3(p - 1)^2$

3 Given $y = -1$, evaluate:

  a $4 - 4y$ **b** $y^2 + y$ **c** $(y - 1)^3$ **d** $6y^2 - 5y$ **e** $6 + 2y^3$ **f** $5(3 - 4y)^2$

4 $a = 3$, $b = -2$ and $c = -4$. Calculate the values of:

  a abc **b** $ab + bc$ **c** $ac - b^2$ **d** $(a + b + c)^2$ **e** $a + 2b - 3c$ **f** $b^3 - c^3$

5 Simplify:

a $a \times b$ **b** $a \times (-b)$ **c** $-a \times b$

d $-a \times (-b)$ **e** $3 \times (-4x)$ **f** $4x \times (-5)$

g $2y \times 3y$ **h** $5m \times (-m)$ **i** $-x \times (-x)$

j $-3a \times 6a$ **k** $4p \times 9q$ **l** $7x \times (-2y)$

m $(-t)^2$ **n** $(-5k)^2$ **o** $(-x)^3$

p $(-x)^4$ **q** $(mn)^2$ **r** $a^2 \times (-b^2)$

6 An oil pipeline comes up from the sea, and then goes through a pumping station. The pipeline is at a constant slope.

Each joint in the pipeline has a number (n), and its height (h m) above sea level is found from the formula $h = 30 - 10n$.

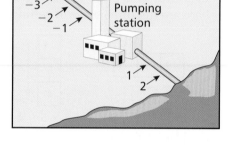

a Calculate the height of joint number:

   i 2   **ii** 6

   iii -1 **iv** -6.

What does your answer to **ii** mean?

b Calculate the difference in height between joints:

   i   5 and 8   **ii** -2 and -5 **iii** -4 and 7.

7 The train is slowing down steadily.

Ron starts his stopwatch as it passes him, travelling at speed u m/s. The formula Ron uses to calculate the train's speed (v m/s) t seconds after passing him is $v = u - 5t$.

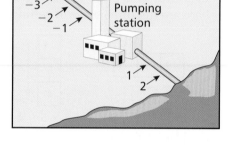

a The train passes Ron at 30 m/s.

Calculate its speed:

   i   2 seconds later

   ii 4 seconds later.

b How many seconds after passing Ron will the train stop?

c **i**   What does $t = -3$ mean?

   ii What was the speed of the train at this time?

d The train started braking 7 seconds before reaching Ron. What was its speed then?

8 A flask is used to store very cold liquids. The label states that liquids should not be stored in it if their boiling point is below -100 °F. The table gives various boiling points in degrees Celsius. The conversion formula is:

$F = 1 \cdot 8 \times C + 32$.

   i   Convert each temperature to Fahrenheit.

   ii Say whether or not the flask is suitable for storing each substance.

	Liquid	Boiling point
a	Ether	35·0 °C
b	Sulphurous anhydride	−10·0 °C
c	Chlorine	−33·6 °C
d	Ammonia	−33·5 °C
e	Carbon anhydride	−78·2 °C
f	Nitrous oxide	−87·9 °C

Challenge

Use each of the numbers 1, 2, 3 and some of the symbols $+$, $-$, $\times$ and ( ) to produce each integer from 0 to -8, for example:
$(2 - 1) \times (-3) = -3$.

Investigations

1 a i If $x = 4$, then $x^2 = 16$. True or false?
  ii If $x = -4$, then $x^2 = 16$. True or false?
  b Only one of the following is true. Which one?
    i If $x^2 = 16$, $x = 4$.
    ii If $x^2 = 16$, $x = -4$.
    iii If $x^2 = 16$, $x = 4$ or -4.

2 a Investigate possible solutions of the equation $x^n = 1$, where n is a whole number.
  b What happens when $x^n = -1$?

3 Study the values $(-1)^2$, $(-1)^3$, $(-1)^4$, $(-1)^5$, ...
  a Investigate the value of $(-1)^n$, where n is a whole number.
  b Investigate whether a^n is positive or negative, where a is an integer and n is a positive whole number.
  c Write up your investigation.

8 Dividing integers

Here is a multiplication table.

$\times$	-5	-4	-3	-2	-1	0	1	2	3	4	5
5	-25	-20	-15	-10	-5	0	5	10	15	20	25
4	-20	-16	-12	-8	-4	0	4	8	12	16	20
3	-15	-12	-9	-6	-3	0	3	6	9	12	15
2	-10	-8	-6	-4	-2	0	2	4	6	8	10
1	-5	-4	-3	-2	-1	0	1	2	3	4	5
0	0	0	0	0	0	0	0	0	0	0	0
-1	5	4	3	2	1	0	-1	-2	-3	-4	-5
-2	10	8	6	4	2	0	-2	-4	-6	-8	-10
-3	15	12	9	6	3	0	-3	-6	-9	-12	-15
-4	20	16	12	8	4	0	-4	-8	-12	-16	-20
-5	25	20	15	10	5	0	-5	-10	-15	-20	-25

Division is the inverse operation of multiplication, for example:
$5 \times 4 = 20 \Rightarrow 20 \div 5 = 4$ and $20 \div 4 = 5$.

We can therefore use the multiplication table in reverse to see that, for example:

a $3 \times (-2) = -6 \Rightarrow -6 \div 3 = -2$ and $-6 \div (-2) = 3$

b $-4 \times (-3) = 12 \Rightarrow 12 \div (-4) = -3$ and $12 \div (-3) = -4$.

In general, we see that the rules for division are the same as the rules for multiplication.

> **When dividing one number by another, where the signs are the same, the quotient is positive; when the signs are different, the quotient is negative.**

Examples: **a** $-36 \div 4 = -9$ **b** $28 \div (-7) = -4$ **c** $-24 \div (-8) = 3$ **d** $\dfrac{-18}{9} = -2$

Exercise 8.1

1 Say whether each of these produces a positive or negative quotient:

a $\dfrac{-7}{1}$ **b** $\dfrac{-4}{-3}$ **c** $\dfrac{9}{5}$ **d** $\dfrac{12}{-6}$ **e** $\dfrac{-3}{15}$ **f** $\dfrac{-1}{-17}$

2 Calculate:

a $8 \div (-2)$ **b** $14 \div 2$ **c** $-12 \div 3$ **d** $-15 \div (-5)$ **e** $-100 \div 25$

f $20 \div (-1)$ **g** $0 \div (-7)$ **h** $100 \div (-10)$ **i** $-18 \div (-9)$ **j** $-27 \div 27$

3 Calculate:

a $\dfrac{-32}{8}$ **b** $\dfrac{-30}{-6}$ **c** $\dfrac{63}{-7}$ **d** $\dfrac{-4}{64}$ **e** $\dfrac{10\,000}{-100}$ **f** $\dfrac{-3}{-81}$

4 Calculate the mean of these scores:

$4, -1, -3, -9, 2, -1, 5, -6, -8, -3$

5 Calculate the mean temperature.

$2\,°C, -1\,°C, -4\,°C, 0\,°C, -7\,°C, 3\,°C, -14\,°C, 0\,°C, -6\,°C$

6 Use the formula $F = \frac{9}{5}C + 32$ and $C = \frac{5}{9}(F - 32)$ to convert:

a i $50\,°F$ **ii** $14\,°F$ **iii** $-13\,°F$ **iv** $-40\,°F$ to degrees Celsius

b i $-5\,°C$ **ii** $-20\,°C$ **iii** $-65\,°C$ **iv** $-200\,°C$ to degrees Fahrenheit.

7 Given $a = 27$, $b = -9$ and $c = -3$, calculate the values of:

a $\dfrac{a}{b}$ **b** $\dfrac{b}{c}$ **c** $\dfrac{a + b}{c}$ **d** $\dfrac{bc}{a}$ **e** $\dfrac{a + b}{b - c}$

f $\dfrac{a + bc}{b}$ **g** $\dfrac{a - b}{b - c}$ **h** $\dfrac{a - bc}{abc}$ **i** $\dfrac{ac}{b^2}$ **j** $\dfrac{5b}{a + b + c}$

8 Here is an example of someone calculating the coordinates of the point midway between two given points:

$$M\left(\frac{-3 + 5}{2}, \frac{4 + (-2)}{2}\right) = M(1, 1)$$

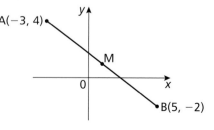

The two end-points have been *averaged*. Use this method to find the midpoint of the line joining:

a $A(-1, 3)$, $B(3, -7)$ **b** $E(3, 4)$, $F(-3, -6)$

c $P(-7, -2)$, $Q(1, -8)$ **d** $V(5, -4)$, $W(-6, 3)$

9 You can find the time of day at any place P in the world from the formula:

$$\text{time at P} = \text{time at London} + \frac{\text{longitude of P}}{15}$$

Going west, the longitude is negative, so 20° W gives (−20).

a Find the time, to the nearest hour, in these places when it is noon in London:

   i Sao Paulo, 45° W

   ii Ottawa, 75° W

   iii St Louis, 90° W

   iv Vancouver, 123° W

   v Kiev, 30° E

   vi Singapore, 105° E

   vii Delhi, 77° E

   viii Sydney, 151° E.

b Comparing times with noon in London, find the time gap between:

   i Cairo, USA, 90° W and Cairo, Egypt, 30° E

   ii Montreal, Canada, 74° W and Osaka, Japan, 135° E.

10 Think about the equation $x + 1 = 0$.

The ancient Greek mathematician Diophantus (AD 275) called such equations 'absurd'.

Negative numbers had not been discovered at that point.

Solve these 'absurd' equations:

a $x + 3 = 0$ **b** $x + 9 = 0$

c $x + 5 = 3$ **d** $x + 8 = 1$

e $x - 1 = -4$ **f** $x - 6 = -7$

g $2x + 12 = 0$ **h** $3x + 27 = 0$

i $2x - 3 = -9$ **j** $5x - 1 = -26$

k $4x + 5 = -7$ **l** $3x + 6 = -6$

---

9 Integers on the button

You can add, subtract, multiply and divide integers on your calculator using the [+/−] button.

It is always good practice to include brackets when they are given in the text.

Example 1 $-6 + (-7)$ [+/−] [6] [+] [(] [+/−] [7] [)] [=] −13

Example 2 $3 - (-4)$ [3] [−] [(] [+/−] [4] [)] [=] 7

Example 3 $2 \times (-6)$ [2] [×] [(] [+/−] [6] [)] [=] −12

Example 4 $-24 \div (-8)$ [+/−] [24] [÷] [(] [+/−] [8] [)] [=] 3

Exercise 9.1

1 Try these without a calculator, then use your calculator to check your answers.

a $-4 + (-11)$ b $3 + (-18)$

c $1 - (-15)$ d $7 - (-25)$

e $-6 - (-36)$ f $-10 - (-15)$

g $-5 + (-17)$ h $-6 - 7$

i $-9 - 8$ j $13 - 15$

k $24 + (-15)$ l $-100 - (-25)$

m $3 \times (-15)$ n $7 \times (-14)$

o $-6 \times (-12)$ p $-8 \times (-30)$

q -7×11 r $-50 \div (-2)$

s $-36 \div (-3)$ t $28 \div (-7)$

u $50 \div (-2)$ v $-64 \div 4$

w $-70 \div 7$ x $-42 \div (-3)$

2 Use a calculator to evaluate:

a $9 + (-12) + (-7)$ b $-5 + (-9) - (-10)$

c $-13 - (-9) - (-6)$ d $7 \times (-3) \times (-5)$

e $-4 \times (-5) \times (-12)$ f $-8 \times 3 \times (-2)$

3 Remembering that integers obey the rules of priority, BODMAS, evaluate the following:

a $-19 + 7 \times 3$ b $-5 + (-4) \times (-2)$

c $-6 - (-5) \times (-4)$ d $(7 - (-3)) \times (-8)$

e $10 \times (-4) + (-7) \times 6$ f $(18 + (-3) - (-5)) \times (-10)$

4 Given $p = -16$, $q = 4$ and $r = -8$, calculate the values of:

a $p - qr$ b $pq - (-r)$ c $\dfrac{qr}{p}$

d $\dfrac{p^2 - r^3}{-pr}$ e $\dfrac{(p + q)^2}{-(q + r)}$

5 a The Vulcan Cave system starts at a height of 345 m and goes down in four stages of 100 m.

   i Evaluate $345 - 4 \times 100$.

   ii What is the height of the end of the cave system?

b The Tubor system starts at a height of 275 m and goes down in steps of 35 m.

   i Form an equation for the height, h, after going down n steps.

   ii Solve your equation to find how many steps down from the top a height of -110 m is.

6 Express the following numbers in scientific notation, i.e. in the form $a \times 10^n$, where a is a number between 1 and 10 ($1 \leq a < 10$) and n is an integer.

a 250 000   b 16 500 000

c 0·000 245   d 0·000 008

e 0·000 000 000 84

◀◀ **RECAP**

Integers are positive or negative whole numbers.
You should be able to:

- order, add, subtract, multiply and divide integers
- use them to solve problems, including algebraic ones.

Integers can be represented on a number line.

$$-10\ -9\ -8\ -7\ -6\ -5\ -4\ -3\ -2\ -1\ \ 0\ \ 1\ \ 2\ \ 3\ \ 4\ \ 5\ \ 6\ \ 7\ \ 8\ \ 9\ \ 10$$

The further to the right a number is on the number line, the bigger it is.

Examples $6 > 4$; $-6 < -4$ ('>' means 'is greater than'; '<' means 'is less than'.)

A number line can help to:
- add integers   Start at the first number and do what the second number tells you.
  Examples   **a** $3 + (-7) = -4$
  b $-1 + (-5) = -6$
- subtract integers   Instead of subtracting an integer, add its negative.
  Examples   **a** $2 - 6 = 2 + (-6) = -4$
  b $-1 - (-3) = -1 + 3 = 2$

When multiplying integers, remember: same signs, positive product; different signs, negative product.

Examples   **a** $-5 \times 4 = -20$
b $3 \times (-2) = -6$
c $-2 \times (-4) = 8$

When dividing integers, remember: same signs, positive quotient; different signs, negative quotient.

Examples   **a** $-12 \div 6 = -2$
b $\dfrac{-24}{8} = -3$
c $-18 \div (-9) = 2$

Using integers in algebra:

Examples   **a** When $x = -3$ and $y = -4$,
$$2x^2y = 2 \times (-3)^2 \times (-4)$$
$$= 2 \times 9 \times (-4)$$
$$= 18 \times (-4) = -72$$
b $-3a - 5a - a = -9a$
c Solve $x + 9 = 2$.
$$x + 9 = 2 \Rightarrow x = 2 - 9$$
$$\Rightarrow x = -7$$
d Solve $3a + 7 = 1$.
$$3a + 7 = 1 \Rightarrow 3a = -6$$
$$\Rightarrow a = -2$$

1 Which of these are true and which are false?

   a $-2 < -1$ **b** $-8 > 4$ **c** $-2 \cdot 4 > -2 \cdot 6$

2 List these numbers in order of size, smallest first: $\quad 2, -3, -5, 0, 4, -7, 1$.

3 Calculate the following without using a calculator:

   a $-4 + (-9)$ **b** $7 - (-1)$ **c** $-16 - (-11)$ **d** $8 \times (-7)$ **e** -5×15
   f $-72 \div 6$ **g** $-96 \div (-3)$ **h** $-15 \div (-15)$ **i** $-2 - 18$ **j** $5(-9 - 2)$

4 The temperatures (in degrees Celsius) at eight places around the world one day at 6 am were:

      $6, -4, -9, -1, 3, -4, 2, -1$.

   a What was the range of temperatures?
   b What was the mean temperature?

5 ΔPQR has vertices P$(-7, -1)$, Q$(6, -5)$ and R$(-3, 4)$.
   The x coordinates are increased by 5 and the y coordinates are decreased by 7.
   Work out the new coordinates of P, Q and R.

6 The table shows the temperatures at which some chemical elements boil.

Element	mercury	nitrogen	oxygen	bromine	helium
Boiling point (°C)	357	-196	-183	59	-269

   a What is the range of temperatures in the table?
   b Which has the higher boiling point, nitrogen or oxygen?
   c How many degrees higher than helium is the boiling point of
      i   oxygen   **ii** bromine?

7 If $p = -2$, $q = 3$ and $r = -4$, calculate the values of:

   a pqr **b** $pq - qr$ **c** $p(q + r)$ **d** $r - pq$ **e** $\dfrac{(p + q + r)^2}{(p - q + r)}$

8 Simplify:

   a $3x \times (-5x)$ **b** $-4a \times (-6a)$ **c** $(-p)^2 \times (-7p)$ **d** $y - 3y - 2y$

9 Solve for x:

   a $x + 7 = 0$ **b** $x - 5 = -9$ **c** $2x - 3 = -11$

10 Use the formulae $F = \frac{9}{5}C + 32$ and $C = \frac{5}{9}(F - 32)$ to convert:
   a **i** $-15\,°C$ **ii** $-45\,°C$ to Fahrenheit
   b **i** $23\,°F$ **ii** $-22\,°F$ to Celsius.

REVISE

3 Brackets and equations

James Maxwell was born in Edinburgh in 1831.

He attended Edinburgh Academy where he had the nickkname 'Dafty'.

In 1873, in a book called *Electricity and Magnetism*, he published four equations.

James Maxwell

$$\nabla \cdot \mathbf{E} = 4\pi\rho$$

$$\nabla \times \mathbf{E} = -\frac{1}{c}\frac{\partial \mathbf{B}}{\partial t}$$

$$\nabla - \mathbf{B} = 0$$

$$\nabla \times \mathbf{E} = -\frac{4\pi}{c}\mathbf{J} + \frac{1}{c}\frac{\partial \mathbf{E}}{\partial t}$$

Maxwell's equations explain how electricity and magnetism work. They are considered to be one of the great achievements of nineteenth-century mathematics.

1 REVIEW

◄◄ **Exercise 1.1**

1 Calculate:

 a $3 + (-4)$ **b** $2 - (-3)$ **c** $-1 + 3$ **d** $-3 + 1$

 e -4×0 **f** $3 \times (-2)$ **g** -5×3 **h** $-1 \times (-6)$

 i $(-6)^2$ **j** $\dfrac{-6}{2}$ **k** $\dfrac{6}{-2}$ **l** $\dfrac{-6}{-2}$

2 Simplify:

 a $4a - a$ **b** $3x - 9x$ **c** $4e - (-5e)$ **d** $m \times 2m$

 e $3c \times 6c$ **f** $4x + 2y - x + y$ **g** $-6w - (-3w)$

3 If $a = -2$ and $c = -5$ find the value of:

 a ac **b** a^2 **c** $a - c$ **d** $\dfrac{c^2}{a}$

4 Write these without brackets:

 a $3(y - 1)$ **b** $9(k - 2n)$ **c** $3(5z + 4)$ **d** $a(3 - b)$

 e $f(f + 5)$ **f** $x(3x + 5)$ **g** $a(2a - 3b)$ **h** $5(x^2 - 4x)$

5 Solve these equations:

 a $3n = 24$ **b** $5x = -15$ **c** $-2y = 18$ **d** $-t = -8$

 e $5y - 1 = -6$ **f** $16 - 3e = 1$ **g** $7x - 18 = 4x$ **h** $8h - 3 = 13h + 22$

6 Solve:

 a $7(y + 8) = 21$ **b** $-15 = 3(a - 2)$ **c** $2(5y - 6) = -2$

7 a In this isosceles triangle the measurements are
in centimetres.
Find the length of the two equal sides.

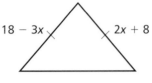

18 − 3x   2x + 8

b For this balance, make an equation and solve it to find
the unknown weight on each side.
All values are in kilograms.

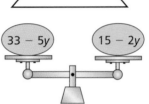

33 − 5y   15 − 2y

8 a Write down an expression for the area of this rectangle.
All measurements are in centimetres.
b If the area is $28x$ cm^2, make an equation and find x.

4

x + 12

9 This shape is made from rectangles.
All lengths are in centimetres.
Find expressions in terms of y for the
lengths:
a AB   **b** CD.

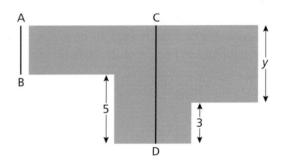

---

2 Getting rid of brackets

Remember:
- $4x$ = four lots of $x = x + x + x + x$
- $4ab$ = four lots of $ab = ab + ab + ab + ab$

Similarly:
- $4(x + 2)$ = four lots of $x + 2 = x + 2 + x + 2 + x + 2 + x + 2$
        = four lots of x and four lots of $2 = 4x + 8$
  so $4(x + 2) = 4x + 8$
- $4(x − 3)$ = four lots of $x − 3 = x − 3 + x − 3 + x − 3 + x − 3$
        = four lots of x minus four lots of $3 = 4x − 12$
  so $4(x − 3) = 4x − 12$

In general, each term within the brackets is multiplied by the term outside the
brackets.
The general pattern is: $a(b + c) = ab + ac$ $a(b − c) = ab − ac$

Example   Remove the brackets: **a** $5(x − y)$ **b** $9(4 − 2x)$ **c** $y(y − 4)$

           a $5(x − y) = 5x − 5y$ **b** $9(4 − 2x) = 36 − 18x$ **c** $y(y − 4) = y^2 − 4y$

Exercise 2.1

1 Remove the brackets:

a $3(y - 7)$	**b** $2(m + 3)$	**c** $5(n - 4)$	**d** $9(x + 1)$
e $7(a + 3)$	**f** $7(b - 4)$	**g** $4(z - 6)$	**h** $10(t - 2)$
i $2(k - 1)$	**j** $11(c - 4)$	**k** $6(7 + y)$	**l** $8(1 + u)$
m $5(5 - h)$	**n** $12(2 - a)$	**o** $7(3 - e)$	**p** $6(x + y)$
q $8(x - y)$	**r** $13(2 - f)$	**s** $20(4 + x)$	**t** $7(a - b)$
u $15(k + a)$	**v** $16(y - 3)$	**w** $19(2 - a)$	**x** $23(m + n)$

2 For each picture below, give the total weight in two different ways (i.e. with brackets, then without brackets).

a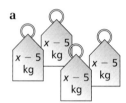

b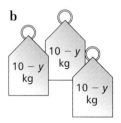

c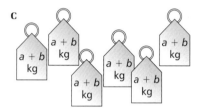

d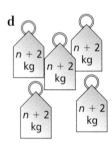

e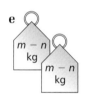

f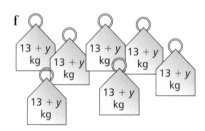

3 For each situation write down an expression for the amount indicated in two different ways.

a

Total volume

b (10 − x) cm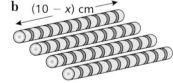

Total length

c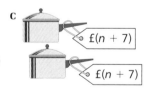

£(n + 7)

£(n + 7)

Total cost

4 In each case write the total area covered by the stamps in two different ways.
   a Each stamp covers $(y - 3)$ mm²   **b** Each stamp covers $(13 + y)$ mm²

Exercise 2.2

1 Remove the brackets:

a $3(4x + 5)$	**b** $5(2y - 1)$	**c** $2(2 + 3m)$	**d** $3(1 - 3k)$
e $8(7w - 2)$	**f** $c(y + 2)$	**g** $a(x + 1)$	**h** $e(f - 3)$
i $r(k - 3)$	**j** $x(y + 4)$	**k** $x(y + z)$	**l** $b(c + d)$
m $e(x - y)$	**n** $k(k + 3)$	**o** $a(a - 5)$	**p** $r(r - s)$
q $e(4 - e)$	**r** $x(x - 8)$	**s** $a(a + 2b)$	**t** $x(4x - 5)$
u $y(6x - 5y)$	**v** $x(2x - 3y)$	**w** $m(5m - 6)$	**x** $x(25 - 2x)$

2 Remove the brackets.
Remember: each term within the brackets is multiplied by the term outside the bracket.

a $3(a + b - 3)$	**b** $4(x + y + 1)$	**c** $2(m - n - 7)$
d $8(x + 2y + z)$	**e** $3(4a - 2b + c)$	**f** $10(5x - 6y + 3)$
g $y(y^2 - 4)$	**h** $a(a^2 + 3)$	**i** $h(h^2 - h)$
j $a(a + a^2)$	**k** $w(w^3 - w)$	**l** $2k(k^3 - 5k^2)$

3 All measurements in the cuboid shown are in centimetres.
Find an expression
  i   with brackets
  ii without brackets for:
a the surface area of the right-hand face A
b the surface area of the top face B
c the volume of the cuboid.

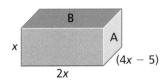

---

3 Negative multipliers

Example 1 $- (x + y)$
           $= -1(x + y)$
           $= -x - y$

Example 2 $-5(a - 7)$
           $= -5a - (-35)$
           $= -5a + 35$

Example 3 $7 + 3 (4 - y)$
           $= 7 + 12 - 3y$
           $= 19 - 3y$

Example 4 $9 - 3(8 - y)$
           $= 9 - 24 + 3y$
           $= -15 + 3y$

Exercise 3.1

1 Remove the brackets:

a $-3(a + 2)$	**b** $-2(k - 1)$	**c** $-7(c + 3)$	**d** $-5(x - 4)$
e $-8(5 + x)$	**f** $- (2 - n)$	**g** $- (14 + x)$	**h** $-4(2 - h)$
i $-2(a + b)$	**j** $-4(m - n)$	**k** $-(x + y)$	**l** $-(w + w^2)$
m $-6(x - x^2)$	**n** $-4(y^2 + y^3)$	**o** $-a(2 - a)$	**p** $-x(x + 5)$
q $-m(m + n)$	**r** $-h(a - b)$	**s** $-k(7 - k^2)$	**t** $-x^2(x + 3)$

2 Simplify by first removing the brackets:

a $7 + 3(a + 1)$ **b** $5 - 2(x - 3)$ **c** $11 - 7(2 - w)$
     $= 7 + 3a + 3$ $= 5 - 2x + 6$ $= 11 - 14 + 7w$
     $= \ldots$ $= \ldots$ $= \ldots$

d $4 - 2(w + 1)$ **e** $5 + 3(y + 7)$ **f** $8 - 3(x - 2)$ **g** $3 + 3(x - 2)$
h $5 + (2 - x)$ **i** $3 - 3(r + 1)$ **j** $7 - 4(3 + y)$ **k** $8 - (5 + k)$
l $2 - (z + 3)$ **m** $7 + (m - 1)$ **n** $12 - 3(6 - f)$ **o** $18 + 3(t - 6)$
p $12 - 8(x + 2)$ **q** $5 + 7(a + 2)$ **r** $8 - 9(b - 2)$ **s** $2 - (h - 1)$
t $5 + 7(y - 3)$ **u** $-3(x + 2) - x$ **v** $-(8 + y) + 2y$ **w** $-4(7 - x) - 3x$

3 a Find an expression for the area of the grey rectangle.

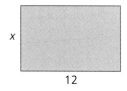 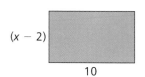

All lengths are in metres.

b Find an expression, with brackets, for the area of the orange rectangle.

c This diagram shows the same two rectangles as above.

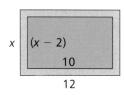

Explain why the grey border area, in m², is given by $12x - 10(x - 2)$.

d Simplify $12x - 10(x - 2)$ by first removing the brackets.

4 Repeat the above steps for these rectangles:

i

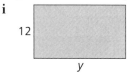 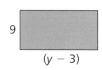 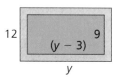

ii

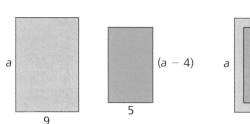

5 A garden area is 15 m long and k m wide.
It consists of a path 1 m wide round a central rectangular grass area.

a Make a sketch and find an expression, with brackets, for the area of the path.
b Simplify this expression.

Exercise 3.2

1 For each pair of rectangles:
   i   find an expression for the difference in their areas
   ii simplify the resulting expression
   iii calculate this difference for the given value of the variable.
All measurements are in centimetres.

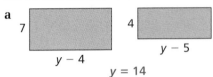
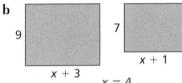

a 7   4   **b** 9   7

$y - 4$ $y - 5$ $x + 3$ $x + 1$

$y = 14$ $x = 4$

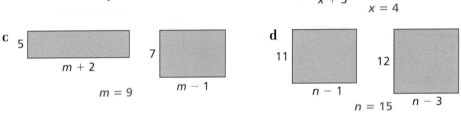

c 5   7   **d** 11   12

$m + 2$ $n - 1$ $n - 3$

$m = 9$ $m - 1$ $n = 15$

2 Simplify:
   a $4(m - 3) - (m + 2)$ **b** $6(x + 4) - 4(x - 1)$ **c** $7(k - 3) + 5(k - 3)$
   d $2(x + 5) - (x + 6)$ **e** $2(w - 1) - 5(w + 2)$ **f** $5(n - 9) - (n + 5)$
   g $3(4 - x) - 4(2 - x)$ **h** $7(7 - r) - 2(2 + r)$ **i** $5(6 - x) - 6(5 - x)$

3 For each pair of pictures:
   i   write down an expression for each pile of money
   ii state how much more valuable the first pile of money bags is than the second
       pile, giving your answer as a simplified expression
   iii evaluate the expression for the given value of the variable.

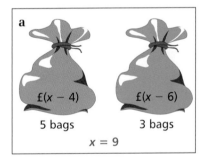

a

£$(x - 4)$ £$(x - 6)$

5 bags   3 bags

$x = 9$

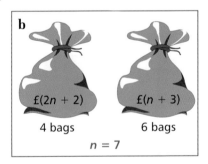

b

£$(2n + 2)$ £$(n + 3)$

4 bags   6 bags

$n = 7$

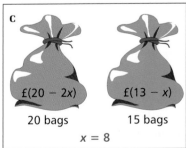

c

£$(20 - 2x)$ £$(13 - x)$

20 bags   15 bags

$x = 8$

4 Equations and brackets

If an equation has brackets then follow this procedure.

Step 1: Remove the brackets.
Step 2: Simplify each side of the equation if possible.
Step 3: Solve the equation.

Example 1   Solve $5(x - 3) = 25$.

$5(x - 3) = 25$
$\Rightarrow 5x - 15 = 25$
$\Rightarrow 5x - 15 + 15 = 25 + 15$
$\Rightarrow 5x = 40$
$\Rightarrow 5x \div 5 = 40 \div 5$
$\Rightarrow x = 8$

Example 2   Solve $-3(2 + 2y) = 6 - (y + 2)$.

$-3(2 + 2y) = 6 - (y + 2)$
$\Rightarrow -6 - 6y = 6 - y - 2$
$\Rightarrow -6 - 6y = 4 - y$
$\Rightarrow -6 - 6y + 6 + y = 4 - y + 6 + y$
$\Rightarrow -5y = 10$
$\Rightarrow -5y \div (-5) = 10 \div (-5)$
$\Rightarrow y = -2$

Exercise 4.1

1 Solve, by first multiplying out brackets:

   a $3(m + 2) = 18$ **b** $2(y - 7) = 4$ **c** $5(x + 1) = 10$
   d $7(x - 5) = 28$ **e** $8(n + 2) = 40$ **f** $9(k - 3) = 63$
   g $2(r - 6) = 2$ **h** $4(w + 3) = 12$ **i** $6(k + 2) = 12$
   j $12(x - 1) = 24$ **k** $7(x + 5) = 35$ **l** $11(n - 2) = 0$

2 Solve:

   a $3(x - 1) = -3$ **b** $2(n + 1) = -2$ **c** $4(k + 4) = 4$
   d $7(w - 1) = -14$ **e** $3(k + 2) = 0$ **f** $9(y + 3) = -18$
   g $8 = 2(x + 5)$ **h** $-15 = 5(x - 2)$ **i** $-18 = 6(r - 1)$
   j $9 = 3(y + 12)$ **k** $-10 = 2(t - 3)$ **l** $-24 = 8(k - 9)$

3 For each picture:
   i form an equation, with brackets
   ii solve it to find the weight of one object.

a

$y - 5$ kg

5 objects
weigh 10 kg

b

$x + 3$ kg

8 objects
weigh 64 kg

c

$x - 10$ kg

7 objects
weigh 42 kg

d

$m - 12$ kg

9 objects
weigh 27 kg

4 Solve:

a $-2(x-1)=4$ b $-3(k+1)=-3$ c $-7(m+4)=14$

d $-5(x-1)=-15$ e $-2(w+3)=0$ f $-6(x+5)=24$

g $-(r+3)=7$ h $-7(x-1)=28$ i $-4(y+4)=-40$

Exercise 4.2

1 Solve:

a $6(x-2)=3(x+1)$ b $4(w+2)=6(w+1)$

c $8(x-5)=4(x-3)$ d $4(r+1)=2(r+5)$

e $5(x+4)=4(x+5)$ f $4(w+2)=7(w-1)$

2 In each picture the two piles of money bags have the same value.

  i   Make an equation and solve it.

  ii Say how much one bag from each pile is worth.

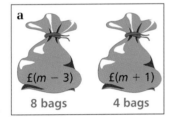

a

£(m − 3)   £(m + 1)

8 bags   4 bags

b

£(f − 7)   £(f + 3)

9 bags   4 bags

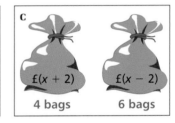

c

£(x + 2)   £(x − 2)

4 bags   6 bags

3 a Find an expression, with brackets, for the area of this rectangle. Units are centimetres.

  b If the area is 88 cm², form an equation and solve it to find x.

  c What are the dimensions of the rectangle?

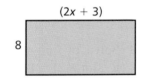

$(2x + 3)$

8

4 a Find an expression, with brackets, for the total area of the two rectangles. Units are centimetres.

  b If this total area is 148 cm², form an equation and solve it to find y.

  c What are the dimensions of each of the rectangles?

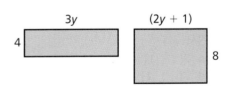

$3y$ $(2y + 1)$

4   8

5 Solve to find x:

a $16 - 3(x+1) = x - 3$ b $6x = 26 - 2(5-x)$

c $9x - 20 = 6 - (4+2x)$ d $3(8-x) + 1 = x + 5$

e $3(x+5) - 1 = 9 + 2x$ f $3x - 4(x-1) = 7(4-x)$

g $8 - (x-2) = x$ h $3x - 5(x-3) = x$

i $2x + 7(x+2) = 4 - x$ j $3(x-2) - 7 = 3 - (4+x)$

k $3 - 2(3-4x) = 5(x+6)$ l $x - 2(3x+2) = x - (x-1)$

5 Pairs of brackets

A rectangle has been partitioned as shown.
The length has been split into two parts, 5 cm and 3 cm.
The height has been split into 2 cm and 4 cm.
The area can be considered in two ways:

- $(2 + 4) \times (5 + 3) = 48$ cm^2
- $2 \times 5 + 2 \times 3 + 4 \times 5 + 4 \times 3 = 48$ cm^2

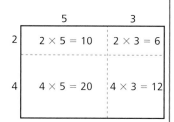

In a similar way we can multiply any pair of brackets.

Example 1 Simplify $(x + 3)(x + 4)$.
From the diagram we see that the answer is

$x^2 + 4x + 3x + 12$

$\quad = x^2 + 7x + 12$

Notice the terms:

$x^2 \quad \ldots \quad (\mathbf{x} + 3)(\mathbf{x} + 4) \quad \ldots$ multiplying the two **F**irst terms

$+ 4x \quad \ldots \quad (\mathbf{x} + 3)(x + \mathbf{4}) \quad \ldots$ multiplying the **O**utside terms

$+ 3x \quad \ldots \quad (x + \mathbf{3})(\mathbf{x} + 4) \quad \ldots$ multiplying the **I**nside terms

$+ 12 \quad \ldots \quad (x + \mathbf{3})(x + \mathbf{4}) \quad \ldots$ multiplying the **L**ast terms

Example 2 Simplify $(2x + 3)(x - 4)$.
From the diagram we see that the answer is

$2x^2 - 8x + 3x - 12$

$\quad = 2x^2 - 5x - 12$

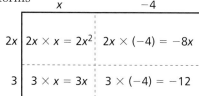

Notice the terms:

$2x^2 \quad \ldots \quad (\mathbf{2x} + 3)(\mathbf{x} - 4) \ldots$ multiplying the two **F**irst terms

$- 8x \quad \ldots \quad (\mathbf{2x} + 3)(x - \mathbf{4}) \ldots$ multiplying the **O**utside terms

$+ 3x \quad \ldots \quad (2x + \mathbf{3})(\mathbf{x} - 4) \ldots$ multiplying the **I**nside terms

$- 12 \quad \ldots \quad (2x + \mathbf{3})(x - \mathbf{4}) \ldots$ multiplying the **L**ast terms

The expression **FOIL** is often used to act as a memory aid.

Exercise 5.1

1 Multiply these brackets:

a $(m + 3)(m + 2)$ **b** $(m + 3)(m - 2)$ **c** $(m - 3)(m + 2)$ **d** $(m - 3)(m - 2)$
e $(a + 2)(a + 1)$ **f** $(a + 2)(a - 1)$ **g** $(a - 2)(a + 1)$ **h** $(a - 2)(a - 1)$
i $(w + 7)(w + 5)$ **j** $(w + 7)(w - 5)$ **k** $(w - 7)(w + 5)$ **l** $(w - 7)(w - 5)$

2 Simplify by first removing the brackets:

a $(x - 6)(x - 4)$ **b** $(x - 6)(x + 4)$ **c** $(x + 6)(x + 4)$ **d** $(x + 6)(x - 4)$
e $(y - 9)(y + 1)$ **f** $(y - 9)(y - 1)$ **g** $(y + 9)(y - 1)$ **h** $(y + 9)(y + 1)$
i $(t - 10)(t - 3)$ **j** $(t + 10)(t + 3)$ **k** $(t + 10)(t - 3)$ **l** $(t - 10)(t + 3)$
m $(n + 2)(n - 2)$ **n** $(n - 2)(n - 2)$ **o** $(n - 2)(n + 2)$ **p** $(n + 2)(n + 2)$

3 Multiply:

a $(m + 3)(m - 7)$ **b** $(n + 2)(n - 3)$ **c** $(p + 1)(p - 6)$ **d** $(r - 7)(r + 8)$
e $(t - 2)(t + 2)$ **f** $(w - 4)(w + 4)$ **g** $(x + 7)(x - 4)$ **h** $(y - 3)(y + 2)$
i $(a + 1)(a + 10)$ **j** $(c + 4)(c - 4)$ **k** $(d - 12)(d + 5)$ **l** $(f - 6)(f - 7)$
m $(h + 1)(h + 1)$ **n** $(x - 6)(x + 6)$ **o** $(y + 8)(y - 3)$ **p** $(a + 3)(a - 3)$
q $(b + 4)(b + 4)$ **r** $(w - 4)(w - 3)$ **s** $(y + 9)(y + 11)$ **t** $(e - 9)(e + 11)$
u $(m + 15)(m - 12)$ **v** $(n - 23)(n + 1)$ **w** $(x + 13)(x - 20)$ **x** $(y + 15)(y - 30)$

Example 3 Simplify $(3x - 4)(5x - 2)$.

F	**O**	**I**	**L**
$3x \times 5x$	$+3x \times (-2)$	$-4 \times 5x$	$-4 \times (-2)$
$= 15x^2$	$-6x$	$-20x$	$+ 8$

$= 15x^2 - 26x + 8$

Example 4 Simplify $(3 + 2x)(5 - 3x)$.

$3 \times 5 + 3 \times (-3x) + 2x \times 5 + 2x \times (-3x)$
$= 15 - 9x + 10x - 6x^2$
$= 15 + x - 6x^2$

Example 5 Simplify $(2x - 3)(3x - 2) - (x - 3)(x + 3)$.

$(2x - 3)(3x - 2) - (x - 3)(x + 3)$
$= (6x^2 - 4x - 9x + 6) - (x^2 + 3x - 3x - 9)$
$= 6x^2 - 4x - 9x + 6 - x^2 - 3x + 3x + 9$
$= 5x^2 - 13x + 15$

Note that brackets were needed in line 2 of the solution.

Exercise 5.2

1 Multiply out these brackets:

a $(3m + 1)(2m - 2)$ **b** $(2y - 3)(y + 3)$ **c** $(6k - 2)(k + 2)$
d $(4x - 5)(3x - 1)$ **e** $(2h - 3)(5h - 4)$ **f** $(y + 3)(2y - 7)$
g $(x - 1)(4x + 2)$ **h** $(m - 6)(3m + 7)$ **i** $(2y + 1)(2y - 5)$
j $(7c + 2)(2c + 3)$ **k** $(4n - 5)(6n - 7)$ **l** $(2n - 8)(7n + 5)$
m $(3 - y)(2 - y)$ **n** $(4 - 2x)(1 + 3x)$ **o** $(8 - 4a)(3 - 5a)$

2 For each rectangle find a simplified expression (no brackets) for the area.
All measurements are in centimetres.

a $2y + 1$ **b** $5x + 3$ **c** $3m - 4$ **d** $8w - 3$

   $3y - 2$

   $2x - 5$

   $2m - 7$

$3w + 1$

3 Copy and complete this 'multiplication table'.

×	$8 - 3w$	$2 + w$	$3 - w$	$3 + w$	$9 - 2w$
$8 - 3w$					
$2 + w$					
$3 - w$					
$3 + w$					
$9 - 2w$					

4 Copy and complete the following.
The table should help.

$(x + 3)(x^2 - 2x + 3)$
$= x(x^2 - 2x + 3) + 3(x^2 - 2x + 3) = \ldots$

	x^2	$-2x$	$+3$
x	$x \times x^2 = x^3$	$x \times (-2x) = -2x^2$	$x \times 3 = 3x$
3	$3 \times x^2 = 3x^2$	$3 \times (-2x) = \ldots$	$\ldots$

5 Multiply out and simplify:
a $(x + 2)(x^2 - 3x + 1)$ **b** $(x - 3)(x^2 + x - 3)$
c $(x - 1)(x^2 - 2x - 4)$ **d** $(x + 3)(x - 5) + (x + 2)(x - 4)$
e $(y - 4)(y - 5) - (y + 3)(y - 3)$ **f** $(2m - 1)(3m + 3) + (m - 5)(m - 1)$
g $(4w - 1)(3w + 2) - (w + 5)(5w - 4)$

6 a Find an expression with brackets for the area of the grey rectangle.
Units are metres.

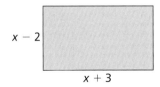 $x - 2$

$x + 3$

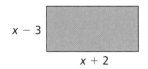 $x - 3$

$x + 2$

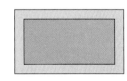

b Find an expression, with brackets, for the area of the orange rectangle.
c The orange rectangle sits inside the grey rectangle.
Explain why the grey border area is given by:

$(x - 2)(x + 3) - (x - 3)(x + 2)$ m^2.

d Simplify the expression for the area of the grey border.

7 Repeat question **6** for the following rectangles.

i

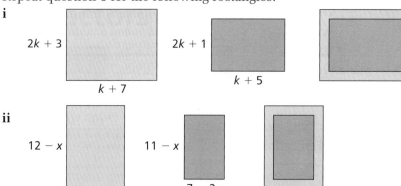

ii

8 A garden area is shown in the sketch. The path is 2 metres wide.
  a The length of the garden is $(5x - 2)$ metres.
    Explain why the length of the flowerbed is $(5x - 6)$ metres.
  b Find an expression for the width of the flowerbed.
  c Find expressions, with brackets, for the area of the whole garden and for the flowerbed.
  d Find a simplified expression for the area of the path.
  e If the width of the garden is 15 metres, find x and calculate the area of the path.

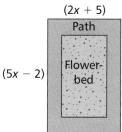

Challenge

The Centred Cube

1 How many spheres do you need to build the fourth Centred Cube?

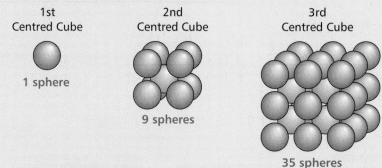

2 Professor Mackenzie came up with a formula.
  He declared that you need $(2n - 1)(n^2 - n + 1)$ spheres to build the nth Centred Cube. Check that this formula works for the first four cubes by substituting: $n = 1$, 2, 3 and 4.

3 His rival Professor McIntosh had a different formula: $n^3 + (n - 1)^3$.
  Check this formula for $n = 1$, 2, 3 and 4.

4 Write each formula without brackets and compare your answers.
  Comment on the result.

6 Squaring brackets

Example 1 $(x + y)^2$
$$= (x + y)(x + y)$$
$$= x^2 + xy + yx + y^2$$
$$= x^2 + 2xy + y^2$$

Example 2 $(x - y)^2$
$$= (x - y)(x - y)$$
$$= x^2 - xy - yx + y^2$$
$$= x^2 - 2xy + y^2$$

Example 3 $(a - 3)^2$
$$= a^2 - 3a - 3a + 9$$
$$= a^2 - 6a + 9$$

Example 4 $(3x + 2y)^2$
$$= 9x^2 + 6xy + 6xy + 4y^2$$
$$= 9x^2 + 12xy + 4y^2$$

Exercise 6.1

1 Multiply out:

a $(t + m)^2$	**b** $(a - b)^2$	**c** $(k + s)^2$	**d** $(u - v)^2$
e $(m - n)^2$	**f** $(c + d)^2$	**g** $(x - y)^2$	**h** $(f - g)^2$
i $(c - w)^2$	**j** $(w + x)^2$	**k** $(e - f)^2$	**l** $(x + y)^2$
m $(a + 3)^2$	**n** $(x + 1)^2$	**o** $(y - 1)^2$	**p** $(e + 8)^2$
q $(w + 5)^2$	**r** $(x - 2)^2$	**s** $(f - 7)^2$	**t** $(a + 9)^2$
u $(e - 9)^2$	**v** $(x - 3)^2$	**w** $(y + 10)^2$	**x** $(w - 8)^2$

2 Find expressions for the areas of each square
  i   with brackets
  ii without brackets.
All lengths are in centimetres.

a $y + 5$ **b** $x - 4$ **c** $m + 7$ 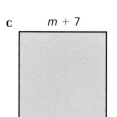   **d** $k - 6$ **e** $w - 1$

3 Multiply out:

a $(8 + x)^2$	**b** $(4 - a)^2$	**c** $(9 + k)^2$	**d** $(1 - y)^2$
e $(1 + m)^2$	**f** $(7 + f)^2$	**g** $(2 - x)^2$	**h** $(3 - c)^2$
i $(10 - d)^2$	**j** $(5 + h)^2$	**k** $(6 - g)^2$	**l** $(12 + x)^2$

Exercise 6.2

1 Expand:

a $(3y + 2)^2$	**b** $(5x + 1)^2$	**c** $(3c - 7)^2$	**d** $(4w + 3)^2$
e $(2f - 1)^2$	**f** $(3d - 6)^2$	**g** $(2 + 4y)^2$	**h** $(5 - 3x)^2$
i $(7 + 3k)^2$	**j** $(10 - 7h)^2$	**k** $(5a + 2b)^2$	**l** $(4a - 5b)^2$
m $(2c - 3d)^2$	**n** $(8d - 3e)^2$	**o** $(2x + 4y)^2$	**p** $(5e - 3f)^2$
q $(9x + 2g)^2$	**r** $(10y - 7x)^2$	**s** $(4a + 2d)^2$	**t** $(4b - 3a)^2$

2 The diagram shows a square pond surrounded by a 3 metre wide border of slabs. The outside edge of the slabs has length $(x + 2)$ metres.

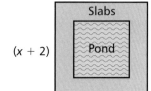

a Explain why the area of the slabs is given by:
$$\text{Area} = \left((x + 2)^2 - (x - 4)^2\right)\text{m}^2.$$

b Simplify this expression.

c Find the area of the slabs when $x = 8$.

3 Multiply out:

a $\left(x + \dfrac{1}{x}\right)^2$ **b** $\left(y - \dfrac{1}{y}\right)^2$ **c** $\left(5 + \dfrac{1}{n}\right)^2$ **d** $\left(3 - \dfrac{1}{w}\right)^2$

e $\left(a + \dfrac{2}{a}\right)^2$ **f** $\left(8 - \dfrac{3}{k}\right)^2$ **g** $\left(m + \dfrac{4}{m}\right)^2$ **h** $\left(2x - \dfrac{1}{x}\right)^2$

i $\left(\dfrac{1}{a} + \dfrac{1}{b}\right)^2$ **j** $\left(\dfrac{2}{x} - \dfrac{3}{y}\right)^2$ **k** $\left(4m + \dfrac{2}{m}\right)^2$ **l** $\left(7x - \dfrac{3}{x}\right)^2$

m $\left(\dfrac{1}{a} + 2\right)^2$ **n** $\left(\dfrac{3}{y} - 7\right)^2$ **o** $\left(\dfrac{2}{m} + m\right)^2$ **p** $\left(\dfrac{3}{h} - 4h\right)^2$

4 Simplify:

a $(y + 3)^2 + (y + 4)^2$ **b** $(x + 5)^2 - (x + 2)^2$ **c** $(3t - 1)^2 - (t + 4)^2$

d $(6y + 1)^2 + (y - 5)^2$ **e** $(3x - 5)^2 - (2x - 1)^2$ **f** $(3w - 7)^2 - (w + 3)^2$

5 A fashion designer wants a border sewn on to a 15 cm square of material as shown in the diagram.

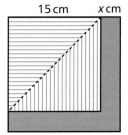

a Find an expression in terms of x for the *increase* in area of the finished article.

b If the side of the square has increased by 10% then find the actual increase in the area.

c What percentage increase is this?

Challenge

A Multiplying Triangle

Look at this pattern:

$(a + b)^1 = \qquad\quad 1a + 1b$

$(a + b)^2 = \qquad 1a^2 + 2ab + 1b^2$

$(a + b)^3 = 1a^3 + 3a^2b + 3ab^2 + 1b^3$

Here is help with the working:

$(a + b)^3 = (a + b)(a + b)^2$

$\qquad\quad = (a + b)(a^2 + 2ab + b^2)$

$\qquad\quad = \ldots$

1 Check that the expression for $(a + b)^3$ in the triangle is correct.

2 Work out the next row of the triangle by calculating $(a + b)^4$.

3 Describe carefully any pattern that appears in the triangle that may help you complete more rows.

7 More equations

Example 1   Solve the equation $(x + 2)^2 = x^2 + 8^2$.

$(x + 2)^2 = x^2 + 8^2$
$\Rightarrow x^2 + 4x + 4 = x^2 + 64$
$\Rightarrow x^2 + 4x + 4 - x^2 = x^2 + 64 - x^2$
$\Rightarrow 4x + 4 = 64$
$\Rightarrow 4x + 4 - 4 = 64 - 4$
$\Rightarrow 4x = 60$
$\Rightarrow x = 15$

Exercise 7.1

1 Solve:

a $m(m + 2) = m^2 + 10$

b $y(y + 3) = y^2 - 9$

c $a(3a + 7) = 3(a^2 - 7)$

d $(x + 1)(x - 3) = x(x - 3)$

e $k(k + 2) = (k + 4)(k - 1)$

f $(n + 1)^2 = n(n + 3)$

g $(b - 2)^2 = b(b + 4)$

h $(a + 4)^2 = (a + 6)(a + 3)$

i $(y - 12)^2 = y^2 + 144$

j $(w - 1)(2w - 3) = w(2w + 1)$

k $(y + 9)(y - 5) = (y + 7)(y - 7)$

l $(2d - 3)^2 = (2d + 1)^2$

Example 2   These two pictures have equal area.
All lengths are in centimetres.
What are the actual dimensions of the paintings?

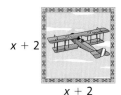

Areas are equal

so $(x + 2)^2 = (x + 7)(x - 2)$
$\Rightarrow x^2 + 4x + 4 = x^2 - 2x + 7x - 14$
$\Rightarrow x^2 + 4x + 4 - x^2 = x^2 + 5x - 14 - x^2$
$\Rightarrow 4x + 4 = 5x - 14$
$\Rightarrow 4x + 4 - 4x = 5x - 14 - 4x$
$\Rightarrow 4 = x - 14$
$\Rightarrow 4 + 14 = x - 14 + 14$
$\Rightarrow x = 18$

So the paintings are 20 m by 20 m and 25 m by 16 m.

Check: both paintings have an area of 400 cm².

Exercise 7.2

1 The photographs in each pair below have the same area. Make an equation for each pair, and find the lengths and breadths of the paintings. All lengths are in centimetres.

a

x

 $x - 10$

2x − 5

2x + 30

b

$x - 12$ $x - 4$

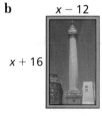 

$x + 16$ x

c

$x + 2$ $x - 7$

$x - 5$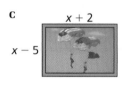

$x + 5$

d

3x − 3   3x − 8

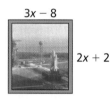

2x − 2   2x + 2

2 Solve:

a $2m^2 - m(2m - 2) = 2$ **b** $4x^2 - 2x(2x + 3) = 6$

c $y^2 - y(2 + y) + 10 = 0$ **d** $(n + 4)^2 = (n + 2)^2$

e $(k + 5)^2 = (k - 1)^2$ **f** $(a + 1)^2 = (a - 2)^2$

g $(w + 3)(w - 3) = (w - 1)^2$ **h** $(3x + 4)(3x - 4) = (3x - 2)^2 + 4$

i $(4d + 3)(d - 1) = (2d - 1)^2 + 2$ **j** $9n^2 - (3n - 4)^2 - 8 = 0$

k $a^2 - (a - 3)^2 = 3$ **l** $h^2 - (h + 7)^2 - 7 = 0$

◀◀ RECAP

Brackets can be removed by multiplying each term within the bracket by the term outside the bracket.

$$a(b + c) = ab + ac \qquad a(b - c) = ab - ac$$

Be careful when the term outside the bracket is negative.

If an equation has brackets then follow this procedure.

Step 1:   Remove the brackets.

Step 2:   Simplify each side of the equation if possible.

Step 3:   Solve the equation.

Pairs of brackets can be multiplied out by multiplying each term in the second bracket by each term in the first bracket.

$(a + b)(c + d) =$	ac	$+$	ad	$+$	bc	$+$	bd
	$(a + b)(c + d)$		$(a + b)(c + d)$		$(a + b)(c + d)$		$(a + b)(c + d)$
	Firsts		Outsides		Insides		Lasts

When the two brackets are the same: $(x + y)^2 = x^2 + 2xy + y^2$; $(x - y)^2 = x^2 - 2xy + y^2$

1 Remove the brackets:

  a $11(w + 3)$ **b** $7(k - 2)$ **c** $2(3h + 1)$

  d $8(2 - d)$ **e** $p(q + r)$ **f** $a(a - 2b)$

  g $-4(h + 3)$ **h** $-5(y - 4)$ **i** $-8(6 - 5x)$

  j $8(x - y + 4)$ **k** $m(m^2 - 3)$ **l** $3n(n^3 - 2n^2)$

2 Multiply out, then simplify:

  a $7 + 3(n - 2)$ **b** $3 - 5(y + 3)$ **c** $7x - (x - 3)$

  d $-5(2 - m) - 3m$ **e** $2(w - 3) - (3w + 2)$ **f** $7(5 - 2y) - 4(2 + 3y)$

3

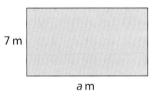 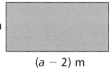 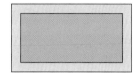

7 m   5 m

        a m $(a - 2)$ m

  a Find an expression for the area of the grey rectangle.

  b Find an expression, with brackets, for the area of the orange rectangle.

  c Find an expression, with brackets, for the area of the grey border.

  d Simplify the area expression in part **c**.

4 Solve:

  a $3(a - 3) = 15$ **b** $7(y + 1) + 2 = 30$ **c** $-18 = 6(p + 8)$

5 The two piles of money bags have the same value.

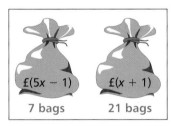

£$(5x - 1)$ £$(x + 1)$

 7 bags   21 bags

  a Make an equation and solve it.

  b Say how much one bag from each pile is worth.

6 Solve:

  a $10 - 2(y + 3) = y + 19$ **b** $3a = 2 - (8 - a)$ **c** $w - 14 = 1 - 2(3 - w)$

7 Multiply out:

  a $(y + 2)(y + 5)$ **b** $(t - 3)(t - 1)$

  c $(m - 7)(m + 3)$ **d** $(4x + 3)(2x + 1)$

  e $(3 + d)(3 - d)$ **f** $(x + 5)^2$

  g $(2c - 5)^2$ **h** $(9y - 8x)^2$

8 Solve:

  a $(x + 1)^2 = x^2 + 13$ **b** $(y - 2)^2 = (y - 4)(y + 1)$

  c $(r + 5)(r - 3) = (r + 1)(r - 1)$ **d** $(m + 1)^2 - (m - 2)^2 = 3$

REVISE

4 Money

The euro became an official currency for non-cash transactions at the beginning of 1999.

In 2002 the euro notes and coins replaced the old currencies of Germany, France, Holland, Eire, Belgium, Luxembourg, Italy, Greece, Finland, Spain, Portugal and Austria.

1 REVIEW

◀◀ Exercise 1.1

1 Calculate:
  a £6·50 + £5·99   **b** £12·20 − £3·49   **c** £64·45 + £7·75
  d £80·35 − £67·99   **e** £2·68 + 75p + £14·32   **f** £6·35 − 49p + £12
  g £52 − £5·75 − £12·25

2 Bob buys a pair of jeans for £22·95, shoes for £26·45 and a sweatshirt for £7·99.
  a How much has he spent altogether?
  b How much change does he get from £60?

3 Round to the nearest 10p:
  a £6·09   **b** £53·74   **c** £80·35   **d** £66·66   **e** £9·92

4 Round each of these amounts to the nearest penny:
  a 38·2p   **b** 7·5p   **c** 83·9p   **d** £2·835   **e** £7·999   **f** £19·081

5 Estimate: **a** £7·95 + £6·38 + £3·79 **b** £91·24 − £27·89
            c £6·95 × 42   **d** £143·50 ÷ 19

6 Calculate: **a** £4·28 × 10   **b** £0·63 × 100   **c** £0·84 × 1000
            d £9 ÷ 10   **e** £305 ÷ 100   **f** £7380 ÷ 1000

7 Calculate: **a** £0·73 × 4   **b** £12·75 × 9   **c** £39·99 × 6   **d** £8·70 ÷ 5
            e £45·22 ÷ 7 **f** £272·40 ÷ 8   **g** £46·72 × 40 **h** £73·50 ÷ 30

8 Calculate   **i** 10%   **ii** 25%   **iii** 30%   **iv** 15% of:
  a £12   **b** £700   **c** £5·60   **d** £8400   **e** £17·20

9 Calculate the discount on these sales items.

a
MODEL
AIRCRAFT
£14·50
DISCOUNT
20%

b
SUNGLASSES
£8·90
Discount 15%

c
Skis
£175□80
Discount
25%

d
2-WEEK
CRUISE
£1449·60
Discount $33\frac{1}{3}$%

10 Write the following fractions as percentages:
  a $\frac{1}{4}$ **b** $\frac{2}{5}$ **c** $\frac{7}{10}$ **d** $\frac{2}{25}$

11 Write the following as fractions in their simplest terms:
  a 10%   **b** 15%   **c** 75%   **d** $33\frac{1}{3}$%

12 Donald earns £345·62 per week.
  a How much does he earn in one year?
  b He receives a pay rise of 4%. Calculate his weekly pay increase.

13 Anna buys £1250 worth of shares in a company.
Their value falls by 12·5%. How much has Anna lost on the shares?

---

2 Profit and loss

Example 1   An art dealer buys a sculpture for £750. He wants to make a profit of 15%.
What price should he put on the sculpture?

Profit = 15% of £750 = 15 ÷ 100 × 750 = £112·50
Selling price = £750 + £112·50 = £862·50

Example 2   The dealer buys a painting for £480.
He sells it in an auction and the highest bid is £450.
Calculate the loss as a percentage of the cost price.

Loss = £480 − £450 = £30

Loss as a percentage of cost price = $\dfrac{£30}{£480} \times 100 = 6·25\%$

$$\text{Percentage profit/loss} = \frac{\text{profit/loss}}{\text{cost price}} \times 100\%$$

Exercise 2.1

1 Calculate: **a** 20% of £60 **b** 30% of £200 **c** 8% of £7   **d** 25% of £85
                 e 75% of £9 **f** 90% of £600 **g** 4% of £8500 **h** 0·5% of £4

2 Calculate **i** the profit
            ii the profit as a percentage of the cost price on each of the following items.

  a Cost price £8   **b** Cost price £10   **c** Cost price £20
     Selling price £12   Selling price £12   Selling price £26

3 OK Electronics aim to make a profit of 20% on their cost prices.
Calculate   **i**   the profit
             ii   the selling price of each of these items.

a    **b**    **c**    **d**

     £36   £6·50   £53·60   £112

4 The Holmes family bought their bungalow for £86 000. They sold it at a loss of 3%.
   a How much did they lose?
   b Calculate their selling price.

5 Dynamo Dragons buy a striker for £6·25 million.
He performs badly and at the end of the season they sell him for £4·5 million.
Calculate the loss as a percentage of the cost price.

 6 **a** Calculate the profit as a percentage of the cost price on each of these items, correct
to 1 decimal place.
   b Which piece earned the greater percentage profit? By how much?

Gold bracelet   Gold necklace
Cost price £87·50   Cost price £52
Selling price £125   Selling price £79·99

7 A florist buys 240 daffodils for £28·50. She sells them in bunches of 12 for £1·99
a bunch.
If she sells all the flowers, what is her profit as a percentage of the cost price, correct
to 1 decimal place?

8 Busy Builders Ltd buy three plots of land for £24 000 each.
They sell the plots individually for £33 000, £28 000 and £21 000.
   a Calculate the profit or loss on each plot as a percentage of the cost price.
   b Express their overall profit or loss as a percentage of the total amount they paid for
the land. Give your answers correct to 1 decimal place.

9 Compare
   a the selling prices
   b the percentage profits, correct to 1 decimal place, of a new Midi at these two garages.

GALACTIC GARAGES      **COSMIC CARS**
NEW MIDI   **NEW MIDI**
Cost price £13 900   Cost price £13 900
Profit 7·5%   Selling price £14 999

10 Smart Computers Plc buy 80 computers costing £575 each.

They start by selling them at £799·99 each and reduce the prices at intervals to clear the stock. The table gives the sales data.

Calculate the overall profit on the computers as a percentage of the total cost price, correct to 1 decimal place.

Number sold	Selling price
32	£799·99
24	£649·95
13	£599·49
11	£425·75

Example 3

Janice buys a gas fire from Perfect Homes for £425·60.
Perfect Homes make a profit of 12% on the sale.
Calculate what it cost Perfect Homes.

Cost price = 100%
Selling price = 100% + 12% = 112%

112 % = £425·60
$\Rightarrow$ 1%   = £425·60 ÷ 112
$\Rightarrow$ 100% = £425·60 ÷ 112 × 100 = £380
The cost price was £380.

Exercise 2.2

1 Amy buys two old fire surrounds for £80 each. She sells one for £120 and the other for £60. Calculate the profit or loss, as a percentage of the cost price, on each fire surround.

2 Ron buys a painting at an auction for £40. He sells it to a dealer for £70.
  a Calculate Ron's profit as a percentage of the cost price.
  b The dealer sells the painting for a profit of 30%.
    How much does the dealer sell the painting for?

3 A coin collector sells a rare coin for £600. He reckons he made a profit of 200%.
  How much did he pay for the coin? Copy and complete:
    Cost price = 100%
    Selling price = 100% + ... % = ...%
    ...% = £600
    $\Rightarrow$ 1% = £600 ÷ ...
    $\Rightarrow$ 100% = £600 ÷ ... × 100 = £...
    $\Rightarrow$ Cost price = £...

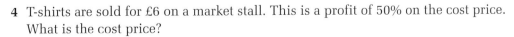

4 T-shirts are sold for £6 on a market stall. This is a profit of 50% on the cost price. What is the cost price?

5 A shop buys pens in bulk. They are sold for 40p each.
  The shop makes a profit of 400% on the cost price.
  Calculate the cost price of one pen.

6 Mega Mechanics Plc is sold for £741 000.
It was bought a year ago and its value has increased by 14%.
Calculate the price paid for the company a year ago.

7 Jenny gets bored with her rollerblades and sells them to a friend for £54.
This was 20% less than she paid for them. How much did she pay?

8 Below are the selling prices of some lamps and the profit made by the shop on each.
Calculate the cost price of each lamp.

a
BEDSIDE LAMP
£14·95
PROFIT 15%

b
DESK LAMP
£38·35
PROFIT 18%

c
STANDARD LAMP
£72·27
Profit 12·5%

9 Two rival companies sell blank video tapes. Their prices are:

Echo Electrics   10 tapes for £29·99
Toptrack Tapes   3 tapes for £10·45

Echo Electrics' profit is 35%. Toptrack Tapes' profit is 40%.
Which of these two stores pays less for each blank video tape?
By how much? Give your answer correct to the nearest penny.

10 The Crofts sell 'Dunroaming' for £120 000.
They bought it from Mrs Hayes a year ago and have made a profit of 25% on what they paid for it.
Mrs Hayes made a loss of 20% on her purchase price.
How much did Mrs Hayes pay?

Brainstormers

1 In question **10** above explain why the percentages used give that particular result.

2 Mr Toad sells his sports car for £7280.
He makes a loss of $\frac{3}{8}$ of the price he paid for it.
How much did it cost him?

3 Value Added Tax (VAT)

Teachers, civil servants, police and fire brigade, nurses, … schools, hospitals, … all these have to be paid for. The government raises money by different taxes. One of these is **Value Added Tax** (VAT).
We pay VAT on most goods and services.

Cars, computers, CDs, electrical goods, furniture, garage bills, restaurant and hotel bills, holidays, phone bills …

17·5%

5%

Gas and electricity bills

School books, medicine, children's clothes, food

0%

Example 1

A new iron is priced at £46·80 + VAT (17·5%). Calculate the total price.

Without a calculator: Note that 17·5% = 10% + 5% + 2·5%

10% of £46·80 = £4·68
  5% of £46·80 = £2·34   (half of 10%)
2·5% of £46·80 = £1·17   (half of 5%)

17·5% of £46·80 = £8·19

Total cost = £46·80 + £8·19 = £54·99

With a calculator: 17·5 ÷ 100 × 46·80 = 8·19.
                Total cost = £46·80 + £8·19 = £54·99

Note that the total price can be obtained by this calculation: 1·175 × £46·80. (Why?)

Exercise 3.1

1 Find 5% of: **a** £40   **b** £7   **c** £230   **d** 80p   **e** £17·60

2 Copy and complete:

a   10% of £52 = £…   **b**   10% of £270 = £…   **c**   10% of £93·80 = £…
   5% of £52 = £…   5% of £270 = £…   5% of £93·80 = £…
 2·5% of £52 = £…   2·5% of £270 = £…   2·5% of £93·80 = £…
17·5% of £52 = £…   17·5% of £270 = £…   17·5% of £93·80 = £…

3 Use the same method as question **2** to find 17·5% of:
   a £20   **b** £6   **c** £840   **d** £6300   **e** £1·60

4 George's gas charges for the year are listed below.
   Calculate   **i** the VAT at 5%   **ii** the total for each bill.
   a £110   **b** £87·40   **c** £59·20   **d** £125·60

5 Calculate   **i** the VAT due (at 17·5%)   **ii** the total cost of each of these items:
   a an exercise bike at £130   **b** a step machine at £96·40
   c lifting weights at £157·20

6 Calculate the total cost of each of these items, including VAT (at 17·5%):
   a £360 fridge
   b £476 cooker
   c £35·60 toaster

7 Copy and complete this garage bill:

```
4 tyres at £37·79                       £...
5 litres of oil at £2·55 per litre      £...
1 oil filter at £8·99                   £...
2 hours labour at £28·50 per hour       £...
Pre-VAT total                           £...
VAT at 17·5%                            £...
Total bill                              £...
```

8 Joe checks his electricity bill and his phone bill.
   By coincidence both bills come to £95·20 before VAT is added.
   How much more is his phone bill when VAT is included?
   (Electricity VAT is 5%; phone bill VAT is 17·5%.)

9 Calculate the total cost including VAT at 17·5%, to the nearest penny, of these items:
   a rocking chair at £174·49 + VAT
   b dining table at £259·75 + VAT
   c carpet at £1265 + VAT
   d 3-piece suite at £1739·99 + VAT

10 The Jacksons compare prices for a family holiday to Florida.

   a Which company is cheaper?
   b By how much?

11 Mrs Robinson's gas bill is £73·60 before VAT is added.
   Her telephone bill before VAT is £140·38.
   On one day she pays both these bills and buys her baby daughter a new outfit costing £28·75.
   How much did she spend altogether?

Example 2

The total cost of Kylie's meal at a restaurant is £73·32.

This includes VAT at 17·5%. Calculate the cost before VAT was added.

This is the process of working out the cost including VAT:

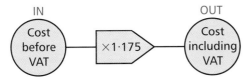

Reversing this process will give the cost before the VAT was added.

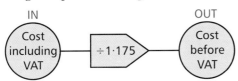

So, the cost of the meal before VAT was added = £73·32 ÷ 1·175 = £62·40.

Exercise 3.2

1 Copy and complete:

a   10% of £850 = £...   **b**   10% of £5200 = £...   **c**   10% of £234·80 = £...

      5% of £850 = £...   5% of £5200 = £...   5% of £234·80 = £...

    2·5% of £850 = £...   2·5% of £5200 = £...   2·5% of £234·80 =£...

   17·5% of £850 = £...   17·5% of £5200 = £... 17·5% of £234·80 = £...

2 Calculate the total price of each of these items.

  a SANDALS   £18 + VAT

  b SHOES   £56·40 + VAT

  c LEATHER BOOTS   £132·80 + VAT

3 In 1993, gas and electricity bills were zero-rated for VAT.

The following year they had 8% VAT added, and the year after that 17·5%.

Now VAT on these bills is 5%. How much would you have to pay, including VAT, in

i 1994   **ii** 1995   **iii** now on a pre-VAT bill of:

a £76   **b**   £224·80?

4 Ali pays £98·70 for a camera.

Calculate the price of the camera before VAT

(at 17·5%) is added.

5 Find the pre-VAT prices, correct to the nearest penny, on these goods.

  a Alarm clock/radio at £15·99 including VAT

  b Bunk beds at £399·95 including VAT

  c Laptop computer at £2499·50 including VAT

6 At Robust Radios the cost of a CD player, including VAT, rises from £59·49 to £65·49. By how much, to the nearest penny, has the VAT increased?

7 Alice's gas bill for one quarter, excluding VAT at 5%, comes to £60.
  a Write 5% as a decimal fraction.
  b By what number is £60 multiplied to calculate the total bill?
  c Calculate the total bill.
  d For the next quarter her total bill is £73·50.
   Starting with £73·50, how is the pre-VAT bill calculated?
  e Find the bill before VAT is added.

8 Graham gets these bills in the post:

   gas bill £105·64; electricity bill £96·47; telephone bill £120·73.

  These bills include VAT.
  Find the total amount, correct to the nearest penny, he would have to pay if VAT wasn't levied on these bills.
  Note: VAT rate on telephone bills is 17·5%.

9 At Better Bikes a Mountain Master bike costs £394·80 including VAT.
  Classic Cycles sell the same bike for £414·54 including VAT.
  How much dearer is a Mountain Master at Classic Cycles before VAT is added?

10 Country Cars make a profit of 11·5% on their 4 × 4 vehicles.
  Calculate the cost price before VAT is added, to the nearest £1, of a 4 × 4 vehicle to Country Cars.

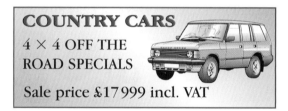

COUNTRY CARS
4 × 4 OFF THE
ROAD SPECIALS
Sale price £17 999 incl. VAT

Brainstormers

1 a John paid £101·50 in VAT on a new garden shed and £240·45 in VAT on a greenhouse.
  Calculate the total price of each item, including VAT.
  b Find the fraction, in its lowest terms, that the amount paid in VAT can be multiplied by to give the total price.

2 The total amount raised by VAT in 2002−03 was £6·36 × 10⁹.
  Calculate the total amount of sales and services that generated this amount of VAT.
  Assume all VAT is charged at 17·5%.

4 Loans and hire purchase

Often goods can be purchased by paying regular instalments.
Sometimes there is an initial payment called a deposit.
This way of buying is called hire purchase (HP).
An alternative is to take out a loan.
This is usually paid back in instalments too.

Example 1
Sean wants to buy a second-hand motorbike.

> **MOTORBIKE**
> CASH PRICE £1499 or HP terms
> 10% DEPOSIT +
> 18 monthly instalments of £84·95

a Calculate the cost of buying the bike on hire purchase.
b How much more does it cost to buy the bike on HP rather than paying the cash price?

a Deposit = 10% of £1499 = £149·90
   Instalments = 18 × £84·95 = £1529·10
   Total HP cost = £149·90 + £1529·10 = £1679
b On HP Sean would pay £1679 − £1499 = £180 more.

Example 2
Sean's bank offers to lend him £1499 to be paid back in 12 instalments of £134·50.
Calculate:
a his total repayments
b how much the loan costs him.

a Total loan repayments = 12 × £134·50 = £1614
b The loan costs him £1614 − £1499 = £115.

Exercise 4.1

1 Helen borrows £2500 to pay for a new central heating system.
   She will pay back the loan by making 12 monthly payments of £224.
   a Calculate the total cost of the instalments.
   b How much does the loan cost her?

2 The Greens want to add a conservatory to their house.
   They borrow £6500 and agree to pay back the loan by making 36 monthly
   repayments of £220.
   a Calculate the total cost of the instalments.
   b How much does the loan cost them?

3 For each item below, calculate:
  i   the hire purchase price
  ii the difference between the HP price and the cash price.

  a Skateboard ... Cash price £49·99 **or** 6 payments of £9·99
  b Rollerblades ... Cash price £89·95 **or** 10 payments of £8·45
  c Mountain bike ... Cash price £259·49 **or** deposit £49 + 12 payments of £19·95
  d Windsurfer ... Cash price £599·90 **or** deposit £79·50 + 20 payments of £29·99
  e Diving wetsuit ... Cash price £230 **or** 10% deposit + 6 payments of £36·95
  f Fishing rod and reel ... Cash price £140 **or** 5% deposit + 12 payments of £12·45

4 Calculate
  i   the deposit
  ii   the total HP cost
  iii how much is saved by paying cash for each of these vehicles.

a
| MIDI HATCHBACK |
| Cash price £8449·95 |
| or 10% deposit |
| + 24 payments of £379·99 |

b
| 4 × 4 LAND ROAMER |
| Cash price £19 999 |
| or 12% deposit |
| + 36 monthly payments of £595·95 |

5 Moira is a keen golfer. She has been saving up for a new set of clubs.
   How much more than the cash price would each of the three HP schemes cost?

EASY BUY
TOP PRO
GOLF CLUBS
£338·45 Cash

EASY PAY

20 weeks at £19·25
or
DEPOSIT of £49·99 +
36 weeks at £9·99
or
DEPOSIT of 20% +
99 weeks at £3·99

Example 3

Carla buys a DVD player on HP.
She will pay a deposit of 10% and 6 monthly payments of £70.
She calculates that she will pay £60 more than the cash price.
What is the cash price?

Total instalments = £70 × 6 = £420
Cash price = £420 − £60 + deposit = £360 + deposit
The deposit is 10% of the cash price
so £360 represents the other 90% of the cash price.

90% of cash price = £360
⇒ 1% of cash price = £360 ÷ 90
⇒ 100% of cash price = £360 ÷ 90 × 100 = £400
Cash price = £400

Exercise 4.2

1 Susan wants to borrow £4500 to convert her loft into an extra room.
She considers two possibilities:

- Shark Loans … 12 instalments of £570
- Beta Bank … 18 instalments of £295

Calculate the difference between the amount repaid and the amount borrowed if
Susan uses:

a Shark Loans   **b** Beta Bank.

2 For each item calculate:
  i the hire purchase price
  ii the difference between the HP price and the cash price.
  a Dishwasher … Cash price £549·99 **or** 10% deposit + 12 payments of £44·95
  b Washing machine … Cash price £375·45 **or** 15% deposit + 24 payments of £13·75

3 Calculate what the monthly instalment would be in each case.

a

NO DEPOSIT 0% INTEREST
3-PIECE SUITE
Cash price £894 or make 12 equal monthly payments

b

FLAT SCREEN TV
0 INTEREST   Cash price £699·80   0 INTEREST
or 10% deposit +
18 equal monthly instalments

4 The Gardeners decide to buy a new greenhouse with a cash price of £1589·25.
They are offered a choice of HP terms:
  a 26 weeks at £64·99 per week   **b** 52 weeks at £34·49 per week
For each option calculate:
  i the HP price
  ii the difference between the HP price and the cost price
  iii the difference as a percentage of the cost price.

5 The cash price of a racing bike is £360.
A shopkeeper works out a 6 month HP plan, with no
deposit, which will return 10% more than the cash price.
How much is each monthly instalment?

6 The Wilsons reckon they will have paid £645 more than the cash price when they
make their last payment for their double-glazing. Their deposit is £310·50 and they
have to make 24 instalments of £116·45. Calculate the cash price.

7 Allsports had a snooker table on sale at £450. The manager offers these HP terms:
deposit 20% of cash price and 24 equal monthly payments. By this method, the total
cost is 25% more than the cash price. How much will each monthly payment be?

8 Peter buys a digital camera on HP. He pays 20% deposit and will make 12 payments
of £55. Using the HP offer he will pay £84 more than the cash price.
Calculate the cash price.

9 The HP terms on a motorbike are advertised as '15% deposit + 24 instalments of £99·99'. If Marianne buys the bike on HP she will pay £275·61 more than the cash price. Calculate the cash price.

Investigation

Annual Percentage Rate (APR)

Credit card companies charge a monthly rate for loans.
5% per month doesn't seem a lot.
However, the interest for one month on £1000 is
£1000 × 5 ÷ 100 = £50.
If the loan isn't repaid, then in the second month the sum owed is £1050 and the interest is £1050 × 5 ÷ 100 = £1052·50.
Calculate the interest due after 12 months if the loan is not repaid.

> **SHARK**
> **CREDIT CARD**
> **ONLY 5%**
> per month

This spreadsheet will make the job easier.
Copy this and then fill down for another ten rows.

	A	B	C
1			owed
2	month	interest	1000
3	1	=C2*5/100	=C2+B3
4	=A3+1	=C3*5/100	=C3+B4

Annual rather than monthly rates are usually quoted for investments and loans.
At 5% per month the Annual Percentage Rate (APR) is calculated by the following method.

Step 1: $1·05^{12} = 1·796$

Step 2: $1·796 - 1 = 0·796 = 79·6\%$

The APR is 79·6%.
Investigate the APRs of various credit cards.

5 Currency exchange

The UK uses pounds and pence. £1 = 100p
The USA uses dollars and cents. $1 = 100 cents
Much of Europe uses the euro and cents. €1 = 100 cents

Example 1 Use an exchange rate of £1 = €1·40 to change:
    a £200 to euro   **b** €1800 to pounds.

    a £200 = 200 × 1·40 = €280

    b €1800 = 1800 ÷ 1·40 = £1285·71 (to the nearest penny)

Exercise 5.1

For this exercise use the exchange rates in this table unless the question says otherwise.

Region	£1 buys
Europe	€1·40
USA	$1·60
Switzerland	2·25 francs
Denmark	10·0 kroner
South Africa	12·5 rand
India	75·0 rupees
Japan	191·5 yen

1 Change £1000 into:
   a euro   **b** dollars   **c** francs   **d** kroner
   e rand   **f** rupees   **g** yen

2 **a** Change £5 into euro.
   b Use your answer to **a** to change €28 into pounds.

3 **a** Change £8 into South African rand.
   b How many pounds are 500 rand worth?

4 This conversion graph changes pounds to euro
and euro to pounds.
Use the graph to change:
   a i £50
      ii £80
     iii £25 into euro
   b i €100
      ii €20
     iii €80 into pounds.

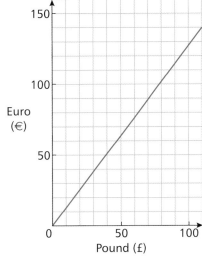

5 On holiday from the USA Janis spends her money on the items below.
Calculate the cost of each in dollars.
   a Hamburger £4   **b** Golf £30 green fee   **c** Plane ticket £200
   d Hotel room £32   **e** Cinema ticket £4·50

6 Change these amounts into pounds:
   a €280   **b** $800   **c** 9000 francs   **d** 45 000 kroner
   e 80 000 rand   **f** 200 000 rupees   **g** 1 000 000 yen

7 Copy and complete this table:

Region	Value in pounds
Euro	€1 = £0·71
Dollar	$1 = £…
Swiss franc	1 franc = £…
Rand	1 rand = £…

8 Mrs Grant changes £475 into euro for a holiday.
  a How much is she given?
  b She returns with €87 and changes it back into pounds.
  How much does she receive, correct to the nearest 10p?

9 Ruth compares the cost of a novel in airport shops in South Africa and Japan.
  The two prices are 112·90 rand and 1725 yen.
  a Which is the better deal?
  b Calculate the difference between the two prices in pence.

10 Several of Jimmy's relatives live abroad. On his birthday he is sent $30, €40, 35 rand, 45 Swiss francs and 10 000 yen.
  How much does he receive altogether, correct to the nearest pound?

Example 2
Ravi visits India. He changes £2400 into Indian currency and is given 185 520 rupees.

Calculate how many: **a** rupees £1 buys
                       b pounds can be bought for 100 rupees, correct to the nearest penny.

a £1 = 185 520 ÷ 2400 = 77·3 rupees.
b 100 rupees = £100 ÷ 77·3 = £1·29

Exercise 5.2

1 Julie flies to Hong Kong. She changes £600 into Hong Kong dollars and gets 7860 dollars.
  a How many Hong Kong dollars does £1 buy?
  b How many Hong Kong dollars would £8000 buy?

2 The fuel tank of Ewan's car holds 62 litres.
  The table gives the typical price of diesel fuel.
  Calculate the cost of a full tank:
  a in the UK   **b** in France.
  Use an exchange rate of £1 = €1·42.
  Give your answers in pounds correct to the nearest penny.

Country	Price per litre
UK	77·9p
France	72·9 cents

3 Copy and complete the following using the rates £1 = €1·40 and £1 = $1·60.
  a $1 = €...   **b** €1 = $...

4 Holly booked a hotel for a few days in New York. Using a rate of £1 = $1·60 she reckoned her bill would be $320.
  a Calculate her estimated cost of the hotel in pounds.
  b However by the time she leaves New York the dollar has dropped in value against the pound by 2 cents. How much does she pay (in pounds)?

5 Before flying to Japan Viv exchanges £400.
She is given 76 480 yen.
On arrival she changes a further £400 and is given 75 800 yen.
How much less does £1 buy in Japan?

6 Brian spends €136·62 in a French supermarket.
He is charged an extra 2·75% for paying with his credit card.
Calculate the total bill:
  a in euro   **b** in pounds, correct to 2 decimal places.
Use an exchange rate of £1 = €1·38.

7 Over a period of a few months the value of the pound drops from €1·53 to €1·41.
Calculate the change in value as a percentage of the original rate, correct to 2 decimal places.

8 A jewellery merchant travels to Switzerland and changes £50 000 into francs at £1 = 2·23 francs. He buys 95 000 francs worth of diamonds and changes his remaining francs into euro at a rate of €1 = 1·62 francs.
How many euro does he receive, correct to the nearest euro?

9 Paul and Paula plan a holiday where they will spend a week in Switzerland and a week in Italy. They list the costs:
Total flights £564·90
Switzerland (7 nights)
Hotel 95·60 Swiss francs per night
Spending money 1200 Swiss francs
Italy (7 nights)
Hotel €63·50 per night
Spending money €600
Use £1 = 2·21 Swiss francs and £1 = €1·43 to calculate the total costs, in pounds, correct to the nearest penny.

10 Mr Wright changes £2000 into dollars at a rate of £1 = $1·60.
However, the bank takes 4·6% of the money for exchanging it.
In the USA he spends $2600.
He changes the remaining money back into pounds at the same rate.
Again the bank takes 4·6% of the transaction.
  a How much does he receive?
  b What is the total amount paid to the bank for the two transactions?
    Give your answer in pounds.

6 Car insurance

By law, drivers must be insured in case they injure other road users or cause damage. This is called 'Third Party Insurance'.

Usually insurance against fire and theft is added to a Third Party policy.

If a car owner wants to insure against damage to himself and his own car he takes out a 'Comprehensive' policy.

Insurance rates vary according to the area where the driver lives and the type of car.

If a driver makes no claims on his insurance he may be given a discount, called a no-claims bonus.

The table gives comprehensive premiums for 12 months of cover with Crazy Car Insurance Plc.

		Area		
		low risk	medium risk	high risk
	small	£380	£487	£625
Car type	saloon	£490	£584	£986
	sports	£683	£839	£1264

Note: Drivers under 25 years of age pay an extra 50%

No-claims bonus table:

No. of years without claim	Discount
1	10%
2	20%
3	30%
4	40%
5	50%
6 or more	60%

Example 1   Harry lives in a medium risk area and drives a sports car.
He gets 8 years no-claims bonus.
Calculate his annual premium.

Premium before no-claims bonus = £839
No-claims bonus = 60% of £839 = £503·40
Annual premium = £839 − £503·40 = £335·60

Exercise 6.1

1 What is the annual cost of a comprehensive policy, before any no-claims bonus, for each of these drivers?
   a Ms Wheeler who lives in a medium risk area and drives a saloon car.
   b Mr Carter who lives in a low risk area and drives a sports car.
   c Miss Turner who lives in a high risk area and drives a small car.

2 Austin lives in a low risk area and drives a saloon car. He has a 5 year no-claims bonus. How much is:
   a his no-claims bonus worth?
   b his annual premium?

3 Mrs Healy qualifies for a 2 year no-claims bonus.
   She drives a sports car and lives in a high risk area. How much is:
   a her no-claims bonus worth?
   b her annual premium?

4 Morris drives a small car and lives in a medium risk area.
   He has 6 years no-claims bonus.
   How much does he pay for 12 months insurance?

5 Donald is under 25 years old.
   He lives in a high risk area, drives a saloon car and has a one year no-claims bonus.
   Calculate his annual premium.

6 Laura is due a no-claims bonus of 20%.
   She drives a small car and moves from a high risk area to a low risk area.
   How much does she save in insurance costs?

7 Mr Morgan pays £441 for his insurance premium.
   This includes a discount for a no-claims bonus of one year.
   a Calculate the premium before the discount.
   b How much is the discount worth?

8 Miss Cooper lives in a medium risk area and qualifies for 4 years no-claims bonus.
   She sells her small car and buys a sports car.
   How much extra will her annual policy cost?

9 Tim's annual premium would be £986 but he only pays £690·20 because of his no-claims bonus. For how many years of no-claims bonus does he qualify?

10 James and Jane each drive sports cars.
   James lives in a high risk area and has a no-claims bonus of 6 years.
   Jane lives in a low risk area and has a one year no-claims bonus.
   Who pays more? By how much?

11 Mr Hillman, who is with Indestructible Insurance, receives a 40% no-claims discount.
   He pays £328·80 for his annual insurance.
   Calculate his premium before the discount is subtracted.

7 Travel and valuables insurance

It is sensible to take out travel insurance when going on holiday in case:

- the trip has to be cancelled
- you are ill or injured and have to pay medical bills
- you lose your money or baggage, or they are stolen.

The table shows how much Tragic Travel Insurance Plc charge **one person** for insurance.
The cost depends on destination and length of stay.

No. of days	UK (£)	Europe (£)	Worldwide (£)
1–3	8·25	14·50	30·50
4–6	9·75	16·80	36·70
7–9	11·52	22·60	39·45
10–17	14·83	24·85	42·50
18–25	18·56	26·90	45·37
26–35	22·85	30·25	48·52
each extra week	5·30	8·25	15·78

Note: these prices do not include skiing holidays.
To include skiing all prices must be doubled.
For children travelling with adults
Tragic Travel charge 60% of the adult insurance.

Example 1
Naomi is going to Italy for 2 weeks.
How much will her insurance cost her?

Cost of European insurance for 14 days = £24·85.

Example 2
Mrs Curtis takes her two children to China.
The total cost of the insurance policy is £93·50.
What is the maximum number of days they are insured for?

Mrs Curtis pays 100%. Each of her children is charged at 60%.
Total percentage = 100% + 2 × 60% = 220%
220% = £93·50
⇒   1% = £93·50 ÷ 220
⇒ 100% = £93·50 ÷ 220 × 100 = £42·50 (the cost for one adult)

From the table, the maximum number of days for worldwide cover is 17.

Exercise 7.1

1 Find the cost of travel insurance for these people:
   a Ron, flying to Rome for a 5 day break
   b Wendy, on holiday in Wales for 8 days
   c Carol, spending 2 weeks in Canada skiing
   d Marcus, on a trip to Morocco for 40 days.

2 Mr and Mrs Ferguson go skiing in France.
   Calculate the cost of insuring them both for 2 weeks.

3 Andy travels to Australia for 4 weeks.
   a How much does it cost him for insurance?
   b Calculate the cost of the insurance per day, to the nearest penny.

4 Janice takes out travel insurance for a 15 day holiday in Jamaica.
   She gets the chance to extend her holiday by 5 days.
   How much extra will her policy cost?

5 How much more expensive is it for 6 weeks worldwide insurance than 6 weeks
   European insurance?

6 Mr and Mrs Forest book a 3 week trip to Florida.
   They insure themselves and their two children.
   Calculate the total cost of their policy.
   (Remember there is a discount for children.)

7 Mr Lees plans to take his son to London for a few days.
   The total cost of the insurance for both of them is £15·60.
   What is the maximum number of days they are insured for?

8 The Adams family, consisting of two adults and three children, go skiing in Austria.
   Tragic Travel give them a family discount of 25%. This saves them £42·94.
   What is the maximum number of days they are insured for?

8 Building and contents insurance

It is wise to insure your home, its contents and valuables.

Building Insurance
This usually covers damage by fire, storm, floods, lightning, subsidence, theft and
vandalism.

Contents Insurance
It is possible to insure furniture and other household items against fire, theft and
accidental damage.
A separate policy is usually taken out for valuables.

Valuables Insurance
It is possible to insure valuable items separately against theft or loss.
These might include cameras, computers, jewellery or sports equipment.
Valuables are often insured for both in and outside the home.

The table shows Helpful House Insurance's annual charges.

Item	Charge
Building per £1000	£0·73
Contents per £1000	£3·57
Valuables per £100	£4·75

Helpful House Insurance give a no-claims bonus of 10% for each year that no claim is made on their buildings and contents policies.
The maximum discount they award is 30%.

Exercise 8.1

1 Find the annual premium for insuring these properties with Helpful House.
   (No-claims discounts do not apply.)
   a a semi-detached house value £88 000
   b a detached house value £105 000
   c a city centre house value £189 000

2 Find the annual premium for insuring contents worth:
   a £9000   b £15 000   c £33 000

3 Calculate the annual premium for insuring the following valuables:
   a a digital camera worth £600
   b a camcorder worth £850
   c jewellery worth £4000

4 Liz takes out both building and contents policies.
   She doesn't qualify for a no-claims bonus.
   Her flat is valued at £40 000 and the contents are valued at £12 000.
   a What is the annual cost of
      i the building   ii the contents premium?
   b What is the total cost of the policies?

5 Hanif insures his home, valued at £150 000, the contents valued at £30 000 and valuables worth £4500 with Helpful House.
   Calculate the total cost of his annual insurance premiums.

6 George pays £105·12 for his building insurance and £96·39 for the contents insurance. He doesn't get any no-claims discount.
Find the value of: **a** his house   **b** the contents.

7 The Harpers' house is worth £124 000. They insure the contents for £25 000.
They receive a one year no-claims discount.
  a What is the annual cost of
    i the building   **ii** the contents premium?
  b What is the total cost of the policies?

8 Carrie pays £97·09 for her building insurance. This includes 3 years of no-claims bonus. Calculate what sum her house is insured for.

9 Mr Temple pays £71·40 for his contents insurance. This includes 2 years of no-claims bonus. Calculate what his contents are insured for.

10 Mr and Mrs Slater pay £102·82 to insure their house contents for one year.
They have a 2 year no-claims bonus.
  a Calculate the value their contents are insured for.
  b During the year the Slaters make no claims.
    The cost of all Helpful House policies rise by 8% before the next year's premium is due. Calculate the cost of their policy next year.

---

9 Life insurance

Many people take out life insurance so that their dependants are taken care of if they die.

Fixed Term Life Insurance is taken out for a fixed number of years for an agreed amount. If the person insured dies in that time, his/her beneficiaries (dependants) receive the amount for which they are insured. If the insured person survives the term, no payment is made.

The table gives the monthly premiums of the Happy Families Insurance Company's policies. The term is 20 years and the sum insured is £10 000.

Age	Male smoker	Female smoker	Male non-smoker	Female non-smoker
20	£1·25	£1·02	£0·77	£0·57
25	£1·36	£1·11	£0·86	£0·66
30	£1·48	£1·20	£0·96	£0·75
35	£1·60	£1·30	£1·05	£0·84

Example 1
Julie is 35 years old and takes out a fixed term policy. She doesn't smoke.
She wants her dependants to receive £150 000 if she dies.
Calculate: **a** her monthly premium
              b the total amount she will pay over 20 years.

  a Monthly premium = 150 000 ÷ 10 000 × 0·84 = 15 × 0·84 = £12·60
  b Total paid over 20 years = £12·60 × 12 × 20 = £3024

Exercise 9.1

1 What are the monthly premiums for each of these people taking out a 20 year term policy, sum insured £10 000, with Happy Families?
  a George, aged 20, who smokes
  b Edward, aged 25, who doesn't smoke
  c Kate, aged 30, who smokes

2 Jack is 25 years old and takes out a fixed term insurance policy. He doesn't smoke. He wants his dependants to receive £200 000 if he dies.
  Calculate:
  a his monthly premium
  b the total amount he will pay over 20 years.

3 Calculate
  i   the monthly
  ii   the annual premium for a £50 000 policy for a non-smoking female aged:
       a 20   b 25   c 30   d 35 years old.

4 On a £200 000 term insurance policy, how much extra is paid
  a per month   b over 20 years
  by a man, aged 30, who smokes compared to a man of the same age who doesn't smoke?

5 Donna is a 35-year-old smoker. She pays a monthly premium of £23·40 to Happy Families for a fixed term insurance policy. Calculate the sum she is insured for.

6 Mr and Mrs Giles both take out 20 year policies at the age of 25 with Happy Families. Each of them is insured for £80 000. Mr Giles smokes. Mrs Giles doesn't.
  Calculate:
  a the difference between
  b the total of the two policies over 20 years.

7 John, who smokes and is aged 35, can afford to pay up to £30 a month for a 20 year life insurance policy. Happy Families only issue policies in multiples of £10 000.
  a Find the amount John could be insured for.
  b Calculate his exact monthly premium if he takes out a policy for this amount.

8 Mike is 30 years old and smokes. Mary is 25 and also smokes.
  They each take out a £250 000 policy for 20 years with Happy Families.
  a Calculate the total amount
    i   Mike
    ii   Mary will pay over 20 years.
  b How much less would
    i   Mike
    ii   Mary pay over 20 years if they didn't smoke?

◀◀ RECAP

Profit and Loss

Cost price is the amount paid for goods.
Selling price is the amount the goods are sold for.
You should be able to calculate the profit or loss made when goods are bought and sold, and work with percentages.

- profit = selling price − cost price (a loss if negative)
- percentage profit $= \dfrac{\text{profit}}{\text{cost price}} \times 100\%$

Value Added Tax (VAT)

You should be able to calculate the VAT on goods and services.
VAT is a tax added to the cost of goods.

- 0% ... school books, children's clothes, medicines
- 5% ... electricity and gas bills
- 17·5% ... most other items

You should be able to calculate the pre-VAT price given the price including VAT and the rate of VAT. For example, for a VAT rate of 17·5%:

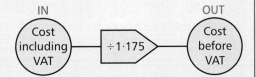

Hire Purchase (HP)

You should be able to calculate the cost of buying goods on HP.
A **deposit** may be asked for. This is often a percentage of the cash price.
The rest of the bill is made up of equal, regular payments called **instalments**.

Insurance premiums

An annual insurance **premium** is a yearly payment made to a company who will then cover you against financial loss.
You should be able to work with insurance premiums involving building and contents, cars, travel and valuables and life insurance.

- The premium for house, contents and valuables depends on the value of goods insured.
- The premium for car insurance depends on car value and the length of time since the last claim was made, and is calculated using **no-claims bonus** tables.
- The premiums for life insurance depend on age, sex, the type of policy, the amount insured and lifestyle habits that may affect health (e.g. smoking).

Foreign currency exchange

You should be able to convert from one currency to another and calculate exchange rates.
The rate of exchange varies all the time and can be found in newspapers, on teletext and on the net.

Percentage increase and decrease

You should be able to calculate the original quantity given the percentage change and the resulting quantity. This situation may arise in any of the above topics.

1 **a** The Top Tackle fishing store buys a fly rod for £48 and makes a profit of 16%.
Calculate the selling price.

   b The cost price of a reel is £26·50. The selling price is £34·95.
Calculate the profit as a percentage of the cost price, correct to 1 decimal place.

   c The selling price of a landing net is £18·17. A profit of 15% is made.
Calculate the cost price.

2

GRAND PIANO

CASH PRICE £3599

or

5% deposit +
24 instalments of
£149·99

   a Calculate the total cost of buying the piano on HP.
   b What is the difference between the HP price and the cash price?

3 The table gives details of
Mr Power's utility bills.
Calculate the missing entries.

Utility	Pre-VAT	Including VAT	VAT rate
Telephone	£84·60	£99·41	
Electricity	£134·68		5%
Gas		£80·14	5%

4 **a** Use an exchange rate of £1 = $1·64 to change
   i £38 to dollars
   ii $750 to pounds, correct to the nearest penny.

   b Marie changes £280 into Swiss currency and receives 635·6 francs.
   i What exchange rate was she given?
   ii She changes 100 francs back into pounds at the same rate.
How much does she get, correct to the nearest penny?

5 Calculate the difference in price, in pounds, of the racing bike in these
two countries

BLUE RACER
SCOTLAND

£275 + VAT at 17·5%

LE BLEU RACER
FRANCE

€375 + VAT at 19·6%

   a before VAT is added
   b after VAT is added. Use a rate of £1 = €1·38.
Give your answers to the nearest penny.

6 The table gives Rock Safe's insurance rates.
Calculate the annual premium for:
   a a bungalow valued at £110 000
   b contents valued at £27 500
   c jewellery valued at £2600.

Item	Charge
Contents per £1000	£4·26
Building per £1000	£0·72
Valuables per £100	£5·25

7 Clyde and Bonnie both qualify for a 20% no-claims bonus on their car insurance.
Clyde's premium is £1054 before his discount.
  a How much does Clyde pay for his insurance?
  b Bonnie's premium is £697·60 after her discount.
    How much is her insurance before her no-claims bonus?

8 The table shows some of Top Trips' travel insurance rates.

No. of days	UK (£)	Europe (£)	Worldwide (£)
1–3	8·36	14·90	32·50
4–6	10·68	17·90	36·80
7–9	13·50	23·40	40·25

  a How much more expensive is it for one week's worldwide insurance compared to
    one week's European insurance?
  b A party of 8 adults plan to spend 6 days in Madrid.
    Top Trips give them a group discount of 12·5%.
    Calculate the total cost of their insurance.

9 The table gives monthly premiums for Happy Families' policies.
The term is 20 years and the sum assured is £10 000.

Age	Male smoker	Female smoker	Male non-smoker	Female non-smoker
20	£1·25	£1·02	£0·77	£0·57

Gill is 20 years old and doesn't smoke. She is insured for £120 000.
How much: a is her monthly premium?
             b will she pay, in total, over 20 years?

5 Factors

Numbers which have only two factors, namely themselves and 1, are called **prime numbers**.

Eratosthenes described a systematic way of sifting out the primes from the other whole numbers. The method is known as the Sieve of Eratosthenes.

The largest known prime (at the time of printing) is $2^{13466917} - 1$, which has over 4 million digits!

Eratosthenes
(276–194 BC)

1 REVIEW

◀◀ **Exercise 1.1**

1 $12 = 1 \times 12 = 2 \times 6 = 3 \times 4$. These are all the pairs of **factors** of 12.
In the same way, write down *all* the pairs of factors of:
   a 6   **b** 4   **c** 10   **d** 18   **e** 20

2 List *all* the factors (including 1 and the number itself) of:
   a 7   **b** 8   **c** 12   **d** 16   **e** 25

3 List all the prime numbers less than 50. (Reminder: primes have only two factors.)

4 $2xy = 1 \times 2xy = 2 \times xy = 2x \times y = 2y \times x$.
The factors of $2xy$ are 1, x, y, $2x$, $2y$, xy and $2xy$.
Find *all* the factors of:
   a $5a$ **b** x^2 **c** ab **d** $4y$ **e** $3mn$

5 $\dfrac{x}{x} = 1; \quad \dfrac{xy}{x} = y; \quad \dfrac{2x^2y}{xy} = \dfrac{2xxy}{xy} = 2x$

In a similar manner, simplify:

   a $\dfrac{ab}{a}$ **b** $\dfrac{m^2}{m}$ **c** $\dfrac{4k}{2}$ **d** $\dfrac{6x}{2x}$ **e** $\dfrac{8x^2y}{2x}$

6 a The nth term of a number pattern is $5n - 3$.
So the 8th term (when $n = 8$) is $5 \times 8 - 3 = 40 - 3 = 37$.
Find the first five terms of the pattern.
b The nth term of a number pattern is $4n + 7$. List the first four terms.
c The nth term of a number pattern is n^2. List the first six terms.
What kind of numbers are these?
d The nth term is $\frac{1}{2}n(n + 1)$. List the first six terms. What are these numbers called?

7 The diagram shows a garden.
Write an expression for the area of the garden
a with brackets
b without brackets.

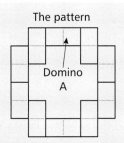

5 m — Grass area — Slabbed area
x m — 4 m

8 Multiply out:
a $5(y - 3)$ **b** $7(x + 4)$ **c** $10(3k + 2)$ **d** $8(2 - n)$
e $x(x + 3)$ **f** $a(a - b)$ **g** $m(2m + 3)$ **h** $7y(2 - 4y)$

9 Multiply out, then simplify:
a $3(m - 1) + 2(m - 1)$ **b** $7(x - 2) - 4(x - 2)$
c $4(x + 2y) - 3(x - 2y)$ **d** $x(y + x) - x(y - x)$

10 Multiply out:
a $(u + 1)(v + 2)$ **b** $(x - 3)(x + 4)$ **c** $(y + 7)(y - 2)$
d $(w - 5)(w - 3)$ **e** $(2x + 1)(3x - 1)$ **f** $(3x - 5)(3x + 5)$
g $(7 - t)(5 + 2t)$ **h** $(x - 3)^2$ **i** $(3 - 2y)^2$
j $(a - 2b)^2$ **k** $(4c + 5d)^2$ **l** $\left(x + \dfrac{1}{x}\right)^2$

11 a Find a formula for the nth term of each sequence:
     i   3, 5, 7, 9, ...   **ii**   1, 6, 11, 16, ...   **iii**   1, 4, 9, 16, ...
b Use your formulae to find the tenth term of each sequence.

Challenge 1: Domino expressions

Domino A is placed centrally at the top of the pattern.
The rest of the dominoes are placed as shown.
Where dominoes touch, the two expressions are equal.

Copy the pattern and show where each domino
is placed to complete the puzzle.

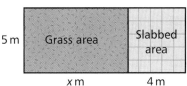

The pattern

Domino
A

Domino A	Domino B	Domino C	Domino D	Domino E
$2ab \times 2ab$: $2 \times ab$	$2b \times b$: $2a \times b^2$	$2a^2 \times 2b$: $2b \times 2ab$	$2a^2 \times 2b^2$: $2b^2 \times 2a$	$2 \times b^2$: $2a \times b$

Domino F	Domino G	Domino H	Domino I	Domino J
$2b \times a^2$: $2a \times b$	$2a \times 2ab$: $2a \times 2b$	$2 \times 2ab$: $2ab \times ab$	$2a \times ab$: $2 \times ab$	$2b \times ab$: $2a^2 \times b^2$

Challenge 2: Numbers of Factors

The expression a has two factors: 1 and a.

The expression ab has four factors: 1, a, b and ab.

a How many factors does the expression abc have?

b How many factors does the expression $abcd$ have?

c Is there a pattern to your answers? Can you predict the number of factors of $abcde$?

d Investigate the number of factors of the expressions a, a^2, a^3, a^4, ...

---

2 Factors and expressions

Factor pairs

Example 1   The factors of a number come in pairs:

$$18 = 1 \times 18$$
$$= 2 \times 9$$
$$= 3 \times 6$$

So the factors of 18 are 1, 2, 3, 6, 9 and 18.

Example 2   The factors of an expression similarly come in pairs:

$$ab^2 = 1 \times ab^2$$
$$= a \times b^2$$
$$= b \times ab$$

So the factors of ab^2 are 1, a, b, ab, b^2 and ab^2.

Exercise 2.1

1 List all the different factor pairs for these numbers:

a 4	**b** 13	**c** 9	**d** 6	**e** 20	**f** 12	**g** 24
h 27	**i** 30	**j** 45	**k** 17	**l** 81	**m** 50	**n** 100

2 Find the missing factor in each product.

a $6 = 2 \times ...$ **b** $ab = a \times ...$ **c** $ab = b \times ...$ **d** $ab = 1 \times ...$

e $2x = ... \times x$ **f** $2x = ... \times 2$ **g** $n^2 = ... \times n$ **h** $n^2 = 1 \times ...$

i $6cd = 3 \times ...$ **j** $6cd = c \times ...$ **k** $6cd = 2 \times ...$ **l** $6cd = 3 \times ...$

m $6cd = ... \times 2$ **n** $6cd = ... \times 2d$ **o** $6cd = 3d \times ...$ **p** $2a^2 = a \times ...$

q $2a^2 = ... \times 2a$ **r** $2a^2 = a^2 \times ...$ **s** $12ab = 3b \times ...$ **t** $12ab = 6b \times ...$

u $12ab = 2ab \times ...$ **v** $8nm = ... \times 4m$ **w** $6x^2 = ... \times 3x$ **x** $a^2b = ... \times ab$

3 For each expression find *all* the different ways it can be written as a product of two factors:

a $3a$	**b** $11x$	**c** cd	**d** $4r$	**e** $14k$	**f** $6n$
g $2xy$	**h** $3kw$	**i** d^2	**j** $2x^2$	**k** $3d^2$	**l** $6ef$

4 List all the factors of each expression.
(Factor pairs should help.)

   a $4x$ **b** $6b$ **c** mn **d** h^2 **e** $9y$ **f** $3w^2$

   g $17h$ **h** $2wx$ **i** $5d^2$ **j** $4n^2$ **k** a^2b **l** ab^2

5 Match expression with factor.
(There is only one matching that gives six pairs.)

Expressions: **1** $8ab$ **2** $6ab$ **3** $4b^2$ **4** $9a^2$ **5** ab **6** a^2b

Factors: **a** $3b$ **b** ab **c** a^2 **d** $2b$ **e** $4a$ **f** $3a^2$

---

3 Highest Common Factor (HCF)

Example 1   18 has factors 1, 2, 3, 6, 9 and 18.

               24 has factors 1, 2, 3, 4, 6, 8, 12 and 24.

               1, 2, 3 and 6 are common to both 18 and 24.

               6 is the highest common factor (HCF).

               Note that $18 \div 6 = 3$ and $24 \div 6 = 4$

               and that the HCF of 3 and 4 is 1.

Example 2 $2x^2y$ has factors 1, 2, x, y, $2x$, $2y$, xy, $2xy$, x^2, $2x^2$, x^2y and $2x^2y$.

               $4y^2$ has factors 1, 2, 4, y, $2y$, $4y$, y^2, $2y^2$ and $4y^2$.

               $2y$ is the HCF.

               Note that $2x^2y \div 2y = x^2$ and $4y^2 \div 2y = 2y$

               and that the HCF of x^2 and $2y$ is 1.

Example 3   Explain why 4 is not the HCF of 20 and 60.

               $20 \div 4 = 5$ and $60 \div 4 = 15$

               The HCF of 5 and 15 is 5 … not 1

               So 4 is not the HCF of 20 and 60 … $4 \times 5 = 20$ … 20 is the HCF.

Exercise 3.1

1 **a** Explain why 4 *is not* the HCF of 16 and 24.

    b Explain why 8 *is* the HCF of 16 and 24.

    c Explain why $2x$ *is not* the HCF of $4xy$ and $6xy$.

    d Explain why $2xy$ *is* the HCF of $4xy$ and $6xy$.

    e Explain why $2a$ *is not* the HCF of $8a^2$ and $4a$.

    f Explain why $4a$ *is* the HCF of $8a^2$ and $4a$.

    g Explain why d *is not* the HCF of $2cd^2$ and $3cd$.

    h Explain why cd *is* the HCF of $2cd^2$ and $3cd$.

2 **a i**   Complete: $6x^2 = 2x \times \dots$ and $4x = 2x \times \dots$

     ii State the HCF of $6x^2$ and $4x$.

   b i   Complete: $9wx = 3x \times \dots$ and $6x^2 = 3x \times \dots$

     ii State the HCF of $9wx$ and $6x^2$.

   c i   Complete: $2ab = \dots \times b$ and $4a = \dots \times 2$

     ii State the HCF of $2ab$ and $4a$.

   d i   Complete: $4x^2 = \dots \times 2x$ and $6xy = \dots \times 3y$

     ii State the HCF of $4x^2$ and $6xy$.

3 Write down the HCF of:

    a 4 and $2x$ **b** ab and ac **c** $4y$ and 8   **d** $6w$ and w

    e 5 and $10d$ **f** $2y$ and y **g** $7c$ and 14   **h** $3m$ and $4m$

    i x and x^2 **j** ab and a^2 **k** $4y$ and $2yx$ **l** h^2 and $6h$

    m $2xy$ and 4   **n** $2xy$ and $4x$ **o** $2xy$ and $4xy$ **p** $2a^2$ and $4a$

    q $8gh$ and $6g$ **r** $4k^2$ and $6km$ **s** $10h^2$ and $15h$ **t** $4x^2y$ and xy^2

    u $5ab$ and $10a^2$ **v** $12xy^2$ and $18x^2$ **w** $16g^2h$ and $20h^2$ **x** $12a^2b$ and $8ab^2$

Challenge

Powerful HCFs

a What is the HCF of: **i** a^4 and a^7 **ii** a^9 and a^5?

b Explain how you would find the HCF of a^n and a^m where n and m are positive whole numbers.

---

4 Factorising ... the common factor

When a number is expressed as a product, it is said to be factorised.

We learned in Chapter 3 that $3(2x + 5) = 6x + 15$.

If we reverse this process and turn $6x + 15$ into $3(2x + 5)$, we say $6x + 15$ has been **factorised**.

Since 3 was the HCF of the terms $6x$ and 15 we say it has been factorised by taking out a **common factor**. The factors of $6x + 15$ are 3 and $2x + 5$.

Example   Factorise: **a** $8a + 6$ **b** $6ab - 9a^2$

    a By inspection 2 is the HCF of $8a$ and 6

         $\Rightarrow 8a + 6 = 2(4a + 3)$ ... check by mentally removing brackets.

    b By inspection $3a$ is the HCF of $6ab$ and $9a^2$

         $\Rightarrow 6ab - 9a^2 = 3a(2b - 3a)$ ... check by mentally removing brackets.

Exercise 4.1

1 For each expression, find the HCF of the two terms, then factorise.

    a $4a + 8$ **b** $6y - 15$ **c** $10e + 8$ **d** $12h + 8$

    e $16 - 8x$ **f** $5 - 15y$ **g** $6a + 8b$ **h** $7m - 14n$

    i $16 - 6c$ **j** $22h + 11$ **k** $28x - 7$ **l** $8w - 20$

    m $24x - 18$ **n** $20y + 12$ **o** $23 - 46t$ **p** $12 + 8y$

2 Factorise by finding the HCF. Remember to check by multiplying out mentally.

    a $4y + 8$ **b** $4x + 6$ **c** $10a + 25$ **d** $5t - 15$

    e $6n - 8$ **f** $4b + 6$ **g** $3 + 9r$ **h** $8 - 12a$

    i $x^2 + x$ **j** $a - a^2$ **k** $2n + n^2$ **l** $y^2 - 3y$

    m $2ef - 4$ **n** $6 - 3kh$ **o** $8t + 12k$ **p** $2ab - 4a$

    q $3mk + 12k$ **r** $2x^2 - 4x$ **s** $7y - y^2$ **t** $3d + 6d^2$

3 Factorise, taking out the common factor:

a $a^2 + a$ **b** $y - y^2$ **c** $m^2 + 7m$ **d** $y^2 - 3y$

e $3k^2 + 6k$ **f** $6t^2 - 8t$ **g** $8a - 6a^2$ **h** $5d^2 - 3d$

i $2d + 8d^2$ **j** $12k^2 + 20k$ **k** $6z^2 - 8z$ **l** $12f + 48f^2$

m $26g - 28g^2$ **n** $16w^2 - 24w$ **o** $46x + 18x^2$ **p** $2a^2 + 6ab$

q $6n^2 - 2n$ **r** $12m + 8n$ **s** $2ab - 4ac$ **t** $6bx - 4by$

u $9xy - 12xz$ **v** $6h^2 + 4h$ **w** $15w^2 - 6wx$ **x** $\frac{1}{2}ab - \frac{1}{2}ac$

4 a Pete challenged Iain to calculate $12 \times 98 + 12 \times 2$ in his head.
He knew about common factors.
Explain why $12 \times (98 + 2)$ gives the same answer. Do the calculation.

b Use the common factor to calculate mentally:

i $32 \times 51 + 32 \times 49$ **ii** $9{\cdot}2 \times 12 - 9{\cdot}2 \times 2$ **iii** $19 \times 13 + 19 \times 87$

iv $1{\cdot}5 \times 82 - 1{\cdot}5 \times 72$ **v** $\frac{1}{3} \times 9{\cdot}3 - \frac{1}{3} \times 6{\cdot}3$ **vi** $2005 \times 7 - 2005 \times 6$

Exercise 4.2

1 Jordan has a calculation to do.
Work it out in your head and write down
the answer.

17 daily papers at
55 pence and 17
magazines at £1·45

2 Megan sold 26 biscuits at 17 pence
each and the same number of cakes
at 83 pence each.
Mentally calculate how much she made.

3 For each of these expressions:

i expand the brackets **ii** simplify **iii** factorise.

a $2(m + 3) + 5(m - 11)$ **b** $4(y + 1) - 2(y + 8)$

c $6(x - 6) + 2(x + 14)$ **d** $7(y + 2) - 3(y - 6)$

e $5(k - 1) - 2(k + 5)$ **f** $10(d - 5) + 2(d + 1)$

Challenge

The HCF cascade

As you travel down the cascade diagram, each circle is filled with the HCF of the
two expressions immediately above it.

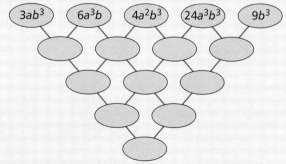

Copy and complete the cascade diagram.

5 Factorising: The difference of two squares

In Chapter 3 we learned to multiply out expressions of the form $(a - b)(a + b)$:

$(a - b)(a + b) = a^2 + ab - ab - b^2 = a^2 - b^2$ … note that the middle terms total zero.

Thus whenever we come across an expression which is the difference of two squares we can automatically factorise it.

$$a^2 - b^2 = (a - b)(a + b)$$

Example 1   Factorise $b^2 - 16$.

$$b^2 - 16 = b^2 - 4^2 \qquad \text{… a difference of two squares}$$
$$= (b - 4)(b + 4)$$

Example 2   Factorise $9y^2 - 4x^2$.

$$9y^2 - 4x^2 = (3y)^2 - (2x)^2 \text{ … a difference of squares}$$
$$= (3y - 2x)(3y + 2x)$$

Exercise 5.1

1 Factorise:

a $c^2 - d^2$	**b** $e^2 - f^2$	**c** $a^2 - b^2$	**d** $y^2 - 2^2$
e $x^2 - 7^2$	**f** $8^2 - a^2$	**g** $3^2 - w^2$	**h** $9^2 - x^2$
i $1 - y^2$	**j** $m^2 - 1$	**k** $h^2 - 9$	**l** $n^2 - 1$
m $w^2 - 16$	**n** $81 - e^2$	**o** $y^2 - x^2$	**p** $b^2 - 16$
q $49 - k^2$	**r** $x^2 - 25$	**s** $a^2 - 100$	**t** $36 - b^2$
u $1 - k^2$	**v** $121 - x^2$	**w** $4 - h^2$	**x** $49 - n^2$

2 Factorise these by first writing them as a difference of two squares:

a $4y^2 - 25$	**b** $9x^2 - 64$	**c** $4a^2 - 1$	**d** $49a^2 - 4$
e $9y^2 - 16$	**f** $16k^2 - 9$	**g** $81x^2 - a^2$	**h** $a^2 - 9b^2$
i $49a^2 - 9b^2$	**j** $100h^2 - 9d^2$	**k** $m^2 - 16n^2$	**l** $d^2 - 36z^2$
m $4w^2 - 9x^2$	**n** $9y^2 - 16x^2$	**o** $100e^2 - 81$	**p** $1 - 121k^2$
q $36x^2 - 1$	**r** $100x^2 - 169y^2$	**s** $64u^2 - 9v^2$	**t** $144x^2 - 225y^2$

3 Do these calculations mentally by first factorising the difference of squares:

a $98^2 - 2^2$	**b** $53^2 - 47^2$	**c** $13 \cdot 5^2 - 3 \cdot 5^2$
d $201^2 - 200^2$	**e** $(\frac{2}{3})^2 - (\frac{1}{3})^2$	**f** $1 \cdot 99^2 - 0 \cdot 01^2$

4 There are 16 different pairings between the two sets of four cards.

For each pairing:

a subtract the numbered card from the lettered card

b factorise the resulting expression.

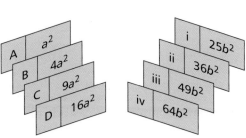

> *Example 3*   Factorise *fully* $75a^2 - 27b^2$.
> $75a^2 - 27b^2$ .... there is a common factor of 3
> $= 3(25a^2 - 9b^2)$
> $= 3((5a)^2 - (3b)^2)$ ... a difference of squares
> $= 3(5a - 3b)(5a + 3b)$

Exercise 5.2

1 Factorise fully. First take out the common factor, then factorise the difference of squares.

a $3a^2 - 12$	**b** $5x^2 - 5$	**c** $7d^2 - 28$	**d** $6y^2 - 24$
e $18 - 2x^2$	**f** $50 - 2y^2$	**g** $8 - 8x^2$	**h** $5 - 20a^2$
i $3a^2 - 3b^2$	**j** $10c^2 - 40d^2$	**k** $2k^2 - 8m^2$	**l** $3c^2 - 27d^2$
m $12a^2 - 12b^2$	**n** $9m^2 - 36n^2$	**o** $10x^2 - 90y^2$	**p** $17d^2 - 17e^2$
q $2e^2 - 98f^2$	**r** $2x^2 - 162y^2$	**s** $80x^2 - 5y^2$	**t** $128u^2 - 8v^2$
u $16y^2 - 36t^2$	**v** $45a^2 - 80b^2$	**w** $48c^2 - 27d^2$	**x** $8a^2 - 50w^2$

2 Factorise fully:

a $ax^2 - ay^2$	**b** $pa^2 - pb^2$	**c** $ax^2 - 4ay^2$	**d** $xw^2 - 9xz^2$
e $2de^2 - 2df^2$	**f** $3ax^2 - 12ay^2$	**g** $2mk^2 - 8m$	**h** $5am^2 - 45a$
i $4x^2y - 9y$	**j** $8a^2b - 50b$	**k** $12kx^2 - 3ky^2$	**l** $18c^2e - 2d^2e$

3 The diagram shows the cross-section of a wooden dowelling. It consists of a large square with a small square area removed.

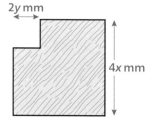

2y mm

4x mm

a Explain why the area, A mm^2, of this shape is given by
   $A = 16x^2 - 4y^2$ mm^2.

b Factorise this expression fully.

c Without using a calculator, use this factorised expression to help you to calculate A when $x = 6\cdot25$ and $y = 2\cdot5$.

Challenge

Powerful factorising patterns

1 Heather noticed the following:

$a^4 - 1$
$= (a^2)^2 - 1^2$ ... a difference of squares
$= (a^2 - 1)(a^2 + 1)$ ... another difference of squares!
$= (a - 1)(a + 1)(a^2 + 1)$

She then tried to factorise $a^8 - 1$, $a^{16} - 1$ and $a^{32} - 1$.
Can you factorise each of these expressions *fully*?

2 a Later Heather tackled these expressions: $a^2 - 1, a^4 - a^2, a^6 - a^4, a^8 - a^6$ ...
   Can you find the answers she got? Is there a pattern?
   b Factorise $a^{2n+2} - a^{2n}$ where $n = 1, 2, 3, 4$ ...

6 Factorising: Trinomials

You saw in Chapter 3 how to remove the brackets from $(x + 3)(x - 4)$:

$$(x + 3)(x - 4) = x^2 - 4x + 3x - 12 = x^2 - x - 12$$

Can we reverse this process to get the factors back?

Examine the terms:

x^2 … is the result of multiplying the first terms in both brackets.

-12 … is the result of multiplying the last terms in both brackets.

$-x$ … is the result of multiplying the outer terms, the inner terms and adding
the results.

Follow these steps to factorise $x^2 - x - 12$.

Step 1:   Find the factors of x^2.
The factors are x and x, giving $(x \quad)(x \quad)$

Step 2:   Find two numbers that multiply to give -12 (for the last term) and add
to give -1 (for the middle term).

$$
\begin{array}{ll}
1 \times (-12): & 1 + (-12) = -11 \ ✗ \\
2 \times (-6): & 2 + (-6) = -4 \ ✗ \\
3 \times (-4): & 3 + (-4) = -1 \ ✓
\end{array}
$$

… a bit of trial and improvement

$$x^2 - x - 12 = (x + 3)(x - 4)$$

Example 1   Factorise $a^2 + 8a - 20$.

The factors of a^2 are a and a, giving $(a \quad)(a \quad)$
Find two numbers which multiply to give -20 (for the last term) and
add to give $+8$ (for the middle term).
Note: the bigger one will be positive. (Why?)

$$
\begin{array}{ll}
20 \times (-1): & 20 + (-1) = 19 \ ✗ \\
10 \times (-2): & 10 + (-2) = 8 \ ✓
\end{array}
$$

So $a^2 + 8a - 20 = (a - 2)(a + 10)$

Example 2   Factorise $m^2 - 5m + 6$.

The factors of m^2 are m and m, giving $(m \quad)(m \quad)$
Find two numbers which multiply to give $+6$ (for the last term) and
add to give -5 (for the middle term).
Note: both numbers will be negative. (Why?)

$$
\begin{array}{ll}
-6 \times (-1): & -6 + (-1) = -7 \ ✗ \\
-3 \times (-2): & -3 + (-2) = -5 \ ✓
\end{array}
$$

So $m^2 - 5m + 6 = (m - 2)(m - 3)$

Exercise 6.1

1 Factorise these trinomials:

a $a^2 + a - 2$ **b** $a^2 - 3a + 2$ **c** $a^2 + 3a + 2$

d $a^2 - a - 2$ **e** $x^2 + 5x + 6$ **f** $x^2 - x - 6$

g $x^2 - 5x + 6$ **h** $x^2 + x - 6$ **i** $m^2 - 6m + 5$

j $m^2 - 4m - 5$ **k** $m^2 + 4m - 5$ **l** $m^2 + 6m + 5$

2 Factorise these expressions, checking your answers by multiplying out:

a $t^2 + 6t + 8$ **b** $q^2 - 4q + 4$ **c** $y^2 + 9y + 20$

d $n^2 + n - 6$ **e** $k^2 - 8k + 16$ **f** $x^2 + 2x + 1$

g $w^2 - 2w + 1$ **h** $y^2 - 9y + 20$ **i** $u^2 - 12u + 35$

j $x^2 + 3x + 2$ **k** $p^2 - 3p + 2$ **l** $x^2 - 6x - 7$

m $y^2 + 8y + 15$ **n** $v^2 - 10v + 16$ **o** $x^2 + 6x + 5$

p $k^2 - 6k + 9$ **q** $x^2 + 7x + 10$ **r** $c^2 + 11c + 10$

s $d^2 + 5d + 6$ **t** $r^2 - 10r + 21$ **u** $t^2 + 9t + 8$

v $u^2 - 10u + 21$ **w** $a^2 - 7a + 6$ **x** $w^2 - 6w + 5$

3 Factorise:

a $w^2 - 6w + 9$ **b** $x^2 + 6x + 9$ **c** $t^2 - t - 56$

d $m^2 + 10m + 16$ **e** $b^2 + 10b + 25$ **f** $a^2 - 10a + 25$

g $n^2 - 2n - 3$ **h** $t^2 + 17t + 16$ **i** $c^2 + 8c + 16$

j $t^2 - 10t + 16$ **k** $b^2 - 17b + 16$ **l** $p^2 - 20p + 100$

m $x^2 + 12x + 36$ **n** $y^2 + y - 6$ **o** $w^2 + w - 72$

p $x^2 + 4x + 4$ **q** $e^2 - e - 2$ **r** $a^2 + 4a - 5$

s $b^2 - 4b - 21$ **t** $r^2 - 3r - 10$ **u** $x^2 - 4x + 4$

v $d^2 - 10d + 16$ **w** $t^2 + 6t + 8$ **x** $u^2 + u - 20$

4 The expression given for the area of each square can be factorised.
The factors will provide an expression for the length of the square.
The dimensions are in centimetres. For each square:

  i   find the expression for the length of a side

  ii use the given value of x to calculate the dimensions of the square.

a

$x^2 + 10x + 25$

$x = 7$

b

$x^2 + 14x + 49$

$x = 4$

c

$x^2 + 4x + 4$

$x = 6$

d

$x^2 + 2x + 1$

$x = 5$

5 Factorise:

a $y^2 - y - 6$ **b** $w^2 + 18w + 65$ **c** $x^2 + 7x + 12$ **d** $n^2 + n - 2$

e $k^2 - k - 20$ **f** $n^2 + n - 30$ **g** $x^2 - 7x + 12$ **h** $y^2 + y - 12$

i $p^2 + 3p - 10$ **j** $n^2 - n - 12$ **k** $b^2 - 8b + 12$ **l** $w^2 - 2w - 24$

m $c^2 + 11c - 12$ **n** $v^2 + 4v - 12$ **o** $q^2 + 2q - 15$ **p** $d^2 - 13d + 12$

q $c^2 - 2c - 15$ **r** $k^2 + k - 20$ **s** $a^2 - 4a - 12$ **t** $r^2 - 5r - 36$

u $b^2 + 8b - 20$ **v** $u^2 - 11u + 18$ **w** $y^2 - 10y - 11$ **x** $c^2 + 9c + 18$

y $g^2 + 14g + 49$ **z** $w^2 + 21w - 72$

Challenge

Does it factorise or not?

a Find all the whole numbers a less than 50 for which $x^2 - x - a$ factorises and write a sentence to describe how you could find others.

b For which numbers b less than 50 does $x^2 - 2x - b$ factorise?

c Do similar investigations for $x^2 - 3x - c$ and $x^2 - 4x - d$.

d Compare all your results and write an account of your discoveries.

> $x^2 - x - 1$ does not factorise
> $x^2 - x - 2 = (x + 1)(x - 2)$
> $x^2 - x - 3$ does not factorise
> $x^2 - x - 4$ does not factorise
> $x^2 - x - 5$ does not factorise
> $x^2 - x - 6 = (x + 2)(x - 3)$
> ...
> ... ?
> ...

7 Harder examples

Consider the expansion of $(3d + 2)(d - 3)$:

$$(3d + 2)(d - 3) = 3d^2 - 9d + 2d - 6 = 3d^2 - 7d - 6$$

$3d^2$ ... is the result of multiplying the first terms, in this case $3d$ and d.
-6 ... is the result of multiplying the last terms, in this case 2 and 3.
$-7d$ ... is the result of multiplying the outer terms, the inner terms and adding the results.

To factorise $3d^2 - 7d - 6$:

Step 1: Find the factors of $3d^2$. The factors are $3d$ and d, giving $(3d \quad)(d \quad)$

Step 2: Find two numbers a and b which multiply to give -6 (for the last term), and for which $3a + b$ gives -7 (for the middle term), then factors will be $(3d + b)(d + a)$.

> $6 \times (-1)$: $18 + (-1) = 17$ ✗
> $3 \times (-2)$: $9 + (-2) = 7$ ✗
> This nearly fits but the sign is wrong.
> Try switching signs ...
> -3×2: $-9 + 2 = -7$ ✓

Thus $3d^2 - 7d - 6 = (3d + 2)(d - 3)$

Example Factorise $6x^2 + 7x + 2$.

> *Step 1:* Find factors of $6x^2$. They could be $6x$ and x or they could be $2x$ and $3x$.
> Try $6x$ and x.

Step 2: Find two numbers a and b which multiply to give $+2$ (for the last term), and for which $6a + b$ gives 7 (for the middle term), then factors will be $(6x + b)(x + a)$.

2×1: $12 + 1 = 13$ ✗
1×2: $6 + 2 = 8$ ✗
There are no other options so it can't be $6x$ and x.

Try $2x$ and $3x$.

Step 2: Find two numbers a and b which multiply to give $+2$ (for the last term), and for which $2a + 3b$ gives 7 (for the middle term), then factors will be $(2x + b)(3x + a)$.

2×1: $4 + 3 = 7$ ✓

So $6x^2 + 7x + 2 = (2x + 1)(3x + 2)$

Exercise 7.1

1 Factorise these expressions:

a $2w^2 + 3w + 1$	**b** $3y^2 - 4y + 1$	**c** $3b^2 - 2b - 1$	**d** $2m^2 + m - 1$
e $3k^2 + 4k + 1$	**f** $3d^2 - d - 2$	**g** $3a^2 + 7a + 2$	**h** $3f^2 + 5f + 2$
i $5e^2 - 6e + 1$	**j** $5x^2 + 11x + 2$	**k** $2p^2 + 9p + 7$	**l** $2x^2 - 7x + 3$
m $2c^2 - 5c + 2$	**n** $2x^2 + 5x + 2$	**o** $3v^2 - 5v + 2$	**p** $5k^2 - 16k + 3$
q $5n^2 + 7n + 2$	**r** $11u^2 + 13u + 2$	**s** $2x^2 - 3x + 1$	**t** $3r^2 + r - 2$
u $5b^2 + 4b - 1$	**v** $13u^2 + 7u - 6$	**w** $17a^2 + 9a - 8$	**x** $7w^2 - 11w - 6$

2 Expressions for the length and breadth of each rectangle can be obtained by factorising the expression for the area.
Lengths are measured in centimetres.
Use the given value of x to find the dimensions of each rectangle.

a
$A = 4x^2 - 4x - 3$

$x = 5$

b
$A = 9x^2 + 7x - 2$

$x = 1$

c
$A = 8x^2 + 10x - 3$

$x = 3$

3 Factorise these quadratic expressions:

a $4d^2 + 5d + 1$	**b** $6x^2 - 5x + 1$	**c** $8d^2 + 10d - 3$	**d** $4y^2 - 7y + 3$
e $9w^2 - 6w + 1$	**f** $4t^2 + 3t - 1$	**g** $12n^2 + 5n - 2$	**h** $8b^2 - 2b - 3$
i $6a^2 + 17a - 3$	**j** $12c^2 - 8c + 1$	**k** $9x^2 - 3x - 2$	**l** $4m^2 + 4m + 1$
m $6w^2 + 7w + 1$	**n** $4x^2 - 8x + 3$	**o** $6h^2 + 7h - 3$	**p** $9b^2 - 10b + 1$
q $6t^2 + 5t + 1$	**r** $12v^2 + 7v + 1$	**s** $24r^2 + 5r - 1$	**t** $24a^2 + 2a - 1$

4 Factorise:

a $25y^2 - 10y + 1$

b $6a^2 - 5a - 6$

c $9e^2 - 19e + 2$

d $1 + 4d + 3d^2$

e $1 - c - 2c^2$

f $4r^2 - 11r + 6$

g $1 - 3w - 18w^2$

h $5 + 11b - 12b^2$

i $10x^2 + 3x - 4$

j $15 - 7d - 2d^2$

k $1 - 8n + 16n^2$

l $6 - 5w - 6w^2$

m $18a^2 + a - 4$

n $12m^2 - 7m - 12$

o $p^2 - pq - 2q^2$

p $a^2 - 2ab + b^2$

q $2x^2 + 11xy + 5y^2$

r $9a^2 + 6ad - 8d^2$

s $6m^2 - 5mn - 6n^2$

t $12e^2 + 13ef - 4f^2$

Challenge

The trinomial factor clock

In this challenge you have to place the 12 trinomial expressions in the correct positions on the clock.

Expression A is placed at the 12 o'clock position.

When correctly placed, each expression shares exactly one factor with the expressions in the positions on either side of it.

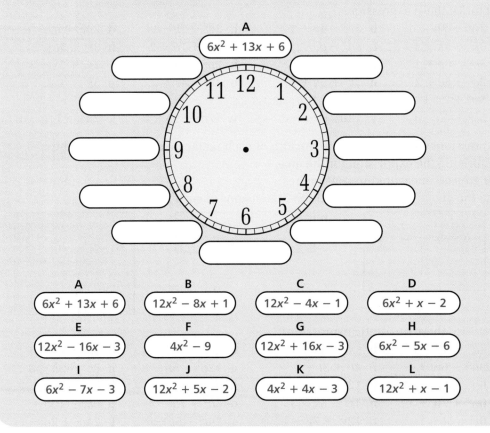

A	**B**	**C**	**D**
$6x^2 + 13x + 6$	$12x^2 - 8x + 1$	$12x^2 - 4x - 1$	$6x^2 + x - 2$
E	**F**	**G**	**H**
$12x^2 - 16x - 3$	$4x^2 - 9$	$12x^2 + 16x - 3$	$6x^2 - 5x - 6$
I	**J**	**K**	**L**
$6x^2 - 7x - 3$	$12x^2 + 5x - 2$	$4x^2 + 4x - 3$	$12x^2 + x - 1$

8 Factorising: A mixture

Example 1
Factorise fully $2ax^2 - 8ay^2$.

$2ax^2 - 8ay^2$
$= 2a(x^2 - 4y^2)$ ... common factor
$= 2a(x - 2y)(x + 2y)$ ... difference of two squares

Example 2
Factorise fully $3x^2 + 3x - 6$.

$3x^2 + 3x - 6$
$= 3(x^2 + x - 2)$ ... common factor
$= 3(x + 2)(x - 1)$ ... trinomial expression

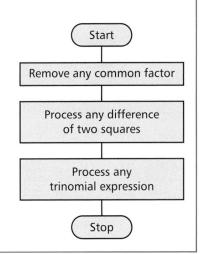

Exercise 8.1

1 Fully factorise these expressions. There is a mixture of types.
   a $4m + 8$ **b** $w - 2w^2$ **c** $2a^2 - 2b^2$ **d** $3k^2 + 18k + 27$
   e $t^2 - tu$ **f** $4d - 2d^2$ **g** $2m^2 + 2m - 12$ **h** $9y^2 + 6y$
   i $5g^2 - 20$ **j** $ab + a^2c$ **k** $4x^2 - 12x + 8$ **l** $8 - 2xy$
   m $x^3 - x$ **n** $72 - 2m^2$ **o** $2p^2 + 12p + 16$ **p** $4b^2 + 2bc$
   q $6p^2 - 3q^2$ **r** $7q^2 - 28q + 28$ **s** $2u^2 - 2v^2$ **t** $3k^2 - 24k + 48$
   u $9c^2 - 900$ **v** $6x^2 + 12x - 90$ **w** $2x^2 - 18$ **x** $x^3 - 2x^2$

2 Factorise fully:
   a $8w^2 + 16w - 24$ **b** $18x^3 - 2x$ **c** $4ab - 6bc$ **d** $2y + 2y^2 + 2y^3$
   e $r^3 - 4r$ **f** $3x^3 - 27x$ **g** $11x^2 + 22x + 11$ **h** $6a^2b - 8ab^2$
   i $8p^2 - 72$ **j** $2n^2 - 2n - 144$ **k** $3xy + 6b^2y$ **l** $3b^2 - 12b$
   m $3f^3 - 27f$ **n** $4w^2 + 6w - 10$ **o** $3u^2 - 36u + 105$ **p** $30a^2 - 30a$

Exercise 8.2

1 Factorise fully:
   a $180 - 5d^2$ **b** $12n^2 - 33n + 18$ **c** $2xyz - 8zyw$ **d** $6v + 16v^3$
   e $28q^2 - 14q - 14$ **f** $16 - 400a^2$ **g** $17 - 34x + 17x^2$ **h** $m^3 - 9mn^2$
   i $6x^2 - 17x + 12$ **j** $u^2w^2 - 4w^2$ **k** $28x^2 + 28x - 168$ **l** $14x^2 + 20x + 6$
   m $9y - 16y^3$ **n** $36 + 72a - 108a^2$ **o** $abc^2 + a^2bc$ **p** $x^2y^4 - x^4y^2$

2 Factorise fully:
   a $(p + q)^2 - r^2$ **b** $x^2 - (x - y)^2$ **c** $(a + b)^2 - b^2$
   d $(x + y)^2 - (x - y)^2$ **e** $(e - f)^2 + (e + f)^2$ **f** $a(x + y) + b(x + y)$
   g $ax + ay + bx + by$ **h** $3p + 3q + ap + aq$ **i** $(e + f)^2 - (f + g)^2$
   j $w^2 - w^6$ **k** $3x^2 + 3xy - 18y^2$ **l** $(p - q)^2 - 4p^2$
   m $x^4 - 1$ **n** $(x - y) - (x - y)^2$ **o** $(a + 1)^3 - 4(a + 1)$
   p $2(x - y) - 18(x - y)^3$

Challenge

Factors and sequences

For the sequence 1, 4, 7, 10, 13 ..., the difference between neighbouring terms is 3.

Using the formula $3n$ gives the sequence 3, 6, 9, 12, 15 ....

In this sequence the difference between neighbouring terms is also 3.

So the nth term formula we want is $3n + $ *some adjustment.*

Comparing 1, 4, 7, 10, 13 ... with 3, 6, 9, 12, 15 ..., we can see that the *adjustment* must be -2.

The nth term $= 3n - 2$.

1 Find the nth term formula for these sequences:

  a 8, 11, 14, 17, 20, ...

  b 3, 8, 13, 18, 23, ...

  c 1, 10, 19, 28, 37, ...

  d 5, 18, 31, 44, 57, ..

In the sequence 6, 24, 52, 90, ...

the difference between terms is not constant.

However there is a pattern in the factors of the terms:

$6 = 2 \times 3$; $24 = 3 \times 8$; $52 = 4 \times 13$; $90 = 5 \times 18$.

2 **a** Find the nth term of 2, 3, 4, 5, ..., the sequence of 1st factors.

  b Find the nth term of 3, 8, 13, 18, ..., the sequence of 2nd factors.

  c Factorise $5n^2 + 3n - 2$ and compare with **a** and **b**. Comment on the result.

3 For each nth term formula:

  i   use it to write down the first four terms of the sequence

  ii factorise the formula, and use this to write down the first four terms as products of factors

  iii check that the four terms in **i** and **ii** match.

  a $4n^2 - 1$ **b** $6n^2 - n - 2$ **c** $4n^3 + 4n^2 - 3n$

4 The diagram shows a spiral of numbers.

From within the spiral, numbers are selected to form a sequence.

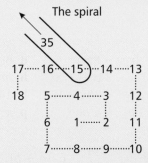

The spiral

  a Continue the spiral to find the next two terms in the indicated sequence.

  b Is there a pattern in the factors of each term?

  c Can you find the formula for the nth term of the sequence?

  d Will there ever be a prime number in this sequence? Prove your answer.

◀◀ RECAP

Factors of numbers and expressions come in **factor pairs**.

Numbers may share factors. These are called **common factors**.
One of these common factors will be the **Highest Common Factor** or **HCF**.
When you divide numbers by their HCF the quotients will have an HCF of 1.

The result of **factorising** an expression is a **product of factors**.
There are several types of factorising patterns.

Type 1:   Common factor ... $ab + ac = a(b + c)$
e.g. $4xy - 6x^2 = 2x(2y - 3x)$

Type 2:   Difference of two squares ... $a^2 - b^2 = (a - b)(a + b)$
e.g. $25a^2 - 9b^2 = (5a)^2 - (3b)^2 = (5a - 3b)(5a + 3b)$

Type 3:   Trinomial expressions
To factorise trinomials trial and improvement must be used, taking into consideration the steps taken when removing brackets.
For example, in the trinomial expression $3d^2 - 7d - 6$

$3d^2$ ... is the result of multiplying the first terms, in this case $3d$ and d.

-6 ... is the result of multiplying the last terms, in this case 2 and 3.

$-7d$ ... is the result of multiplying the outer terms, the inner terms and adding the results.

This consideration leads to the factors $(3d + 2)(d - 3)$.

Factorising *fully* means you must examine each factor to see if it can be factorised further, e.g.

$3y^2 + 3y - 6 = (3y + 6)(y - 1) = 3(y + 2)(y - 1)$

The common factor could have been removed initially:

$3y^2 + 3y - 6 = 3(y^2 + 3y - 2) = 3(y + 2)(y - 1)$

- Look for common factors first.
- Then check for difference of two squares.
- Finally check if the trinomial expressions have factors.

1 Find the missing factor in these products:
   a $63 = 7 \times \ldots$ b $pq = p \times \ldots$ c $6xy = 2 \times \ldots$ d $6xy = \ldots \times 2x$
   e $2m^2 = m \times \ldots$ f $12wx = 3x \times \ldots$ g $6p^2 = \ldots \times 3p$ h $c^2d = \ldots \times cd$

2 List all the factors of:
   a 24 b de c w^2 d $2g^2$ e $4a^2b$

3 Find the HCF of:
   a 24 and 30 b $4x$ and $18y$ c $6a$ and $27a^2$ d $6n^2m$ and $8nm^2$

4 Factorise by removing the common factor:
   a $5a - 25$ b $7 - 7a$ c $b^2 + 2b$ d $12c^2 + 20c$
   e $apR - apr$ f $2xy - 4xz$ g $56 - 7x^2$ h $g^2h + gh^2$

5 Factorise these differences of squares:
   a $k^2 - h^2$ b $n^2 - 1$ c $a^2 - 9b^2$ d $4b^2 - 49c^2$

6 Factorise these quadratic expressions:
   a $d^2 + 10d + 21$ b $u^2 + 4u - 21$ c $y^2 - 12y + 27$ d $k^2 - 7k - 8$
   e $3m^2 - m - 2$ f $13x^2 + 7x - 6$ g $6n^2 - 5n + 1$ h $6u^2 - 5u - 6$

7 A rectangle has an area which can be calculated using the formula:

   Area $= (6n^2 - 19n - 7)$ cm^2

   a Factorise the area expression.
   b In this case, the two factors give expressions for the length and breadth of the rectangle. If $n = 5$ find its dimensions.

8 Fully factorise:
   a $a^2 - ab$ b $4w^2 - 12w + 8$ c $8d^2 - 8e^2$ d $y^3 - y$
   e $4a^2 - 400$ f $8b^2 + 16b - 24$ g $3e^3 - 27e$ h $196 - 4d^2$

6 Statistics – charts and tables

The table gives the date of Easter over a period of 17 years (from 2000 to 2017).
It is full of information, but patterns are hard to see.

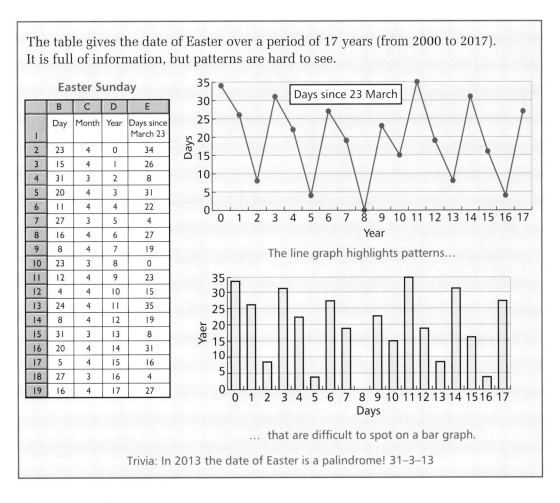

Easter Sunday

	B	C	D	E
1	Day	Month	Year	Days since March 23
2	23	4	0	34
3	15	4	1	26
4	31	3	2	8
5	20	4	3	31
6	11	4	4	22
7	27	3	5	4
8	16	4	6	27
9	8	4	7	19
10	23	3	8	0
11	12	4	9	23
12	4	4	10	15
13	24	4	11	35
14	8	4	12	19
15	31	3	13	8
16	20	4	14	31
17	5	4	15	16
18	27	3	16	4
19	16	4	17	27

Days since 23 March

The line graph highlights patterns…

… that are difficult to spot on a bar graph.

Trivia: In 2013 the date of Easter is a palindrome! 31–3–13

1 REVIEW

◄◄ Exercise 1.1

1 The chart shows the money collected by a charities committee in one year.

   a Which season produced the most funds?

   b How much was collected in autumn?

   c What is the difference between the amount collected in winter and the amount collected in autumn?

   d What name is given to this sort of diagram?

This year's collection

Winter   Spring   Summer   Autumn

represents £100

e What would a quarter coin represent?

f Give one i advantage ii disadvantage of using this kind of diagram.

2 A sample of bottles from the recycling bottle
bank is inspected.
The chart represents the data collected.
a Which colour of glass occurs the most?
b How many bottles are in the whole sample?
c What fraction of the bottles were white?
d What is the ratio of green to brown bottles?
e If the x axis was rearranged to give the colours
with highest frequency first, would it affect
the information in the chart?
f Give one i advantage ii disadvantage of using
this kind of diagram.

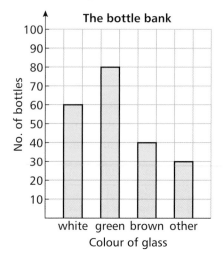

3 This line graph shows the number of
hours of sunshine recorded by a
weather station over a year.
a Would it matter here if the x axis
was labelled in a different order?
b Taking December, January and
February as winter, write out the
hours of sunshine for each season.
c What was the increase in hours of
sunshine from April to June?
d Give one i advantage ii disadvantage
of using this kind of diagram.

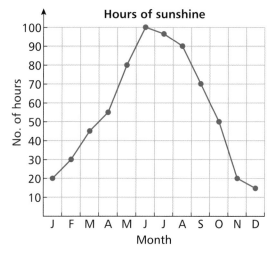

4 The table gives a breakdown of the pupils in class 1A.
The pie chart shows the same data in diagrammatic
form.
a There are 30 pupils in the class.
What is the angle at the centre of the sector
representing boys
i aged 11
ii aged 12?
b How many girls aged
i 11 years
ii 12 years are there?
c What fraction of the class are girls?
d Give one
i advantage ii disadvantage
of using this kind of diagram.

	A	B
1	Gender (age)	No. of pupils
2	boy (11)	15
3	boy (12)	6
4	girl (11)	5
5	girl (12)	4

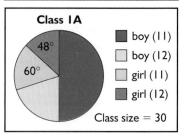

5 The table shows both the absences for class A1 for the week and the absences for the whole school.

Day	Absences for A1	Absences from school
Monday	6	30
Tuesday	7	40
Wednesday	2	16
Thursday	4	28
Friday	5	38

   a Using the symbol to represent 5 pupils, make a pictograph of the 'whole school' data.

   b Make a bar graph of the absences for class A1.

   c Why would it not be a good idea to draw bar graphs of both 'whole school' and 'A1' absences on the one chart?

6 The table gives the monthly average rainfall records for 2002 and 2003 in one city.

Month	J	F	M	A	M	J	J	A	S	O	N	D
2002 rain (mm)	90	70	50	30	20	10	20	30	50	50	60	70
2003 rain (mm)	70	60	40	40	30	20	10	0	10	30	50	80

   a Draw a line graph of both years on the one grid.

   b What is the advantage of doing this rather than using two grids?

   c For how many months were the 2003 figures greater than the 2002 figures?
   Is this easier to answer by looking at the table or by looking at the graph?

   d For what month was the difference in the figures greatest?

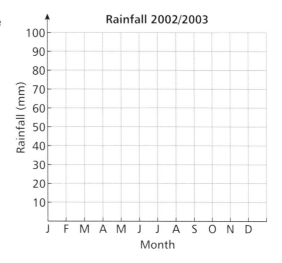

7 The precipitation is recorded at a weather station every day of November, December and January. For example, on 18 days in this period it was dry.

   a For how many days were records kept?

   b Make an accurate pie chart to represent the data. (Work to the nearest degree.)

Dry	18
Rain	24
Sleet	35
Snow	15

2 Misleading statistics

'There are three kinds of lies: lies, damned lies and statistics.'
Benjamin Disraeli (1804−81)

Different charts follow different conventions. The reader of a chart usually makes assumptions about these conventions when interpreting the chart.

- Scales are uniform.
- The origin is the point (0, 0).
- In a pictogram, each icon represents the same frequency.
- In a bar chart and line graph, height is directly proportional to frequency.
- In a pie chart, area is proportional to frequency.
- The units on both axes are meaningful and can be measured.

When these conventions are disregarded, the result is a graph that misleads the reader.

Exercise 2.1

1 After a recent budget a newspaper carried the chart shown.

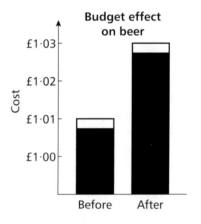

a At a glance, what seems to have happened to the price of beer − by what factor has it apparently increased?

b i What was the cost before the budget?
  ii What was the cost after the budget?
  iii What fraction of the original cost is the increase?

c Which of the above conventions are being broken?

2 This chart would seem to show the preferences of a group of pupils in S1 and S2 when asked what they would like as a Christmas treat.

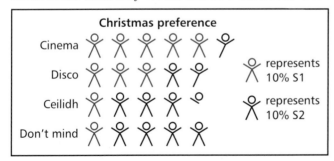

a What would appear to be the most popular choice?

b What percentage of i S1 ii S2
  chose the cinema?

c There were 10 people in S1 and 40 people from S2 in the sample.
  To the nearest whole number, how many i S1 ii S2 chose the cinema?

d Copy and complete this table.

e Comment on the actual order of preference.

f What convention is being broken here?

	Ci	Di	Ce	Do
S1 (%)	50			
S2 (%)	8			
Totals (%)	58			
S1 actual	5			
S2 actual	3			
Totals (actual)	8			

3 This line graph was found in an advertisement for a headache tablet.

It shows how the pain recedes after taking a pill.

a How many minutes does it take to remove all pain?

b How much pain was the sufferer in to start with?

c What convention is being broken here?

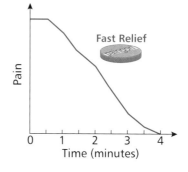

4 Honest Harry is trying to impress his clients. The chart shows his profits over three years.

a Describe your first impression of the trend in Harry's profits.

b What were his profits in

    i 2002   **ii** 2003   **iii** 2004?

c Are the profits increasing or decreasing with time?

d What convention is being broken here?

e Make a chart which properly shows the trend.

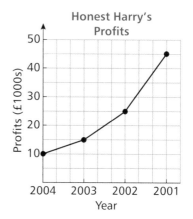

5 The chart shows the trend in dropping profits before and after a new management took over a business.

a At a glance, what is the difference in the trends before and after the takeover?

b By how much did the profits drop in

    i 2001

    ii 2002

    iii 2003?

c What is wrong with the graph?

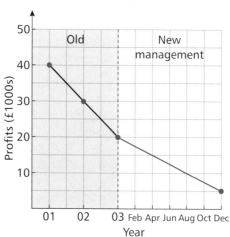

6 This novelty chart shows an airline's profits.

   a What would seem to be the case as the year progresses?

   b Transfer the graph to an ordinary square grid.

   c What aspects of the data have been distorted?

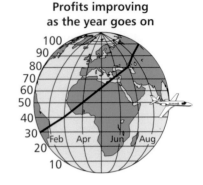

Profits improving as the year goes on

7 A novelty pie chart compares the sales of Easter eggs at four outlets.

   a From first impressions, list the outlets in order of their sales with the one with most sales first.

   b Measure the angle at the centre of each sector to the nearest 10°.

   c Given that there were a million sales, work out how many sales were made at each outlet.

   d Comment on the order of the outlets.

   e What convention is not being followed this time?

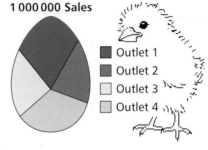

1 000 000 Sales

■ Outlet 1
■ Outlet 2
□ Outlet 3
□ Outlet 4

8 a What were the sales of stamps
   i last year **ii** this year?

   b By what factor have they increased?

   c By what factor has the area of the stamp increased?

   d State why this chart is misleading.

Christmas stamp success story

Sales (millions)

200

100

Last year   This year

---

3 Tables

A table helps us to organise and order data. When the table records how often each outcome or score occurs then it is referred to as a **frequency table**.

Tally marks are often used to help in the creation of frequency tables.

Example   A survey into shoe size in an S1 class produced the following responses:

9	8	7	8	9
8	8	6	6	10
5	8	9	9	10
8	5	7	6	9
9	8	7	5	10

Arranging the data in a frequency table helps us to see at a glance how many there were of each size.

Size	Tally	Frequency
5					3
6					3
7					3
8	⅏ ||	7
9	⅏		6
10					3

It is often useful to add a relative frequency column which gives the fraction of the time each score has occurred. This is useful when constructing pie charts. The fraction can be given as a common or a decimal fraction.

Size	Tally	Frequency	Relative frequency
5	|||	3	$\frac{3}{25} = 0 \cdot 12$
6	|||	3	$\frac{3}{25} = 0 \cdot 12$
7	|||	3	$\frac{3}{25} = 0 \cdot 12$
8	⅏ ||	7	$\frac{7}{25} = 0 \cdot 28$
9	⅏		6	$\frac{6}{25} = 0 \cdot 24$
10	|||	3	$\frac{3}{25} = 0 \cdot 12$
	Total	25	1

Note that the sum of the relative frequencies is 1.
Note also that a sector with an angle of $0 \cdot 24 \times 360 = 86°$ (to the nearest degree) would represent size 9 shoes in a pie chart.

Exercise 3.1

1 Sort each set of data into a frequency table.

a
29	27	25	27	27
25	27	28	27	29
26	28	29	26	29
25	27	26	27	27
27	28	25	29	29

b
left	right	right	right	right
right	ahead	ahead	right	right
left	left	left	right	ahead
left	ahead	ahead	ahead	return
ahead	right	ahead	right	left

c
♠	♥	♥	♣	♣
♥	♥	♣	♣	♣
♣	♣	♥	♥	♦
♥	♣	♣	♠	♦
♣	♦	♦	♣	♥

2 The time (in minutes) it took each candidate to complete a test was noted.

30	45	50	40	45
40	35	45	45	35
50	40	50	50	50
50	30	45	55	45
50	50	35	50	40
50	35	45	50	45

    a Sort the data using a frequency table.
    b How many candidates were timed?
    c Add a relative frequency column, working to 2 decimal places.
    d Draw a pie chart of the data, working to the nearest degree.
    e How many candidates took less than 40 minutes to complete the test?
    f How many took between 40 and 50 minutes, inclusive?

3 In a study of the common cold, the number of days the symptoms persisted was noted for several patients.

5	6	8	6	6	3	5	5	8	4
3	6	6	6	5	6	8	6	5	6
8	7	8	6	4	4	6	7	3	6
6	7	7	5	5	6	8	7	5	6
6	6	6	6	7	7	4	5	5	6
4	6	5	5	5	7	5	6	4	4

    a Sort the data using a frequency table.
    b How many patients were observed?
    c How many patients had the cold for more than 4 days?
    d How many had the cold for more than 3 but less than 8 days?
    e Add a relative frequency column to your table.
    f What fraction of the patients had the cold for 5 days?
    g They say that with medicine you can clear a cold in 7 days.
       Without the medicine it can take a week to clear.
       What fraction of the patients had a cold for exactly 7 days?

4 The table shows the heights, in millimetres, of a sample of daisies.

Height (mm)	35	36	37	38	39	40	41
Frequency	2	6	7	8	7	3	2

    a How many daisies had a height
      i   less than 37 mm
      ii more than 39 mm
      iii 38 mm or more but less than 41 mm?
    b How many daisies were measured?
    c What fraction of the daisies were
      i   37 mm high   **ii** more than 39 mm high?
    d What is the most commonly occurring height?
    e A gardener removed half of the sample. They were all x mm high or less.
       The other half were all x mm or more. What is the value of x?

Cumulative frequency

It is often useful to keep a running total of the frequencies as the score or value being measured increases. For each score we then know how many scores are equal to or less than it. This is known as the **cumulative frequency** (c.f.) of that score.

For example, consider the data in question **4**:

Height	35	36	37	38	39	40	41
Frequency	2	6	7	8	7	3	2
Cumulative freqency	2	8	15	23	30	33	35

A third row has been added, giving a running total of the frequencies. This shows that:
- 2 daisies were 35 mm high or less
- 8 daisies were 36 mm high or less
- 15 daisies were 37 mm high or less
- 23 daisies were 38 mm high or less
- 30 daisies were 39 mm high or less
- 33 daisies were 40 mm high or less
- all 35 daisies were 41 mm high or less.

Note that if we are given cumulative frequencies we can work out the actual frequencies.

Example 1   How many daisies were 39 mm high?

c.f. for 39 = 30; c.f. for 38 = 23
$\Rightarrow$ 30 − 23 = 7 were 39 mm high.

Example 2   How many daisies were between 39 mm and 37 mm high (inclusive)?

c.f. for 39 = 30 $\Rightarrow$ 30 daisies were 39 mm or less
c.f. for 36 = 8 $\Rightarrow$ 8 daisies were 36 mm or less
$\Rightarrow$ 30 − 8 = 22 daisies were between 39 mm and 37 mm high.

Exercise 3.2

1 Add a cumulative frequency column to each table.

a

Score	Frequency	Cumulative frequency
21	8	
22	5	
23	2	
24	12	
25	1	
26	3	

b

Score	Frequency	Cumulative frequency
50	14	
60	12	
70	9	
80	6	
90	3	
100	2	

c

Score	Frequency
7·6	11
7·7	26
7·8	31
7·9	48
8·0	14
8·1	8

2 In this table the cumulative frequencies are given.
Work out the actual frequencies.

Height		18	19	20	21	22	23	24
Frequency								
Cumulative freqency		1	4	12	22	29	35	40

3 A civil engineer has to assess the condition of a kilometre of road with a view to repairs.
Each 10 m stretch is given a score of 0 to 5 depending on the amount of work needed.
(0 represents no work needed; 5 means complete resurface needed.)
The table shows the results of his survey.

Score	0	1	2	3	4	5
Frequency	15	21	31	23	8	2
Cumulative freqency						

a Add a cumulative frequency row.
b Show how the results can be used to calculate:
  i how often a condition 3 stretch occurred
  ii the amount of times a stretch of road worse than condition 3 was encountered
  ii how often the road was worse than condition 1 but not as bad as condition 4.
c In the first 500 m all of the stretches were condition x or less.
In the other 500 m they were all condition x or more.
What is the value of x?

4 Stem-and-leaf diagrams (stem plots)

Another useful way of sorting a collection of data and getting order into it is by means of the **stem-and-leaf diagram**.

Example   Sort the following exam marks into ascending order by means of a stem-and-leaf diagram.

21	38	42	20
40	29	23	4
44	2	28	35
13	13	41	41
32	34	17	47
16	18	19	45

First, noting the scores run from 2 to 47, we form a stem 0 1 2 3 4 to represent 0, 10, 20, 30, 40. In this case the unit digits form the leaves.

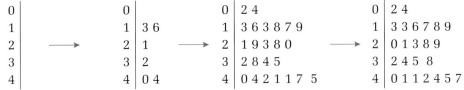

0		0		0	2 4		0	2 4
1		1	3 6	1	3 6 3 8 7 9		1	3 3 6 7 8 9
2	→	2	1	→ 2	1 9 3 8 0	→ 2	0 1 3 8 9
3		3	2	3	2 8 4 5		3	2 4 5 8
4		4	0 4	4	0 4 2 1 1 7 5		4	0 1 1 2 4 5 7

| Form a stem. | Add the leaves … | … until all the data is included. | Sort the leaves in ascending order coming from the stem. |

The completed stem-and-leaf diagram will look like this:

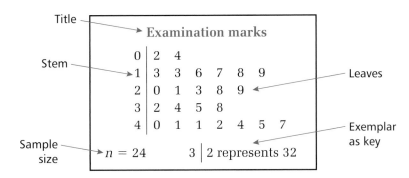

Each row of the diagram is referred to as a **level**.
The '1' level records the numbers 13, 13, 16, 17, 18 and 19.
The original 24 pieces of data have now been sorted in ascending order and can be read from the diagram: 2, 4, 13, 13, 16, 17, 18, 19, 20, 21, 23, 28, 29, 32, 34, 35, 38, 40, 41, 41, 42, 44, 45, 47.

Using the stem as the basis for a horizontal axis, and replacing the leaves by dots, produces a quick diagram to represent the distribution of scores. This is referred to as a **dot plot**.

Using the above as an example gives:

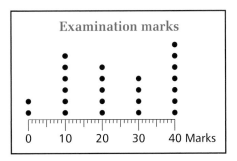

Exercise 4.1

1 This stem-and-leaf diagram records the result of a survey on car tyre treads.
Note that 1 | 3 represents 1·3 mm and not 13 mm.

    a What was the deepest tread measured?

    b How many cars were in the survey?

    c What numbers does the '2' level record?

    d List the data in order, lowest number first.

Depth of tread					
1	3	3	5		
2	3	3	4	6	7
3	1	3	4	5	5	8
4	2	2	5	6	
5	0	7			

$n = 20$ 1 | 3 represents 1·3 mm

    e Since there are 20 numbers there will be two numbers sharing the middle position in this list. What are these two numbers?

    f Make a dot plot to illustrate the distribution.

2 The stem-and-leaf diagram shows the times, in seconds, attained by a runner practising for a 200 m race.

    a What was his **i** fastest **ii** slowest time?

    b What time did he achieve the most often?

    c The diagram helps arrange the times in order.
      If we call 20·1 s the first time, what is

      i the 4th time   **ii** the 10th time

      iii the 15th time   **iv** the 20th time?

Running time							
20	1	2					
21	0	1	2	8	9		
22	2	2	3	4	6	6	6
23	0	5	7	7	9		
24	2	3	4	4	4	4	8	9
25	6	6	7				

$n = 30$ 20 | 1 represents 20·1 s

3 a Make use of a stem-and-leaf diagram to arrange the following list of scores in order.

5·7	9·6	5·9	5·2	9·5	9·5	8·6
9·1	6·5	6·8	5·9	9·9	5·9	7·8
8·1	6·7	9·3	5·6	6·7	5·3	5·2
9·2	5·5	7·9	7·8	7·4	5·9	7·9
8·3	9·2	7·5	5·1	7·3	7·1	5·3

    b Since there are 35 scores then the 18th number is in the middle.
      With the scores now in order, what is the middle score?

    c What is the   **i** lowest   **ii** highest score?

    d Make a dot plot to illustrate the distribution of scores.

4 Several books have their number of pages recorded.

257	251	258	258	281
256	274	240	280	242
273	241	260	283	269
242	265	287	247	246
271	248	279	273	255

    a Sort the list out using a stem-and-leaf diagram.

    b How many books were surveyed?

    c With the list in order, what score is in:

      i the first position   **ii** the last position   **iii** the middle position?

Back-to-back stem-and-leaf diagrams

Often two sets of figures can be compared by setting two stem-and-leaf diagrams back-to-back.

Example
In a school's rugby competition the heights of those players from Scott House and those from Burns House are being compared in a back-to-back stem-and-leaf diagram.
Notice that in both cases the leaves get bigger coming away from the stem.

Scott House		Burns House
4 2 1	14	0 2 6 7 8
7 6	15	3 4
8 5 0	16	0 1 6
6 4 3 3 1	17	1 6
7 0	18	1 4 4

$n = 15$ $\qquad$ $n = 15$

14 | 1 represents 141 cm

We can see that, with the lists in order, half the people in Scott House are bigger than 168 cm and half the people in Burns House are bigger than 160 cm. The tallest person in Scott House is 187 cm but the tallest in Burns House is 184 cm. The shortest person in Scott house is 141 cm; the shortest in Burns House is 140 cm. You get the feeling that Scott House people are *typically* taller than those of Burns House.

Exercise 4.2

1 The stem-and-leaf diagram shows the ages of 21 people selected at random from an audience at the cinema one Wednesday. The figures below show another sample made the following Friday.

Friday		Wednesday
	3	0 1 1 4 6
	4	1 5
	5	2 2 9 9
	6	0 1 1 1 4 5 7
	7	0 1 1

$n = 21$

3 | 0 represents 30 years old

60	35	40	56	38	39	38
35	40	59	51	32	41	44
53	43	48	55	38	33	35

a Copy and complete the diagram to form a back-to back stem-and-leaf diagram.

b Compare the ages of the two samples by considering the ages in the
   i lowest   ii highest   iii middle positions in the lists.

c Would you say that either of the samples was typically younger than the other?

2 In an experiment with speed and time, a student measured his reaction times before and after a meal. The diagram shows his measured results.

a What was his best reaction time before the meal?

b How often did he score below 0·3 second
   i before   ii after the meal?

c What was his worst time
   i before   ii after the meal?

d How easy is it to compare the 'middling' results?

Before		After
1	2	2 3 5 5
8 4	3	0 1 2 4
7 3 1	4	0 1 1
8 3 2 2 0	5	0
0	6	

$n = 12$ $\qquad$ $n = 12$

2 | 1 represents 0·21 s

3 Each fortnight an electrical shop records its sale of satellite dishes.
An advertising campaign took place in December of 2002.
The figures show the 12 month period before and after the campaign.

2002				
26	27	15	21	15
20	16	13	29	30
30	28	12	15	27
26	13	14	28	25
14	14	27	24	

2003				
12	23	22	26	19
27	28	24	28	28
28	17	24	11	17
25	24	25	22	13
20	25	27	11	

a Make a back-to-back stem-and-leaf diagram with this data.
b Use your diagrams to help you compare the sales figures.
  Do you think the campaign was successful?

5 Five-figure summaries

When we have a large amount of data it is often useful to summarise it by quoting
five numbers. First the list is sorted into ascending order. Then the five numbers
are:
- the lowest value
- the highest value
- the middle value, called the **median** – this splits the list into two halves
- the middle value of the lower half, called the **lower quartile**
- the middle value of the upper half, called the **upper quartile**.

When we have an even number of items in a list, there will be two middle values.
We should use the mean of these two values.
The median and the two quartiles split the list into four smaller lists of equal length.

Example 1   1, 2, 3, 3, 4, 5, 6, 6, 7, 9, 9, 10

- There are 12 numbers in the list so it splits into two lists of six:
  1, 2, 3, 3, 4, 5 and 6, 6, 7, 9, 9, 10; the median is the mean of 5 and 6 … **5·5**
- There are 6 numbers in the lower list so it splits into two lists of three:
  1, 2, 3 and 3, 4, 5; the lower quartile is the mean of 3 and 3 … **3**
- There are 6 numbers in the upper list so it splits into two lists of three:
  6, 6, 7 and 9, 9, 10; the upper quartile is the mean of 7 and 9 … **8**
- The lowest number is **1** and the highest is **10**.

The five-figure summary is 1, 3, 5·5, 8, 10.

Example 2   1, 2, 3, 3, 4, 5, 6, 6, 7, 9, 9, 10, 14

- There are 13 numbers in the list, giving two lists of six and one in the middle:
  1, 2, 3, 3, 4, 5   **6**   6, 7, 9, 9, 10, 14; the median is **6**
- There are 6 numbers in the lower list so it splits into two lists of three:
  1, 2, 3   and   3, 4, 5; the lower quartile is the mean of 3 and 3 … **3**

- There are 6 numbers in the upper list so it splits into two lists of three: 6, 7, 9 and 9, 10, 14; the upper quartile is the mean of 9 and 9 ... **9**
- The lowest number is **1** and the highest is **14**.

The five-figure summary is 1, 3, 6, 9, 14.

Example 3   1, 2, 3, 3, 4, 5, 6, 6, 7, 9, 9, 10, 14, 18

- There are 14 numbers in the list, giving two lists of seven:
  1, 2, 3, 3, 4, 5, 6 and 6, 7, 9, 9, 10, 14, 18;
  the median is the mean of 6 and 6 ... **6**
- There are 7 numbers in the lower list, giving two lists of three and a middle one:
  1, 2, 3   **3**   4, 5, 6; the lower quartile is **3**
- There are 7 numbers in the upper list, giving two lists of three and a middle one:
  6, 7, 9   **9**   10, 14, 18; the upper quartile is **9**
- The lowest number is **1** and the highest is **18**.

The five-figure summary is 1, 3, 6, 9, 18.

We often use the following symbols: $L = 1$; $Q_1 = 3$; $Q_2 = 6$; $Q_3 = 9$; $H = 18$.

Exercise 5.1

1 Make five-figure summaries of each of the following lists:
  a 6, 6, 7, 8, 8, 8, 9, 11, 13, 14, 15, 15, 17, 18, 25, 28
  b 12, 12, 13, 13, 14, 14, 14, 15, 16, 18, 24, 24, 25, 25, 26, 27, 29
  c 22, 22, 23, 25, 25, 27, 28, 32, 34, 36, 38, 41, 43, 44, 56, 57, 59, 63
  d 46, 47, 49, 55, 57, 66, 71, 72, 74, 76, 79, 80, 82, 84, 85

2 a Use a stem-and-leaf diagram to help you arrange the following data into ascending order:

58	55	1	30	27	35
15	12	27	44	4	41
46	40	55	57	38	34
40	10	25	47	29	20
16	50	48	18	23	10

  b Form a five-figure summary of the data.

3 An airport logged the number of minutes late 35 different flights were departing.

Minutes delayed

29	26	2	35	23	9	31
39	25	23	17	27	21	9
3	27	18	28	40	8	39
16	4	22	8	14	32	32
17	14	32	19	15	35	16

  a Sort the list using a stem-and-leaf diagram.
  b Use the stem-and-leaf diagram to help you form a five-figure summary.

4 The stem-and-leaf diagram shows the result of a survey into hotdog sales at the tuck shop.
The figures were collected over 23 days.
  a From the diagram identify
   i Q_1, the lower quartile
   ii Q_2, the median
   iii Q_3, the upper quartile.
  b Write out a five-figure summary of the data.

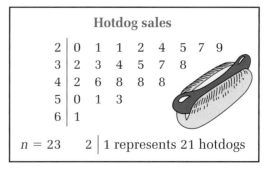

Hotdog sales

```
2 | 0  1  1  2  4  5  7  9
3 | 2  3  4  5  7  8
4 | 2  6  8  8  8
5 | 0  1  3
6 | 1
```

$n = 23$ $2 \mid 1$ represents 21 hotdogs

5 The back-to-back stem-and-leaf diagram shows how much Bryan and Kirsty spent each month on sending each other text messages.
  a Make up a five-figure summary for
   i Bryan's expenditure
   ii Kirsty's expenditure.
  b Use the summary to help you compare both people's use of text messaging.

Bryan		Kirsty
2	1	3 6 7 7
9 1	2	0 6 8 9
8 8 2	3	6 7 7
7 4 4 3 1	4	3
7	5	

$n = 12$ $n = 12$

$1 \mid 3$ represents £1·30

6 Box plots

Once a five-figure summary has been obtained, the data can be well represented by a diagram called a **box plot**.

Example   A planner wanted to check the timing of a set of traffic lights.
He counted the number of vehicles in the queue as the lights turned green.
He did this for 13 light changes.
His observations arranged in ascending order were: 1, 2, 3, 3, 4, 5, 6, 6, 7, 9, 9, 10, 14.
The list can be summarised by the five-figure summary:
$L = 1$; $Q_1 = 3$; $Q_2 = 6$; $Q_3 = 9$; $H = 14$.

The following diagram represents his findings:

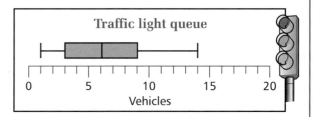

The diagram includes:
- a suitable number line, graduated and with units noted (namely vehicles)
- a set of five vertical lines indicating the values of the five-figure summary
- a box whose sides are the vertical lines marking the quartiles.

From the diagram we can easily see that:
- the middle 50% of the data lies in the box
- the lower 25% of the data is in the 'whisker' to the left of the box
- the upper 25% is in the whisker to the right of the box.

We get a feeling for how the data is spread out.

Exercise 6.1

1 Make box plots to illustrate sets of data with the following five-figure summaries.
   a $L = 3$; $Q_1 = 8$; $Q_2 = 14$; $Q_3 = 16$; $H = 22$
   b $L = 20$; $Q_1 = 30$; $Q_2 = 36$; $Q_3 = 41$; $H = 46$
   c $L = 120$; $Q_1 = 125$; $Q_2 = 138$; $Q_3 = 146$; $H = 157$
   d $L = 23 \cdot 3$; $Q_1 = 23 \cdot 7$; $Q_2 = 24 \cdot 4$; $Q_3 = 24 \cdot 8$; $H = 25 \cdot 4$
   e $L = 300$; $Q_1 = 340$; $Q_2 = 400$; $Q_3 = 480$; $H = 510$

2 At a local cinema the number of people going to the evening showing of *Pirates of Gold* was recorded each night over a period of 24 days.

52	79	79	79	68	69
62	67	64	85	51	53
78	58	63	54	70	52
64	82	84	84	74	60

   a Organise the data using a stem-and leaf diagram.
   b Use this to help you make a five-figure summary.
   c Copy and complete the box plot to illustrate the audience numbers.

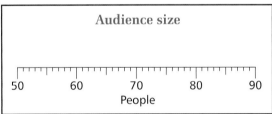

Audience size

50   60   70   80   90
People

3 The stem-and-leaf diagram shows the number of caterpillars found in 19 different vegetable plots in an allotment.

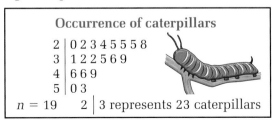

Occurrence of caterpillars

```
2 | 0 2 3 4 5 5 5 8
3 | 1 2 2 5 6 9
4 | 6 6 9
5 | 0 3
```
$n = 19$ 2 | 3 represents 23 caterpillars

   a State the highest and lowest scores.
   b Calculate the median and quartiles.
   c Draw a box plot to illustrate how the data is spread out.

4 In a survey, the following typing speeds were recorded.

Typing speeds									
19	3	4	8	9	9				
20	0	1	1	2	5	6	7	9	9
21	4	4	7	7	8				
22	0	1							

$n = 21$ 19 | 3 represents 193 words/minute

   a Make a five-figure summary of the data.
   b Draw a box plot to illustrate the distribution of the data.

Comparing data sets

Often two sets of data can be compared more easily if box plots are drawn of each set over the same number line.

Example   Some research was carried out at two different fish and chip shops into the contents of a bag of chips. Several bags were bought at each outlet and the contents counted.
The resulting data was used to make this diagram.

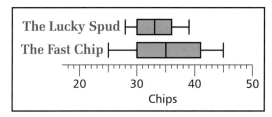

Write a few sentences to compare the data sets.

* The median number of chips at the Lucky Spud was less than that of the Fast Chip. Typically you get more at the Fast Chip.
* However, the content of the bag of chips at the Lucky Spud was more consistent. Buy there and you're not likely to get a bag with fewer than 28 chips.

Exercise 6.2

1 Afternoon temperatures in June and July are being compared in this box plot.
   a State the median temperature for
      i June   **ii** July.
   b What is the lower quartile for
      i June   **ii** July?
   c Write a few sentences comparing the temperatures.

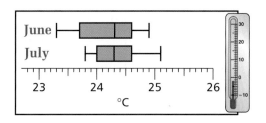

2 The box plots show the results of a survey into how long each child has with Santa at Supa Shop and Mega Stores.

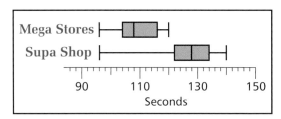

a Make a five-figure summary for each store.
b If both stores charge the same amount for a visit to Santa, which offers better value for money? Give a few reasons.

Investigation

Choose a reading book suitable for an S1 pupil and another book suitable for an S6 pupil and compare their sentence length. Pick about 30 sentences at random from each book and count the number of words in each. Make five-figure summaries and box plots. Write a short report on your findings.

7 Scatter diagrams

Often two variables are examined to see if there is any connection between them. A good way of doing this is to make a **scatter diagram**.

Example   Twenty S1 pupils are asked their height and their shoe size.
This table is a summary of the answers given.

Pupil	1	2	3	4	5	6	7	8	9	10	11	12	13	14	15	16	17	18	19	20
Shoe size	7·5	8·5	7	8	10	6·5	6	8·5	9·5	8	9	7	9	7·5	6	8	8·5	9·5	10	6·5
Height (cm)	135	143	131	145	160	135	120	147	152	140	150	135	152	143	129	137	150	155	155	126

Is there a connection between *shoe size* and *height*?

Plot each data pair as a point on a coordinate grid. Although it is not perfect, we can see that there is indeed a connection. In general, the taller you are, the bigger your size of shoe.

Such a connection is called a **correlation**.
If the points very nearly form a straight line we say the correlation is strong.
If one variable increases as the other increases we call the correlation positive.
Between *height* and *shoe size* there is a strong, positive correlation.

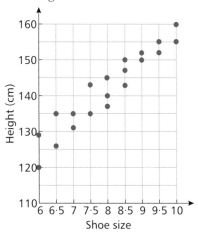

If we wish to highlight the relation we can use our judgment to draw a line of best fit on the graph ... a line to relate typical shoe size to typical height.

We can then use this line to estimate:

- height given shoe size
- shoe size given height.

For example, it looks like someone who is 130 cm tall will wear a shoe of size 6·5.

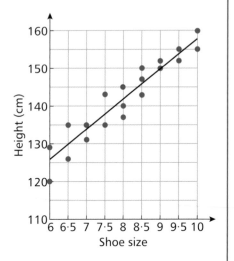

Other possible outcomes include:

- a negative correlation, where as one variable increases, the other decreases (we can use a line of best fit again)
- no correlation, where the variables show no sign of being related.

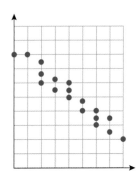

A strong negative correlation ... as one variable gets bigger the other gets smaller.

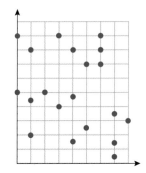

No correlation

Exercise 7.1

1 i Make scatter diagrams using the data in the tables.
ii Describe any correlation you find.

a

	1	2	3	4	5	6	7	8	9	10	11	12	13	14	15
Variable 1	9	11	12	10	12	8	11	9	14	8	15	10	14	13	13
Variable 2	7	6	5	8	6	8	7	8	5	7	4	6	4	5	4

b

	1	2	3	4	5	6	7	8	9	10	11	12	13	14	15
Variable 1	37	20	35	5	40	18	22	5	28	13	45	43	40	10	25
Variable 2	80	55	75	40	80	40	40	25	60	40	90	80	70	30	60

c

	1	2	3	4	5	6	7	8	9	10	11	12	13	14	15
Variable 1	5	25	13	30	20	35	40	5	15	27	20	35	45	37	10
Variable 2	55	50	53	47	51	48	52	48	51	53	49	51	47	50	50

d

	1	2	3	4	5	6	7	8	9	10	11	12	13	14	15
Variable 1	17	11	30	26	9	35	40	28	13	34	45	19	37	12	21
Variable 2	35	30	26	78	54	43	85	53	79	71	52	15	20	41	52

2 State what kind of relation you would expect between:
   a the value of a teddy bear and its age
   b the number of visitors to a tourist attraction and the cost of entry
   c the amount of beetles in a pond and the amount of pollution.

3 A study was undertaken to see how long candles would burn.
Different length candles were lit and then timed to see how long they lasted.

Candle no.	1	2	3	4	5	6	7	8	9	10	11	12	13	14	15
Candle length (mm)	10	14	34	3	78	25	32	20	59	30	50	68	50	56	70
Lifetime (min)	20	17	40	14	86	35	44	24	71	32	58	79	53	60	75

   a Make a scatter diagram using the data.
   b Add a line of best fit.
   c Describe the correlation between candle length and the lifetime of
      the candle.
   d Use the line of best fit to estimate the length of time a 40 mm candle
      would burn.

4 The table shows the times taken to do similar jobs with different widths of paint
brushes.

Brush no.	1	2	3	4	5	6	7	8	9	10	11	12	13	14	15
Brush width (cm)	8	6	3	8	9	4	2	7	10	4	7	5	4	6	3
Time taken (min)	6	7	10	7	5	9	12	7	5	11	6	9	10	9	11

   a Make a scatter diagram using the data.
   b Describe the correlation between brush width and the time taken
      to do the job.
   c Add a line of best fit.
   d Use the line of best fit to estimate the time it will take to do the job
      using a 6 cm brush.

5 This scatter diagram shows a connection
between the length of time an antique clock
will run and the number of times its key is
turned.
 a Describe the correlation.
 b Copy the diagram and add a line of best fit.
 c Use your line to estimate how long a clock
   will run if its key is given five turns.

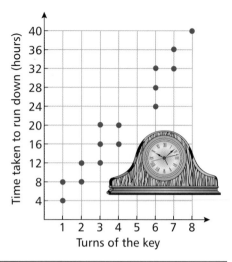

◀◀ RECAP

Conventions
If the following conventions are disregarded when drawing a graph, the result can
be misleading.
● Scales are uniform.
● The origin is the point (0, 0).
● In a pictogram, each icon represents the same frequency.
● In a bar chart and line graph, height is directly proportional to frequency.
● In a pie chart, area is proportional to frequency.
● The units on both axes are meaningful and can be measured.

Tables
The formation of a table helps us to organise and order data.
When the table records how often each outcome or score occurs then it is referred
to as a **frequency table**.
It is often useful to add a **relative frequency** column, which gives the fraction of the
time each score has occurred.
It can be useful to keep a running total of the frequencies as the score or value
being measured increases. This is known as the **cumulative frequency** of that score.

Example

Score	Frequency	Relative frequency	Cumulative frequency
5	2	$\frac{2}{20} = 0.1$	2
6	4	$\frac{4}{20} = 0.2$	6
7	7	$\frac{7}{20} = 0.35$	13
8	6	$\frac{6}{20} = 0.3$	19
9	1	$\frac{1}{20} = 0.05$	20
Total	20	1	

Stem-and-leaf diagrams

A useful way of sorting a collection of data and getting order into it is by means of the **stem-and-leaf diagram**.

Using the stem as the basis for a horizontal axis, and replacing the leaves by dots, gives a quick diagram to represent the distribution of scores. This is referred to as a **dot plot**.

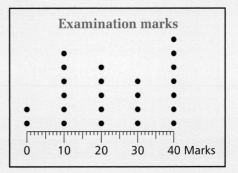

Stem-and-leaf diagrams can be drawn back-to-back to compare sets of data.

Five-figure summaries

Once a set of data has been put in order then it can be summarised using five figures:

- the lowest value (L)
- the highest value (H)
- the middle value, the **median**, which splits the list into two halves (Q_2)
- the middle value of the lower half, the **lower quartile** (Q_1)
- the middle value of the upper half, the **upper quartile** (Q_3).

Once a five-figure summary has been obtained, the data can be well represented by a diagram called a **box plot**.

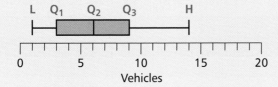

Scatter diagrams

These diagrams can be used to highlight **correlation** between different data sets.

Correlation may be **positive** … as one variable increases in value then so does the other.

Correlation may be **negative** … as one variable increases in value then the other decreases.

The correlation may be weak, strong or non-existent.

1 Comment on the graph opposite.

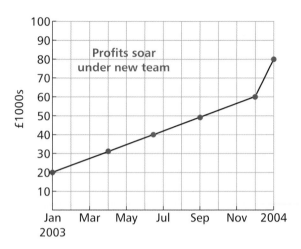

2 A dice is thrown 25 times to see if it is fair.

2	1	5	1	3
2	2	4	1	3
2	1	6	3	2
1	5	3	1	2
1	1	1	1	4

a i Make a frequency table of the scores.
  ii Which score happened least often?
b i Add a relative frequency column to your table.
  ii Use it to help you draw a pie chart to illustrate the data.
c Add a cumulative frequency column.

3 Each week Thomas notes the number of minutes he spends watching news programmes.

70	45	69	58	69
68	46	52	74	50
48	51	71	78	67
72	62	70	60	44
66	42	60	44	78

a Arrange the data in ascending order by first drawing a stem-and-leaf diagram.
b Illustrate the data using a dot plot.
c Give a five-figure summary of the data.
d Draw a box plot to illustrate the distribution of the times.

4 Fifteen pupils were surveyed. They were asked
  i how many dental fillings they had and
  ii how much they spent a week on sweets.

Number of fillings	7	1	8	1	9	3	4	8	2	3	9	10	7	1	10
Spent on sweets (£)	3·00	1·00	3·50	1·50	3·50	1·50	2·50	3·00	2·00	2·50	4·00	3·50	3·50	2·50	4·00

a Make a scatter diagram to illustrate the data.
b Describe the relationship between 'Number of fillings' and 'Spent on sweets'.
c Add a line of best fit to the diagram.
d Use your line of best fit to estimate how much is spent by a pupil with five fillings.

REVISE

7 Proportion and variation

The Scottish parliament is based on
Proportional Representation (PR).

PR is a system of voting designed so that the
number of MPs elected from each party
reflects the share of votes cast for each party.

1 REVIEW

◀◀ **Exercise 1.1**

1 An expedition takes enough supplies to last for 10 days.
   a If the amount of supplies is doubled how long will they last?
   b If the number of people on the expedition is doubled how long will the supplies last?

2 Which of the following are examples of direct proportion?
   a The distance walked and the time taken when walking at a constant speed.
   b The amount each National Lottery winner receives and the number of winners.
   c The age of a tree and the number of rings in its trunk.

3 Which of these pairs vary in direct proportion?
   a 3 golf lessons for £36; 5 lessons for £60
   b 2 items cleaned for £7; 3 items cleaned for £10
   c 8 hours of work for £52; 7 hours for £45·50
   d 300 g jar of coffee for £2·10; 500 g jar for £3·50

4 80 cm^3 of calcium weigh 120 g.
   a Calculate the weight of 60 cm^3.　　**b** What volume of calcium weighs 270 g?

5 The table shows the height a car is lifted by a jack and the number of turns of the handle.

Number of turns (n)	0	5	10	15	20	25	30
Height lifted (h mm)	0	12·5	25	37·5	50	62·5	75

   a Draw a graph to illustrate the table.
   b Is the height directly proportional to the number of turns?
   c How does the graph show this? (Give two reasons.)
   d By what height would 50 turns of the handle raise the car?

6 Copy and complete the table.

x	1	4	16	25	100
x^2					
$\sqrt{x}$					
$\dfrac{1}{x}$					

7 Solve each of the following equations:

a $5a = 35$ **b** $\dfrac{b}{4} = 9$ **c** $0·5c = 14$ **d** $8d = 0·5$

e $10 = 100e$ **f** $8 = \dfrac{f}{0·4}$ **g** $0·4 = 0·05g$ **h** $0·075 = \dfrac{h}{80}$

8 a $P = RI^2$ Calculate P when $R = 5$ and $I = 0·5$.

   b $L = \dfrac{V}{B^2}$ Calculate L when $V = 144$ and $B = 4$.

   c $A = \dfrac{2S}{\sqrt{T}}$ Calculate A when $S = 1·8$ and $T = 0·64$.

9 Calculate k for each of the following when $m = 12$ and $n = 2$.

a $m = kn$ **b** $m = \dfrac{k}{n}$ **c** $m = kn^2$ **d** $m = \dfrac{k}{n^2}$

10 In which of these graphs is y directly proportional to x?

a 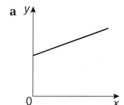   **b** 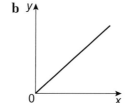   **c** 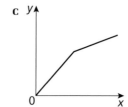   **d**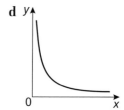

2 Inverse proportion

Keith has a table that shows him how long it takes to get to work at different average speeds.

Speed (mph)	20	30	40	50	60
Time (min)	60	40	30	24	20

Note that with each pair of values speed × time is a constant:

$$20 \times 60 = 30 \times 40 = 40 \times 30 = 50 \times 24 = 60 \times 20 = 1200$$

If the speed is doubled then the time is halved.

When the product of corresponding values of two variables is a constant we say the variables are in **inverse proportion**.

In this example, time and speed are inversely proportional.

Example

Four people need to invest £30 000 each to set up a new business.

However, they decide to increase the number of partners to six.

How much does each person need to invest to raise the same total amount?

4 partners → £30 000 each

1 partner → £30 000 × 4 = £120 000 (total amount needed)

6 partners → £120 000 ÷ 6 = £20 000 each

> If one variable doubles when the other variable is halved, we
> have **inverse proportion**.

Exercise 2.1

1 Which of these relationships involve inverse proportion?
- **a** The number of days it takes a ship to cross the Atlantic and its average speed
- **b** The number of cleaners in an office block and the time taken to clean the offices
- **c** The value of a car and its age
- **d** The number of glasses that can be filled from a jug and the size of the glass

2 Marie is a chess champion.
She plays simultaneously against several opponents.
If she plays against two opponents she can spend an
average of 50% of her time on each game.
What percentage of her time can she spend on each game,
on average, when she plays against

- **a** 4
- **b** 5
- **c** 8
- **d** 10 opponents?

3 A school year is divided into 8 classes of 27 pupils.
If there were 9 classes of equal size, how many pupils would be in a class?
(Hint: find the total number of pupils first.)

4 At a DIY store one truck load of sand can fill 60 bags each weighing 25 kg.
How many 20 kg bags could be filled from the same load?

5 It takes a team of 20 people 4·5 hours to clean a stadium after a concert.
How long should it take if the workforce is increased by 10?

6 At 8 m/s Steve can run one lap of a track in 48 s.
- **a** How long would it take at 6 m/s?
- **b** What average speed would be needed to cycle it in 30 s?

7 An art gallery allocates a budget of £2500 per day for the costs of a 24 day exhibition.
- **a** If the same total amount had to last 25 days, how much would there be for each day?
- **b** If the running costs were reduced by £500 per day, for how many more days could the exhibition run?

8 A lottery has a fixed total payout each month.
In May six winners each receive £18 000.
  a In June the number of winners increases by 2. How much do they each win?
  b In July the individual prizes are £3600 greater than in May.
      How many winners are there in July?

9 A 2 litre container of liquid tomato food will feed 12 of Jack's plants for 30 days.
  a How many days would the 2 litre container last if he had 20 tomato plants?
  b How long would a 3 litre container last with 12 plants?
  c What volume of liquid food is needed to last 18 plants 40 days?

10 Nigella is varnishing wooden floors.
On one area of 9 m² she puts 2 coats and uses 1500 ml of varnish.
  a How much varnish does she need to cover 15 m² with 3 coats of varnish?
  b Applying 4 coats, what area could 2500 ml of varnish cover?

---

3 Direct proportion (or variation) graphs

Example 1

The voltage for different currents in an electrical circuit is recorded in a table.

Current (I amps)	0	0·5	1	1·5	2	2·5
Voltage (V volts)	0	4	8	12	16	20

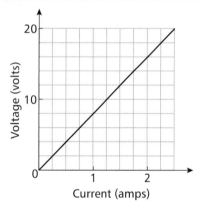

The graph is a straight line passing through (0, 0).
This tells us that voltage (V) is directly proportional to current (I)
or that V varies directly as I.

The mathematical symbol for proportion is $\propto$. We write $V \propto I$.
When V varies directly with I we can say $V = kI$ where k is a constant, called the
constant of proportion, i.e. $V \propto I \Rightarrow V = kI$

The value of k is equal to the ratio $\dfrac{V}{I}$ for any point on the line.

From the table or the graph $\dfrac{V}{I} = \dfrac{4}{0\cdot5} = \dfrac{8}{1} = \dfrac{12}{1\cdot5} = \dfrac{16}{2} = \dfrac{20}{2\cdot5} = 8$

$k = 8$, so $V = 8I$ is the equation connecting V and I.

Exercise 3.1

1 The table shows the earnings of several part-time workers at a warehouse.

Hours (*H*)	8	10	12	16	20
Earnings (£*E*)	60	75	90	120	150

   a Draw a graph of earnings against hours.

   b Do the earnings vary directly with the hours?
      How does the graph show this?

   c Check by calculating the constant of proportion by considering $\dfrac{E}{H}$.

2 This currency graph converts between pounds and dollars.

   a Use the graph to complete the table.

£ (*P*)	10	20	30	40	50
$ (*D*)					

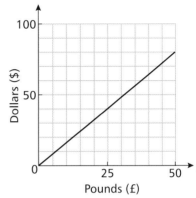

   b $D \propto P \Rightarrow D = kP$. Find the value of k. $\left(\text{Calculate the ratio of } \dfrac{D}{P}\right)$

   c Write down an equation connecting D and P.

3 Melvin is paid petrol expenses for any driving done in connection with his job.
The table shows how much he receives for various distances.

Distance (*d* km)	16	25	32	34	40
Expenses (*e* pence)	288	450	576	612	720

   a Draw a graph of expenses (*e* pence) against distance (*d* km).

   b How does the graph show that $e \propto d$? Check the ratios of $\dfrac{e}{d}$ in the table.

   c Express e in terms of d.

4 In an experiment a 1 m aluminium rod is heated. The expansion is measured for each
10 °C rise in temperature. The table shows the results.

Rises in temperature (*t* °C)	0	10	20	30	40	50
Expansion (*E* mm)	0	0·23	0·46	0·69	0·92	1·15

   a Draw a graph of expansion (*E* mm) against rise in temperature (*t* °C).
   b How does the graph show that $E \propto t$?
   c In the equation $E = kt$, what is the value of k?
   d Write down the formula connecting E and t.

5 The table shows European Energy's charges for different amounts of gas.

Gas (G units)	500	650	750	800	1000
Charge (£C)	9·00	11·70	13·50	14·40	18·00

a Draw a graph of charge (£C) against amount of gas (G units).
b Does the charge vary directly as the number of units? Check by calculating ratios.
c Find the formula for C in terms of G.

Example 2
At ABC Engineering the research team test a
length of metal.

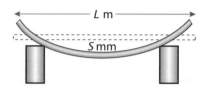

T he table shows the amount of sag for different lengths of the metal.

	A	B	C	D	E
I	Length (L m)	Sag (S mm)	L^2	$\sqrt{L}$	L^3
2	0	0	0	0	0
3	I	0·4	I	I	I
4	2	3·2	4	1·4142	8
5	3	10·8	9	1·7321	27
6	4	25·6	16	2	64

A graph of S against L is not a straight line (graph **i**).
The team plot S against L^2 (graph **ii**) and S against $\sqrt{L}$ (graph **iii**) but still don't get a straight line.

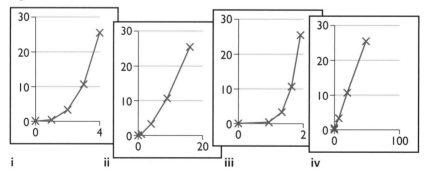

i   ii   iii   iv

Then they try S against L^3 (graph **iv**).

The straight line through (0, 0) shows that $S \propto L^3 \Rightarrow S = kL^3$.
Pick a pair of values (L^3, S), e.g. (1, 0·4):

$$k = \frac{S}{L^3} = \frac{0·4}{1} = 0·4$$

The formula for S is $S = 0·4L^3$.

Exercise 3.2

1 The table shows how the volume of Sharon's car stereo is increased by turning the volume control.

Angle (a degrees)	45	90	135	180	225	270
Volume (v decibels)	15	30	45	60	75	90

a Draw a graph to illustrate the data in the table.

b Explain how the graph shows that volume varies directly as the angle turned through from the 'off' position.

Check by calculating the ratios $\dfrac{v}{a}$ in the table.

c Find a formula connecting v and a.

d Calculate the volume when the control is turned $126°$ from the 'off' position.

2 A train must not go too fast when going round a bend. The maximum speed allowed by Toptrains (S m/s) varies directly as the square root of the radius (R m) of the bend.

$$S \propto \sqrt{R}$$

The graph of S against $\sqrt{R}$ is a straight line.

a Copy and complete the table.

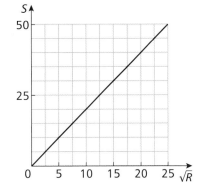

R	100			
$\sqrt{R}$	10	15	20	25
S	20			

b Find a formula for S.

c What is the maximum speed allowed on a bend with a radius of 484 m?

3 The distance it takes a car to brake depends on how fast it is travelling.

The table shows the braking distances for various speeds.

Speed (S mph)	10	20	30	40
Distance (D feet)	5	20	45	80

a Check the ratios $\dfrac{D}{S}$. Does D vary directly as the speed?

b Copy and complete this table of D and S^2.

S^2				
D	5	20	45	80

c Check the ratios of $\dfrac{D}{S^2}$. Are the ratios constant?

d Draw a graph of D against S^2. How does it tell us that D varies directly as S^2?

e Find a formula connecting D and S^2.

f Use your formula to calculate the braking distance for a car travelling at 70 mph.
(Note: these distances do not include the distance travelled before a driver reacts.)

4 The time it takes a pendulum to make one swing depends on the length of the pendulum.
Penny records the swing times for different lengths in a table.

Length (*L* cm)	9	16	25	36
Time (*T* s)	0·6	0·8	1·0	1·2

a Is the relationship
   i $T \propto L$ **ii** $T \propto L^2$ **iii** $T \propto \sqrt{L}$?

b For the correct relationship make a new table and draw a graph to illustrate it.

c Find a formula connecting *T* and *L*.

d Calculate the time taken for one swing for a length of 64 cm.

Investigation

A famous scientist, Johannes Kepler, studied the motion of the planets in their orbits round the Sun. One of Kepler's 'laws' is that the square of the time, *T* years, a planet takes to circle the Sun varies directly as the cube of its distance from the Sun, *R* astronomical units (AU). The Earth takes 365 days for one orbit, and is at a distance of 1 AU from the Sun.

a $T^2 \propto R^3 \Rightarrow T^2 = kR^3$. Calculate *k*.

b Mars is 1·52 AU from the Sun. Calculate the number of days it takes Mars to complete one orbit of the Sun.

c Investigate the time taken for other planets to complete one circle of the Sun.

4 Inverse proportion and variation graphs

The sponsors of Bluebell Rovers' 'Spot the Ball' competition are considering how to divide the £1200 prize money.

Number of prizes (*N*)	1	2	3	4	5
Value of each (£*V*)	1200	600	400	300	240

From the table we see that, as *N* increases, *V* decreases.
V does not vary directly as *N*, as the graph shows.

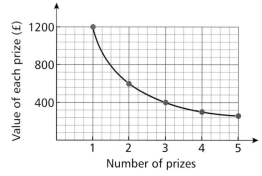

For each pair of values in the table $V \times N = 1200$.

This tells us that V is **inversely proportional** to N or V varies inversely as N.

We write $V \propto \dfrac{1}{N}$

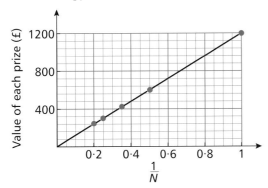

The graph of V against $\dfrac{1}{N}$ is a straight line through O, so $V \propto \dfrac{1}{N} \Rightarrow V = \dfrac{k}{N}$

Notice $V \div \dfrac{1}{N} = 1200$, so $k = 1200$

We can thus express V in terms of N, namely $V = \dfrac{1200}{N}$.

Exercise 4.1

1 The following week Bluebell Rovers have a total of £1800 to share among the winners.
   a Make a table of prize money for 1 to 6 winners.
   b Draw a graph of the value of each prize (£V) against the number of winners (N).
   c Make a new table of V against $\dfrac{1}{N}$.
   d Draw a graph to illustrate the table.
   e Copy and complete: $V \times N = ...$ so $k = ...$
   f Calculate V when $N = 8$.

2 Dave is marking out equally spaced points on circles to draw 'mystic roses'.

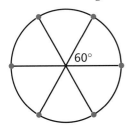

A mystic rose with
radii every 60°

He makes a table showing the number of points (n) and the angle separating the radii ($d°$).

Number of points	2	3	4	5	6	8	9	10	12
Degrees between points	180	120	90	72	60	45	40	36	30

a Check that $d \times n = 360$.

b Copy and complete this table of d against $\dfrac{1}{n}$.

$\dfrac{1}{n}$	0·50	0·33							
d	180	120	90	72	60	45	40	36	30

c Draw a graph of the degrees ($d°$) against $\dfrac{1}{n}$.

Use scales of 0 to 180 on the d axis (vertical) and 0 to 0·50 on the $\dfrac{1}{n}$ axis (horizontal).

d Is the graph a straight line passing through (0, 0)? What does this show?

e Use the equation $d = \dfrac{360}{n}$ to calculate the angle between the radii when there are 15 points.

3 To keep fit Andy does press-ups at the gym. He counts the number he can do in 60 seconds. The table shows the number of press-ups and the time each one takes.

Time for each (t s)	1	2	3	4	5	6
Number completed (n)	60	30	20	15	12	10

a Make a new table of n against $\dfrac{1}{t}$.

b Draw a graph to illustrate the table.

c How does the graph show that n is inversely proportional to t?

d Copy and complete: $n \times t = \dots$ so $n = \dfrac{\dots}{t}$

e Each press-up takes 2·5 s.
At this rate, how many will he complete in the minute?

4 In an electric circuit, Hannah measures the current (I amps) as she varies the resistance (R ohms) while keeping the voltage fixed.

Resistance (R ohms)	0·4	0·8	1·2	1·6	2·0
Current (I amps)	30	15	10	7·5	6

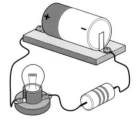

She knows that the current is inversely proportional to the resistance.

a Make a new table and plot the graph which shows that $I \propto \dfrac{1}{R}$.

b Find a formula for I in terms of R.

5 A set of solid brass cylinders is made, each with a volume of 100 cm³. The table shows the heights for different diameters.

Diameter (D cm)	4	6	8	10
Height (H cm)	7·96	3·54	1·99	1·27

Here the height varies inversely as the square of the diameter.

$$H \propto \dfrac{1}{D^2} \;\Rightarrow\; H = \dfrac{k}{D^2}$$

A table of values of $\dfrac{1}{D^2}$ and H is made.

$\dfrac{1}{D^2}$	0·0625	0·028	0·0156	0·01
H	7·96	3·54	1·99	1·27

a Find the value of k to the nearest 10.
b Express H in terms of D.
c Estimate the height of such a cylinder with diameter 12 cm.

5 Direct variation

Example 1   A water storage tank is filled from a hose. The depth of water (D cm) in the tank varies directly as the time (t seconds). After 30 seconds the water is 6 cm deep.
a Find a formula for D in terms of t.
b Use the formula to calculate the depth after 250 seconds.

a $D \propto t \Rightarrow D = kt$
  When $t = 30$, $D = 6$
  $\Rightarrow 6 = k \times 30$
  $\Rightarrow k = 6 \div 30 = 0\cdot2$
  $\Rightarrow D = 0\cdot2t$
b After 250 s $D = 0\cdot2 \times 250 = 50$ cm

Exercise 5.1

1 C varies directly as m. When $m = 10$, $C = 85$.
  a Write down a formula for C in terms of m.
  b Calculate C when $m = 24$.

2 y is directly proportional to x. When $x = 20$, $y = 92$.
  a Write down a formula for y in terms of x.
  b Calculate y when $x = 16$.

3 Electricians know that for copper wire of a given cross-section the electrical resistance (R ohms) is proportional to the length of the wire (L metres). For example, 50 m of a certain wire has a resistance of 20 ohms.
  a Find a formula for R in terms of L.
  b Calculate the resistance of 30 m of wire.

4 In silver plating, the number of grams (N) of silver deposited is proportional to the number of minutes (M) the current flows. 5 g of silver are deposited in 20 minutes.
  a Find a formula connecting N and M.
  b Calculate the weight deposited in 28 minutes.
  c Calculate the time required for a deposit of 12 g.

5 The distance a screw goes into a piece of wood (*d* mm) is directly proportional to the number of turns (*n*).
After 8 turns the screw has gone in 3 mm.
   a Construct a formula for *d* in terms of *n*.
   b How far has the screw gone in after 10 turns?
   c How many turns will it take for the screw to go in 10·5 mm?

6 A balloonist knows that when he ascends, the fall in temperature (*t* °C) varies directly as the height risen (*h* m).
On one day he climbs 500 m and the temperature falls by 1·5°C.
   a Find a formula for *t* in terms of *h*.
   b Calculate the fall in temperature when his balloon ascends 3600 m.
   c On another flight the temperature on the ground is 24 °C. At what height above the ground does he reach freezing point?

Example 2
At a terminal, the rate (*R* litres/s) at which oil can be pumped through a pipe varies directly as the square of the radius of the pipe (*r* cm). A pipe with a radius of 2 cm will pump 1·8 litres/s.
   a Find a formula connecting *R* and *r*.
   b What rate could be pumped through a pipe with a radius of 3 cm?

   a $R \propto r^2 \Rightarrow R = kr^2$
      When $r = 2$, $R = 1·8$
      $\Rightarrow 1·8 = k \times 2^2$
      $\Rightarrow k = 1·8 \div 2^2 = 1·8 \div 4 = 0·45$
      $\Rightarrow R = 0·45r^2$
   b When $r = 3$ cm, $R = 0·45 \times 3^2 = 0·45 \times 9 = 4·05$ litres/s

---

Exercise 5.2

1 Use the symbol $\propto$ to express the relationships in **a** to **d**, and then write down an equation for each using *k* as the constant of variation.
   a The cost of renting an office (£*C*) varies directly as the area of the floor (*A* m²).
   b The distance travelled down a slide (*d* metres) is directly proportional to the square of the time (*t* seconds) in motion.
   c The volume of a sphere (*V* cm³) varies directly as the cube of the radius (*r* cm).
   d Over a 10 day period the height of a plant (*h* cm) varies as the square root of the number of days' growth (*d* days).

2 A car accelerates from traffic lights. The distance it travels (*d* m) varies directly as the square of the time (*t* s). In 2 seconds a sports car goes 10 m.
   a Find a formula for *d* in terms of *t*.
   b How far does the car travel in 6 seconds?

3 If the train travels round the curve too quickly it will leave the rails. But how quickly should it go?
A working model is 'safe speed (V m/s) is proportional to the square root of the radius (r m) of the curve'.
  a Construct a formula connecting V and r, given that for a radius of 400 m the safe speed is 40 m/s.
  b Calculate the safe speed for a radius of 80 m (to the nearest m/s).

4 The weight (W kg) of a lead ball varies directly as the radius (r cm) cubed.
A lead sphere of radius 10 cm weighs 47·3 kg.
  a Find a formula for W in terms of r.
  b Calculate the weight, correct to the nearest kilogram, of a lead ball of radius 16 cm.

5 A stone falls D metres in t seconds, and it is known that D varies directly as the square of the time (t s). After 3 seconds the stone has fallen 45 m.
  a Find the formula for D in terms of t.
  b How far will the stone fall in 6 seconds?
  c How long will it take to fall 125 m?

Brainstormer

Jacobini, the Swiss diamond cutter, knows that the value of a diamond is directly proportional to the square of its weight.
He has to cut a diamond weighing 6 g into two parts in the ratio 2 : 1.
Express the value of the diamond after cutting as a fraction of the value before cutting.

---

6 Inverse variation

The time taken for a journey (t min) is inversely proportional to (varies inversely as) the speed of travel (s km/h).

$$t \propto \frac{1}{s} \Rightarrow t = \frac{1}{s}$$

Example 1 At 5 km/h it takes Darren 24 minutes to walk to school.
  a Find a formula connecting t and s.
  b How long would it take him at 6 km/h?

  a $t = \dfrac{k}{s}$

  When $s = 5$, $t = 24$

  $\Rightarrow 24 = \dfrac{k}{s}$

  $\Rightarrow k = 24 \times 5 = 120$

  $\Rightarrow t = \dfrac{120}{5}$

  b When $s = 6$, $t = \dfrac{120}{s} = 20$. It would take him 20 minutes.

Exercise 6.1

1 M varies inversely as N.
   a Write down a formula for M in terms of N using k as the constant of variation.
   b When $N = 40$, $M = 0.9$. Find the value of k.
   c Calculate M when $N = 48$.

2 H is inversely proportional to w. When $w = 12$, $H = 8.5$.
   a Find a formula for H in terms of w.   b Calculate H when $w = 60$.

3 Pressure (P kg/m^2) varies inversely as area (A m^2).
   When a force is applied to an area of 0.2 m^2 the pressure is 30 kg/m^2.
   a Find a formula for P in terms of A.   b Calculate P when $A = 0.5$.

4 The current (I amps) in a circuit is inversely proportional to the resistance (R ohms).
   The current is 2 amps when the resistance is 250 ohms.
   a Find a formula for I in terms of R.   b Calculate I when $R = 200$.
   c Calculate R when $I = 4$.

5 At a fixed temperature, the pressure P of a given mass of gas varies inversely as its
   volume, V. When $P = 600$, $V = 2$.
   a Find a formula for P in terms of V.   b Calculate P when $V = 3$.
   c Calculate V when $P = 800$.

6 On a railway curve of radius R m, the outer rail is H cm higher than the inner rail.
   Also, H varies inversely as R, and when $R = 500$, $H = 12$.
   a Find a formula for H in terms of R.   b Calculate H when $R = 400$.
   c Calculate R when $H = 10$.

Example 2
The number (n) of ball bearings that can be made from a fixed amount of molten
metal varies inversely as the cube of the radius r (mm).
When $r = 2$ mm, $n = 168$.
a Find a formula connecting n and r.
b How many ball bearings, radius 4 mm, can be made from this same amount of
   metal?

a $n \propto \dfrac{1}{r^3} \Rightarrow n = \dfrac{k}{r^3}$

   When $r = 2$, $n = 168$

   $\Rightarrow 168 = \dfrac{k}{2^3}$

   $\Rightarrow k = 168 \times 2^3 = 1344$

   $\Rightarrow n = \dfrac{1344}{r^3}$

b When $r = 4$, $n = \dfrac{1344}{4^3} = 21$.

Exercise 6.2

1 Danielle carries out an experiment involving measuring the volume of a gas under different pressures. She keeps the temperature fixed.

She knows that the volume (V) varies inversely as the pressure (P).

She finds that $V = 2 \cdot 7$ when $P = 200$.

a Find a formula for V in terms of P.

b When P is 300 what should she expect the value of V to be?

2 Q varies inversely as E^3. When $E = 3$, $Q = 50$.

    a Find a formula for Q in terms of E.   **b** Calculate Q when $E = 5$.

3 $y \propto \dfrac{1}{\sqrt{x}}$. When $x = 25$, $y = 3$.

    a Find a formula for y in terms of x.   **b** Calculate y when $x = 100$.

    c Calculate x when $y = 3 \cdot 75$.

4 As you go further away from a light source, the dimmer it becomes.

The intensity of illumination (I lumens/m^2) is inversely proportional to the square of the distance (D metres) from the light source.

At a distance of 4 m the intensity is measured to be 5 lumens/m^2.

    a Find a formula for I in terms of D.   **b** Calculate I when $D = 8$ m.

    c Calculate D when $I = 3 \cdot 2$ lumens/m^2.

5 After a tyre is punctured, the air pressure (P units) varies inversely as the square root of the time (t s).

John drives over a nail. Four seconds later the tyre pressure is 24 units.

    a Construct a formula for P in terms of t.

    b What is the pressure 9 seconds after the puncture?

    c How long after the puncture is $P = 12$ units?

6 In an electrical circuit the resistance (R ohms) is inversely proportional to the square of the radius (r m) of the wire the current is flowing through.

In an experiment, Rachel measures R to be $0 \cdot 8$ ohm when $r = 0 \cdot 1$ mm.

    a Find a formula connecting R and r.

    b Calculate the resistance in a wire of the same material with a radius of $0 \cdot 2$ mm.

    c What is the value of r when $R = 0 \cdot 05$?

Brainstormers

1 The weight (W kg) of a body varies inversely as the square of its distance (d km) from the centre of the Earth. Isaac weighs 75 kg. The radius of the Earth is 6400 km. Calculate Isaac's weight when he is 1600 km above the Earth's surface.

2 What happens to the value of y when x is

    i doubled   **ii** halved

in each of these relationships?

    a $y \propto x$ **b** $y \propto \dfrac{1}{x}$ **c** $y \propto x^2$ **d** $y \propto x^3$

Investigation

a Copy and complete this table for the sequences of regular polygons:

Number of sides (n)	3	4	5	6
Size of an exterior angle (x)				

b Find a formula for x in terms of n.

7 Joint variation

How long will Viv take to type the manuscript?

The greater the number of pages, the longer she will take.
The time (T minutes) varies directly as the number of pages (N).
So $T \propto N$

Also the greater her typing speed, the shorter the time she will take.
The time varies inversely as the speed (S words/minute).
So $T \propto \dfrac{1}{S}$

T varies directly as N **and** inversely as S.

We also say T varies **jointly** as N and $\dfrac{1}{S}$.

$$T \propto \frac{N}{S} \Rightarrow T = \frac{kN}{S}$$

Example 1 Viv types a 24-page manuscript in 2 hours 24 minutes at a speed of 50 words/minute.
  a Find a formula for T (the time taken) in terms of S (her speed) and N (the number of pages).
  b How long would she take to type 30 pages at 40 words per minute?

  a $T = \dfrac{kN}{S}$

  When $N = 24$ and $S = 50$, $T = 144$

  $\Rightarrow 144 = k \times \dfrac{24}{50}$

  $\Rightarrow k = 144 \times 50 \div 24 = 300$

  $\Rightarrow T = \dfrac{300N}{S}$

  b When $N = 30$ and $S = 40$,

  $T = 300 \times \dfrac{30}{40}$

  $= 225$

  She would take 3 hours 45 minutes.

Exercise 7.1

1 Write these relationships in symbolic form using $\propto$.
 a P varies directly as T and inversely as V.
 b A varies directly as L and as W.
 c V varies jointly as h and the square of r.
 d W varies directly as the square root of A and inversely as B.

2 Write these relationships in words:

 a $E \propto ab$ **b** $S \propto \dfrac{D}{T}$ **c** $T \propto W\sqrt{L}$ **d** $h \propto \dfrac{V}{R^2}$

3 $J \propto MN$. $J = 40$ when $M = 5$ and $N = 4$.
 a Find the value of k, the constant of variation and hence write down a formula for J in terms of M and N.
 b Calculate J when $M = 6$ and $N = 10$.

4 $y \propto \dfrac{x}{z}$. When $x = 3$ and $z = 21$, $y = 8$.

 a Find a formula for y in terms of x and z.
 b Calculate y when $x = 16$ and $z = 14$.

5 The weight of wafer (W g) needed to make an ice-cream cone varies directly as the diameter (D cm) of the top of the cone and as the slant height of the cone (S cm).

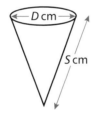

 a Write down a formula for W in terms of D, S and a constant k.
 b Given that when $W = 18$, $D = 4$ cm and $S = 10$ cm, find the value of k.
 c Calculate the weight of wafer when $D = 5$ cm and $S = 12$ cm.

6 When gas is heated it expands. When pressurised, it contracts.
 In fact the volume (V cm^3) of a gas varies directly as the temperature ($T°$) and inversely as the pressure (P units).
 a Write down a formula for V in terms of T, P and a constant k.
 b Given that $V = 80$ when $T = 300$ and $P = 900$ find the value of k.
 c Calculate V when $T = 270$ and $P = 1200$.

7 The Safe and Secure Insurance Company provides pensions (£P) for its employees which are directly proportional to their length of service (Y years) and to their final salary (£S).
 a Find the formula for P in terms of Y, S and a constant k.
 b Mrs Jackson has 20 years' service and a final salary of £24 000.
  Her pension is £6000. Find the value of k.
 c Calculate the pension for 30 years' service and a final salary of £32 000.

Example 2   The height (h cm) of a cone varies directly as the volume (V cm³) and inversely as the square of the radius of the base (r cm).
When $r = 3$ cm and $V = 47\cdot1$ cm³, $h = 5$ cm.

a Find a formula for h in terms of V and r.

b Calculate h, correct to 1 decimal place, when $r = 4$ cm and $V = 75$ cm³.

a $h \propto \dfrac{V}{r^2} \Rightarrow h = \dfrac{kV}{r^2}$

when $r = 3$ and $V = 47\cdot1$, $h = 5$

$\Rightarrow 5 = \dfrac{k \times 47\cdot1}{3^2}$

$\Rightarrow k = 5 \times 9 \div 47\cdot1 = 0\cdot96$ (to 2 decimal places)

$\Rightarrow h = \dfrac{0\cdot96V}{r^2}$

b When $r = 4$ and $V = 75$, $h = 0\cdot96 \times 75 \div 4^2 = 4\cdot5$ cm.

Exercise 7.2

1 Write these relationships using the proportional symbol '$\propto$'.

a B varies jointly as the square root of C and as D.

b y varies directly as the square of x and inversely as the square of z.

c F varies directly as M_1 and as M_2 and inversely as the square of d.

2 Write these relationships in words:

a $W \propto Dr^3$ **b** $V \propto LWH$ **c** $y \propto \dfrac{x^2}{\sqrt{z}}$

3 V varies directly as A and as T^3.

a Write down a formula for V in terms of A, T and a constant k.

b Given that $V = 120$ when $A = 10$ and $T = 4$, find the value of k.

c Calculate V when $A = 12$ and $T = 6$.

4 y varies directly as $\sqrt{x}$ and inversely as z^3.

a Write down a formula connecting y, x, z and a constant k.

b When $y = 40$, $x = 25$ and $z = 3$. Find the value of k.

c Calculate y when $x = 36$ and $z = 4$.

5 The number of litres of petrol (L) used by the new Super Sports Saloon is in direct proportion to the distance travelled (d kilometres) and to the square root of the average speed (s km/h).

a If 10 litres are required for a journey of 80 km travelled at an average speed of 100 km/h, find a formula expressing L in terms of d and s.

b Calculate L when $d = 200$ and $s = 64$ km/h.

6 A scientist has investigated how long it takes to barbecue beefburgers.
He claims that the cooking time (T min) varies directly as the diameter of the burger (d cm) and as the square of the thickness (t cm).
On his BBQ it takes 12 minutes to cook an 8 cm diameter burger which is 1 cm thick.

a Find a formula for T in terms of d and t.

b How long should he cook a burger which is 12 cm in diameter and 1 cm thick?

c How long should he cook a burger which is 8 cm in diameter and 1·5 cm thick?

7 The simple interest (£I) in a bank account varies directly as the principal amount (£P), the time (T years) and the rate of interest per annum (R%). The interest on £8000 for 3 years at 4% p.a. is £960.

    a Find the formula for I.   **b** Calculate the interest on £5000 for 2 years at 6% p.a.

8 Craig rides on the Daredevil Drum.
His speed, weight and the radius of the track all matter.
The force on him (F newtons) varies directly as the square of his speed (S m/s) and as his mass (M kg), and inversely as the radius of the curve (R m).

    a Given that $F = 20$ when $S = 10$, $R = 5$ and $M = 75$, find the formula for F.

    b Calculate the force on Craig, whose mass is 72 kg, when his speed is 15 m/s and the radius of the curve is 6 m.

Brainstormer

The electrostatic force (F newtons) between two charges (Q_1 and Q_2 coulombs) varies directly as Q_1 and Q_2 and inversely as the square of the distance between them (d metres).

a Write down a formula for F in terms of Q_1, Q_2, d and a constant k.

b When $Q_1 = 8 \times 10^{-9}$, $Q_2 = 5 \times 10^{-9}$, $d = 0.25$ m and $F = 5.76 \times 10^{-6}$.
Find the value of k.

c Calculate F when $Q_1 = 7.5 \times 10^{-9}$, $Q_2 = 7.5 \times 10^{-9}$ and $d = 0.08$ m.

d In these questions both charges are positive so the force between them repels one from the other. Say whether the force would attract or repel in each of these cases:

    i one charge positive, the other negative   **ii** both negative.

◀◀ RECAP

Direct and inverse proportion
You should be able to recognise where **direct** or **inverse proportion** applies and make calculations involving these relationships.

Direct and inverse proportion graphs
You should be able to:
- recognise and draw graphs which involve direct and inverse proportion
- find k, the **constant of proportion**.

Direct and inverse proportion formulae
You should be able to:
- use the proportional symbol ... $y \propto x$ and $y \propto \dfrac{1}{x}$
- construct formulae, including powers and roots

$$y \propto x \Rightarrow y = kx \text{ and } y \propto \frac{1}{x} \Rightarrow y = \frac{k}{x}$$

- find the constant of proportion, k, given a set of data
- use the formulae to make calculations
- work with more than two variables (joint variation).

1 **a** A photocopier prints 10 worksheets in 40 seconds.
How long will it take to print 25 worksheets?
b It takes 14 hours for 3 ticket sales desks to sell the tickets for an event.
How long would it take 4 desks to sell the same number of tickets?

2 Write these relationships in words:
a $H \propto n$ **b** $D \propto mt^2$ **c** $B \propto \dfrac{\sqrt{R}}{S}$

3 Use the proportion symbol to express these relationships:
a C varies directly as u^2
b P varies inversely as the square root of r
c V varies directly as m and g and inversely as the square of e.

4 Sketch a graph showing:
a direct proportion   **b** inverse proportion.

5 Isaac Newton discovered that the force varies directly as the acceleration produced.
Heather carries out an experiment to verify this. The table shows her results.

Acceleration (a m/s^2)	0	10	20	30	40
Force (F newtons)	0	1·6	3·2	4·8	6·4

a Draw a graph to illustrate her results.
b How does the graph show that F varies directly as a?
c Find a formula for F in terms of a.

6 The weight of barley (W tonnes) a farmer harvests is directly proportional to the area planted (h hectares). When $h = 8$, $W = 52$.
a Find a formula connecting W and h.
b What weight of barley should the farmer expect from 11 hectares?
c One area yields 39 tonnes of barley. How many hectares are harvested?

7 Wavelength (W metres) varies inversely as the frequency (f kHz).
Ian's local radio station broadcasts on a wavelength of 250 m at a frequency of 1200 kHz.
a Find a formula for W.
b Another station has a wavelength of 400 m. Calculate its frequency.
c Calculate the wavelength for a frequency of 1500 kHz.

8 The air resistance (R newtons) to a vehicle varies directly as the square root of its speed (S km/h).
a Write down a formula for R in terms of S and a constant k.
b At 64 km/h the resistance is 1440 newtons. Calculate k.
c Find the resistance at 100 km/h.

9 L varies directly as M and inversely as B and H.
    $L = 12$ when $M = 1200$, $B = 8$ and $H = 5$.
a Construct a formula for L.
b Calculate L when $M = 1500$, $B = 10$ and $H = 6$.

8 Pythagoras

Pythagoras (who was born around 570 BC) was originally from the Greek island of Samos. After travelling around the known world he settled in Croton in Italy where he formed a school.

As well as being a mathematician he was also a philosopher, but perhaps he is best known for discovering the relationship between the three sides of a right-angled triangle.

1 REVIEW

◀◀ **Exercise 1.1**

1 Write down the value of:
  a 3^2 **b** 7^2 **c** 5^2 **d** $2 \cdot 5^2$ **e** $0 \cdot 3^2$

2 Find the value of:
  a $\sqrt{81}$ **b** $\sqrt{36}$ **c** $\sqrt{2 \cdot 25}$ **d** $\sqrt{729}$

3 Calculate the area of each square below.

  a
    7·3 cm

  b
    4·5 cm

  c
    0·7 cm

4 Work out the length of the side of a square with area:
  a 121 cm^2 **b** 144 cm^2 **c** $210 \cdot 25 \text{ cm}^2$

5 Use your calculator to find the value of:
  a 9^2 **b** 8^2 **c** $8^2 + 9^2$ **d** $\sqrt{8^2 + 9^2}$

6 Name all the right-angled triangles in the diagrams below (**b** is a cuboid).

  a
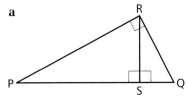

  b
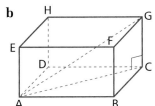

7 The diagram shows a square within a square.
  The area of each white triangle is $6\,\text{cm}^2$. Calculate:
  a the area of the larger square
  b the area of the smaller square
  c the length of side of the smaller square.

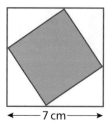

$\longleftarrow$ 7 cm $\longrightarrow$

2 Pythagoras' theorem

The side opposite the right angle in a right-angled triangle is known as the **hypotenuse**.
Given any right-angled triangle, hypotenuse a units and shorter sides b units and c
units, we can always use four copies to help form the large squares shown below.
Both large squares have a side of length $(b + c)$ units and so are of equal area.

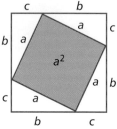

Area of large square
$= a^2 +$ area of
4 triangles

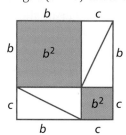

Area of large square
$= b^2 + c^2 +$ area of
4 triangles

So $a^2 = b^2 + c^2$

Since there was nothing special about the right-angled triangle used, the finding
must be true for all right-angled triangles.

This result is known as **Pythagoras' theorem**. It states that:

> in any right-angled triangle, the square on the hypotenuse is equal to the sum
> of the squares on the other two sides.

The theorem is useful for calculating the length of a side in a right-angled triangle
when we know the lengths of the other two sides.

Example 1 Calculate the value of a in this right-angled
  triangle. (All lengths are in centimetres.)

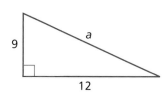

  The triangle is right-angled so we can use
  Pythagoras' theorem:
  $$a^2 = 9^2 + 12^2$$
  $$\Rightarrow a^2 = 81 + 144$$
  $$\Rightarrow a^2 = 225$$
  $$\Rightarrow a = \sqrt{225}$$
  $$\Rightarrow a = 15$$
  The hypotenuse is 15 cm long.

Exercise 2.1

In this exercise all lengths are in centimetres.

1 Use Pythagoras' theorem to help you write down the relation between the sides of these right-angled triangles.

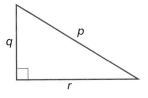

a

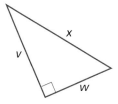

b

c

2 Calculate the length of the hypotenuse in each triangle below.

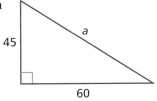

a

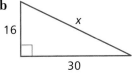

b

c

3 Calculate a, giving your answer correct to 1 decimal place.

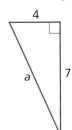

a

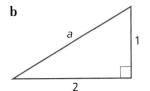

b

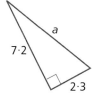

c

Example 2 Triangle ABC is right-angled at C.
AC = 8·4 cm and BC = 7·9 cm.
Calculate the length of AB.

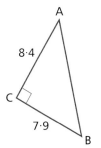

By Pythagoras' theorem
$AB^2 = AC^2 + BC^2$
$\Rightarrow AB^2 = 8·4^2 + 7·9^2$
$\Rightarrow AB^2 = 70·56 + 62·41$
$\Rightarrow AB^2 = 132·97$
$\Rightarrow AB = \sqrt{132·97}$
$\Rightarrow AB = 11·5$ (to 1 decimal place)
AB is 11·5 cm.

Exercise 2.2

Give your answers to 1 decimal place.

1 Calculate the length of the hypotenuse in these right-angled triangles. (Lengths are in centimetres.)

a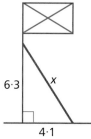

b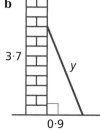

c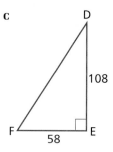

2 Calculate x and y in these triangles. (All lengths are in metres.)

a **b**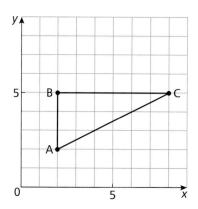

3 Calculate the length of AC.

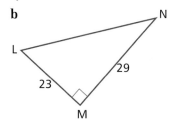

---

3 Calculating a shorter side

Example   Calculate x.
The triangle is right-angled, so by Pythagoras' theorem

$$51^2 = x^2 + 43^2$$
$$\Rightarrow x^2 = 51^2 - 43^2$$
$$\Rightarrow x^2 = 2601 - 1849$$
$$\Rightarrow x^2 = 752$$
$$\Rightarrow x = \sqrt{752}$$
$$\Rightarrow x = 27{\cdot}4 \text{ (to 1 d.p.)}$$

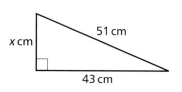

Exercise 3.1

1 Calculate x, y and z in these triangles.
(All measurements are in millimetres.)

a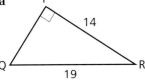

b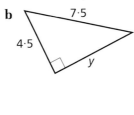

c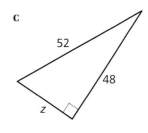

2 Calculate m in each triangle. Give your answer to 2 significant figures.
(All lengths are in centimetres.)

a

b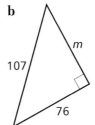

c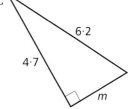

3 Calculate the length of PQ in each of these diagrams, correct to 1 d.p.
(All measurements are in millimetres.)

a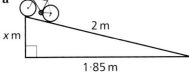

b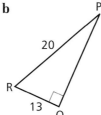

4 Calculate the value of x in each diagram, correct to 2 d.p.

a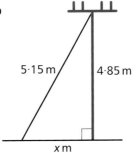

b

Exercise 3.2

Sometimes you are asked to work out the length of the hypotenuse and sometimes a shorter side. Give your answers correct to 3 significant figures and *always make sure your answer is sensible.*

1 In each of the following diagrams
    i   name the hypotenuse
    ii calculate the length of AB.

a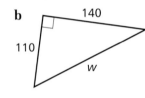

b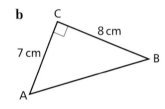

2 Calculate the length of the lettered side in each right-angled triangle.
    (All lengths are in centimetres.)

a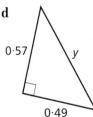

b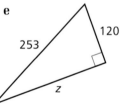

c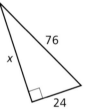

d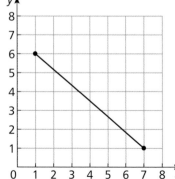

e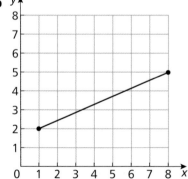

3 Calculate the distance between each pair of points.

a

b

4 A farmer has an L-shaped section of wall as shown in this plan view.
He uses a strip of fencing to close off a triangular area.
How long does the section of fencing need to be?
(All lengths are in metres.)

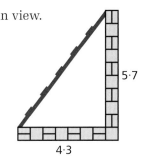

5·7

4·3

Exercise 4.1

Give your answers to 1 decimal place.

1 In a barn an elevator carries bails of
straw to the top of the stack.
How high is the stack?

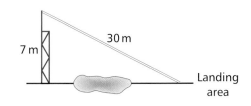

6·7 m

5·2 m

2 A death slide is set up over a pond using
a wire 30 metres long. The wire is fixed
at a height 7 metres higher than the ground
at the other side of the pond.

How far is it to the landing area?

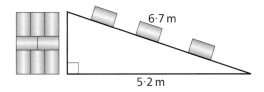

30 m

7 m

Landing
area

3 A janitor decides put up some hanging
baskets around the school. He needs to make
brackets from some metal rods. The centre of
the basket must be 45 cm from the wall and the
rod in contact with the wall must be 35 cm long.

What length will he need to make the third rod?

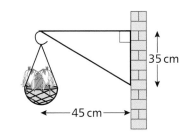

35 cm

45 cm

4 Mr Williamson has damaged the tyres of his car
on the kerb at his gateway. He needs to put down
a piece of wood to stop his tyres bumping into the
kerb as he drives through his gate. The kerb is
17 cm high and the block of wood has to reach no
more than 25 cm into the road.

Calculate the length of the sloping edge of the block of wood.

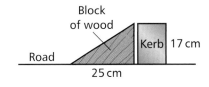

Block
of wood

Road

Kerb 17 cm

25 cm

5 A yacht sails south from Southerness.
It then turns and sails the *same* distance west.
It is now 5·7 km from Southerness.
How far south and west did it sail?

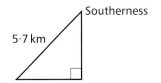

Southerness

5·7 km

Exercise 4.2

1 Mr Oddie's bird table has stays which are 37 cm long and reach
   29 cm up the leg of the table.
   How far apart are the bottom of these stays, to the nearest
   centimetre?

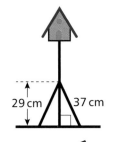

2 The front of this tent is an isosceles triangle.
   Calculate the height of the tent, correct to 2 d.p.
   (Hint: half an isosceles triangle is a right-angled triangle.)

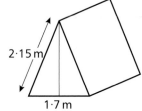

3 The ramp for wheelchair access to the Mossat
   Shop is 3·35 metres long and rises 45 cm.
   How far is the foot of the ramp from the
   shop door? Give your answer to 2 d.p.

4 What is the length of side of the biggest square jigsaw
   puzzle that can fit onto a circular coffee table of diameter
   75 cm? Give your answer to the nearest centimetre.

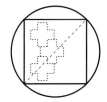

5 The diagonals of a rhombus are 8 cm and 6 cm long.
   Calculate:
   a the length of one side of the rhombus
   b the perimeter of the rhombus.

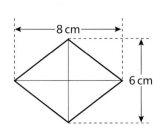

6 Two trees are planted in a patio as shown.
   The square slabs have a side of 150 cm.
   What is the distance between the trees?

7 Calculate the perimeter of the kite.
   (Lengths are in centimetres.)

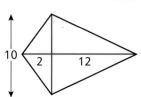

8 Ross, Blair and Kirsty were at Sandgreen with their Auntie Sheila. They parked the car and walked 850 metres west and set up a picnic. They walked 925 metres south to have a paddle in the sea. Ross was stung by a jellyfish so his aunt took him directly to the car. Kirsty and Blair walked back to pick up the picnic gear before returning to the car. How much further than Ross and Auntie Sheila did Blair and Kirsty walk on their way back to the car?
Give your answer to the nearest metre.

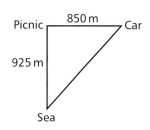

9 The Rennies' central heating runs on oil which is stored in a cylindrical tank.
The tank has a radius of 90 cm.
When the oil is 50 cm deep what is the length of AB, to the nearest centimetre?
(Hint: triangle AOB is isosceles.)

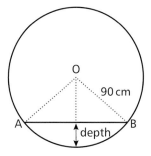

---

5 Pythagoras ... twice!!

Occasionally we encounter a situation where we need to use Pythagoras' theorem more than once to solve a problem.

Example 1   Find the value of y in this diagram.

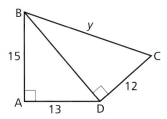

y belongs to right-angled triangle BCD about which we know only one side. So we must first find another side. BD belongs to triangle ABD about which we know two sides. Let us first find BD.

By Pythagoras' theorem
$$BD^2 = 15^2 + 13^2$$
$$\Rightarrow BD^2 = 225 + 169$$
$$\Rightarrow BD^2 = 394$$
$$\Rightarrow BD = \sqrt{394} \quad \text{(don't bother working it out)}$$

Now, also by Pythagoras' theorem
$$y^2 = BD^2 + 12^2$$
$$\Rightarrow y^2 = 394 + 144 \quad \text{(see above)}$$
$$\Rightarrow y^2 = 538$$
$$\Rightarrow y = \sqrt{538} = 23{\cdot}2 \text{ (to 1 d.p.)}$$

Example 2   Find the length of space diagonal AH in this cube. The cube has edges of length 5 cm.

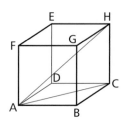

ΔABC is right-angled

⇒ $AC^2 = AB^2 + BC^2$

⇒ $AC^2 = 5^2 + 5^2$

⇒ $AC^2 = 25 + 25$

⇒ $AC^2 = 50$

ΔACH is right-angled,

⇒ $AH^2 = AC^2 + CH^2$

⇒ $AH^2 = 50 + 5^2$

⇒ $AH^2 = 50 + 25$

⇒ $AH^2 = 75$

⇒ $AH = \sqrt{75}$

⇒ $AH = 8.66$ cm to 3 s.f.

Exercise 5.1

1 Use Pythagoras' theorem to calculate x and then y in each diagram. Remember that, when working out y, you have an exact value for x^2. All measurements are in centimetres. Give your final answers to 1 d.p.

a
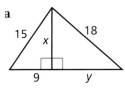

b
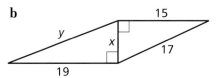

c
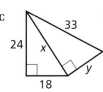

d
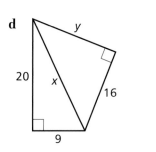

2 Calculate the length of a space diagonal in a cube with edges 7 cm long.

3 Calculate the length of the space diagonals marked in these cuboids.

a
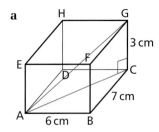

b
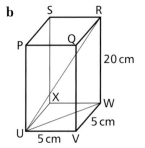

4 Elaine bought a carpet in a sale.
To save on the delivery charge she
asked her friend David to collect it in
his stock trailer. The trailer measures
3 metres by 1·5 metres by 2 metres
and the carpet comes in a 4 metre
long roll. Can the carpet be fitted into
the trailer without bending it?
(Hint: is it shorter than the space diagonal?)

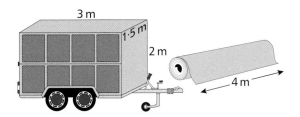

6 The converse of Pythagoras' theorem

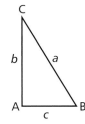

Pythagoras' theorem
If ∆ABC is right-angled
at A then $a^2 = b^2 + c^2$

The converse
If in ∆ABC $a^2 = b^2 + c^2$ then
angle A is a right angle

To show that the converse is true, consider these two triangles. AC = DF and AB = DE.

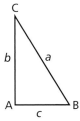

Suppose that in this triangle
$a^2 = b^2 + c^2$
So $a^2 = b^2 + c^2 = d^2$ and thus $a = d$

Suppose that in this triangle ∠D = 90°
then by Pythagoras' theorem $d^2 = b^2 + c^2$

The two triangles must be congruent since their three sides are equal.
So ∠A = ∠D = 90°
So if $a^2 = b^2 + c^2$ then the triangle is right-angled.
The converse of Pythagoras' theorem is true.

Example 1   Chippie the joiner is making a door frame.
The frame measures 1·92 m by 0·8 m.
To check that the frame has 90° corners he measures
the diagonal. It is 2·08 m. Show that ∠ABC = 90°.

Longest side: AC² = 2·08² = 4·3264

The shorter sides: AB² + BC² = 1·92² + 0·8² = 3·6864 + 0·64 = 4·3264
so AC² = AB² + BC²
⟹   by the converse of Pythagoras' theorem
∆ABC is right-angled at B.

Example 2   Charlie is laying paving slabs to make a
path round the corner of a flower bed.
The slabs have sides of 1 metre.
Is the corner a right angle?

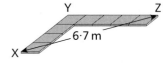

Longest side: $XZ^2 = 6\cdot7^2 = 44\cdot89$

The shorter sides: $XY^2 + YZ^2 = 4^2 + 5^2 = 16 + 25 = 41$
so $XZ^2 \neq XY^2 + YZ^2$
$\Rightarrow \angle Y$ is not right-angled.

Exercise 6.1

1 By using the converse of Pythagoras' theorem, decide which of these triangles is right-angled.

a   **b**   **c** 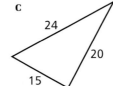   **d** 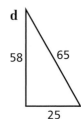   **e**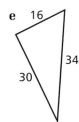

2 a Calculate the length of:
   i   AC
   ii AB
   iii BC.
   (Lengths are in centimetres.)
b Is ΔABC right-angled?

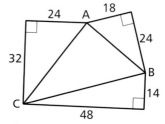

3 When marking out a football pitch, Titch the groundsman measures the pitch diagonally to check if the corners are right angles.
He measures the diagonal to be 118·79 metres.

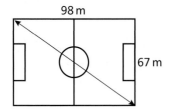

a Is the pitch a rectangle?
b Should he re-line the pitch?

4 A mobile phone mast stands on a flat piece of ground and is supported by wires which are anchored to the ground.
One wire is 35 metres long, is attached to the mast at a height of 28 metres and anchored to the ground 21 metres from the foot of the mast. Is the mast perpendicular to the ground?

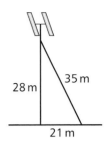
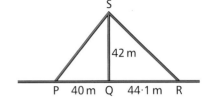

5 This diagram shows part of a bridge.
  a Calculate the length of each sloping girder.
  b Prove that ∠PSR between these girders is a right angle.

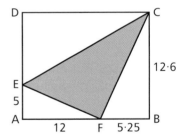

Exercise 6.2

1 A triangle has a perimeter of 11·2 cm. Two of its sides are 1·4 cm and 5 cm. Is this a right-angled triangle?

2 The points A (3, 1), B (5, 5) and C (11, 2) are the vertices of a triangle. Prove that this is a right-angled triangle and name the right angle.

3 Prove that ΔCEF is right-angled given that ABCD is a rectangle.

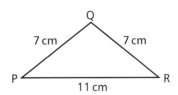

4 In ΔPQR prove that ∠QRP is *not* 45°.

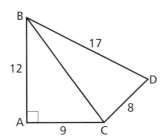

5 Show that ∠DCB is 90°.

◀◀ RECAP

Pythagoras' theorem states that:
In any right-angled triangle, the square on the hypotenuse is equal to the sum of the squares on the other two sides.

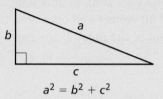

$$a^2 = b^2 + c^2$$

Calculating the hypotenuse

Example   Calculate the value of x.

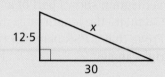

The triangle is right-angled so by Pythagoras' theorem
$$x^2 = 12 \cdot 5^2 + 30^2$$
$$\Rightarrow x^2 = 156 \cdot 25 + 900$$
$$\Rightarrow x^2 = 1056 \cdot 25$$
$$\Rightarrow x = \sqrt{1056 \cdot 25}$$
$$\Rightarrow x = 32 \cdot 5$$

Calculating a shorter side

Example   Calculate the value of y correct to 3 s.f.

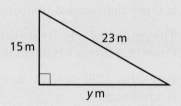

The triangle is right-angled so by Pythagoras' theorem
$$y^2 = 23^2 - 15^2$$
$$\Rightarrow y^2 = 529 - 225$$
$$\Rightarrow y^2 = 304$$
$$\Rightarrow y = \sqrt{304}$$
$$\Rightarrow y = 17 \cdot 4 \text{ (to 3 s.f.)}$$

The converse of Pythagoras' theorem

If in $\triangle ABC$ $a^2 = b^2 + c^2$ then angle A is a right angle.
If in $\triangle ABC$ $a^2 \neq b^2 + c^2$ then angle A is not a right angle.

1 Find the length of the lettered side in each right-angled triangle, correct to 2 significant figures. All lengths are centimetres.

a 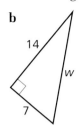 **b** 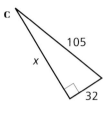 **c** **d** 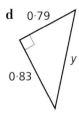 **e**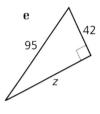

2 A 3·45 metre ladder leans against a wall.
How far must the foot of the ladder be from the foot of the wall if the ladder is to reach a window sill 3·35 metres above the ground?

3 A fishing trawler, *The Queen of Berwickshire,* leaves Eyemouth harbour and sails 75 km due east. It then sails 27 km due north.
a Draw a diagram of the situation.
b Calculate how far the trawler needs to sail in a straight line to return to Eyemouth, correct to 1 d.p.

4 A local council put up bunting for the Fair straight across the High Street, in a zig-zag pattern. The High Street is 14 m wide and the zig-zags form congruent isosceles triangles. The High Street is 754 metres long.
What is the total length of bunting required?

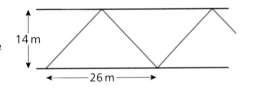

5 What is the distance between A and B (to 1 d.p.)?

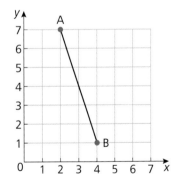

6 Use the converse of Pythagoras' theorem to find out which triangle is right-angled. Lengths are in centimetres.

a 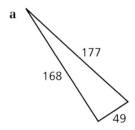   **b**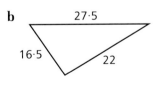

REVISE

9 Time, distance and speed

The greatest speed at which a human has travelled is 39 897 km/h and that was by the crew of *Apollo 10* in 1969.
At this speed you could go from Edinburgh to Glasgow in 6 seconds.

I do not *believe* it!

1 REVIEW

◄◄ Exercise 1.1

1 The table shows the distances, in kilometres, between certain towns.
  a How far is it between Barns and Yetby?
  b Which of these towns are 53 km apart?

Edmonton

74	Barns		
53	21	Fairholm	
101	63	48	Yetby

2 How long does each of these bus journeys take?

	a	b	c
Depart	07 40	11 35	17 53
Arrive	09 55	12 05	22 26

3 This timetable shows the times of trains from Dufftown to Levenworth on a Sunday.

Dufftown	06 30	07 15	08 15	10 05	12 12	14 20	16 15
Johnstown	07 12	07 57	08 58	10 45	12 55	15 04	16 57
Dungarven	07 27	...	09 11	11 00	...	15 15	17 12
Levenworth	08 18	09 00	10 02	11 50	14 21	16 05	18 02

  a When does the second train arrive in Johnstown?
  b At which station does the train not always stop?
  c How long does the third train take to get from Dufftown to Levenworth?
  d Jeanne must be in Dungarven by 2.30 pm.
    i What is the latest she can leave Johnstown?
    ii How much time does she have in Dungarven before her appointment?

4 Nidou set out from Glasgow at 22 55 to drive to Portsmouth.
He stopped for a rest at 03 20.
  a For how long had he been driving?
  b The whole journey, including rests, took 10 hours 23 minutes.
    When did he arrive in Portsmouth?

5 The graph shows the distance travelled by a car at a steady speed.

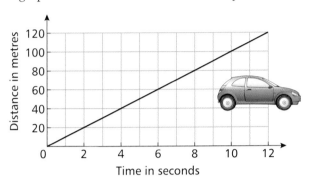

Work out:
  a the distance travelled in
    i   4 seconds   **ii**   9 seconds
  b the time it took to travel
    i   80 metres   **ii**   110 metres.

6 a How many minutes are in
    i   3 hours
    ii $4\frac{1}{2}$ hours
    iii 300 seconds?
  b How many hours are in
    i   2 days
    ii   450 minutes
    iii 1 year?
  c How many days are in
    i   144 hours
    ii   April
    iii June, July and August?

7 Write these fractions as decimals:
  a $\frac{1}{2}$ **b** $\frac{1}{4}$ **c** $1\frac{3}{4}$ **d** $3\frac{1}{10}$ **e** $\frac{18}{60}$

8 What is Nicola's steady speed, in miles per hour, if she drives:
  a 60 miles in 2 hours
  b 250 miles in 5 hours?

9 Estimate, then calculate the following, rounded to the given degree of accuracy:
  a 4·55 × 13·4, to the nearest whole number
  b 539 ÷ 18·4, to 1 decimal place
  c 343 × 0·26, to 2 significant figures.

2 Average speed

Ailidh drives from Glasgow to London, a distance of 400 miles, in 10 hours.
The graph shows her actual journey as a solid line.
There were times when she slowed down, speeded up, stopped, etc.
The straight dotted line shows what the journey would be like if she travelled at a constant speed.

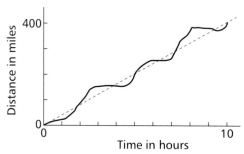

She travelled 400 miles in 10 hours.
We say she averaged 40 miles per hour ... or that her **average speed** was 40 mph.

$$\text{Average speed} = \frac{\text{Distance}}{\text{Time}} \qquad S = \frac{D}{T}$$

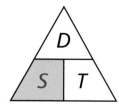

Note: units must be consistent, i.e. the units of all three variables must agree.
If distance is measured in **metres** and time in **seconds**, then the speed must be measured in **metres per second**.

Exercise 2.1

1 Anne-Marie drives 150 miles in 3 hours.
   Calculate her average speed in miles per hour (mph).

2 Calculate the average speed for each of these journeys in kilometres per hour (km/h).

	a	b	c	d
Distance (km)	40	68	540	345
Time (h)	2	4	9	5

3 The best times recorded in a number of races at a school sports were:
   a 80 metres in 10 seconds   **b** 100 metres in 15 seconds
   c 200 metres in 35 seconds   **d** 1500 metres in 5 minutes 20 seconds

   Calculate the average speed of each of the winners in metres per second, correct to 2 decimal places.

4 At a steady trot a horse can cover 150 metres in 24 seconds.
Calculate the average speed of the horse in metres per second,
rounded to 2 significant figures.

5 Concorde, the supersonic aircraft, could fly from London to New York, a distance of
5520 km, in 3 hours. Calculate the average speed of the flight.

6 Calculate the average speed of each journey, correct to
1 d.p. where necessary.
Remember to use the correct unit for speed in each answer.
  a cycling 40 miles in 4 hours
  b running 500 metres in 72 seconds
  c walking 16 km in 3 hours
  d driving 275 km in 4 hours
  e flying 1484 miles in 3 hours

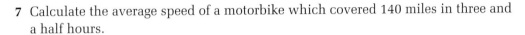

7 Calculate the average speed of a motorbike which covered 140 miles in three and
a half hours.

8 Diana set off from home at 14 25 to drive to her friend's house, a distance of 150 km
away. She arrived at 16 55.
  a How long did her journey take?
  b Calculate her average speed for the journey.
  c She returned home next day by the same route in a time of two and a quarter
     hours.
     Calculate her average speed on the return journey, correct to 3 significant
     figures.

9 Whales take 64 days to swim 6000 miles from the
Mexican coast to their feeding gounds in the Bering Sea.
Calculate their average speed in:
  a miles per day
  b miles per hour.

Decimal times

When carrying out time calculations, we often have to change hours and minutes
into hours so that they can be entered into a calculator.

Example 1   12 minutes = $\frac{12}{60}$ of an hour = 12 ÷ 60 = 0·2 of an hour

Example 2   4 hours 33 minutes = 4 hours + $\frac{33}{60}$ hour = 4 + 0·55 hour = 4·55 hours

Example 3   Express 3·2 hours in hours and minutes.

              0·2 of an hour = 0·2 × 60 minutes = 12 minutes
              3·2 hours = 3 hours 12 minutes

Exercise 2.2

1 Change the following minutes into decimal parts of an hour:
 a 30 minutes **b** 45 minutes **c** 15 minutes **d** 18 minutes
 e 54 minutes **f** 27 minutes **g** 6 minutes **h** 39 minutes

2 Change these times, given in hours and minutes, into hours:
 a 3 hours 12 minutes **b** 1 hour 57 minutes **c** 10 hours 9 minutes

3 Write these times in hours, rounding your answers to 2 decimal places:
 a 52 minutes **b** 6 hours 28 minutes **c** 2 hours 46 minutes

4 Convert the following into hours and minutes:
 a 3·2 hours **b** 5·15 hours **c** 1·3 hours **d** 3·25 hours **e** 6·65 hours

5 A group of friends travelled 130 km to see their favourite band in concert.
 The journey took them 2 hours 36 minutes.
 a Write the time taken in hours.
 b Calculate the average speed for the journey.

6 Calculate the average speed for each of these journeys:
 a 90 km in 1 hour 15 minutes **b** 132 km in 2 hours 24 minutes
 c 2 hours 54 minutes to travel 145 km **d** 6 km in 12 minutes.

7 Use the distance chart opposite to calculate the
 average speed, to 1 decimal place, for these journeys:
 a London to Bristol in 2 hours 6 minutes
 b London to Edinburgh in 8 hours 36 minutes
 c Aberdeen to York in 6 hours 15 minutes
 d Manchester to York in 58 minutes
 e Aberdeen to Bristol in 10 hours 23 minutes.

Aberdeen					
514	Bristol				
125	381	Edinburgh			
545	120	411	London		
353	172	219	202	Manchester	
322	226	193	211	50	York

Distance in miles

8 An aircraft flies 1550 km in the first hour, 1730 km
 in the second hour and 470 in the last quarter of an hour.
 a Calculate the total distance travelled and the time
  taken for the flight.
 b Calculate the average speed of the flight.

9 Calculate the speeds of the following in kilometres per hour.
 a Horse **b** Runner **c** Ant

 4 km in 12 minutes   8 km in 1h 45 minutes   5 m in 1 minute

10 Which is faster in each case? (Show all your working.)
 a 45 km/h or 13 m/s **b** 80 km/h or 22 m/s

Brainstormer

The distance round a circle is approximately three times the size of the diameter.
The Earth circles the Sun in approximately 365 days.
Its distance from the Sun is approximately $9 \cdot 3 \times 10^7$ miles.

a Show that there are $8 \cdot 8 \times 10^3$ hours in 365 days (approximately).
b Calculate the speed of the Earth as it orbits the Sun.

---

3 Speed graphs

Speed–time graphs can be used to give a picture of how speed changes over time.
This graph shows how the speed of a car changes as it travels along.
Note the following points on the graph:

a the car is parked
b the car reaches a steady speed
c it slows down then speeds up
d it maintains a steady speed
e it slows down and stops
f it continues at a constant speed

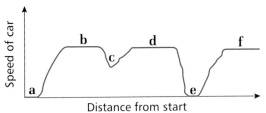

Exercise 3.1

1 Copy and complete each graph to show the change in speed of a car as it travels through the various labelled points.

a

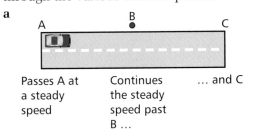

Passes A at a steady speed   Continues the steady speed past B ...   ... and C

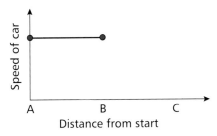

b

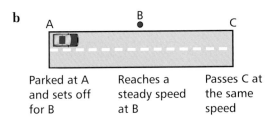

Parked at A and sets off for B   Reaches a steady speed at B   Passes C at the same speed

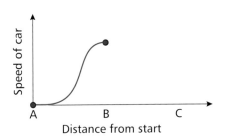

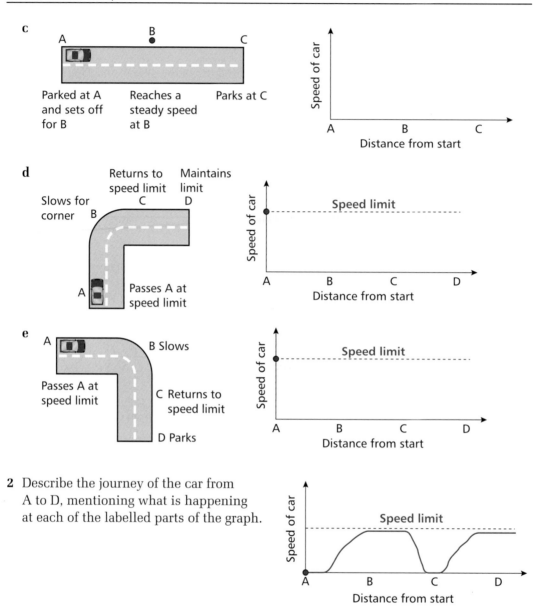

2 Describe the journey of the car from A to D, mentioning what is happening at each of the labelled parts of the graph.

3 a There are two routes from A to D, one past B and the other past C. Which route does this graph show?

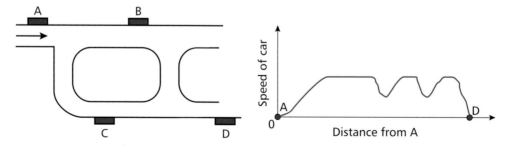

b Draw a graph to show the progress of the car by the other route.

4 Calculating time

Lloyd wants to visit a friend who lives 275 km away.
He thinks he could drive his car at an average speed of
55 km/h.
How long will it take him?

55 km in 1 hour
$\Rightarrow$ 110 km in 2 hours
$\Rightarrow$ 275 km in 5 hours

$$\text{Time taken} = \frac{\text{Distance}}{\text{Time}} \qquad T = \frac{D}{S}$$

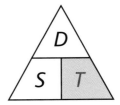

Example Returning home, Lloyd takes a different route using the motorway.
He travels the 292 km at an average speed of 68 km/h.
How long does it take him?

$$T = \frac{D}{S} = \frac{292}{68} = 4.294 \text{ hours} = 4 \text{ hours } 18 \text{ minutes}$$

$0.294 \times 60 = 17.64 = 18$ (to the nearest minute)

Exercise 4.1

1 Toni drives her car at an average speed of 48 mph.
How long will it take her to drive 192 miles?

2 Calculate the time taken to travel:
   a 245 km at 35 km/h   **b** 250 metres at 5 m/s
   c at 189 miles at 54 mph   **d** at 8 m/s for 200 metres.

3 How long, in hours and minutes, would it take to travel:
   a 155 miles at 50 mph   **b** 450 km at 68 km/h   **c** 252 km at 80 km/h?

4 Andrew jogged at a steady 10 km/h.
How long, in hours and minutes, would he take to cover:
   a 25 km   **b** 17 km   **c** 3 km?

5 How long would each of these journeys take?
   a   **b**

a bee flying 147 metres at 3·5 m/s   a tortoise walking 2·25 metres at 7·5 cm/s

6 Caitlin cycled 8 km at an average speed of 24 km/h.
How many minutes did it take her?

7 Andrew left his house at 18 45 to go to a concert.
The venue was 34 km from his home. He drove at an average speed of 42 km/h.
a When did he arrive at the venue?
b If the concert started at 20 30, how long did he have to find a parking space and get into the concert before it started?

8 Jo has an interview for a job at 14 30. She wants to be there a quarter of an hour beforehand.
She will have to travel 13 km to get to the interview and reckons she should be able to drive at an average speed of 42 km/h.
What is the latest time she should leave home?

9 The speed of sound is roughly 340 m/s.
Khali shouts 'Hello' very loudly towards a cliff 150 metres away.
The sound goes to the cliff and bounces back as an echo.
How long, to the nearest tenth of a second, will it be before he hears his echo?

10 Light travels at nearly 3×10^8 m/s.
How long does it take for light to travel to the Earth from the Sun, 1.5×10^{11} m away?

---

5 Calculating distance

Lorna runs at 8·5 m/s. How far can she run in 10 seconds?

In 1 second she runs 8·5 m
$\Rightarrow$ in 10 seconds she runs 8·5 × 10 = 85 metres

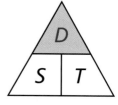

| Distance travelled = Speed × Time taken $\quad$ $D = ST$ |

Example   How far would you get travelling at 44 km/h for 2 hours 54 minutes?

$$D = S \times T = 44 \times 2\tfrac{54}{60} = 44 \times 2.9 = 127.6 \text{ km}$$

Exercise 5.1

1 What distance is travelled:
a at 52 mph for 4 hours
b at 10·5 m/s for 30 seconds
c for 6 hours at 144 mph
d for 25 seconds at 4 feet/second?

2 A long distance coach can average a speed of 62 mph on a motorway journey.
How far would it travel in 3 hours 24 minutes?

3 Erin ran at 8·4 m/s for half a minute. How far did she run?

4 An oilrig supply ship left harbour at 12 35 and arrived at the rig at 15 53.
Its average speed was 24 km/h.
How far is the oilrig from the harbour?

5 Ginny's train took 50 minutes to get from Hull to Leeds.
She was told the train averaged a speed of 72 km/h.
How far apart are the towns?

6 Migrating swallows can keep up an average of 20 mph for 45 hours without stopping for food.
How far will they have travelled in that time?

7 Rae ran to the shops at a speed of 5·5 m/s.
She took 3 minutes 45 seconds to get there.
How far, in kilometres rounded to the nearest tenth, did she run?

8 Dave flew his plane at an average speed of 370 km/h.
He took off at 16 50 and landed at 17 56. How far did he fly?

9 A group of joggers took 58 minutes to do their practice run.
They jogged at an average speed of 6·5 km/h.
How far did they jog, to the nearest tenth of a kilometre?

10 Sarah was practising for a half-marathon (13 miles) race.
She wanted to run twice this distance in the week prior to the race.
On Monday she ran for 1 hour 20 minutes at an average speed of 7·5 mph.
On Wednesday she ran at 8 mph for 1 hour 42 minutes.
How far would she have to run on Friday to achieve her target?

6 Distance–time graphs

The graph shows the journey made by the Rogers family.
Features of the graph to be noted are:

- the scales on the axes are different
  - each division on the time axis represents 15 minutes
  - each division on the distance axis represents 20 km
- the steeper the slope, the faster the speed (more distance in less time)
- the horizontal section indicates they stopped (no distance covered as time passes).

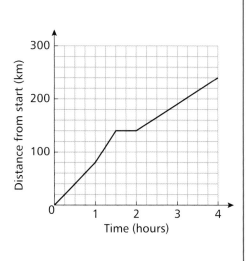

Exercise 6.1

1 Aaron jogged to the shops. The graph illustrates his journey.

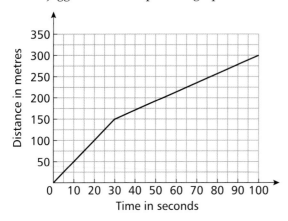

a How far did Aaron run in the first 30 seconds?
b Calculate his speed in metres per second for this part of his journey.
c How far did he run altogether?
d How far had he gone after 65 seconds?
e How long did it take him to run 250 metres?

2 The graph illustrates the journey made by
Siobhan from her home to the airport.
a How far did she travel in the first hour?
b For how long did she stop?
c How far had she gone when she stopped?
d How far did she travel altogether?
e Calculate her average speed
  i   in the first hour
  ii over the whole journey.
f If she left home at 09 13, when did she get
to the airport?

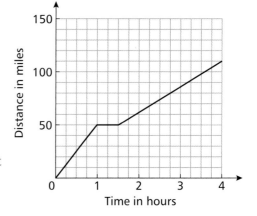

3 A journey takes 6 hours by coach, 4 hours by train
or 1 hour by plane.
a Copy the graph for the coach, then draw graphs
for the train and the plane on the same diagram.
b Which line is the steepest? Comment.
c Calculate the average speed for
  i   the coach
  ii the train
  iii the plane.

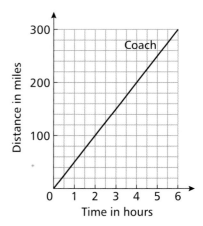

4 Mark rode his motorbike from Carlisle to Kendal and back again.

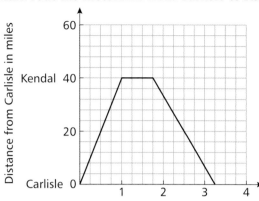

   a How long did it take Mark to get to Kendal?
   b How far is it from Carlisle to Kendal?
   c How long did he stay in Kendal?
   d How long did the return journey take him?

5 Ellie waked to the library, stayed for a while then walked back home again.

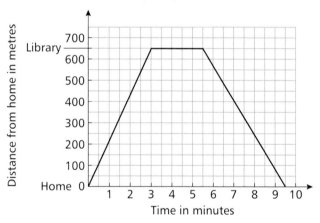

   a How long did Ellie stay at the library?
   b Did she walk faster going to or returning from the library?
   c At what times was she 550 metres from home?

6 Use the axes and scales shown to draw
   a distance–time graph to illustrate
   Gordon's visit to the dentist.
   Gordon walked 2 km in 15 minutes,
   then waited at the bus stop for
   5 minutes.
   His bus took him the 5 km to the
   dentist's surgery in 10 minutes.
   He was in the surgery for 20 minutes,
   before returning directly home.
   He arrived home an hour and a half after leaving.

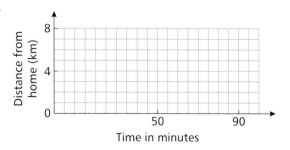

Exercise 6.2

1 Mr McLean drove from his office to a meeting
   in Oban.
   a How long did it take him to get to Oban?
   b How far did he travel in the first hour?
   c For how long did he stop?
   d How far had he gone when he stopped?
   e Which part of his journey was the fastest?
   f Calculate the speed for this part of the
      journey.

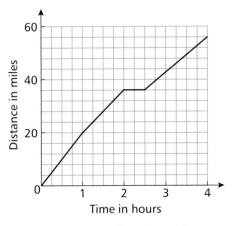

2 The graph shows the journey Jerome made between Salthill and Ballinrobe and
   back again.

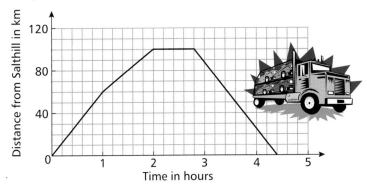

   a How far is Ballinrobe from Salthill?
   b For how long did Jerome stop in Ballinrobe?
   c What was his average speed for his journey
      i to Ballinrobe   **ii** back?
   d If he left at 11 35, when did he get back?

3 Two salesmen set out from their office in London at the same time to drive to Gloucester,
   170 km away. One drives directly there, the other stops for a while in Oxford.
   a How far is it from London
      to Oxford?
   b After what times are the
      salesmen the same distance
      from London?
   c How far from London are
      they then?
   d What is the difference in
      their arrival times in
      Gloucester?

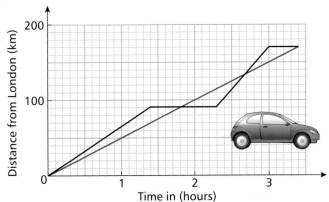

4 The graph below shows the journeys Peter and Paul made.
Peter left Brighton at 10 am to travel to Dorchester, while Paul left Dorchester at 11.36 am for Brighton.

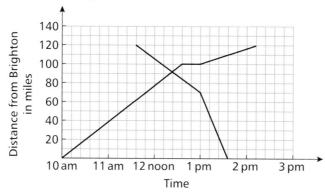

a When did they meet?
b How far from Brighton were they then?
c How much quicker did Paul do the journey than Peter?
d Calculate the average speed for
   i the first part of Peter's journey
   ii the last part of Paul's journey.

5 Amir and Ny are having a race. Describe the race in as much detail as you can.

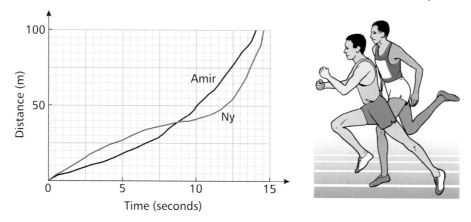

6 Keira jogs the 21 miles from Hawick to Kelso, while Cara cycles from Kelso to Hawick by the same route.
  a Use the information below to draw a graph of each girl's journey.
     Use the same set of axes.
  b Estimate how far from Hawick they were when they met.
  c At what time did they meet?
  d Compare the girls' average speeds.

Time	11 am	11.15	11.30	11.45	12.00	12.15	12.30	12.45	1 pm
Keira's distance	0	3	6	8	11	14	16	19	21
Cara's distance	–	–	–	21	15	11	6	0	–

7 Which formula?

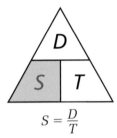 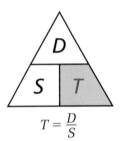 

$$S = \frac{D}{T} \qquad T = \frac{D}{S} \qquad D = S \times T$$

When you know two of the quantities you can work out the third.
Remember: the units must be consistent.

Exercise 7.1

1 Work out the missing quantity in each of the following:

    a Speed = 15 m/s   **b** Speed = 48 km/h   **c** Speed = ?
       Distance = 285 m   Distance = ?   Distance = 56 miles
       Time = ?   Time = 2 hours 15 minutes   Time = $3\frac{1}{2}$ hours

2 A meteor travels at $6 \cdot 7 \times 10^5$ m/s.
   How far does it travel in 5 seconds?

3 A plane flies 3444 km at an average speed of 820 km/h.
   a How long, in hours and minutes, will the journey take?
   b If the flight leaves at 17 20, when will it arrive at its destination?

4 A dart flies through the air for $0 \cdot 18$ second.
   If it travels 3 metres calculate its speed, correct to
   3 significant figures.

5 The Hillertons leave home at Lochinlea to visit Charlesfield, Deanhead and Flint
   before returning home.

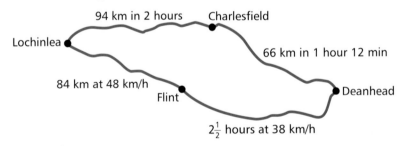

   a Find the missing distance, speed or time for each part of the journey.
   b Work out the total distance travelled.
   c How long did it take the Hillertons to drive this route?

6 Leyton is practising his return of serve against an automatic serving machine.
He stands 26 metres from the machine.
How long, to the nearest 0·1 s, does it take the ball to reach him at:
a 15 m/s **b** 40 m/s **c** 55 m/s?

7 Anthony leaves home at 13 30 to drive the 38 miles to
his girlfriend's house.
He drives at an average speed of 45 mph.
a How many minutes will the journey take him?
b When will he arrive at her house?
c On the way home Anthony takes the same route but drives it in 46 minutes.
Calculate his average speed, correct to the nearest mph.

8 Uma hopes to cycle 100 km in 5 hours. She averages 21 km/h for the first 4 hours.
a How far has she travelled in the first 4 hours?
b What average speed will she need to do in the fifth hour, if she is to succeed?

Exercise 7.2

1 Calculate the missing entries:

	a	b	c	d
Distance	159 miles	200 m		4 km
Speed	53 mph		42 km/h	10 km/h
Time		16 seconds	1 hour 15 min	

2 These world records were recently recorded:
100 metres in 9·86 seconds; 200 metres in 19·47 seconds.
Calculate the average speed of each, in kilometres per hour, correct to 1 decimal place.

3 The distance from Jupiter to the Sun is $7·79 \times 10^8$ km.
If light travels at $3·0 \times 10^5$ km/s, how long will it take light to travel from the Sun to
Jupiter? Give your answer in scientific notation, rounded to 2 significant figures.

4 Concorde, the supersonic aircraft, travelled 3290 km in
1 hour 24 minutes.
a Calculate its speed in kilometres per hour.
b Supersonic aircraft speed is often given as a Mach number.
Mach 2 means twice the speed of sound.
If the speed of sound is 1050 km/h, calculate the Mach
number, to 3 s.f., of this flight.

5 Michael Coulthard, the racing driver, was driving at 125 km/h when he sneezed.
His eyes were shut for 0·8 s.
For how many metres did he travel with his eyes shut?
Give your answer to 1 decimal place.

6 In a recent 100 metre race the winner and runner-up had times of 9·88 seconds
and 9·91 seconds.
When the winner crossed the line, how far behind him was the runner-up?

Challenge

Mr James arranges handicaps for the 100 m event so that each competitor has the same chance of running the race in the same time.

He does this by shortening the race for some competitors, by giving them a 'start' of several metres.

Four athletes have reached the final. In the semi-finals their times were:

Tom 12 seconds, Ian 13 seconds, Bill 12·5 seconds and Angus 12·2 seconds.

Tom has to run the full 100 metres.

Calculate how far each of the others will have to run.

Remember that each runner, theoretically, should run the race in the same time.

Include a diagram of the staggered start of the race.

Investigations

1 Investigate the speed of travel of a clockwork toy. If you use a model train or car, find the scale of the model to calculate a 'realistic' speed.

2 Plan a charity walk between two places. Work out a route and find out the distances between places. How would you work out how long each stage would take you? What factors would have to be considered?

◀◀ RECAP

Given any two of speed, distance and time, the third can be calculated using one of these formulae:

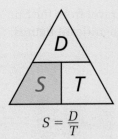

$$S = \frac{D}{T}$$

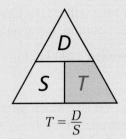

$$T = \frac{D}{S}$$

$$D = S \times T$$

Remember: the units must be consistent.

Decimal time

In order to use the formulae above, time given in hours and minutes may have to be expressed as a decimal part of an hour and *vice versa*.

Example 1 3 hours 36 minutes = $3\frac{36}{60}$ hours = 3·6 hours (36 ÷ 60 = 0·6)

Example 2 3·7 hours = 3 hours and 0·7 × 60 minutes = 3 hours 42 minutes

Speed–time graphs

You should be able to interpret and construct speed–time graphs.

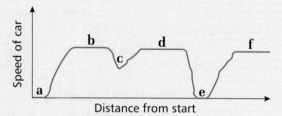

In this example the key features are:

- **a** the vehicle sets off
- at **b, d** and **f** the speed is constant
- at **c** the vehicle slows down
- at **e** the vehicle stops.

Distance–time graphs

You should be able to interpret and construct distance–time graphs.
Such a graph shows the distance from the starting place against time.
The steeper the line, the greater the speed.
A horizontal line indicates zero speed.
Where the line slopes down to the right, the traveller is heading in the direction of the start.

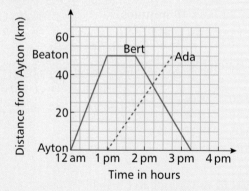

The journeys made by two people can be represented on the same graph.
Where lines cross it indicates that the two people are at the same place at the same time.

1 Calculate the missing quantity in each of the following sets of data:
  a distance = 150 km, time = 6 hours, speed = ?
  b distance = ?, time = 25 seconds, speed = 8·5 m/s
  c distance = 98 miles, time = ?, speed = 28 mph
  d distance = 3·6 × 10⁶ km, time = 12 hours, speed = ?

2 Helen ran at 7·2 m/s for 3 minutes. How far did she run?

3 Calculate Steve's speed, to 3 s.f., when he ran 200 metres in 24·3 seconds.

4 How long, in hours and minutes, would it take to drive 135 miles at 50 mph?

5 Ross drove from Aberdeen to Edinburgh in two and a half hours.

Aberdeen

87	Perth		
125	42	Edinburgh	
147	62	48	Glasgow

Distances are in miles.

  a Calculate his average speed.
  b He continues from Edinburgh to Glasgow at an average speed of 36 mph.
    How long does it take him?
  c He then returns directly to Aberdeen in 3 hours 18 minutes.
    Calculate his average speed, correct to 1 decimal place.

6 This is part of the Hawick to Carlisle bus timetable.

Hawick	06 55	08 45	11 05	14 00	18 05
Langholm	07 35	09 25	11 40	14 40	18 45
Longtown	08 00	09 50	12 05	15 05	19 10
Carlisle	08 27	10 12	12 27	15 27	19 32

  a How long does the first bus take to travel from Hawick to Carlisle?
  b The fourth bus was delayed by 23 minutes because of snow.
    When would it arrive in Langholm?
  c i How long does it take the last bus to travel from Langholm to Carlisle?
    ii The distance between Langholm and Carlisle is 22 miles.
      Calculate the average speed of the bus, to 1 decimal place, over this part of
      the journey.

7 David left home at 13 17 and arrived at his office at 13 52.
  His average speed for the journey was 58 km/h.
  Calculate, to 3 s.f., the distance he travelled.

REVISE

8 A bus left Edinburgh to take holidaymakers to York.
At the same time a bus left York for Edinburgh using the same route.

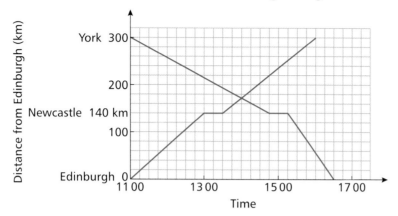

a At what time did the buses pass each other?
b How far from Edinburgh was this?
c Calculate the average speed of the bus from York, excluding the stop in Newcastle.
d For how long did the Edinburgh to York bus stop in Newcastle?
e Calculate the average speed of the Edinburgh to York bus on
   i the first part
   ii the last part of its journey.

REVISE

10 Angles and circles

Finding the area of a circle is an important skill.

The secret of squaring the circle (to draw a square the same area as a circle) was the holy grail of ancient mathematicians.

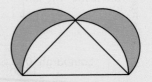

Hippocrates of Chios (fifth century BC) thought he had the answer when he discovered that if you draw a semicircle on each side of an isosceles right-angled triangle as shown, the area of the lunes (shaded) was equal to the area of the triangle.

1 REVIEW

◀◀ **Exercise 1.1**

1 Find the missing angles in these triangles.

a

68°
74°

b

68°
Isosceles

c

28°
Right-angled triangle

2 Find the value of x in each diagram.

a

$x°$ $x°$ $x°$ $x°$ $x°$ $x°$ $x°$ $x°$

b

$x°$ $x°$ $x°$ $x°$ $x°$

c

$x°$ 114°

3 Draw round a circular object.
Can you describe how you might find the centre of the circle you have drawn?

4 Use Pythagoras' theorem to calculate x in each right-angled triangle.

a

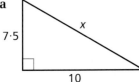

7·5
x
10

b

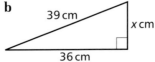

39 cm
x cm
36 cm

2 Isosceles triangles in the circle

When two radii are drawn to the ends of a chord, an isosceles triangle is formed.

Example
O is the centre of the circle and A and B are points on the
circumference. Calculate the value of ∠OBA.

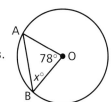

Since OA and OB are radii, OA = OB and triangle AOB is isosceles.
⇒   ∠OAB = ∠OBA
Now   ∠OAB + ∠OBA + 78 = 180
⇒   ∠OBA + ∠OBA + 78 = 180
⇒   2∠OBA = 180 − 78 = 102°
⇒   ∠OBA = 102 ÷ 2 = 51°

Exercise 2.1

In this exercise, O is the centre of the circle and A, B, C and D are points on the
circumference.

1 Calculate *a*, *b* and *c* in these diagrams.

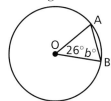

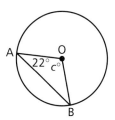

2 Find *x*, *y* and *z* in these diagrams.

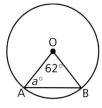

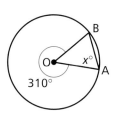

BC is a diameter

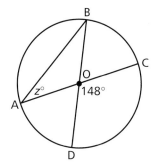

BD and AC are diameters

3 A reptile house at a zoo is circular and is divided up into five congruent enclosures each
of which has a viewing area. Calculate the size of the angles in the enclosures (*a* and *b*).

Viewing area

Enclosure

4 a Copy these diagrams and fill in the sizes of all the angles.

i 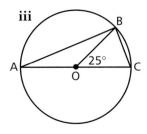 ii 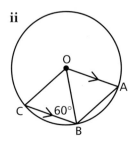 iii

b In part **iii** what is ∠ABO + ∠OBC?

3 The angle in a semicircle

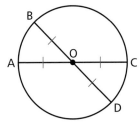 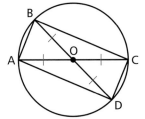 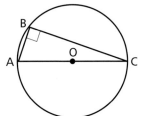

This circle has centre O and diameters AC and BD.

AC and BD have the same length and bisect each other, so ABCD is a rectangle.

∠ABC is 90° since all angles in a rectangle are right angles.

∠ABC is formed by joining a point on the circumference (B) of a circle to the ends of a diameter (AC). Any angle which is formed in this way is known as **an angle in a semicircle**.

> **Every angle in a semicircle is a right angle.**

Exercise 3.1

In this exercise O is the centre of the circle, AB is a diameter and C and D are points on the circumference.

1 Calculate ∠OAC in these diagrams.

a 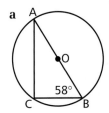 **b** 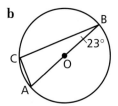 **c**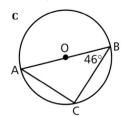

2 Find a, b, c, d, e and f.

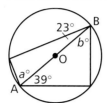
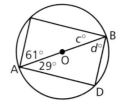
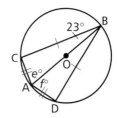

3 Calculate x and y.

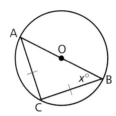
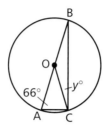

4 a Why can we use Pythagoras' theorem to calculate the length of the diameter of this circle?
b Calculate the length of the diameter.

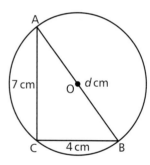

5 Calculate the value of x in each diagram.
All measurements are in centimetres.

a
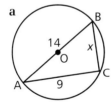

b
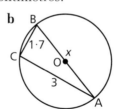

6 A carpenter is making a circular pine plinth of diameter 26 cm.
It is to have a triangular oak section inlaid.
Which of these triangular sections would fit?
(Hint: use the converse of Pythagoras' theorem to identify the right-angled triangle.)

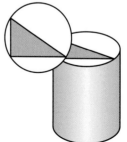

a
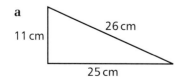

b
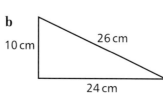

7 Follow these steps for another proof that an angle in a semicircle is always a right angle. AB is a diameter. O is the centre, and C is a point on the circumference.

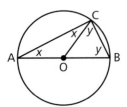

  a State why the angles marked x are equal.
  b State why the angles marked y are equal.
  c Why is $2x + 2y = 180$?
  d So what is the sum of $x° + y°$?

---

4 Tangents to a circle

A **tangent** is a line that touches a circle at only one point.

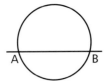   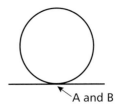

Notice that as the chord moves down, A and B get closer together.
When A and B are the same point then the line is a tangent to the circle.

In the diagrams below the red line is a diameter. Note that it is an axis of symmetry.

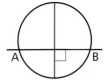 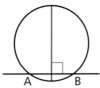 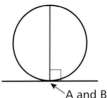

By the last diagram we see that the tangent and the diameter, at the point of contact, are perpendicular (at right angles). We usually say that the radius at the point of contact is perpendicular to the tangent.

Note that if the line was not at right angles to the radius then the radius would not meet the tangent at the point of contact with the circle.

Example 1
O is the centre of the circle and AB is a tangent to that circle at A. Calculate the value of x.

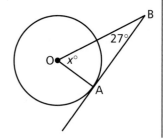

$\angle OAB = 90°$ (radius meeting tangent at point of contact)
$\Rightarrow\ x = 180 - (90 + 27)$
$\Rightarrow\ x = 180 - 117$
$\Rightarrow x° = 63°$

Example 2
MN is a tangent at M to the circle, centre O.
Calculate the length of OM.

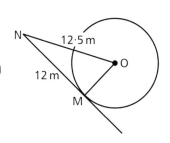

$\angle$OMN = 90° (radius meeting tangent at point of contact)
so by Pythagoras' theorem
$$12{\cdot}5^2 = 12^2 + OM^2$$
$$\Rightarrow OM^2 = 12{\cdot}5^2 - 12^2$$
$$\Rightarrow OM^2 = 156{\cdot}25 - 144$$
$$\Rightarrow OM^2 = 12{\cdot}25$$
$$\Rightarrow OM = \sqrt{12{\cdot}25}$$
$$\Rightarrow OM = 3{\cdot}5 \text{ m}$$

Exercise 4.1

In this exercise A is the point of contact of the tangent with circle centre O.

1 Calculate the value of x in each diagram.

a

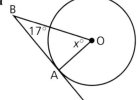

b

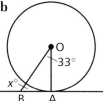

c

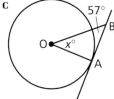

2 Sketch the following diagrams and fill in the sizes of all the angles.
(B and C are points on the circumference.)

a

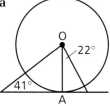

b

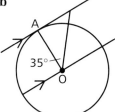

c

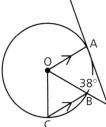

d

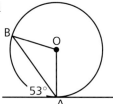

e

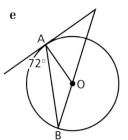

f

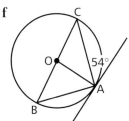

BC is a diameter

3 Calculate the value of *x*. All lengths are in centimetres.

a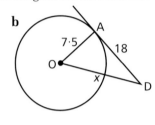

b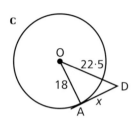

c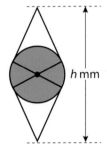

4 An earring is made from a circular stone which has strands of silver attached so that they are tangents to the circle.
The stone has a radius of 5 mm and the silver strands each measure 10 mm in length.

What is the overall height of the earring?

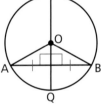

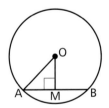

---

5 The diameter as an axis of symmetry

The diameter PQ bisects AB at right angles.
PQ is an axis of symmetry of the diagram.

The following statements are always true.
1 A line drawn through the centre of a circle through the midpoint of a chord will cut the chord at right angles.
2 A line drawn through the centre of a circle at right angles to a chord will bisect that chord.
3 A line bisecting a chord at right angles (a perpendicular bisector) will pass through the centre of a circle.

Example
In a circle of radius 10 cm, find the distance from the centre O to a chord 12 cm long.
The shortest distance from the centre O to the chord AB can be measured along OM, a line at right angles to the chord.

So OM bisects the chord (by **2** above) and AM = 6 cm.

By Pythagoras' theorem
$$OA^2 = OM^2 + AM^2$$
$$\Rightarrow \quad 10^2 = OM^2 + 6^2$$
$$\Rightarrow OM^2 = 10^2 - 6^2$$
$$\Rightarrow OM^2 = 100 - 36$$
$$\Rightarrow OM^2 = 64$$
$$\Rightarrow \quad OM = \sqrt{64} = 8$$

So the distance from the centre O to the chord is 8 cm.

Exercise 5.1

1 Copy and complete the following statements.

a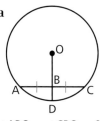

∠ABO = ∠CBO = 90°
since the radius OD
... the chord AC.

b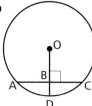

AB = BC since the
radius OD cuts the
chord at B at ... ...

c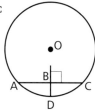

BD extended will pass
through centre O since
BD ... chord AC at ... ...

2 Copy these diagrams and fill in the sizes of all the angles.

a

b

c

3 Calculate the shortest distance from the centre of the circle to each chord.

a

b

c

4 Calculate the length of each chord to 1 decimal place.

a

b

5 Calculate the radius of each circle.

a

b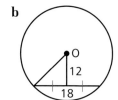

6 Calculate the value of *x* by first finding the radius.

a

b

7 The 'D' on the edge of the penalty box on a football pitch is to ensure that players are 10 metres from the penalty spot. What is the distance between a player standing at A and a player standing at B?

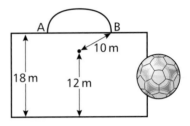

8 The diagram shows the cross-section of a paperweight. Find its height.

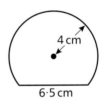

9 The span of this bridge (AB) is 100 m, and the radius of the curve, OA, is 200 m.
Sketch OAB and calculate the rise in the bridge, to the nearest metre.

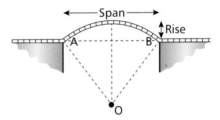

Exercise 5.2

1 The designers on a make-over TV show have decided to have a circular shelf feature in their latest house.
The shelves measure 80 cm and 60 cm and are both horizontal.
The radius of the shelf feature is 50 cm.
They want to place an ornament on the bottom shelf.
The ornament is 75 cm tall.
Will it fit in under the top shelf?

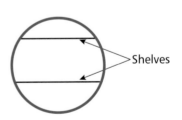

2

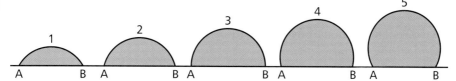

A stall at a fairground offers a prize if you can hit a circular target which slowly comes into view from behind a board. In position 1 the top of the circle is 10 cm above the board and the diagram shows it rising at 10 cm intervals. The radius of the target is 30 cm. Calculate the length of the chord AB in each of the positions.

3 A car with wheels of diameter 60 cm has gone off the road and its wheels have sunk in the soft grass verge as shown in the diagram. The chord AB is 14 cm long. How far below the surface of the verge is the bottom of the wheel?

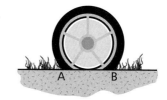

4 The radius of each circle is 10 cm.
Which chord is longer in **a** and by how much?
Which chord is nearer the centre in **b** and by how much?

a

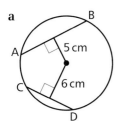

b

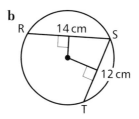

6 Finding the centre of a circle

Example

Follow these steps to find the centre of a circle.
1 Draw two chords … not parallel.
2 Use a ruler and a pair of compasses to draw the perpendicular bisector of each chord.
3 Since the centre of a circle lies on any perpendicular bisector of a chord, the centre must be located where the two perpendiculars intersect.

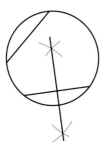  

Exercise 6.1

1 Draw round a circular object and use the method described on page 189 to find the centre of the resulting circle.

2 A gardener is planting standard rose bushes in a park flowerbed.
He has already planted three and he wants the fourth one to be equidistant from the other three.
Trace the position of the three already planted and find the position of the fourth.

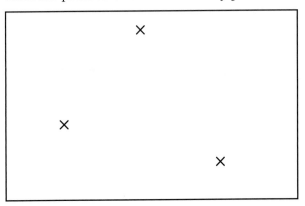

7 The circumference of a circle

The diameter of a circle is twice the radius. $D = 2R$

Mathematicians have known for thousands of years that there is also a simple connection between the diameter and the circumference. In fact the circumference is approximately three times the diameter.

$C = 3D$ … this is good enough for rough work.

With better measurement however, it was found that this factor wasn't 3, but 3·141 592 6…

In fact the decimals go on forever. Scientists test their new computers by getting them to calculate this number to large numbers of decimal places. The record at the moment is over a trillion places.

The number is referred to by the symbol π (pronounced 'pie'). For reasonably accurate answers the value 3·14 is used. Calculators have a π button which is used for very accurate answers.

$C = \pi D$

> *Example*   Find, correct to 1 d.p., the circumference of a circle of:
>   **a** diameter 12·6 cm   **b** radius 4·2 m.
>
>   **a** diameter = 12·6 ⇒ $C = \pi \times 12 \cdot 6 = 39 \cdot 6$ cm (to 1 d.p.)
>   **b** radius = 4·2 ⇒ diameter = 8·4 ⇒ $C = \pi \times 8 \cdot 4 = 26 \cdot 4$ m (to 1 d.p.)
>
> In the above example, the π button on the calculator was used. Check that using
> 3·14 for π produces the same result correct to 1 d.p.

Exercise 7.1

1 Using 3·14 for π, calculate (to 1 d.p.) the circumference of the circle with diameter:
   a 12 cm   **b** 18·4 m   **c** 125 mm   **d** 26 km

2 Calculate, correct to 1 d.p., **i** the diameter **ii** the circumference of a circle with radius:
   a 14 cm   **b** 22·6 m   **c** 144 mm   **d** 45 km

3 The Earth has a radius of 4000 miles.
   Calculate, correct to 2 significant figures:
   a the diameter of the Earth
   b the circumference round the equator.

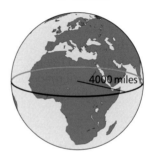

4 A tin of beans has a diameter of 84 mm.
   a What is its circumference?
   b The tin is 8 cm high. What are the dimensions of the label that wraps round the tin?

5 A boy spins a toy plane round his head.
   The length of the string is 1·4 m.
   a Working to 2 decimal places, calculate the distance
   the plane travels in one turn round his head.
   b The boy extends the string by a further 20 cm.
   What is the extra distance travelled by the plane in one turn?

6 Knowing that $C = \pi D$ we can find the diameter for a given circumference by division.
   $$D = C \div \pi$$

   Calculate, to 1 d.p., the diameter of a circle with circumference:
   a 40 cm   **b** 100 mm   **c** 23·6 m   **d** 742 km

7 At what radius would you set a pair of compasses to draw a circle
   with circumference:
   a 5 cm   **b** 8 cm
   c 54 mm   **d** 3·6 cm?
   Give your answers to 1 d.p.

8 A groundsman wants to mark out a circular running track so that the inside of the track has a circumference of 500 m.
  a What is the radius, to the nearest metre, of the circle?
  b The track is 6 m wide. How much longer is the distance round the outside of the track than round the inside?

9 In each of the following work to an appropriate accuracy.
  a What is the circumference of a circle of radius 1 cm?
  b A circular hoop has a radius of 2 m.
    i What is its circumference?
    ii The hoop is stretched so that its radius increases by 1 cm.
      By how much is the circumference increased?
  c A circular enclosure of radius 100 m is to be made.
    i What total length of fencing is required?
    ii An error is made in measuring the radius. It is 1 cm too small.
      What extra fencing is required?
  d Imagine an elastic band all the way round the world at the equator.
    Imagine that little sticks are used to raise the elastic band by 1 cm right round the world. By how much would the elastic band stretch?

10 A waste bin is in the shape of a truncated cone.
    The diameter of the opening is 880 cm.
    a Calculate, to the nearest centimetre, the circumference of the opening.
    b The circumference of the base is 310 cm shorter than that of the opening.
      What is the radius of the base?

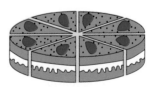

8 The length of an arc

An **arc** is a part of the circumference of a circle.
The radii drawn to the ends of the arc define an angle.
This angle allows us to work out what fraction the arc is of the circumference.

Examples

$\dfrac{90}{360} = \dfrac{1}{4}$

$\dfrac{60}{360} = \dfrac{1}{6}$

$\dfrac{40}{360} = \dfrac{1}{9}$

$\dfrac{120}{360} = \dfrac{1}{3}$

Example
A slice has been taken from a circular cake.
The radius of the cake is 10 cm. Each slice is a **sector** of the circle making an angle of 45° at the centre.

Find the length of the curved edge of one slice.

Fraction of circumference $= \dfrac{45}{360} = \dfrac{1}{8} \,(= 0{\cdot}125)$

so length of arc $= \dfrac{1}{8} \times$ circumference of circle
$\qquad\qquad\quad = 0{\cdot}125 \times \pi d$
$\qquad\qquad\quad = 0{\cdot}125 \times \pi \times 20$
$\qquad\qquad\quad = 7{\cdot}9$ cm, correct to 1 decimal place

Arc

45° 10 cm

Exercise 8.1

1 In each of these diagrams work out the length of the arc.

a
5 cm
180°

b
45°
3 cm

c
90°
7 cm

d
60°
2 cm

e
14 cm
270°

2 The pendulum on a grandfather clock swings through an angle of 50°.
The length of the pendulum is 90 cm.
What is the length of the arc traced out by the end of the
pendulum?

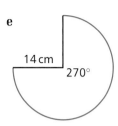

50°
90 cm

3 The diagram shows a workstation.
It is based on a circular table from which a
140° sector is removed. The radius of the table
is 70 cm. The table is to have a trim fixed to the
curved edge. How long will this trim need to be?

70 cm
140°

4 A flowerbed in a garden is the sector of a circle. The straight edges
of the sector are 5 metres long. The angle between them is 35°.
The curved edge is to be planted with geraniums. The geraniums
should be 15 cm apart. How many geranium plants will be required?

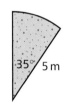

35° 5 m

5 A sign for Charlie's Night Club has a big letter 'C' on it.
The 'C' is a circular arc which has a radius of 1·2 metres and
an angle at the centre of 135°.
Calculate the length of the C.

harlie's

6 Here is a sector of a circle, radius 12 cm.
  a What is the circumference of the circle, to the nearest centimetre?
  b The arc length of the sector is 10 cm.
    What fraction of the circle is the sector?
    $\left(\text{Hint: } \dfrac{\text{arc length}}{\text{circumference}}\right)$
  c The sector angle is the same fraction of 360°.
    Calculate the size of $x°$, the sector angle.
  d Repeat these steps to calculate the angle of a circular
    sector of radius 4 m and arc length 15 m.

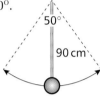

10 cm
$x°$ 12 cm

4 m
15 m

7 Ian and Irma make and sell party hats.
They make the cones from sectors of circles.
Note that the arc of the sector is the
circumference of the base of the cone.
Calculate:

35 cm

35 cm

a the arc length of the sector
b the angle of the sector.

Base radius = 11 cm   Net of cone

---

9 The area of a circle

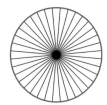

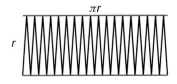

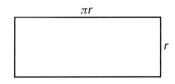

A circle, radius r units, is cut into 36 equal sectors.
Its circumference, marked in red, is $2\pi r$ units long.

The sectors can be rearranged to form a shape that is very nearly a rectangle. Note that its height is r units long and its length is πr units (half of the circumference of the circle).

The smaller the angle used, the closer the circle can be formed to look like a rectangle
… with area $L \times B = \pi r \times r = \pi r^2$.

The area of a circle of radius r units can be calculated using the formula:

$$A = \pi r^2$$

Example   Calculate, to 1 d.p., the area of a circle of:
a radius 12 cm   **b** diameter 20 m

a $A = \pi r^2 \Rightarrow A = \pi \times 12^2 = 452 \cdot 4$ cm^2 (to 1 d.p.)
b $D = 20 \Rightarrow r = 10 \Rightarrow A = \pi \times 10^2 = 314 \cdot 2$ m^2 (to 1 d.p.)

Exercise 9.1

Unless otherwise stated, work to 1 decimal place.

1 Calculate the area of a circle of radius:
   a 30 cm   **b** 45 mm   **c** 7·2 m   **d** 85 km

2 Calculate the area of a circle of diameter:
   a 16 cm   **b** 88 mm   **c** 19·4 m   **d** 90 km

3 In the strawberry fields, a sprinkler rotates and squirts out jets of water which reach a distance of 23 m. What is the area of the circular patch being watered?

4 The lid of a tin can is a circle of radius 3·8 cm.
   Calculate the area of the tin required to make the lid.

5 A spotlight casts a circular beam of light onto the stage.
The diameter of the spot lit up is 5 m.
a What area is lit up?
b A stage hand reduces the diameter to 4 m.
What area is now not lit up?

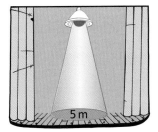

6 Washers are made by taking discs of metal and punching a circular hole in the centre.

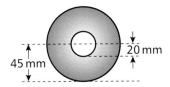

a If the original disc has a radius of 45 mm, what is its area?
b If the hole has a radius of 20 mm, what area has been removed?
c What is the area of the washer?
d What is the area of a washer made from a disc of radius 55 mm with a hole of radius 34 mm?
e What is the area of a washer of external radius 50 mm and width 10 mm?

7 A lawn is rectangular with length 15 m and breadth 12 m.
Two circular flowerbeds are cut out of the lawn.
They both have a diameter of 5 m.
a What is the area of each bed?
b What area is grass?

8 $A = \pi r^2$. If we know the area then we can work out the radius using $r^2 = \dfrac{A}{\pi}$
or, even better, $r = \sqrt{\dfrac{A}{\pi}}$.
a Calculate the radius of a circle of area:
   i   100 cm²   **ii**   26 mm²   **iii**   4000 m²
b Calculate the diameter of a circle of area:
   i   30 cm²   **ii**   99 mm²   **iii**   75·3 m²

9 A £2 coin is made from a silver disc of diameter 20 mm imbedded in a bronze disc of diameter 28 mm.
What is the area of the bronze surrounding the silver disc?

10 A trundle wheel has a circumference of 1 metre.
a Calculate its radius.
b Calculate its area.

11 A kilometre of fencing is used to enclose a circular arena.
What is the area enclosed?

10 The area of a sector

If we know what fraction the **sector** is of the circle then we can work out its area.
As already shown, this can be worked out if you know the angle at the centre or the
arc length and the radius.

$$\text{The fraction the sector is of the circle} = \frac{\text{area of sector}}{\text{area of circle}} = \frac{\text{angle at centre}}{360°}$$

$$= \frac{\text{arc length}}{\text{circumference}}$$

Example
Andy is making a new breadbin.
He needs to calculate the area of the end of the
breadbin, which is a sector of a circle.

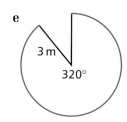

The sector is $\frac{90}{360} = \frac{1}{4} (= 0.25)$ of the circle.

Area of the sector $= 0.25 \times \pi \times r^2$

$\qquad\qquad\quad = 0.25 \times \pi \times 15^2$

$\qquad\qquad\quad = 176.7 \text{ cm}^2$ to 1 decimal place

Exercise 10.1

Give your answers to 1 decimal place, where necessary.

1 Calculate the area of each sector.

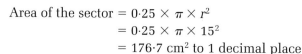

2 Another nightclub is opening.
This one is called The Crimson Sector.
Here is the sign on the wall outside the club.
The logo is a sector of a circle.
The radius of the circle is 1·1 m.
The angle at the centre is 110°.
Calculate the area of the sector.

3 A garden gate is 85 cm wide and opens through an angle of 95°.
A view from above (plan view) is shown here.
What area of ground does the gate cover as it opens?

4 A van has only one windscreen-wiper, which sweeps through 111°.
Calculate, to the nearest square centimetre, the area of:
a the large sector covered (radius 60 cm)
b the small sector (radius 17 cm)
c the actual area of windscreen cleared by the wiper blade.

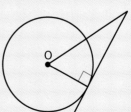

5 The areas of these circular sectors are given.
For each calculate
i the area of the circle
ii what fraction the sector is of the circle
iii the angle at the centre
iv the length of the arc.

a

3 cm
16 cm²

b

0·26 m²
1 m

c

7 m
130 m²

d

42 m²
6·5 m

e
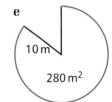
10 m
280 m²

6 A cone is made from cloth. Its net is shown.
Calculate:
a the angle in the sector
b the area of the sector
c the radius of the base of the cone.

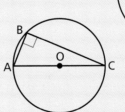
13 cm

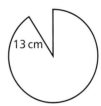
13 cm
Arc length
= 73 cm

◀◀ RECAP

The triangle formed by drawing radii to the ends of a chord is isosceles.

The angle in a semicircle is a right angle.

The angle between a tangent and the radius drawn to the point of contact is a right angle.

A line drawn from the centre of a circle to the midpoint of a chord will be at right angles to the chord.

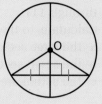

A line drawn from the centre of a circle at right angles to a chord will bisect the chord.

A line bisecting a chord at right angles will pass through the centre of a circle.

The centre of a circle can be found by drawing the perpendicular bisectors of two chords.
The centre will be at the point of intersection.

The circumference of a circle can be found using:
- $C = \pi D$ where D is the diameter of the circle
- $C = 2\pi r$ where r is the radius of the circle.

$\pi =$ 3·141 592 653 589 793 238 462 64 338 32 79 502 884 197 169 399 375 105 820 974 944 592 307 816…

A reasonable approximation for π is 3·14.

The area of a circle can be found using: $A = \pi r^2$

The length of an arc and the area of a circular sector can be calculated if the radius is known and the fraction that the sector is of the circle can be established.

The fraction the sector is of the circle $= \dfrac{\text{area of sector}}{\text{area of circle}}$

$= \dfrac{\text{angle at centre}}{360°}$

$= \dfrac{\text{arc length}}{\text{circumference}}$

1 Calculate *a* and *b*.

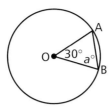 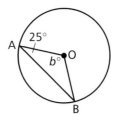

2 Calculate the size of ∠BAC in each diagram.

a   **b**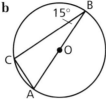

3 Calculate the value of *x* in each of these diagrams.

a 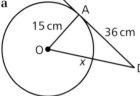   **b** 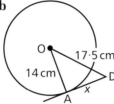   **c**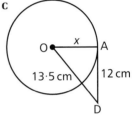

4 Calculate the value of *y* in these diagrams.

a 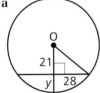   **b**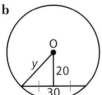

5 Calculate, to 1 decimal place, the circumference of a circle:
   a with a radius of 56·8 cm   **b** with diameter 81 m.

6 What is the area, correct to 3 significant figures, of a circle:
   a with a radius of 21 cm   **b** with diameter 4·2 m?

7 Calculate, to the nearest whole number …

a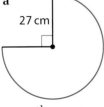
… the area

b
… the arc length

c
… the angle

d
… the area

e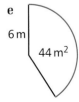
… the arc length

REVISE

11 Angles and triangles

We can use scale drawings to find angles and distances.

The yacht, Y, is 1600 m from the lifeboat, L, on a bearing of 052°.
The harbour, H, is due north of the lifeboat and due west of the yacht.
A scale drawing can help us find the distance of the yacht from the harbour.

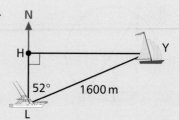

In this chapter we shall discover a quicker and more accurate way to find angles and distances in a right-angled triangle.

1 REVIEW

◀◀ Exercise 1.1

1 Write down the 3-figure bearing of the directions described by these compass points:
   a east   **b** south   **c** west   **d** north   **e** south-west

2 The diagram is a scale drawing showing the positions of a ship, S, in distress and a lifeboat, L. Find, by measurement, the distance and bearing of the ship from the lifeboat.

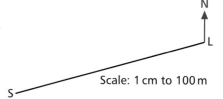

3 Calculate a in each triangle below:

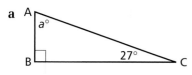

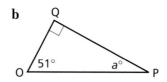

4 Name the hypotenuse of each triangle in question **3**.

5 Use Pythagoras' theorem to calculate ST, correct to 1 decimal place.

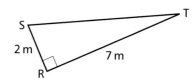

6 Use a calculator to find x, correct to 2 decimal places.

  a $x = \frac{4}{11}$ **b** $x = 0.67 \times 8$ **c** $x = \frac{12}{0.17}$

7 a Solve $\frac{x}{6} = 12$ by multiplying each side by 6.

  b Use this method to solve **i** $\frac{x}{9} = 0.74$ **ii** $\frac{x}{2.5} = 7$.

8 A search party is looking for an injured climber.

  a Mark a point X near the centre of a page of your jotter.
    X represents the search party.

  b Show the positions of the following using a scale of 1 cm to 100 m:
    i injured climber, C, 780 m from X on a bearing of 105°
    ii campsite, S, 930 m from X on a bearing of 294°
    iii bridge, B, 460 m from X on a bearing of 238°
    iv ambulance, A, 220 m from X on a bearing of 342°.

9 a Make a scale drawing to help Toni find the height
    of her school, to the nearest metre.
    Remember to add on her height.

  b Compare your answers with others in the class.
    Then list some drawbacks of scale drawings.

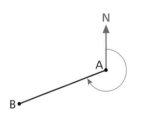

---

2 More about bearings

Reminder
The three-figure bearing of B from A is the angle measured
clockwise from the north line at A.

When making scale drawings:

- always start with a sketch
- draw in the necessary north lines.

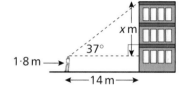

Exercise 2.1

1 A helicopter flies 58 km from A to B on a bearing of 083°.
  It then flies 65 km from B to C on a bearing of 197°.

  a Using a scale of 1 cm to represent 10 km, make a scale
    drawing to show the positions of A, B and C.
    (Start by marking a point A and its north line.)

  b Find the bearing and distance of C from A.

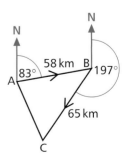

2 A boat sails 45 km from P to Q on a bearing of 130°.
It then changes course and sails 65 km on a bearing
of 042° until it reaches R.

   a Make a sketch of the journey.
     (Remember to draw in the north lines at P and Q.)
   b Using a scale of 1 cm to 10 km, make a scale drawing
     of the journey.
   c Find: **i** the bearing of R from P
            ii the distance from P to R.

3 Mungo the explorer sets out from camp C on a bearing of 306° and walks for
890 metres until he meets a tiger at T.
He walks a further 650 metres on a bearing of 224° to L and then realises he is lost.
   a Make a sketch of Mungo's journey.
   b Using a scale of 1 cm to 100 m, make a scale drawing of Mungo's journey.
   c Help Mungo find his way back to camp by finding how far he is from camp and
     the bearing he will need to take to get there.

4 A ship at A is 75 km due west of a ship at B.
Both ships pick up a distress signal from a boat at C.
The bearing of the boat from A is 128° and from
B is 223°.
Use a scale drawing to find how far the boat is
from both ships.

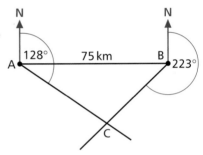

5 The town of Gailes is 19 km due south of the town of Darley.
Kerry is a village on a bearing of 062° from Gailes and on a bearing of 136° from Darley.
   a Make a sketch showing the relative positions of Gailes, Darley and Kerry.
   b Make a scale drawing to find the distance of
     i   Kerry from Gailes   **ii**   Kerry from Darley.

6 An airport runway, PQ, is 3800 m long. It runs from north-east to south-west with P
north-east of Q. A cottage at C bears 165° from P and 095° from Q.
   a Make a sketch showing the position of the runway and the cottage.
   b Using a scale of 1 cm to represent 500 m, make a scale drawing.
   c From the scale drawing find the distance of the cottage from the runway.

7

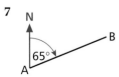 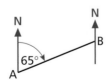

   a The bearing of B from A is 065°.
     What is the size of the acute angle at B in the second diagram?
     Give a reason for your answer.
   b So what is the bearing of A from B?

8 In a similar way to question **7**, find the bearing of A from B if the bearing of B from A is:

    a 040°   **b** 070°   **c** 082°   **d** 100°   **e** 120°   **f** 158°

    g 180°   **h** 190°   **i** 205°   **j** 240°   **k** 290°   **l** 320°

9 What is the bearing of A from B if the bearing of B from A is $x°$?

10 A boat is lost at sea. The coastguard spots it and gives the boat's position as on a bearing of 179° from the harbour.

    What bearing must the boat set so that it can head towards the harbour?

---

3 Trigonometry

Trigonometry is the name given to the study of measurement in triangles. The origins of trigonometry lie in the desire to calculate the positions of stars and planets; scale drawings were not very helpful in achieving this.

We usually refer to the sides of a right-angled triangle with reference to their relation to the angles.

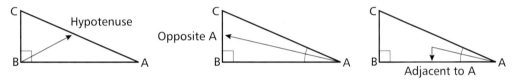

In the right-angled triangle ABC, AC is opposite the right angle. AC is called the **hypotenuse**.

CB is the side **opposite** $\angle$A. AB is the side next to, or **adjacent** to, $\angle$A.

Note that AB is the side opposite $\angle$C, and CB is the side adjacent to $\angle$C.

Exercise 3.1

A class discussion

1

 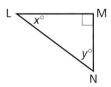 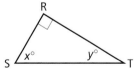 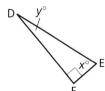

In each right-angled triangle above name the:

a hypotenuse

b side opposite angle x

c side adjacent to angle x

d side opposite angle y

e side adjacent to angle y.

2 In $\triangle$RST, the ratio $\dfrac{\text{opposite S}}{\text{hypotenuse}} = \dfrac{10}{26} = 10 \div 26 = 0 \cdot 385$

to 3 d.p.

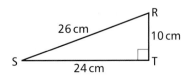

In a similar way, calculate the ratio:

a $\dfrac{\text{adjacent to S}}{\text{hypotenuse}}$

b $\dfrac{\text{opposite S}}{\text{adjacent to S}}$

3 $\triangle$KLM is isosceles. KN is the axis of symmetry.
In the appropriate right-angled triangle, calculate
(to 3 d.p. where appropriate) the ratio:

a $\dfrac{\text{opposite L}}{\text{hypotenuse}}$

b $\dfrac{\text{opposite M}}{\text{adjacent to M}}$

c $\dfrac{\text{opposite L}}{\text{adjacent to L}}$

d $\dfrac{\text{adjacent to } \angle\text{MKN}}{\text{hypotenuse}}$

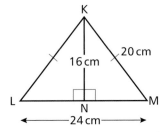

4 The tangent

Exercise 4.1

A class activity

1 a Draw an angle of 33° with arms of reasonable length.
b Draw three lines at right angles to AB, namely B_1C_1,
B_2C_2 and B_3C_3.
c Copy and complete the table below, measuring the
lengths as accurately as you can.
Give your answers to Opp ÷ Adj correct to 3 d.p.

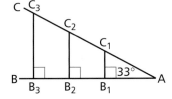

Triangle	Opposite A (Opp)	Adjacent to A (Adj)	Opp ÷ Adj
AB_1C_1	$B_1C_1 =$	$AB_1 =$	
AB_2C_2	$B_2C_2 =$	$AB_2 =$	
AB_3C_3	$B_3C_3 =$	$AB_3 =$	

d You should find that each time you divided the opposite side by the adjacent side
you got approximately the same answer.
Check your answers with others in the class.
You should all have approximately the same answer.

2 On your calculator key in   tan 3 3 =

You should get $0 \cdot 649\ 407\ 6$, to 7 decimal places.
Compare this with the answers to question **1** above.

3 Repeat questions **1** and **2** for different acute angles.

In each case you should find that, for equal angles, the ratio $\dfrac{\text{opposite side}}{\text{adjacent side}}$ is equal.

For a particular angle, $\angle P$, the ratio $\dfrac{\text{opposite side}}{\text{adjacent side}}$ is a fixed value known as the **tangent** of P. It is usually written as tan P.

For example, tan 33° = 0·649 (to 3 decimal places).

Example 1   Calculate the tangent of D.

$$\tan D = \tfrac{7}{24} = 0\text{·}292 \ \text{(to 3 d.p.)}$$

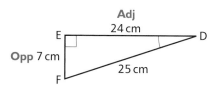

Example 2   Calculate tan $\angle$SRT.

$$\tan \angle SRT = \tfrac{4}{3} = 1\text{·}333 \ \text{(to 3 d.p.)}$$

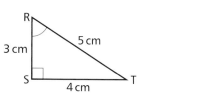

Exercise 4.2

1 In this right-angled triangle,

$$\tan P = \frac{\text{opposite side}}{\text{adjacent side}} = \frac{4}{7} = 0\text{·}571, \text{ correct to 3 d.p.}$$

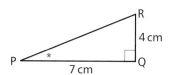

For each triangle below,
i   write down the ratio for tan P
ii   give the value of the ratio correct to 3 d.p.
   (All measurements are in centimetres.)

a   **b** 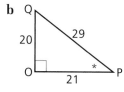   **c** 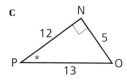   **d**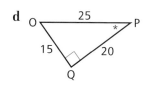

2 Calculate the value of tan B, correct to 3 d.p., for each of these right-angled triangles.

a 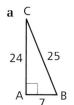   **b** 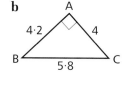   **c** 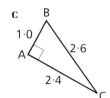   **d**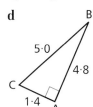

3 Your calculator will give you the tangents of angles.
Copy and complete the table, using your calculator to help you list the tangents of these angles, correct to 3 decimal places.

Angle A	0°	10°	20°	30°	40°	50°	60°	70°	80°
tan A									

4 Find the tangents of these angles, correct to 3 decimal places:
  a 5°   **b** 37°   **c** 48°   **d** 63°   **e** 72·5°   **f** 87·5°

5 Find the values of these tangents, correct to 3 decimal places:
  a tan 26°   **b** tan 52°   **c** tan 68·2° **d** tan 3·7°

> Given tan A = 0·385, you can find the acute angle A:
>
> Key 【2nd】 【tan】 0·385 to get 21·1°, to 1 decimal place.

6 Use your calculator to find the acute angles, correct to the nearest degree, when:
  a tan A = 0·6   **b** tan H = 0·75   **c** tan P = 1
  d tan K = 1·25   **e** tan T = 2·08   **f** tan W = 465.

7 For each triangle in question **2**:
  i   calculate the value of tan C to 3 decimal places
  ii calculate angle C, correct to the nearest degree.
  For example:
  a i $\frac{7}{24} = 0·292$ **ii** Key 【2nd】 【tan】 【(】 【7】 【÷】 【24】 【)】 to get 16°.

Challenge

1 a On squared paper draw a square and one of its diagonals.
  b Mark all the 45° angles.
  c Explain why the value of tan 45° is always 1.

2 a Try to find the value of tan 90°. How does the calculator respond to typing tan 90?
  b Find the tangents of 89°, 89·9°, 89·99°, 89·999°, … How far can you go?
  c Explain what is happening in terms of the definition of the tangent.

---

5 The tangent ratio in action

Example   How high is the tree (correct to 2 d.p.)?

From the diagram we see

$\tan 47° = \dfrac{h}{8}$

$\Rightarrow h = 8 \times \tan 47°$

$\Rightarrow$ height of tree = 8·58 m (to 2 d.p.)

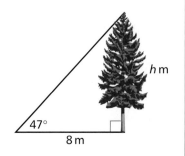

Exercise 5.1

1 Copy and complete the following to find the height of the chimney, to the nearest metre. From the diagram we see

$$\tan 52° = \frac{h}{18}$$

$$\Rightarrow h = \ldots \times \tan \ldots°$$

$$\Rightarrow \text{height of chimney} = \ldots \text{ m (to the nearest metre)}$$

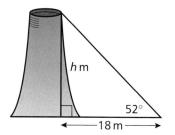

In your answers, give lengths to 1 decimal place unless instructed otherwise.

2 Use the tangent ratio to calculate the value of x in each triangle below.
All the lengths are in centimetres.

a

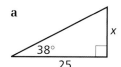

b

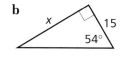

c

3 Calculate the height of each flagpole.

a

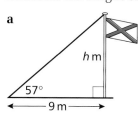

b

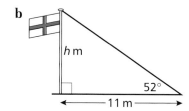

c

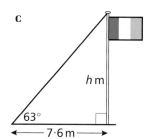

4 How high up the wall does each ladder reach?

a

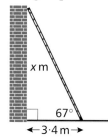

b

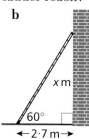

5 Which river is widest? By how much?

a

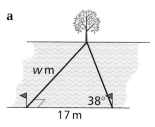

b

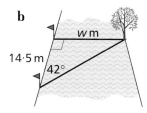

c

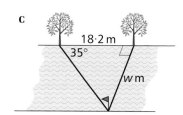

6 If you are looking up at an object, then the angle between the horizontal and your line of sight is called the **angle of elevation** of the object.

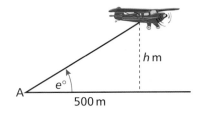

e is the angle of elevation of the plane from A.

The plane is over a spot 500 m from A.
What is the height of the plane when *e* equals
a 30° **b** 35° **c** 40°?

7 At 150 m from the base of the building, the angle of elevation of its top is 37°.
Calculate the height of the building, to the nearest metre.

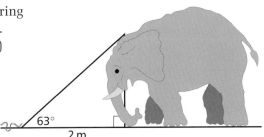

8 There are practical difficulties in measuring the angle of elevation from ground level.
The angle of elevation from the worm (!) to the top of the elephant's head is 63° when they are 2 m apart.
Calculate the height of the elephant's head.

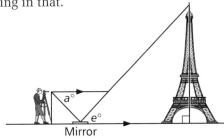

9 In the olden days, a surveyor would place a mirror on the ground and take his siting in that.

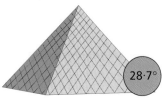

Mirror

a The angle *a* is easy to measure … and it is equal to the angle of elevation.
Can you see why?
b What is the height of the tower when the mirror is placed 200 m from it and the angle, *a*°, is 56°?

10 Here are some famous structures.
The angle of elevation of their tops, measured from a distance of 250 m, is circled.
Use the tangent to calculate the height of each structure, to the nearest metre.

a The Pyramid of Cheops **b** St Paul's Cathedral **c** The Eiffel Tower

28·7°

30·8°

50·2°

11 If you are looking down at an object, then the angle between the horizontal and your line of sight is called the **angle of depression** of the object.

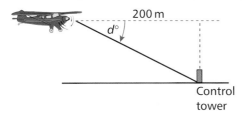

The pilot looks down from horizontal to see the control tower. *d* is the angle of depression of the control tower from the plane. The plane is 200 m from the tower. How high is the plane when the angle of depression is

a 32° **b** 27° **c** 21°?

12 The angle of depression of the wreck at the bottom of the ocean from the *Vital Spark* is 49°. How deep is the water in which the wreck lies?

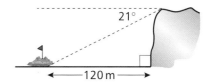

13 A buoy is anchored to a rock 120 m from the foot of a cliff. From the top of the cliff the angle of depression of the buoy is 21°.
Calculate the height of the cliff, to the nearest metre.

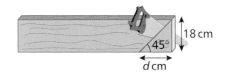

Calculating the adjacent side

Example
A plank of wood 18 cm across has a corner sawn off at an angle of 42° to the side. Calculate *d*, correct to the nearest whole number.

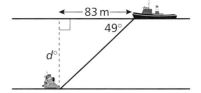

Method 1

$\tan 42° = \dfrac{18}{d}$

$\Rightarrow d \tan 42° = 18$ (multiplying each side by *d*)

$\Rightarrow d = \dfrac{18}{\tan 42}$ (dividing each side by tan 42°)

$\Rightarrow d = 20$ cm

Method 2

Use $\tan 48° = \dfrac{d}{18}$, then $d = 18 \times \tan 48° = 20$ cm

Exercise 5.2

Give your answers to 1 decimal place unless instructed otherwise.

1 Calculate x in each triangle. All measurements are in centimetres.

a

b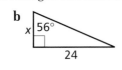

c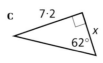

d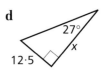

2 Calculate:
   a the length of rectangle ABCD   **b** the breadth of rectangle PQRS.

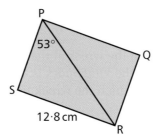

3 The plane is flying at a height of 12 000 feet. Calculate its distance, d feet, from the airport.

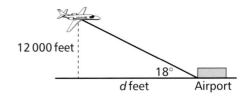

4 A day in the life of the measuring mouse!
The angle of elevation from the mouse to the top of the giraffe's head is 72°.
The giraffe is 4·2 m tall.
How far is the mouse from the giraffe?

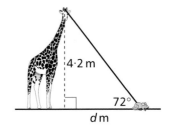

5 A rescue helicopter at a height of 175 m spots a dinghy at an angle of depression of 31°.
Calculate the horizontal distance between the dinghy and the helicopter, to the nearest metre.

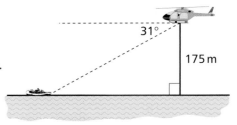

6 Eastport is due east of Westport.
Midway bears 024° from Westport.
Calculate the distance from Westport to Midway, to the nearest kilometre.

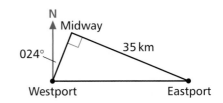

6 Calculating an angle

Example Calculate the angle which the support wire makes with the ground.

$$\tan x° = \frac{11}{4}$$

Using the calculator

$\Rightarrow x° = \tan^{-1} = \left(\frac{11}{4}\right)$ (asking the calculator 'Which angle has a tan of $\frac{11}{4}$?')

$\Rightarrow x° = 70°$, to the nearest degree.

Key (2nd) (tan) (1 1 ÷ 4) =

Exercise 6.1

1 Calculate, to 1 d.p., the value of x in each triangle. All lengths are in centimetres.

 a

 b 4·5, 8

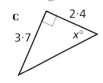 **c** 2·4, 3·7

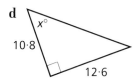 **d** 10·8, 12·6

2 Calculate the marked angles.

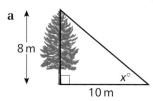 **a** 8 m, 10 m

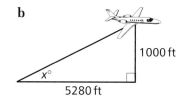 **b** 1000 ft, 5280 ft

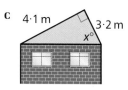 **c** 4·1 m, 3·2 m

3 Asha is 168 cm tall. In sunshine, the shadow she casts on the ground is 470 cm long. What is the angle of elevation of the sun?

4 Calculate all the angles in **a** the kite **b** the rectangle.

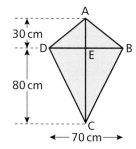

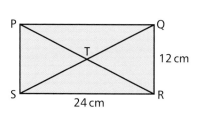

7 The sine of an angle

The ladder will slip if the angle it makes with the ground is less than 40°. Can we calculate the angle?

We do not know the side adjacent to the angle, so we cannot use the tangent ratio.

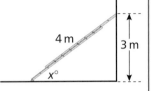
4 m   3 m   x°

We do know the side *opposite* the angle and the *hypotenuse*.

We define a new ratio, $\dfrac{\text{opposite side}}{\text{hypotenuse}}$, called the **sine** of the angle, usually shortened to **sin**.

$$\sin A = \frac{\text{opposite side to A}}{\text{hypotenuse}}$$

Hypotenuse   Opposite A

B

A   C

Your calculator will give you the sine of any angle.

Exercise 7.1

1 Use the $\boxed{\sin}$ key to help you complete this table of sines correct to 3 d.p.

Angle A	0	10	20	30	40	50	60	70	80	90
sin A										

2 Use the $\boxed{\text{2nd}}$ $\boxed{\sin}$ keys to help find, to the nearest degree, the acute angles which have the given values of sines.

Angle A							
sin A	0·5	0·9	0·1	0·25	0·77	0·469	0·956

3 Will the ladder mentioned in the introduction to this exercise slip?

4 In the right-angled triangle ABC,

$$\sin A = \frac{\text{opposite side to A}}{\text{hypotenuse}} = \frac{BC}{AC} = \frac{4}{5}$$

In a similar manner, write down the ratio for sin A in each triangle below.

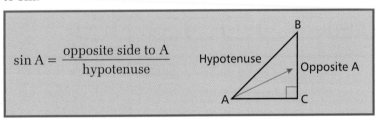
Opposite   B   4   C   5   A   Hypotenuse

a
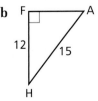
E   11   6   A   C

b
F   12   15   A   H

c
A   10   D   6   8   G

d
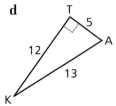
T   5   A   12   13   K

5 For each triangle

i write down the ratio for sin P

ii calculate the size of angle P.

a

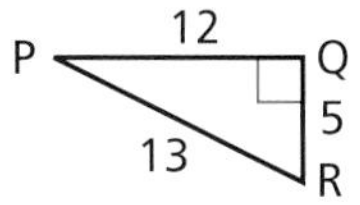

b

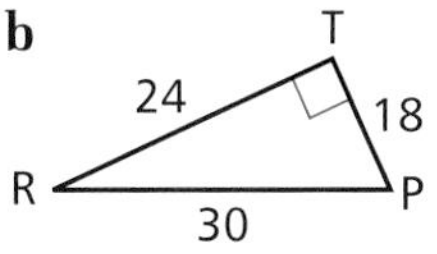

c

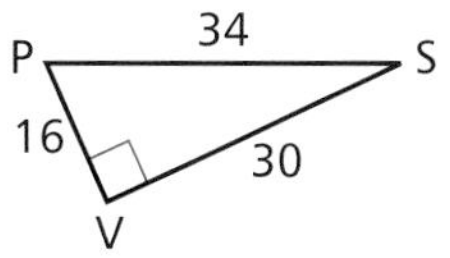

d

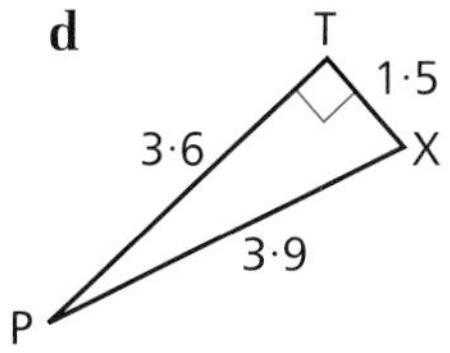

6 Calculate the size of angle x in each right-angled triangle.

a

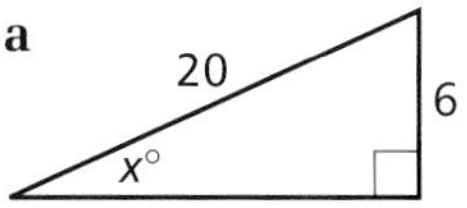

b

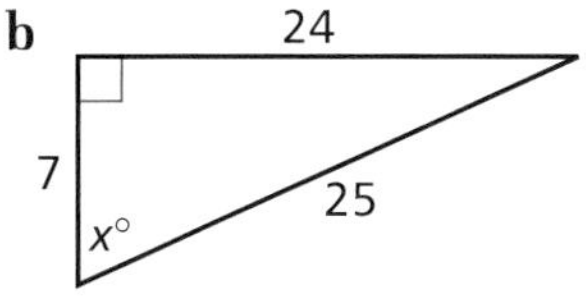

7 Calculate the length of the diagonal KM of kite KLMN.

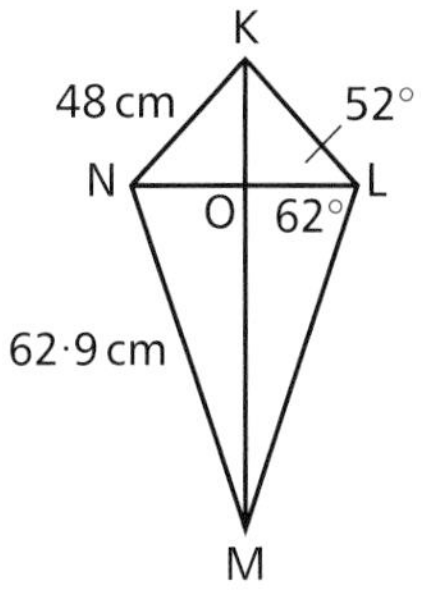

8 **a** Calculate the breadth of rectangle EFGH.

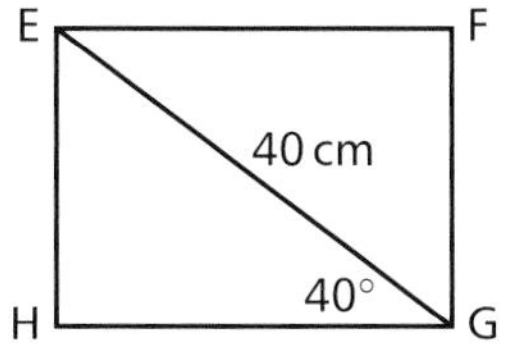

b Use Pythagoras' theorem to calculate the length of rectangle EFGH.

The sine ratio in action

Example The gangway is 24 metres long.
It makes an angle of 23° with the horizontal.
Calculate its height above the quayside (CB).

In ΔABC, $\angle B = 90°$

$$\Rightarrow \sin A = \frac{\text{opposite side to A}}{\text{hypotenuse}} = \frac{BC}{AC}$$

$$\Rightarrow \sin 23° = \frac{h}{24}$$

$\Rightarrow h = 24 \times \sin 23°$

$\Rightarrow h = 9{\cdot}4$, correct to 1 decimal place.

The required height is 9·4 m.

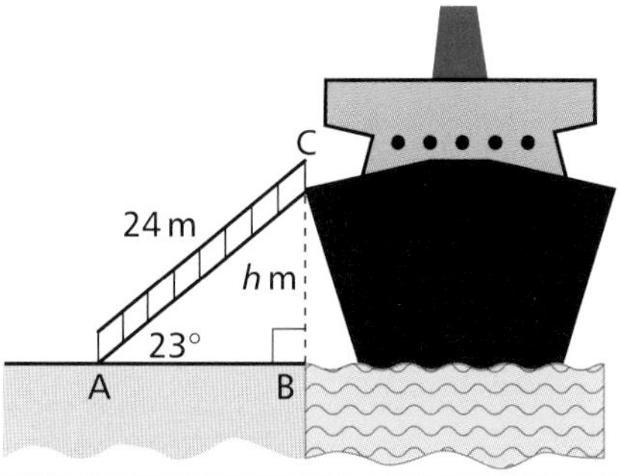

Exercise 7.2

Give your answers to 1 decimal place where appropriate.

1 Calculate the value of x in each triangle.

a

b

c

d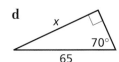

2 Calculate the value of d in each triangle.

a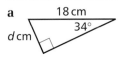

b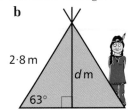

c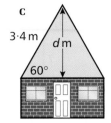

d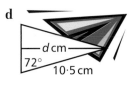

3 A straight road rises steadily for 900 m.
Its angle of slope is 26°.

a Calculate the vertical rise, v m, of the stretch of road.

b Use the sine ratio with the third angle in the diagram to find the value of d m, the horizontal distance travelled.

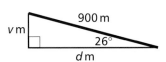

4 The cable car climbs at 38° to the horizontal.
AB = 70 m and BC = 50 m.
Calculate the vertical height the car has gained from:

a A to B

b B to C.

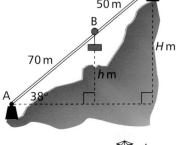

5 A TV mast is 45 m high.
It is supported by a wire 55 m long, as shown in the diagram.
Calculate the angle the wire makes with the ground.

6 This sign shows that the road rises 1 metre for every 9 metres of road.
Calculate the angle between the road and the horizontal.

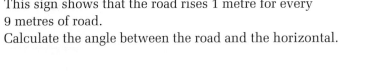

7 A yacht is 750 m west of Devil's Rock, and is following a course of 132°.

a What is the size of ∠RXY when the yacht is closest to Devil's Rock?

b How close to the rock does the yacht sail?

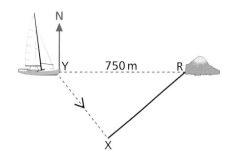

8 Calculating the hypotenuse

Example The road from A to B is at right angles to the road from B to C, which is 5 km long. A new road is being built from A to C, as shown in the diagram.
Calculate the length of this new road, to the nearest tenth of a kilometre.

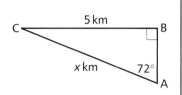

$$\sin A = \frac{\text{opposite side to A}}{\text{hypotenuse}}$$

$$\Rightarrow \sin 72° = \frac{5}{x}$$

$$\Rightarrow x \sin 72° = 5$$

$$\Rightarrow x = \frac{5}{\sin 72} = 5\cdot3, \text{ to 1 d. p.}$$

The new road is 5·3 km long.

Exercise 8.1

1 Calculate d, correct to 1 decimal place, in each triangle.

a 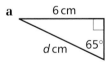 **b**  **c** 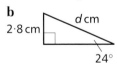 **d**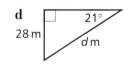

2 Use trigonometry to calculate the length of the hypotenuse of each right-angled triangle.

a 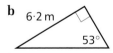 **b**  **c** 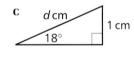 **d**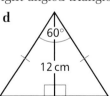

3 Calculate to 1 decimal place:
  a the length of the sloping edge of the roof
  b the height of the house.

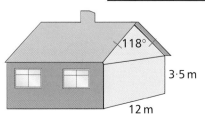

4 The *Mary Ann* sets course from the harbour, O,
on a bearing of 040°, and sails for 80 km.
She then changes course to 135° and sails
until she is due east of the harbour.

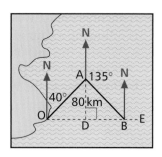

   a What is the furthest north the *Mary Ann* goes from
the harbour?

   b What is the length of her journey from A to B?

   c How far is she from the harbour at B?

     Give your answers to 1 decimal place.

9 The cosine of an angle

Example

A bridge 12·5 m long spans a stream at an angle
of 21° to the horizontal. How wide is the stream?
This time we have to link the hypotenuse with
the side adjacent to the given angle.

So we define another new ratio, $\dfrac{\text{adjacent side to A}}{\text{hypotenuse}}$,

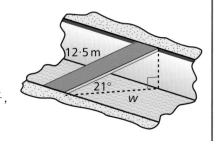

called the **cosine** of the angle.

$$\cos A = \frac{\text{adjacent side}}{\text{hypotenuse}}$$

For the bridge, $\cos 21° = \dfrac{\text{adjacent side to } 21°}{\text{hypotenuse}} = \dfrac{w}{12\cdot5}$

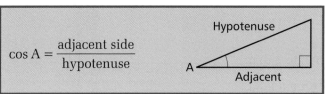

So $w = 12\cdot5 \cos 21°$

     $= 11\cdot7$, to 1 d.p.

The width of the stream is 11·7 m.

Your calculator will give you the cosine of any angle.

Exercise 9.1

1 Use the $\boxed{\cos}$ key on your calculator to help you list these cosines, correct to 3 d.p.

Angle A	0	10	20	30	40	50	60	70	80	90
cos A										

2 Use the $\boxed{\text{2nd}}$ $\boxed{\cos}$ keys to help you find, to the nearest degree, the acute angles
which have the given values of cosines.

Angle A							
cos A	0·5	0·7	0·2	0·35	0·82	0·276	0·943

3 i Write down the ratio for cos A in each triangle.
   ii Calculate the size of angle A.

a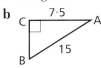

b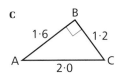

c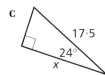

d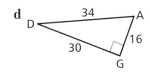

4 Use the cosine ratio to calculate the value of x in each right-angled triangle.
   Give lengths to 1 decimal place and angles to the nearest degree.

a

b

c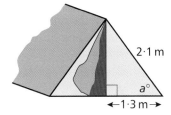

d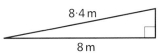

5 Calculate the angle the side of the tent makes with
   the ground.

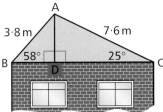

6 The ramp to get into a shopping mall must make
   an angle of less than 16° with the ground.
   Is the ramp opposite suitable?

7 A dinghy leaves a harbour on a bearing of 230° and travels for 15 km. How far
   a west   **b** south is it from the harbour then?
   Give your answers to 1 decimal place.

8 Calculate the length of BC, the horizontal part of
   the roof, to 1 decimal place.

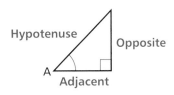

---

10 Which ratio?

$$\sin A = \frac{\text{opposite side}}{\text{hypotenuse}}$$

$$\cos A = \frac{\text{adjacent side}}{\text{hypotenuse}}$$

$$\tan A = \frac{\text{opposite side}}{\text{adjacent side}}$$

SOH – CAH – TOA

Exercise 10.1

1 Decide which trigonometric ratio to use and then calculate *d* to 1 decimal place.

a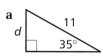
b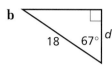
c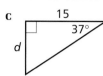
d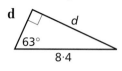

2 Calculate the value of *a* in each triangle.

a
b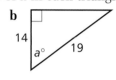
c
d

3 i Which television has the wider screen?
  ii What is the height of each screen?

a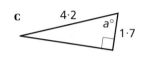
b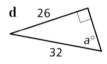

4 Calculate the submarine's angle of dive.

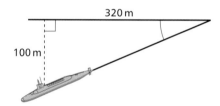

5 From a helicopter vertically above P,
the angle of depression of the helipad is 26°.
Calculate the height of the helicopter,
to the nearest metre.

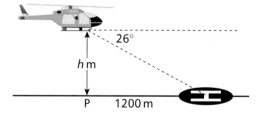

6 Is it easier to score from the penalty spot at
football (A) or hockey (B)?
Calculate the angles at A and B to compare
the shooting angles.
What do you think?
Are there other things to consider in this
situation?

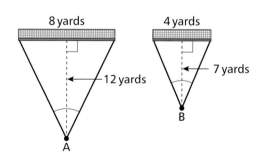

7 A railway line runs straight for 3500 m at an angle of elevation of 7°.
Calculate (to 1 decimal place) how far:
a it rises vertically over this distance
b it travels horizontally.

8 Farmer Brown's field is rectangular.
Calculate:
a a
b d, using trigonometry
c d, using Pythagoras' theorem
d the area of the field, to 3 s.f.

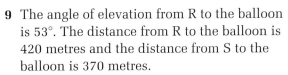

9 The angle of elevation from R to the balloon
is 53°. The distance from R to the balloon is
420 metres and the distance from S to the
balloon is 370 metres.
Calculate:
a the height of the balloon
b the angle of depression from the balloon to S
c the distance between R and S.

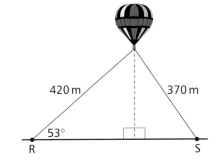

Exercise 10.2

1 A helicopter is flying 70 m above a traffic
jam which is 850 m long on a straight
section of motorway.
The angle of depression from the
helicopter to end A of the traffic jam
is 23°.

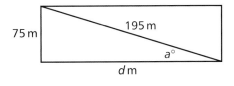

a Calculate the distance of the helicopter
  i   from A   **ii**   from B.
b Calculate the angle of depression from the helicopter to B.

2 a Show that the angle between the roof of the car-port and
  the horizontal is 27°, to the nearest degree.
b Calculate the length of the sloping roof by:
  i   trigonometry   **ii**   Pythagoras' theorem.

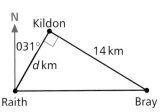

3 Bray is due east of Raith. Kildon is on a bearing of
031° from Raith.
Calculate the distance from Raith to Kildon, to the
nearest kilometre.

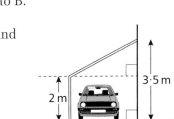

4 In this V-kite calculate the length of:

  a ST   **b** QS.

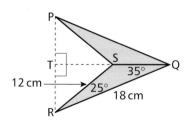

5 a Copy the isosceles triangle DEF, and draw its axis of symmetry meeting EF at G.

  b Calculate:

  i DG

  ii the area of ΔDEF

  iii the angles of ΔDEF.

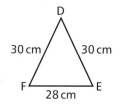

6 A rectangle is 24 cm long and 16 cm broad. Calculate the angles between:

  a the diagonals and the sides

  b the diagonals.

7 From the window of his house, 150 m from a factory chimney, Nick estimates that the angle of elevation of the top is 36°, and the angle of depression of the foot is 6°.

Calculate the height of the chimney to the nearest metre.

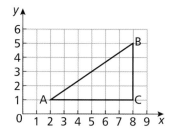

8 The slope or gradient of the straight line AB is measured by the tangent of the angle which AB makes with the horizontal line AC.

  a Calculate the gradient of AB, and the size of ∠BAC.

  b Calculate the gradient of the line joining:

  i P(1, 2) and Q(9, 5)

  ii R(−3, −3) and S(2, −1)

  iii T(−4, 3) and U(4, 6).

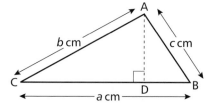

9 a Prove that AD = $b \sin C$.

  b Find a formula for the area of ΔABC which involves a, b and $\sin C$.

  c Use your formula to calculate the area of ΔABC, given $a = 6·4$, $b = 5·6$ and ∠ACB = 43°.

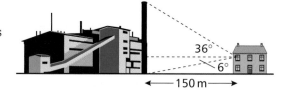

10 The area of the triangle opposite is 144 cm². Calculate the value of:

  a x

  b a.

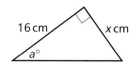

Investigations

1 As angle A increases from 0° to 90°, what happens to sin A, cos A and tan A?

2 **a** Copy and complete the table, giving your answers correct to 2 decimal places.

Angle A	0	10	20	30	40	50	60	70	80	90
sin A										
cos A										

b Can you spot a connection between cosines and sines?

Cosine means the complement of the sine.
Remember: two angles are complementary if they add up to 90°.

sin 0° = cos 90°, sin 10° = cos 80°, sin 20° = cos 70°, etc.

c What angle has the same value for its sine and its cosine?

d Copy and complete:

   i   sin 15° = cos ...°

   ii   cos 25° = sin ...°

   iii cos 1° = sin ...°

   iv sin 37° = cos ...°.

e Use your table of values for A and sin A to help you draw a graph of A against sin A.

f Draw a graph of A against cos A.

◄◄ RECAP

Three-figure bearings are a method of describing
the direction from one place to another.
It is the angle, measured clockwise, from the north
line to the desired direction.
It is always expressed using three digits.
If an angle has less than three digits, then leading
zeros are added.

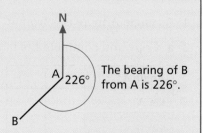

The bearing of B
from A is 226°.

Trigonometry can be used to calculate sides and angles of right-angled triangles.

$$\sin A = \frac{\text{opposite side}}{\text{hypotenuse}}; \quad \cos A = \frac{\text{adjacent side}}{\text{hypotenuse}}; \quad \tan A = \frac{\text{opposite side}}{\text{adjacent side}}$$

SOH-CAH-TOA is an easy way to remember the three ratios.

Example 1 Find h, the height of the building.

$$\tan 40° = \frac{h}{28}$$

$$\Rightarrow h = 28 \times \tan 40°$$

$$\Rightarrow h = 23{\cdot}5$$

The height is 23·5 m, to 1 d.p.

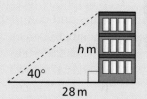

Example 2 Calculate the value of a.

$$\sin a° = \frac{11}{16}$$

$$\Rightarrow \sin a° = 0{\cdot}6875$$

$$\Rightarrow a = 43{\cdot}4 \qquad \text{(using 2nd and sin keys)}$$

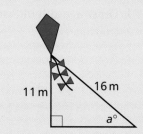

Example 3 Calculate the length of the ladder.

$$\sin 53° = \frac{2{\cdot}4}{h}$$

$$\Rightarrow h \times \sin 53° = 2{\cdot}4$$

$$\Rightarrow h = \frac{2{\cdot}4}{\sin 53°}$$

$$\Rightarrow h = 3{\cdot}0$$

The ladder is 3·0 m, to 1 d.p.

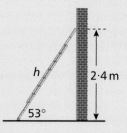

Where appropriate, give answers correct to 1 decimal place.

1 A log cabin, L, is 880 m from a well, W, on a bearing of 210°.
A cave, C, is 620 m from the log cabin on a bearing of 340°.
  a Using a suitable scale, make a scale drawing to show the positions of L, W and C. (Start by marking W and its north line.)
  b From your scale drawing find how far the cave is from the well.

2 The *Mona Mae*, M, is 8·5 km due west of the *Sea Spray*, S.
The bearing of a lighthouse, L, from the *Mona Mae* is 038° and from the *Sea Spray* is 295°.
  a Make a scale drawing to show the positions of the *Mona Mae*, the *Sea Spray* and the lighthouse.
  b Use your scale drawing to find how far each boat is from the lighthouse.

3 The bearing of the youth club from the sports centre is 135°.
What is the bearing of the sports centre from the youth club?

4 Write down ratios for:
  a sin A   **b** cos C   **c** tan D   **d** cos F   **e** tan G   **f** sin H.

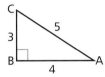
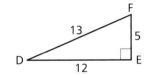
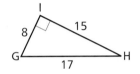

5 Calculate the value of x in each triangle.

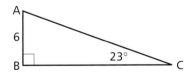

6 Calculate the length of the hypotenuse of each right-angled triangle.

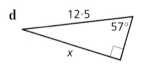

7 The diagonals of a rhombus are 24 cm and 16 cm.
Calculate:
  a the angles of the rhombus
  b the length of side of the rhombus.

8 a Calculate the value of x.
  b Calculate the length of the diagonal, using trigonometry.

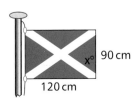

REVISE

9 From the top of the cliff the angle of elevation to
a hot air balloon is 48° and the angle of depression
to a yacht directly below the balloon is 42°.
The cliff is 60 m high.
Calculate:
   a the distance of the yacht from the foot of the cliff
   b the distance between the balloon and the yacht.

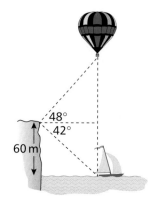

10 Farmer Bull's field is a parallelogram.
Calculate:
   a the altitude of the parallelogram
   b the area of the field, to the nearest 10 m²
   c its perimeter, to the nearest metre, using
      i   trigonometry
      ii Pythagoras' theorem.

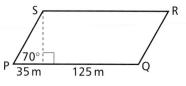

12 More statistics

Holly and Helen were sisters. Holly was in S1 and Helen in S2. They both sat an exam. Each exam had a non-calculator and a calculator component.
The table summarises the results.

	Holly	Helen
Non-calculator	$\frac{12}{20}$	$\frac{14}{25}$
Calculator	$\frac{9}{30}$	$\frac{7}{25}$

Holly turns the scores into percentages to show her father that on both components she is doing better.

	Holly	Helen
Non-calculator	60%	56%
Calculator	30%	28%

Helen, however, gives the scores for the total exam to show they both scored $\frac{21}{50}$ (= 42%).
You can sort and process data but if you misuse it, you can apparently prove anything

1 REVIEW

◄◄ Exercise 1.1

1 Peter read this short sentence and carefully recorded the number of letters to be found in each of the words.
    a Make a frequency table of the data.
    b What was the most common word length?
    c What was the
        i longest   ii shortest word length?

5	4	4	5	8
3	9	8	3	6
2	7	2	2	5
2	4	2	3	5

2 Fifteen students were asked what they scored in a short test. Their replies, when put in order, were 26, 27, 29, 31, 31, 32, 33, 35, 35, 37, 38, 38, 38, 39, 40.
    a State the value of
        i the lowest score   ii the highest score.
    b Which mark splits the list into two smaller lists of equal length (the median)?
    c Find
        i the lower quartile   ii the upper quartile.

3 The box plot shows the result of a survey into the number of passengers found to be travelling on a bus on a busy route.

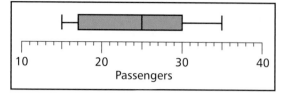

Passengers

a What is the lowest number of passengers counted on a bus?

b What is the median number of passengers?

c State the quartiles of the data set.

d The least busy 25% of the buses carried between 15 and 17 passengers. Make a similar statement about the most busy 25% of the buses.

4 People's opinions were sought on the statement: 'There are too many news programmes on TV.'

Reply	Frequency	Relative frequency	Cumulative frequency
Strongly disagree	4	$\frac{4}{40} = 0\cdot1$	4
Disagree	8		12
Don't care	12		
Agree	10		
Strongly agree	6		
Total	40		

a How many people in total disagreed with the statement?

b What fraction of those asked didn't care?

c Copy and complete the table.

d What is the total of the relative frequency column?

5 Weeds are randomly pulled from a lawn and their lengths measured. The stem-and-leaf diagram records the findings.

a How many weeds were measured?

b What was the length of
i the shortest
ii the longest weed?

c State the median length.

d Calculate the quartiles.

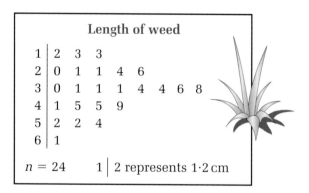

Length of weed

```
1 | 2  3  3
2 | 0  1  1  4  6
3 | 0  1  1  1  4  4  6  8
4 | 1  5  5  9
5 | 2  2  4
6 | 1
```

$n = 24$ 1 | 2 represents 1·2 cm

6 Janet noted the length of commercial breaks between programmes on TV:
5 min, 3 min, 4 min, 4 min, 2 min, 5 min, 6 min, 7 min, 4 min, 3 min.

a What would you consider a typical length of break?

b What is the median time?

c What is the mean time?

2 Putting data in context

If you were to report home that you scored 70 in your maths exam, your parents would be pleased until you told them that everyone else scored over 80.

A single piece of data on its own has no real meaning.

We must put it into some context.

- We might mention the highest or lowest score.
- We might mention the middle score.
- We might be asked 'What was the average?'
- We might be asked 'How close is everyone else to the average?'

In this chapter we will look at ways of giving data a context.

One average that you have already examined is called the **mean**.

$$\text{Mean score} = \frac{\text{total score}}{\text{number of scores}}$$

Exercise 2.1

1 Calculate the mean for each data set.

    a 1, 3, 5, 5, 7, 9

    b 127, 138, 139, 144, 146, 151, 198

    c 2·6, 2·8, 3·4, 3·8, 4·9

    d 0·5, 0·5, 0·6, ,0·7, 0·8, 1, 9, 9·3

2 Sita had some cousins over for a birthday party.

    The ages of those at the party were:

        5 years, 5 years, 6 years, 6 years, 6 years, 7 years, 7 years, 8 years, 32 years, 35 years.

    a What is the mean age at the party?

    b Would you think that this age is typical for those attending?

    c What would you consider is a good guess at Sita's age?

3 Sarah kept a log of her daily use of her phone:

        10 min, 20 min, 8 min, 9 min, 9 min, 12 min, 14 min, 11 min, 22 min, 24 min, 4 min, 12 min, 18 min, 4 min.

    a For how many days did she keep a note?

    b What was her mean use per day?

    c How much longer is her longest phone call than the mean?

    d The next week she averaged 16 minutes per day.
        Is this more or less than the above period?

4 The number of worms found in soil is usually a good indication of how healthy the soil is. Fifteen soil samples were taken before and after the soil had been treated to improve it. The number of worms in each sample was counted. The back-to-back stem-and-leaf diagram shows the data.

	Before			After		
8 7 6 5 4	1	2 3
5 3 3 1	2	2 5 6
7 2 1	3	1 1 1 6 7
1 0 0	4	0 1 2 8
	5	0

$n = 15$ $\qquad$ $n = 15$

1 | 2 represents 12 worms

a Calculate the mean number of worms in the
  i 'before'   ii 'after' samples.
b Would you say that the mean number of worms per sample has increased?

Using a frequency table

The table shows the result of a survey into the number of light bulbs used in people's living-rooms.

Number of bulbs	Frequency
1	7
2	5
3	5
4	2
5	1

The scores could be written out as a long list:

  1, 1, 1, 1, 1, 1, 1, 2, 2, 2, 2, 2, 3, 3, 3, 3, 3, 4, 4, 5.

From this we can get a total of 45 bulbs for 20 rooms, giving a mean of $45 \div 20 = 2 \cdot 25$ bulbs per room.

When the frequencies increase, this method would quickly become too clumsy.

However, look at this table:

Number of bulbs	Frequency	Bulbs × frequency
1	7	7
2	5	10
3	5	15
4	2	8
5	1	5
Totals	20	45

20 rooms   45 bulbs

The mean is the total number of bulbs in the survey ÷ the number of rooms
= $45 \div 20 = 2 \cdot 25$ bulbs per room.

Exercise 2.2

1 For each table

  i   complete or add a third column score × frequency

  ii find the totals of both the frequency and score × frequency columns

  iii calculate the mean correct to 1 d.p.

a

Score	Frequency	Score × freq.
5	3	
6	6	
7	7	
8	1	
Total		

b

Score	Frequency	Score × freq.
45	1	
50	2	
55	4	
60	5	
Total		

c

Score	Frequency
2	1
4	2
6	5
8	3
10	1
Total	

d

Score	Frequency
21	8
22	3
23	1
24	1
25	7
Total	

e

Score	Frequency
3·6	1
3·7	2
3·8	8
3·9	7
4·0	2
Total	

2 A can of juice is advertised as holding 250 ml.
As a quality control exercise several cans are opened and their contents measured.

Score (ml)	Frequency (No. of cans)	Score × freq.
248	8	
249	9	
250	6	
251	4	
252	2	
Total		

a How many cans were examined?

b What was the total volume measured?

c Calculate the mean contents (to 1 d.p.) of a can.

d Is the advertising claim justified?

3 A batch of pots is being glazed.
The frequency of reported minor flaws is recorded in the table.
  a Add a frequency × score column.
  b Use it to help you work out the mean number of flaws
    per pot.
  c If the mean exceeds 3 flaws per pot then
    the whole batch will be sold off as seconds.
    Will this happen?

Score (flaws)	Frequency (No. of pots)
2	6
3	8
4	4
5	2
6	1
Total	

4 The bar chart shows the number of cars in a small
  car park, counted on the hour, over 28 hours.
  a Use the graph to help you form a frequency
    table.
  b Use your table to help you calculate the mean
    number of cars per hour in the car park.
  c If this mean is bigger than 5 then the car park
    will be extended.
    Will it be extended?

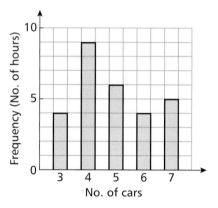

5 A company makes metal wire. A new method is being trialled.
  The strength of a sample of the wire is measured on a scale of 1 to 10.
  Several samples of both the new and the old wire are tested.
  The table gives the results.

Strength	3	4	5	6	7	8	9	10
Frequency (Old method)	1	2	2	3	5	6	9	5
Frequency (New method)	0	1	1	4	7	8	5	5

  a Calculate the mean strength of
    i   the old batch   ii   the new batch.
  b Is there any sign that the new method is better?

3 The mode

Any average should guide us to what is typical of a situation.
If it doesn't do that then it is misleading.

A shoe shop sells ten pairs of shoes. Their sizes are: 6, 6, 6, 6, 6, 6, 6, 6, 10, 12.
So the mean shoe size sold is $70 \div 10 = 7$.
Should the shopkeeper replace his stock with size 7 shoes?
In this instance, a better measure of what is average, or typical, would be a size 6.

This average we call the **mode**. It is the score with the highest frequency. It is often referred to as the **modal score**.

Example   State the mode in each data set.
       a 2, 2, 3, 3, 3, 3, 4, 4, 5, 6
       b yes, no, yes, yes, no, no, yes, yes, yes, no
       c 1, 2, 2, 2, 3, 4, 4, 4, 5, 6

       a 3
       b yes (note you can get the mode of a list which is not numerical)
       c 2 and 4 (note you can get two modes)

Exercise 3.1

1 State the mode of each data set.
  a 1, 2, 3, 4, 4, 5, 5, 6, 6, 6, 7
  b 1, 6, 3, 5, 4, 4, 5, 2, 6, 7, 6, 4, 2, 4
  c red, green, amber, amber, green, green, red, red, amber, amber
  d 1·2, 1·8, 2·4, 1·2, 2·6, 3·5, 2·4, 1·7, 1·9, 2·7

2 A teacher gave her class an exam and graded her pupils' performances A to E.

      C   D   B   D   C
      D   C   C   D   C
      A   E   A   A   E
      D   A   C   C   D
      C   C   E   B   C
      D   E   E   B   D

  a Make a frequency table of the information.
  b Which grade is the mode?
  c Why would the mean not be an appropriate average to get here?

3 Kevin kept a note of the length of his last 20 phone calls in minutes.

      6   2   1   4   4
      2   4   2   2   6
      4   4   4   4   2
      3   5   1   2   4

  a Calculate the mean time.
  b What is the modal time of a call?
  c How many scores were above
    i   the mean
    ii   the modal time?
  d Which of the averages gives a better idea of the typical length of a phone call?

4 The number of light bulbs sold at two outlets is shown.

Outlet A

Type (watts)	Frequency
40	10
60	40
100	20
150	2

Outlet B

Type (watts)	Frequency
40	31
60	41
100	48
150	0

a Calculate the mean number of watts for both outlets. Comment.

b State the mode for each outlet.

c Which of the averages provides a better basis for comparing what is happening at the two outlets?

---

4 The range

Look at the two sets of data given in this table.
They show the rainfall (in millimetres) in two different places over a year.

Place	J	F	M	A	M	J	J	A	S	O	N	D
London	64	50	52	48	44	40	30	42	51	56	58	59
Fort William	125	110	63	12	1	1	0	2	20	40	100	120

The mean rainfall is the same in both cases (49·5 mm) but the monthly pattern is quite different.
In London the values run from 30 mm to 64 mm, a difference of 34 mm.
In Fort William the values run from 0 mm to 125 mm, a difference of 125 mm.
This difference is called the **range** and is used as a measure of how variable a situation is.

Range = maximum score − minimum score

Exercise 4.1

1 Calculate the range of each data set.

  a 48, 23, 35, 43, 39, 18, 50

  b 159, 13, 6, 187, 8, 126, 61, 126, 119, 158, 147, 94

  c 2·2, 2·8, 11·7, 12·6, 1·3, 10·9, 3·6, 16·1

2 The tables show the scores (percentages) achieved by 20 pupils at a particular type of exercise, before practice and after practice.

Before

33	12	37	1
39	32	41	17
50	31	35	11
40	40	8	40
39	45	50	40

After

21	65	67	54
33	45	57	41
64	24	23	65
61	32	34	46
45	60	24	67

a Calculate the mean of both sets.
b Calculate the range of both sets.
c If there has been an improvement in performance, the mean should increase. Has the performance improved?
d If the second exam was harder you would expect the better pupils to do better and the poorer pupils to do worse, i.e. you would expect the range to increase. Was the second exam harder?

3 A machine fills tins with baked beans. It is supposed to put 500 g in each. There is some variation, and the faster the machine works the worse this gets. The table shows the weights of samples taken at two different machines.

Machine 1	460	456	456	458	460	459	456	460	460	458	460	458
Machine 2	452	451	452	450	451	451	450	450	451	450	451	450

a State the modal weight of each data set.
b Calculate the mean of each.
c What is the range of each set?
d Which machine do you think is working faster?

4 A secretary is sent on a course to improve her typing rate. The table gives the figures for several trials before and after the course.

Before course	122	128	122	122	128	124	125	123	128	124	124	126
After course	133	133	131	134	133	134	131	134	132	134	131	131

a Find the mean of each set of trials. Comment.
b Find the range of each set of data. Comment.
c Do you think it was worthwhile going on the course? Make two observations.

5 Two makes of watch are being tested. They are set to the correct time.
After 24 hours it is noted how much they differ from the correct time.
(A negative number means the watch is slow by that number of minutes.)

Prima watch	−3	0	−2	0	0	−1	−2	−3	−3	0	−2
Chronos watch	−4	−2	−5	−6	−5	−3	1	−6	−4	−5	−6

  a Calculate the mean 'score' for both watches.
  b Find the range for both watches.
  c Write a few sentences to compare the watches.

6 In a darts competition, the Flying Tigers need 36 to win.
The previous scores of two of the team are shown.

Philip	47	31	34	44	42	41	32	49	39	55	48	60
Mairi	37	34	35	35	38	33	37	33	34	38	35	37

Which player should the team leader name to go up to play to make their chances of winning as good as it can be? Give reasons.

7 A 44-year-old teacher takes ten students (each 16 years old) and his 4-year-old son on an excursion one Saturday.
  a What is the mean age of the group?
  b What is the range in ages?
  c When the teacher and his son go home what is
    i the mean age   **ii** the range in ages
    of the group that is left?
  d What do you think is meant by saying that the range is sensitive to very small changes?

5 The median and quartiles

In Chapter 6 another average, the **median**, was introduced.
To find the median, the data list is first put in numerical order.
The median is the score that splits this list into two smaller lists of equal length.
If the original list has an odd number of members then the median is the middle number in the list.
If the original list has an even number of members then there will be two middle numbers and the median will be the mean of these two numbers.

The **quartiles** were also described.
The lower quartile splits the list below the median into half and is denoted by Q_1.
The upper quartile splits the list above the median into half and is denoted by Q_3.
The median itself is denoted by Q_2.

The quartiles can be used to give another measure of how the data set is spread out.

> The **interquartile range** = $Q_3 - Q_1$

This is less affected by small changes in the data set, unlike the range (see question **7** opposite).
Sometimes the semi-interquartile range is used:

$$SIQR = \frac{Q_3 - Q_1}{2}$$

Example   The cost of a calculator is found in several different shops:

£6, £6, £6·50, £7, £7, £7·50, £7·50, £8·50, £8·50,£9, £9, £10, £10, £11.

a State the median and quartiles.
b Calculate the semi-interquartile range of the prices.

a There are 14 scores.
The two middle scores are £7·50 and £8·50.
The median is (£7·50 + £8·50) ÷ 2 = £8.
The list below the median has 7 items.
The lower quartile Q_1 = £7.
The list above the median has 7 items.
The upper quartile Q_3 = £9.

b The $SIQR = \dfrac{Q_3 - Q_1}{2} = \dfrac{9 - 7}{2} = 1$

Exercise 5.1

1 For each data set find the median and quartiles.
   a 1, 1, 2, 2, 3, 3, 3, 3, 4, 5, 6, 7, 8, 8, 11
   b 2·7, 3·6, 5·7, 5·8, 5·9, 6·0, 7·0, 10·2, 12·0, 12·0
   c 125, 128, 131, 137, 139, 140, 143, 147, 152
   d 712, 734, 736, 756, 781, 799, 884, 900
   e 10, 7, 5, 24, 8, 12, 13, 27, 35, 36, 12, 11, 42, 4
   (The list needs to be ordered.)

2 Calculate the semi-interquartile range of each data set.
   a 12 kg, 17 kg, 20 kg, 24 kg, 29 kg, 31 kg, 33 kg, 36 kg, 40 kg, 41 kg, 47 kg, 51 kg
   b 243 m, 254 m, 257 m, 259 m, 264 m, 266 m, 278 m, 278 m, 279 m, 281 m
   c 0·45 s, 0·08 s, 0·21 s, 0·62 s, 0·48 s, 0·55 s, 0·09 s, 0·13 s, 0·26 s
   d £72, £98, £81, £65, £88, £24, £33, £75, £70, £63, £81, £64, £60, £89, £90

3 When the number of pieces of data is large, a stem-and-leaf diagram is useful for putting it in order.
Here are the prices, in pounds, of a particular toaster at different outlets.

```
21   28   57   39   51
46   34   22   11   38
35   35   33   30   38
58   31   56   37   28
29   34   34   58   39
```

a Use a stem-and leaf diagram to sort the data.

b Find the median and quartiles.

c Calculate
   i   the range
   ii the semi-interquartile range.

d The price of one more toaster is added to the list. It is £65.
   i   Calculate the new range and semi-interquartile range.
   ii Which one is most affected by the addition of one piece of data?

4 Nineteen students took a test.
The percentage results are:

18, 20, 23, 32, 40, 41, 42, 48, 51, 52, 53, 55, 57, 58, 60, 72, 80, 84, 90.

a Find the median and quartiles of the distribution of marks.

b Calculate the semi-interquartile range.

c A score is considered exceptional when it is three times the SIQR or more beyond the median. Which of the scores are exceptionally
   i   large   (Exceptional score $> Q_2 + 3 \times$ SIQR)
   ii small? (Exceptional score $< Q_2 - 3 \times$ SIQR)

5 Some market research into personal stereos is undertaken.
By considering several features each machine is awarded a percentage score.
Fourteen machines were examined with the following results:

38, 40, 46, 48, 48, 48, 49, 51, 56, 57, 58, 64, 68, 77.

a Calculate the median and quartiles.

b Calculate the semi-interquartile range.

c The people doing the research award 'stars' to machines according to these rules.
   5 stars: score $\geq Q_2 + 3 \times$ SIQR
   4 stars: $Q_2 + 1 \times$ SIQR $\leq$ score $< Q_2 + 3 \times$ SIQR
   3 stars: $Q_2 - 1 \times$ SIQR $\leq$ score $< Q_2 + 1 \times$ SIQR
   2 stars: $Q_2 - 3 \times$ SIQR $\leq$ score $< Q_2 - 1 \times$ SIQR
   1 star: score $< Q_2 - 3 \times$ SIQR
   Turn each score into a 'star award'.

Using a frequency table

In Chapter 6 we saw how to add a cumulative frequency column to a frequency table. This can be used to help you find Q_1, Q_2 and Q_3.

Example   The frequency table shows the distribution of heights in a class.
A cumulative frequency column has been added and a column of notes.

Height (cm)	Frequency	Cumulative frequency	Notes
160	1	1	1 person is 160 cm or less
161	4	5	5 persons are 161 cm or less
162	6	11	11 persons are 162 cm or less
163	8	19	19 persons are 163 cm or less
164	7	26	26 persons are 164 cm or less
165	3	29	29 persons are 165 cm or less
166	1	30	30 persons are 166 cm or less

Use the table to help you find the median, quartiles and SIQR.

A graph is drawn of cumulative frequency against height (cm).

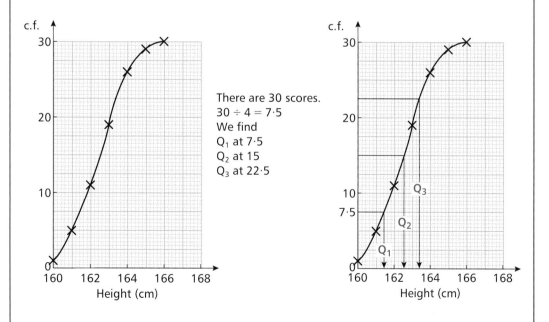

There are 30 scores.
$30 \div 4 = 7 \cdot 5$
We find
Q_1 at $7 \cdot 5$
Q_2 at 15
Q_3 at $22 \cdot 5$

From the graph we estimate $Q_1 = 161 \cdot 5$, $Q_2 = 162 \cdot 5$, $Q_3 = 163 \cdot 5$ and the SIQR = 1.

Exercise 5.2

1 For each frequency table
  i add a cumulative frequency column
  ii draw a cumulative frequency graph
  iii use it to find the median, quartiles and SIQR.

a

Score	Frequency
5	6
10	8
15	6
20	10
25	7
30	3

b

Score	Frequency
10	1
20	5
30	7
40	6
50	4
60	1

c

Score	Frequency
100	5
150	8
200	14
250	12
300	10
350	7

2 The table shows the findings of a survey into the prices (in pounds) of second-hand bikes.
  a Draw a cumulative frequency curve using the data.
  b Use your curve to help you estimate the median and quartiles.
  c Calculate the semi-interquartile range.
  d We would consider a price more than 3 SIQRs above the median as excessively expensive.
    What price is this?
  e A real bargain is more than 3 SIQRs below the median.
    Are any of the prices real bargains?

Cost	Frequency
120	1
125	4
130	12
135	16
140	3
145	1

3 The weights of 50 apples were recorded in grams. A cumulative frequency diagram was constructed.
  a Read the median value.
  b Read the lower quartile (Q_1).
  c Read the upper quartile (Q_3).
  d Calculate the interquartile range ($Q_3 - Q_1$).
  e Calculate the semi-interquartile range.
  f One particular apple in the sample weighs 100 g.
    Compare this weight to the rest of the sample.

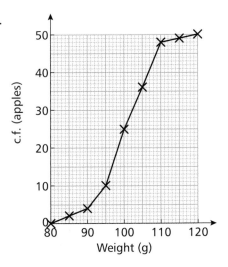

4 Simon was clocking up the kilometres on
his bike for charity.
A cumulative frequency diagram is plotted of his
progress over 60 days.
a i What is a quarter of 60?
ii Read the median distance.
b Read the lower and upper quartiles.
c Calculate the interquartile range.
d Calculate the semi-interquartile range.
e Draw a box plot to illustrate the distribution
of distances covered.
f One day he cycled 16 km.
How does this compare with his performance
in general?

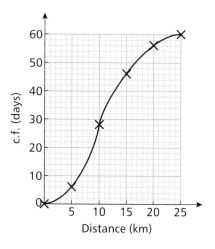

5 The scores of the top 30 candidates in
mathematics last year and this year are
to be compared. Cumulative frequency
curves for both groups are made on the
same grid.
a Read the median score for each group.
b Read the lower and upper quartiles
and calculate the interquartile range
and semi-interquartile range.
c Draw box plots for both years.
d Assuming both sets of pupils were of
equal ability, comment on the difficulty
level of the exams.

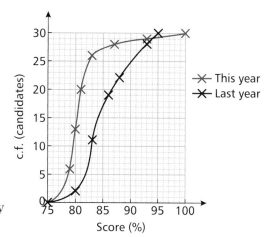

6 An agriculture research lab claims to have produced a pest-resistant cabbage.
An experiment is set up. Two test beds are each sown with 200 plants.
At the height of the season the number of pests on each plant is noted.

Pest-resistant

Pests/plant	1	2	3	4	5	6	7	8	9	10
Frequency	0	10	10	10	20	30	40	30	30	20

Non pest-resistant

Pests/plant	1	2	3	4	5	6	7	8	9	10
Frequency	5	15	25	30	30	20	10	5	20	40

a Construct cumulative frequency diagrams for both tables.
b Find the median number of pests per plant for each type.
c Calculate the interquartile range of each.
d Would you say that the lab's claim is reasonable? Why?

6 Standard deviation

We have seen the range, based on only the highest and lowest score, is sensitive to a change in either.
We see that the semi-interquartile range is less affected by the changing of a single piece of data, but it still only uses two pieces of the data set.
A measure of spread which uses all the data is the **standard deviation**.
The deviation of a score is how much that score differs from the mean.

Example 1 Find the standard deviation of: 9 cm, 12 cm, 15 cm, 19 cm, 20 cm.

	Score	Deviation (score − mean)	(Deviation)^2
	9	−6	36
	12	−3	9
	15	0	0
	19	4	16
	20	5	25
Totals	75	0	86

Step 1: Calculate the mean ... $75 \div 5 = 15$ cm.
Step 2: Calculate the deviations (score − mean).
If we tried to find the mean of the deviations we would get an unhelpful 0.
Step 3: Square the deviations. (These are all positive.)
Step 4: Add the squared deviations and divide by the number of scores (to give the mean square deviation) ... $86 \div 5 = 17 \cdot 2$ cm^2.
Whatever the units of the original scores, this value must be in squared units.
Step 5: Take the square root (to return to the original units).
The standard deviation $= \sqrt{17 \cdot 2} = 4 \cdot 1$ cm (to 1 d.p.).

When the standard deviation is low, it means the scores are close to the mean.
When it is high, it means the scores are spread out from the mean.

Exercise 6.1

1 Five pots of homemade jam are weighed. The weights are 201 g, 216 g, 219 g, 221 g, 223 g.
   a Confirm that the mean weight of a pot is 216 g.
   b Copy and complete the table.
   c Find the mean square deviation. (Hint: the mean of the last column)
   d Calculate the standard deviation (to 2 d.p.).

Weight (g)	Deviation (score − mean)	(Deviation)^2
201		
216		
219		
221		
223		
Totals		

2 a The number of students absent from school each day for one week was noted as

85, 94, 95, 96, 100.

  i Calculate the mean number of absences per day.
  ii Calculate the standard deviation of the absences (to 1 d.p.).

  b The next week the figures were 82, 83, 93, 100, 102.
  i   Calculate this week's mean.
  ii Calculate the standard deviation (to 1 d.p.).
  iii Which week had the bigger mean?
  iv Which week was more variable?

---

7 The standard deviation from a sample

A class activity

The 100 employees of Supa Savers Supermarket all live within a 20 km radius of the store.
The table below gives the actual distances correct to the nearest kilometre.
The standard deviation has been calculated as 5·84 km.

Second random number

	0	1	2	3	4	5	6	7	8	9
0	19	2	10	2	3	19	9	1	12	10
1	13	14	1	14	6	1	20	6	14	15
2	20	8	18	16	9	15	8	16	8	6
3	13	2	16	17	1	8	10	6	13	5
4	13	5	17	7	19	18	3	16	19	8
5	13	16	18	20	13	11	6	2	7	15
6	3	6	3	15	4	16	19	10	16	5
7	11	6	13	4	9	19	19	17	6	1
8	8	15	14	13	11	5	16	7	1	17
9	10	1	12	18	6	18	6	4	16	19

First random number (row labels). Standard deviation = 5·84

It costs time and money to collect this complete set of data.
It would be cheaper to just take a sample.

How is the standard deviation of the sample related to the standard deviation of the population?

1 Set your calculator to FIX mode with 0 decimal places.
2 RAND $\times$ 10 = will generate a random number between 0 and 9.
3 Use this method to generate a pair of random numbers.
  Use the pair as coordinates to help you to pick out one of the distances above.
4 Repeat this to collect a sample of six distances.

5 Calculate the standard deviation of the six distances using the formula:

$$\sqrt{\frac{\text{sum of squared deviations}}{n}}$$

6 Now use the formula: $\sqrt{\dfrac{\text{sum of squared deviations}}{n-1}}$

Try this several times. Average the results of your trials.

Over many trials you should find that, on average, the second formula provides a better estimate for the standard deviation of the whole set of numbers.

For the rest of the chapter we will assume we are always working with a sample and therefore will always work with the second formula.

When you find the mean (sum of scores ÷ n) and standard deviation in this manner, you are also finding an estimate for the mean and standard deviation of the underlying population.

Notation
When dealing with samples, the following symbols are fairly standard.

n ... the number of pieces of data in the sample

x ... this is used to represent a typical piece of data in the sample

$\bar{x}$ ... read as 'x bar', the mean of the sample

s ... the standard deviation of the sample

Σ ... pronounced sigma, this stands for the phrase 'the sum of',
e.g. Σx represents 'the sum of the x values', i.e. the sum of the data.

Using this notation our formulae become:

i for the mean: $\bar{x} = \dfrac{\Sigma x}{n}$

ii for the standard deviation: $\sqrt{\dfrac{\Sigma(x-\bar{x})^2}{n-1}}$

Note that $\Sigma(x-\bar{x})^2$ means the sum of the squared deviations.

When working with real data, and rounding as you calculate, this formula can lead to a build-up of relatively large errors. The formula can be rearranged to a form which is:

- more convenient for calculation
- doesn't require that the mean be calculated first
- cuts down the rounding error.

This form is often referred to as the 'one-pass' formula:

$$s = \sqrt{\frac{\Sigma x^2 - \frac{(\Sigma x)^2}{n}}{n-1}}$$

Example   Find the standard deviation of the data: 1, 3, 3, 4, 5, 5, 6, 7, 7, 7.

x	x^2
1	1
3	9
3	9
4	16
5	25
5	25
6	36
7	49
7	49
7	49
$\sum x = 48$	$\sum x^2 = 268$

$$s = \sqrt{\frac{\sum x^2 - \frac{(\sum x)^2}{n}}{n-1}}$$

$$\Rightarrow s = \sqrt{\frac{\left(268 - \frac{48^2}{10}\right)}{9}}$$

$$\Rightarrow s = 2{\cdot}04 \text{ to 2 d.p.}$$

Exercise 7.1

1 The contents in a sample of ten tubes of sun cream are measured.
   The results are: 150 ml, 152 ml, 154 ml, 154 ml, 155 ml,
                    155 ml, 156 ml, 156 ml, 157 ml, 157 ml.
   Calculate: **a** the mean volume
                   b the standard deviation correct to 1 d.p.

2 A machine in a factory is stamping out components.
   The quality controller counts the number of rejects per minute made by the machine:

   3, 4, 5, 5, 6, 8, 10, 11.

   a i   Calculate the mean number of rejects per minute.
   ii   Calculate the standard deviation (to 1 d.p.).
   b The machine is stopped and adjusted.
   Again a record is kept of the number of rejects per minute:

   5, 6, 6, 6, 7, 7, 7, 8.

   i Calculate the mean and standard deviation.
   ii Has the mean improved?
   iii Has the machine's consistency improved?

3 On 21 June the Arctic Circle enjoys 24 hours of daylight. At 49° N there are 16 hours
   of daylight; at the equator 12 hours; at 49° S 8 hours; at the Antarctic Circle 0 hours.
   Use this sample to estimate the mean and standard deviation number of hours of
   daylight.

4 The number of feral cats in various city centres was counted in a survey:

10, 14, 20, 25, 28, 36, 67.

  a Calculate:
    i the range
    ii the semi-interquartile range
    iii the sample standard deviation.

  b A year later a second survey was done with these results:

9, 16, 19, 26, 30, 42, 72.

  Calculate the new:
    i range
    ii semi-interquartile range
    iii sample standard deviation.

  c Which measure of spread was affected most by the small changes in the data?

5 The number of pondskaters at various sites on a loch is counted:

33, 43, 77, 79, 81, 81, 89, 91.

  a Calculate (to 1 d.p.): **i** the mean **ii** the standard deviation.

  b These insects are sensitive to pollution. To examine the effects of a chemical spillage a second survey is done with the following results:

29, 41, 62, 69, 73, 77, 79, 81.

  Calculate (to 1 d.p.) the new **i** mean **ii** standard deviation.

  c **i** By how much is the mean altered?
    ii Comment on the effect of the spillage.

Using a calculator

Check how to put your calculator into STAT mode.
It is good practice to clear all memories.

Example   You wish to enter the list of numbers: 3, 4, 5, 6, 6, 7, 7, 8, 8, 9.

This is done using the M+ or Data key:
   3 M+ 4 M+ 5 M+ 6 M+ 6 M+ 7 M+ 7 M+ 8 M+ 8 M+ 9

Now if you wish to know how many pieces of data are entered press n … you will be told 10.
If you wish to know the sum of the data then press Σx … the answer is 63.
If you wish to know the sum of the squared data then press Σx^2 … the answer is 429.
If you wish to know the mean then press $\bar{x}$ … the answer is 6·3.
If you wish to know the standard deviation (sample) then the key may be s or σ_{n-1} or s_x … the answer is 1·89 (to 2 d.p.).

Exercise 7.2

1 True Fit make shoes.
To control the quality of their product, they select samples of
100 pairs and look for flaws.
The number of flaws for each batch are:

  5, 6, 4, 7, 3, 7, 4, 3, 5, 8, 5, 5, 3, 4, 4.

  a Calculate the mean number of flaws per batch.
  b Calculate the standard deviation.
  c If the standard deviation is greater than 2, the process of
  making the shoes has to be improved.
  What do the results of these samples suggest should happen?

2 The fuse in a light fitting is set to blow at 3 amps.
When tested, a batch of fuses blew at the following readings:

  2·8, 2·9, 2·9, 2·9, 3·0, 3·0, 3·1, 3·2, 3·3, 3·3.

  a Calculate
    i   the mean
    ii   the standard deviation (to 2 d.p.).
  b The mean should be 3 ± 0·1 amp and the standard deviation should
  be less than 0·2 amp. What does this sample suggest?

3 A firm tests the life of its batteries.
The number of hours for which they supply power is noted.
These times are:

  200, 206, 192, 201, 196, 192, 195, 205, 202, 194,
  200, 193, 199, 202, 193, 192, 204, 208, 203, 190.

  a Calculate
    i   the mean life of a battery
    ii   the standard deviation (to 1 d.p.).
  b If the mean life is within 2 hours of the advertised life of 200 hours, and the
  standard deviation is less than 5 hours, then the batch of batteries from which the
  sample is taken is pronounced good. If not, another sample must be taken.
  What happens here?

4 Two ski resorts keep a note of their snowfall in millimetres
over a fortnight of the season.

Glen Flow   7   16   17   18   18   20   20   20   21   21   22   23   23   24
Bendhui   8   9   9   10   14   14   15   18   18   20   20   25   27   30

  a Calculate the mean and standard deviation (to 1 d.p.)
  for both resorts.
  b If it is a case of the more snow the better, which of the resorts
  would you be likely to pick?

8 Probability

Probability is a measure of how likely an event is to happen.
One could use terms like 'impossible', 'very unlikely', 'unlikely', 'just as likely as it is unlikely', 'likely', 'very likely', 'certain'. In mathematics we like to be more precise.

The likelihood of every event is placed on a scale which goes from 1 (certain) to 0 (impossible).
To help us place events on the scale the following definition is used.

> If all outcomes are equally likely, the probability that E will occur is:
>
> $$P(E) = \frac{\text{number of ways } E \text{ can occur}}{\text{total number of outcomes}}$$

Example 1   A coin is tossed. What is the probability that it will come up heads?
Two things can happen (and they are equally likely), H or T.
Only one of these ways gives heads, H, so

$$P(\text{heads}) = \tfrac{1}{2}$$

Example 2   A pack of cards is cut. What is the probability that a king is selected?
There are 52 cards in a pack and each is equally likely to be picked.
There are 4 kings in the pack.

$P(\text{king}) = \tfrac{4}{52} = \tfrac{1}{13}$. This can also be expressed as a decimal, 0·077 (to 3 d.p.).

Exercise 8.1

1 Consider the standard pack of cards.
What is the probability of picking:
   a a red card   **b** a spade
   c the Jack of Spades   **d** a face card
   e a number divisible by 5?

2 Peter is trying to get three cards to make 21. He has 6♥ and 7♠.
   a How many cards are there left from which to pick?
   b How many cards will make his hand add up to 21?
   c What is his probability of being successful?

3 **a** What is the probability that:
       i   a day of the week selected at random has a T in its name?
       ii there is an 'R' in the month?
   b What us the probibility that a word selekted at random from this sentence has a spelling eror?

4 In a game, two dice are thrown and their scores added.
   a Copy and complete the following table to show all 36 things that can happen.
   b i How many ways can you get a total of 3?
     ii What is the probability of scoring 3?
   c Calculate:
     i P(total = 5) ii P(total = 6) iii P(total = 1)
   d What is:
     i P(total < 5) ii P(total < 11) iii P(total ⩽ 12)?

+	1	2	3	4	5	6
1	2	3	4	5		
2	3	4	5			
3	4	5				
4						
5						
6						12

5 In Tim's class there are 30 pupils. The ratio of girls to boys is 3 : 2.
   a How many of the class are
     i boys   ii girls?
   b If one pupil is selected at random, what is the probability that the pupil is
     i a boy   ii a girl?
   c The ratio of those taking school dinners to those not is 5 : 1.
     What is the probability that a pupil selected at random takes school dinners?

Estimating probability

The probability of an event can be estimated from a frequency table by using the **relative frequency**.

Example   64 boxes of matches were opened and their contents counted.
The frequency table shows the findings.

Score (number of matches)	Frequency	Relative frequencies
44	6	$\frac{6}{64} = \frac{3}{32}$
45	12	$\frac{12}{64} = \frac{3}{16}$
46	24	$\frac{24}{64} = \frac{3}{8}$
47	18	$\frac{18}{64} = \frac{9}{32}$
48	4	$\frac{4}{64} = \frac{1}{16}$
Total	64	$\frac{64}{64} = 1$

Using this table as a basis, estimate the probability that a box of matches contains:
   a 46 matches   b more than 46 matches.

A relative frequency column is added.
   a We see $\frac{24}{64} = \frac{3}{8}$ of the boxes held 46 matches. We use this as our estimate.
     P(number of matches = 46) = $\frac{3}{8}$
   b $\frac{22}{64}$ of the boxes held more than 46 matches.
     P(number of matches > 46) = $\frac{11}{32}$ = 0·34 (to 2 d.p.)

Exercise 8.2

1 Thirty hotels were surveyed. The number of 'stars' they merited was noted.
The table gives the findings.

Score (number of stars)	Frequency	Relative frequencies
1	6	
2	5	
3	12	
4	6	
5	1	
Total	30	

    a Copy the table and complete the relative frequency column.
    b Use this to estimate
      i P(No. of stars $= 1$)
      ii P(No. of stars $= 3$)
      iii P(No. of stars > 2)

2 The travel habits of bus passengers were surveyed.
The number of stops a passenger passes on his or her journey is noted.
The results are given in the table.
    a Estimate the probability that a passenger picked at random will be passing 4 stops.
    b Estimate:
      i P(No. of stops $= 2$)
      ii P(No. of stops > 3)
      iii P(No. of stops < 3)
      iv P(No. of stops $\leqslant 3$)
      v P($1 <$ No. of stops < 5)
      vi P($1 \leqslant$ No. of stops $\leqslant 5$)

Score (number of stops)	Frequency
1	15
2	12
3	6
4	5
5	2
Total	40

3 In a game it is possible to score 10, 20, 30, 40 or 50 points.
The table shows how the scoring went over several trials.
    a What is the most difficult score to get?
    b What is the probability of scoring
      i 10
      ii 50?
    c Estimate:
      i P(score < 30)
      ii P(score > 30)
      iii P($10 \leqslant$ score < 30)

Score	Frequency
10	10
20	5
30	1
40	10
50	24
Total	50

4 A computer was used to simulate a dice.
Here are several 'throws' made by the computer.
  a Make a frequency table of the data.
  b Calculate the actual probability of scoring
    i 6   **ii** more than 4.
  c Use your frequency table to estimate
    i P(6)   **ii** P(more than 4).
  d By comparing answers to **b** and **c** comment on
  how realistic the computer simulation is.

2	5	3	4	1	2	1	5
3	5	3	2	6	3	3	2
3	5	2	2	1	1	1	5
5	6	4	3	5	4	4	4
3	5	2	4	1	4	2	5
2	4	3	6	4	3	4	6
5	6	1	2	1	1	3	1

◀◀ **RECAP**

Data can be summarised by mentioning:
a an average score   **b** a measure of how spread out the data is.

Averages
● **mean** $\text{mean} = \dfrac{\text{total of the data}}{\text{number of pieces of data}}$

If a frequency table is used, then

$$\text{mean} = \frac{\text{total of the } fx \text{ column}}{\text{total of } f \text{ column}} = \frac{\Sigma fx}{\Sigma f}$$

● **mode**   The mode is the score with the highest frequency.

● **median**   When the data is sorted in order, the median is the score that splits the
list into two equal smaller lists.
When there is an odd number of scores, the median is the middle score.
When there is an even number of scores, the median is the mean of the
middle two scores.

The two smaller lists each have their own median.
These are called the lower and upper quartiles, Q_1 and Q_3.

Measures of spread
● **range**   range = highest score − lowest score

● **semi-interquartile range** $\text{SIQR} = \dfrac{Q_3 - Q_1}{2}$

● **standard deviation** for a sample $s = \sqrt{\dfrac{\Sigma(x - \bar{x})^2}{n - 1}}$

or a more convenient form, the 'one-pass' formula, $s = \sqrt{\dfrac{\Sigma x^2 - \frac{(\Sigma x)^2}{n}}{n - 1}}$

Measures of likelihood
● The **probability** of E happening $P(E) = \dfrac{\text{number of ways } E \text{ can happen}}{\text{total number of possible outcomes}}$
assuming all outcomes are equally likely.
● An estimation for $P(E)$, obtained from a frequency table, is the **relative frequency**
of E.

1 The table shows the ages of pupils at a meeting.
  a Calculate the mean age of the group to 2 d.p.
  b State the modal age of the group.

Age	Frequency
14	8
15	12
16	14
17	6

2 The thicknesses of different booklets are measured in centimetres:

  | 1 | 1 | 0·9 | 0·6 | 1 | 0·3 | 0·2 | 0·6 | 0·7 | 0·8 |
  | 0·1 | 0·5 | 0·1 | 0·8 | 0·1 | 0·4 | 1 | 0·4 | 0·7 | 0·9 |

  a Calculate **i** the mean thickness   **ii** the modal thickness.
  b What is the range of thicknesses?
  c Calculate the median and quartiles.
  d Calculate the semi-interquartile range.
  e Any thickness which is more than 3 SIQRs from the median is considered
    exceptional. Are there any exceptional results in our sample?

3 In a biology investigation, the heights of 30 low-lying
  weeds are measured.
  The table summarises the results.
  a Copy the table and add a cumulative frequency column.
  b Draw a cumulative frequency diagram and use it to
    estimate the median and quartiles of the distribution.
  c Estimate the semi-interquartile range.

Size (cm)	Frequency
5	1
6	4
7	10
8	8
9	6
10	1

4 The number of cars in a queue at traffic lights, just before
  they turn green, are counted:
        6, 3, 5, 5, 6, 3, 1, 3, 5, 6.
  a Calculate the mean number of cars in the queue.
  b Calculate the standard deviation.
  c Three standard deviations away from the mean is considered an exceptional case.
    Did any exceptionally long or short queues occur during observations?

5 A dice and a coin are thrown up in the air at the same time.
  a Copy and complete the table to help
    you list all possible outcomes.
  b What is the probability that:
    i   a head and a 6 occur together
    ii a tail and an even number occur?

	1	2	3	4	5	6
H	H1	H2				
T	T1					

6 The frequency table shows the results of a spelling test.
  Everyone scored between 5 and 10.

Score	5	6	7	8	9	10
Frequency	2	4	6	10	2	1

Estimate the probability that someone picked at random scored less than 8.

REVISE

13 Simultaneous equations

A Welshman, Robert Recorde (1510−58), invented the '=' sign.
He introduced it in a book written in 1557 called *The Whetstone of Witte*.
His reason for using two parallel lines was 'bicause noe 2 thynges can be moare equalle'.
Apart from being a mathematician he was also a Royal Physician, a Greek scholar and an astronomer.

1 REVIEW

◀◀ **Exercise 1.1**

1 Calculate
  a $5 + (-3)$ **b** $-5 + 3$ **c** $(-5) + (-3)$ **d** $(-5) - (-3)$ **e** $(-3) - (-5)$

2 Copy and complete this table:

x	−3	−2	−1	0	1	2	3
$3x$							
$x - 1$							
$4 - x$							
$2x + 4$							

3 **a** Draw a coordinate grid for values of x and y from −4 to +4.
  b Plot the points A(4, 2) and B(−2, −4). Draw the straight line AB.
  c Plot the points C(−4, 4) and D(4, −4). Draw the straight line CD.
  d Write down the coordinates of the point where AB meets CD.

4 Add these pairs of terms:
  a $4x$ **b** $3x$ **c** $-2x$ **d** $-5x$
     $\underline{x}$ $\underline{-2x}$ $\underline{3x}$ $\underline{-2x}$

5 Subtract these pairs of terms:
  a $5x$ **b** x **c** $-3x$ **d** $-2x$
     $\underline{4x}$ $\underline{3x}$ $\underline{2x}$ $\underline{-4x}$

6 Given $x = 3$, find the value of y if:
  a $y = 2x - 1$ **b** $y = -x + 2$ **c** $y = 3 - x$ **d** $y = -2 - 2x$

7 Given $y = -2$, find the value of x if:

   a $x = 3y$ **b** $x = -3y$ **c** $x = 3 + 2y$ **d** $x = -2 - 2y$

8 Remove brackets by multiplying terms:

   a $3(x + 4)$ **b** $2(x - 3)$ **c** $4(3x - 1)$ **d** $2(4 - 3x)$ **e** $-3(2 - 5x)$

9 Solve the following equations:

   a $4x = 8$ **b** $2x = -12$ **c** $4x = 3x + 2$ **d** $5x = 3x + 6$

   e $2y = 9 - y$ **f** $4y + 3 = 3y + 7$ **g** $5y - 7 = y - 5$ **h** $2y - 8 = 12 - 3y$

10 Sam is x years old. His mother is 3 times his age.

    Write down an expression for:

   a his mother's age

   b the difference between his mother's age and Sam's age.

11 Bags of sand weigh x kg. Bags of stone each weigh y kg.

    Jane buys 4 bags of sand and 6 bags of stone.

    Write down an expression for the total weight of the bags bought.

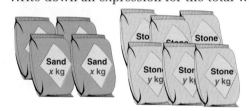

2 Solving simultaneous equations graphically

Example 1   The sum of two numbers is 6.

                 The difference of the two numbers is 2.

                 Find the two numbers.

Let the two numbers be x and y.

Two equations can be formed: $x + y = 6$ (or $y = x - 6$)

                       and $y - x = 2$ (or $y = x + 2$)

There are infinitely many pairs of numbers that make the first equation true. The table shows some of these.

$x + y = 6$

x	0	1	2	3	4	5	6
y	6	5	4	3	2	1	0

There are infinitely many pairs of numbers that make the second equation true. Again this table shows some.

$y - x = 2$

x	0	1	2	3	4
y	2	3	4	5	6

The question is 'Is there a pair of numbers which makes them both true at the same time?'

In the tables, each pair of numbers can be treated as a point.
Points can be joined so that the set of all possible solutions can be considered.
A point that lies on the graph of both tables must fit both equations.

The two sets of points are plotted.
When the points are joined they form two
straight lines.

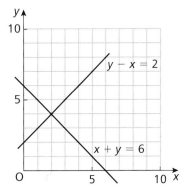

The lines cross at (2, 4) so $x = 2$, $y = 4$ is the
solution.
Check the values fit both descriptions:

$2 + 4 = 6$ ✓ and $4 - 2 = 2$ ✓

Note: the word simultaneously means 'at the same time'. When we try to find
numbers that make a set of equations all true at the same time, we are said to
be solving the equations simultaneously.
The equations are referred to as **simultaneous equations**.

Exercise 2.1

1 a Use the graph to help you solve this pair of
equations simultaneously:

$x + y = 5$ and $y = x + 1$

b Check that the solution fits both of the equations.

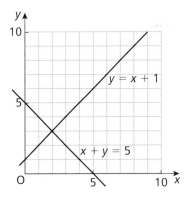

2 a Find the solution to this pair of equations:

$x + y = 6$ and $y = x - 3$

b Check that the solution fits each of the equations.

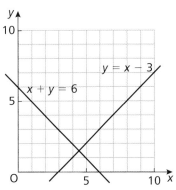

3 a For each equation copy and complete the table:

i $y = x$

x	0	1	2	3	4	5	6
y	0						

ii $x + y = 4$

x	0	1	2	3	4
y	4				

b On the same grid draw the graphs of the solutions to the two equations.

c Which numbers are solutions to both equations $y = x$ and $x + y = 4$?

d Check that the solution fits each of the equations.

4 a Copy and complete the tables for these equations:

i $y = x + 2$

x	0	1	2	3	4
y					

ii $y = 2x - 1$

x	1	2	3
y			

b Use graphs to help you write down the solutions to the simultaneous equations $y = x + 2$ and $y = 2x - 1$.

c Check that the solution fits each of the equations.

5 For the equations $y = 2x$ and $y = 6 - 2x$:

a make tables of values for $x = 0, 1, 2$ and 3

b plot the points and draw the lines (use scales from 0 to 6)

c write down the coordinates of the point where the lines cross

d check that these values for x and y fit both the equations.

6 For the equations $y = x + 1$ and $y = 4 - \dfrac{x}{2}$:

a make tables of values for $x = 0$ to $x = 6$

b plot the points and draw the lines

c write down the values of x and y where the lines cross

d check that the solution fits both equations.

Example 2

The sum of two numbers is 2. $x + y = 2$

The difference of the two numbers is 5. $y - x = 5$

Find the numbers.

$x + y = 2$

x	−3	−2	−1	0	1	2	3
y	5	4	3	2	1	0	−1

$y - x = 5$

x	−3	−2	−1	0	1	2	3
y	2	3	4	5	6	7	8

Note: the lines can be drawn by plotting a few points and extending the lines.

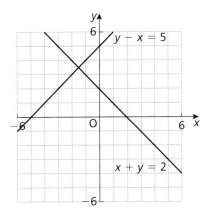

Lines seem to cross at $(-1.5, 3.5)$ so $x = -1.5$ and $y = 3.5$.
Check that the solution fits the pair of equations.
$x + y = -1.5 + 3.5 = 2$ ✓ $y - x = 3.5 - (-1.5) = 3.5 + 1.5 = 5$ ✓

Exercise 2.2

1 For each pair of equations:
  i draw graphs of solutions over the range suggested
  ii use your graphs to help you solve the pair of equations simultaneously
  iii check, by substitution, that the solution fits both equations.

  a $y = x - 2$ and $y = 1 - x$ $(-3 \leqslant x \leqslant 3)$
  b $y = x - 3$ and $y = 3x$ $(-6 \leqslant x \leqslant 6)$
  c $y = x + 3$ and $y = -2 - x$ $(-3 \leqslant x \leqslant 3)$
  d $y = 2x - 4$ and $y = -4 - x$ $(-6 \leqslant x \leqslant 6)$
  e $y = 2x + 3$ and $y = -x$ $(-3 \leqslant x \leqslant 3)$
  f $y = -3x$ and $y = 3 - x$ $(-6 \leqslant x \leqslant 6)$

3 Shortcuts

To quickly sketch the line which represents the solutions to the equation $y = ax + b$, we need only find two points to join. If possible, where $x = 0$ and where $y = 0$ are easy to find.

Example 1
Solve this pair of equations simultaneously: $x - 2y = 4$ and $x + 2y = -2$
For the equation $x - 2y = 4$:

  $x = 0 \Rightarrow -2y = 4 \Rightarrow y = -2 \Rightarrow (0, -2)$ is on the line.
  $y = 0 \Rightarrow x - 2 \times 0 = 4 \Rightarrow x = 4 \Rightarrow (4, 0)$ is on the line.

For the equation $x + 2y = -2$:

$x = 0 \Rightarrow$ $\quad 2y = -2 \Rightarrow y = -1 \Rightarrow (0, -1)$ is on the line.

$y = 0 \Rightarrow$ $\quad x + 2 \times 0 = -2 \Rightarrow x = -2 \Rightarrow (-2, 0)$ is on the line.

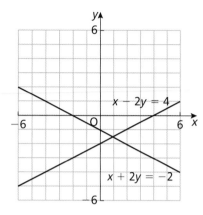

The lines appear to cross at $(1, -1.5)$.

Check: $\quad x - 2y = 4 \qquad 1 - 2 \times (-1.5) \Rightarrow 1 + 3 = 4$ ✓

$\qquad\qquad x + 2y = -2 \qquad 1 + 2 \times (-1.5) \Rightarrow 1 - 3 = -2$ ✓

The solution is $x = 1$ and $y = -1.5$.

Exercise 3.1

1 Solve each set of simultaneous equations graphically.

a $x - 2y = -6$ and $x + y = 6$ **b** $2x + y = 6$ and $2x - y = 0$

c $x + y = 6$ and $x - y = 4$ **d** $y = x$ and $x + y = -4$

e $x + y = 5$ and $3x - y = 3$ **f** $3x - y = 0$ and $x - y = 2$

g $2x - y = 3$ and $x - 2y = -6$ **h** $3x + 4y = 12$ and $x - 2y = -1$

i $2x + 2y = 3$ and $x + 2y = 5$ **j** $y = x + 2$ and $2x + y = -4$

k $y = 4x - 6$ and $y = 4 - x$ **l** $4x - y - 2 = 0$ and $4x + y + 6 = 0$

Brainstormers

1 Is there a solution to the pair of equations $2x - y = 6$ and $y = 2x - 4$?
Draw lines to help you look for a solution.
Explain what happens.

2 Can you find the pair of values for x and y that fits all three equations:
$y = x + 1$, $x + y = 4$ and $3y - x = 6$?

4 Solving simultaneous equations by substitution

It is often impractical to solve pairs of equations graphically. Algebraic methods must be found.

Example 1   Sam's Sunday newspaper costs three times as much as his daily paper.
The Sunday paper costs 90p more than the daily paper.
How much does each paper cost?

Cost of the daily paper $= x$ pence.
Cost of the Sunday paper $= y$ pence.

Clue 1 gives the equation: $y = 3x$ … A
Clue 2 gives the equation: $y = x + 90$ … B

Equation A tells us that $3x$ can be exchanged for y.
Substituting $y = 3x$ in equation B, $y = x + 90$, gives

$3x = x + 90$
$\Rightarrow 2x = 90$
$\Rightarrow \ x = 45$

Equation A tells us that $y = 3x$

$\Rightarrow y = 3 \times 45 = 135$

Check: $45 + 90 = 135$ (Use equation B to check the solution.)
The daily paper costs 45 pence and the Sunday paper costs 135 pence.
Note: using algebra rather than drawing graphs is quicker and more accurate.

Exercise 4.1

1 Solve each pair of simultaneous equations by substitution.

a $y = 2x$
$y = x + 2$

b $y = 3x$
$y = 2x + 2$

c $y = 2x + 1$
$y = x + 3$

d $y = 3x + 3$
$y = 2x + 4$

e $y = 2x$
$y = x + 6$

f $y = 4x$
$y = x + 15$

g $y = 3x$
$y = x - 8$

h $y = 2x + 3$
$y = x + 7$

i $y = 3x - 5$
$y = 2x + 8$

j $y = 4x - 1$
$y = 2x + 3$

k $y = 5x - 4$
$y = x - 16$

l $y = x - 7$
$y = 5 - x$

m $y = 3x - 5$
$y = -x - 3$

n $y = 4 - 2x$
$y = -4x - 1$

2 Don is twice as tall as his younger sister Donna.
He is 78 cm taller than her.
Let Donna's height $= x$ and Don's height $= y$.
a Form a pair of simultaneous equations.
b Solve them to find
    i Donna's   **ii** Don's height.

3 Wayne is 12 kg heavier than Wali.
If Wali's weight is subtracted from 100 kg, Wayne's weight is obtained.
Let Wali's weight $= x$ and Wayne's weight $= y$.
a Form a pair of simultaneous equations.
b Solve them to find:
   i Wali's   **ii** Wayne's weight.

Example 2   Solve this pair of equations simultaneously:

$$y = 2x - 5 \quad \dots \text{A}$$
$$2x + 3y = -7 \quad \dots \text{B}$$

Equation A tells us that y can be exchanged for $2x - 5$.
Substituting $y = 2x - 5$ in the second equation

$$\Rightarrow 2x + 3(2x - 5) = -7$$
$$\Rightarrow 2x + 6x - 15 = -7$$
$$\Rightarrow 8x = -7 + 15$$
$$\Rightarrow 8x = 8$$
$$\Rightarrow x = 1$$

Substituting this value for x in equation A

$$\Rightarrow y = 2 \times 1 - 5 = -3$$
$$\Rightarrow x = 1, y = -3 \text{ is the solution.}$$

Check in equation B that $2x + 3y = -7$

$$\Rightarrow 2 \times 1 + 3 \times (-3) = 2 - 9 = -7 \checkmark$$

Exercise 4.2

1 Solve these simultaneous equations by substitution.

a $y = 2x$
$x + y = 12$

b $y = 5x$
$x + y = -6$

c $y = x + 1$
$x + y = 11$

d $y = x - 1$
$x + y = 19$

e $y = 3x$
$x + 2y = -14$

f $y = x + 2$
$x + 2y = 16$

g $y = x - 1$
$x + 3y = 5$

h $y = x + 4$
$x - 2y = -11$

i $2x - y = 9$
$y = x - 5$

j $3x - 2y = 19$
$y = 3x - 17$

k $y = -2x$
$x - 3y = -14$

l $y = -5 - x$
$x - 3y = 9$

2 In each case,
  i rearrange the first equation into the form $y = \dots$
  ii solve the pair of equations.

a $x - y - 1 = 0$
$3y - 2x = 2$

b $y - 3x = 0$
$4x + y = -28$

c $2y + 4x - 1 = 0$
$x - y = 1$

3 Tim takes four times longer than Toni to get to school.
Tim's time is 45 minutes longer than Toni's.
Form a pair of simultaneous equations and solve them to find how long it takes:
a Toni   **b** Tim to get to school.

Brainstormers

1 In an exam, the percentage of questions Ken gets right is three times greater than the percentage he gets wrong.
   Form *two* simultaneous equations and solve them to find the percentage that are correct. (Hint: let the percentage wrong = x and the percentage correct = y.)

2 In the same exam the percentage of questions Kate gets right is seven times greater than the percentage she gets wrong.
   Form two equations and find the percentage she has correct.

5 Solving simultaneous equations by elimination

Solving equations by substitution can sometimes lead to awkward algebra.
An alternative method is called 'elimination'.

Example 1   The sum of a father's age and his son's age is 59.
   The difference between their ages is 31.
   How old is each person?
   Note that if $P = Q$ and $R = S$ then $P + R = Q + S$.
   Let the father's age be x years and the son's age be y years.
   Construct two equations:

$$x + y = 59 \quad \dots \text{A}$$
$$x - y = 31 \quad \dots \text{B}$$

Since $x + y$ is equal to 59 and $x - y$ is equal to 31, then by addition:

$$(x + y) + (x - y) = 59 + 31$$
$$\Rightarrow \quad x + y + x - y = 90$$
$$\Rightarrow \quad 2x = 90$$
$$\Rightarrow \quad x = 45$$

Put $x = 45$ in equation A, $x + y = 59$,

$$\Rightarrow 45 + y = 59 \quad \Rightarrow y = 59 - 45 = 14$$

Check: $x - y = 31 \Rightarrow 45 - 14 = 31 \checkmark$
The father is 45 and his son is 14 years old.

Example 2   Solve $3x + y = 8$ and $x + y = 2$.
   Note that if $P = Q$ and $R = S$ then $P - R = Q - S$.
   We can see that if the second equation is subtracted from the first then y will be eliminated:

$$(3x + y) - (x + y) = 8 - 2$$
$$\Rightarrow \quad 3x + y - x - y = 6$$
$$\Rightarrow \quad 2x = 6$$
$$\Rightarrow \quad x = 3$$

Substitute $x = 3$ in $x + y = 2$ (choosing one of the equations)

$$\Rightarrow 3 + y = 2 \quad \Rightarrow y = 2 - 3 = -1$$

Solution is $x = 3$, $y = -1$.
Check the solution in the other equation:
$3x + y = 8 \Rightarrow 3 \times 3 + (-1) = 9 - 1 = 8 \checkmark$

Exercise 5.1

1 Solve each pair of equations simultaneously by adding them.
  a $x + y = 9$ and $x - y = 1$
  b $x + y = 7$ and $x - y = 3$
  c $a + b = 2$ and $a - b = 6$
  d $c + 2d = 8$ and $3c - 2d = 0$

2 Solve each pair of equations simultaneously by subtracting them.
  a $2x + y = 9$ and $x + y = 5$
  b $3x + y = 15$ and $x + y = 9$
  c $2e + f = 5$ and $e + f = 3$
  d $4g - 3h = 16$ and $2g - 3h = 2$

3 Solve each pair of simultaneous equations by adding or subtracting to eliminate one of the variables.
  a $3x + y = 1$ and $x + y = 3$
  b $2x + y = 12$ and $x - y = 3$
  c $3x - y = 6$ and $2x - y = 6$
  d $3p + 2q = 7$ and $p + 2q = 1$
  e $3m - 2n = -1$ and $3m + 2n = -29$
  f $u - v = -2$ and $3u - v = -8$ (subtract first equation from second)
  g $4s + 3t = 9$ and $2s + 3t = 3$
  h $5w + 4z = -13$ and $6w - 4z = 2$
  i $2i - 5j = 4$ and $4i - 5j = -2$

Example 3   Solve $x + y = 11$ and $3x - 2y = 18$ simultaneously.

Note that:
- neither addition nor subtraction eliminates a variable
- if $P = Q$ then $a \times P = a \times Q$ for any number a
- if $x + y = 11$ is doubled to get $2x + 2y = 22$, then added to $3x - 2y = 18$, y will be eliminated.

A typical layout to the problem:

$$x + y = 11 \qquad \dots \text{A}$$
$$3x - 2y = 18 \qquad \dots \text{B}$$

$$\begin{array}{lll} \text{A} \times 2: & 2x + 2y = 22 & \dots \text{C} \\ \text{B}: & 3x - 2y = 18 & \\ \hline \text{C} + \text{B}: & 5x \qquad = 40 & \\ \Rightarrow & x = 8 & \end{array}$$

Substituting $x = 8$ in equation A, $x + y = 11$,

$$\Rightarrow \qquad 8 + y = 11$$
$$\Rightarrow \qquad y = 3$$

The solution is $x = 8$, $y = 3$.
Check the solution in $3x - 2y = 18 \Rightarrow 3 \times 8 - 2 \times 3 = 24 - 6 = 18$ ✓

Exercise 5.2

1 Solve each pair of simultaneous equations.

    a $3x + 2y = 26$ **b** $3x + 2y = 26$ **c** $3x - y = 10$ ($\times 3$)
         $x - y = 2$ ($\times 2$) $x + y = 11$ ($\times 2$) $2x - 3y = 2$

    d $4x + 2y = 10$ **e** $3x - 2y = 10$ **f** $5x - 2y = 11$
         $x + y = 3$ $x + y = 5$ $x - y = 1$

    g $5a + 4b = 33$ **h** $2c + d = 3$ **i** $2e - 5f = 1$
         $a + 2b = 9$ $4c - 3d = 31$ $5e + f = 16$

    j $3g - 4h = 8$ **k** $2j - k = 9$ **l** $4m + 3n = -25$
         $2g - h = 7$ $4j + 3k = -7$ $5m + 6n = -38$

    m $2p + q = 14$ **n** $4s - t = 16$ **o** $5u - 8v = -14$
         $3p - 4q = -23$ $5s + 3t = 3$ $7u - 4v = 2$

2 Solve each pair of simultaneous equations.
    Rearrange the equations where necessary.

    a $4w - z = 1$ **b** $4x + 3y + 4 = 0$ **c** $8x = 3y - 11$
         $3z + 2w = 11$ $8x - 9y - 22 = 0$ $6y = 2x + 1$

---

6 More solutions by elimination

Example 1   Solve these simultaneous equations: $2x + 5y = -9$ and
                $5x - 3y = 24$.

              To eliminate y (or x) there must be the same quantity of y (or x)
              in both equations.
              To eliminate y:

                 $2x + 5y = -9$ ... A
                 $5x - 3y = 24$ ... B

                 A $\times$ 3: $6x + 15y = -27$ ... C
                 B $\times$ 5: $\underline{25x - 15y = 120}$ ... D
                 C + D: $\overline{31x \quad\quad = \quad 93}$

                 $\Rightarrow x = 3$

              Substituting $x = 3$ in equation A, $2x + 5y = -9$,

                 $\Rightarrow 2 \times 3 + 5y = -9$
                 $\Rightarrow \quad\quad 6 + 5y = -9$
                 $\Rightarrow \quad\quad\quad\quad 5y = -9 - 6$
                 $\Rightarrow \quad\quad\quad\quad 5y = -15$
                 $\Rightarrow \quad\quad\quad\quad\quad y = -3$

              The solution is $x = 3$, $y = -3$.

              Check the solution in $5x - 3y = 24 \Rightarrow 5 \times 3 - 3 \times (-3) = 15 + 9 = 24$ ✓

Exercise 6.1

Solve each pair of simultaneous equations.

1 $5x + 2y = 9$ $(\times 3)$
   $2x + 3y = 8$ $(\times 2)$

2 $3x + 5y = 22$ $(\times 2)$
   $5x - 2y = 16$ $(\times 5)$

3 $7x - 4y = 2$ $(\times 3)$
   $5x - 6y = -8$ $(\times 2)$

4 $3x + 2y = 7$
   $2x + 3y = 8$

5 $x + 3y = 6$
   $3x - 4y = 5$

6 $5x - 3y = 19$
   $3x - 2y = 11$

7 $5a + 2b = 17$
   $2a + 3b = 9$

8 $2m + 3n = -1$
   $5m - 4n = 9$

9 $3p - 4q = -10$
   $4p - 5q = -13$

10 $2r - 9s = -5$
   $5r + 6s = 16$

11 $5u - 3v = 12$
   $7u - 2v = 19$

12 $3c - 2d = -2$
   $4c + 7d = 36$

13 $3g - 2h = 12$
   $7g - 5h = 29$

14 $4i + 7j = -2$
   $5i + 2j = 11$

15 $7s - 3t = -5$
   $5s + 4t = -22$

Example 2   Solve this pair of simultaneous equations:

$$3y = -1 - 4x \qquad \ldots \text{A}$$
$$5y + 6x + 2 = 0 \qquad \ldots \text{B}$$

Rearrange the equations:

$$4x + 3y = -1 \qquad \ldots \text{A}$$
$$6x + 5y = -2 \qquad \ldots \text{B}$$

$\text{A} \times 5$: $20x + 15y = -5$ $\ldots \text{C}$
$\text{B} \times 3$: $18x + 15y = -6$ $\ldots \text{D}$
$\text{C} - \text{D}$: $\quad 2x \qquad\quad = 1$

$$\Rightarrow x = \tfrac{1}{2}$$

Substituting $x = \tfrac{1}{2}$ in equation A, $3y = -1 - 4x$,

$$\Rightarrow 3y = -1 - 4 \times \tfrac{1}{2} = -1 - 2 = -3$$
$$\Rightarrow y = -1$$

The solution is $x = \tfrac{1}{2}$, $y = -1$.

Check the solution in

$$5y + 6x + 2 = 0 \Rightarrow 5 \times (-1) + 6 \times \tfrac{1}{2} + 2 = -5 + 3 + 2 = 0 \ \checkmark$$

Exercise 6.2

Find the solution to each pair of equations.

1 $2a + 5b = 11$
   $3a - 4b = -18$

2 $3c - 4d = 4$
   $5c + 6d = 13$

3 $5e - 3f = 2$
   $9e + 2f = -26$

4 $3g + 4h = -22$
   $7g - 6h = 10$

5 $4m + 15n = -7$
   $7m - 10n = 24$

6 $7i + 8j = -5$
   $9i + 10j = -7$

7 $5p = 12 + 4q$
   $7p = 6q + 18$

8 $3s = 8r - 13$
   $5s + 3r - 11 = 0$

9 $6t + 5u - 9 = 0$
   $2u - 9t + 42 = 0$

10 $y + x = 0$
   $1 - 4x = 6y$

11 $5k - 8z - 11 = 0$
   $27 = 7k + 12z$

12 $4 + 9v = 4w$
   $10w = 3 + 12v$

7 Choosing the best method

Example 1   Solve simultaneously: $y = x + 7$ and $3x + 4y = 14$.

$y = x + 7$ ... A

Since y is easily expressed in terms of x, substitution may be used here.

$3x + 4y = 14$ ... B

Replace y by $x + 7$ in equation B

$\Rightarrow 3x + 4(x + 7) = 14$
$\Rightarrow 3x + 4x + 28 = 14$
$\Rightarrow 7x = -14$
$\Rightarrow x = -2$

Substituting $x = -2$ in equation A, $y = x + 7$,
$\Rightarrow y = -2 + 7 = 5$

The solution is $x = -2$, $y = 5$.

Check the solution in
$3x + 4y = 14 \Rightarrow 3 \times (-2) + 4 \times 5 = -6 + 20 = 14$ ✓

Example 2   Solve the pair of equations $4x + 3y + 8 = 0$ and $3x - 5y = 23$ simultaneously.

$4x + 3y + 8 = 0$ ... A
$3x - 5y = 23$ ... B

It is awkward to express one variable in terms of the other so elimination is used here.

Rearrange each equation into the form $ax + by = c$:

$4x + 3y = -8$ ... A
$3x - 5y = 23$ ... B

A $\times$ 5: $20x + 15y = -40$ ... C
B $\times$ 3: $9x - 15y = 69$ ... D
C + D: $29x \qquad = 29$

$\Rightarrow x = 1$

Substituting $x = 1$ in equation A, $4x + 3y + 8 = 0$,
$\Rightarrow 4 \times 1 + 3y + 8 = 0$
$\Rightarrow 3y = -12$
$\Rightarrow y = -4$

The solution is $x = 1$, $y = -4$.

Check the solution in
$3x - 5y = 23 \Rightarrow 3 \times 1 - 5 \times (-4) = 3 + 20 = 23$ ✓

Exercise 7.1

Solve these pairs of simultaneous equations by the most suitable method.

1 $x - y = 1$
$x + y = 11$

2 $y = 2x$
$x + y = 9$

3 $2x + y = 10$
$3x + y = 14$

4 $y = 3x$
$2x + y = -5$

5 $x + y = -1$
$x - y = -9$

6 $y = x + 2$
$x + 2y = 25$

7 $2x + 5y = -6$
$x + y = 0$

8 $3x - 4y = 14$
$5x - 3y = 27$

9 $y = 2x + 8$
$x - y = -5$

10 $2y = 7x + 12$
$3x - 2y = -4$

11 $4x - 5y = -22$
$3x + 2y = -5$

12 $5x - 6y = 20$
$8x - 9y = 29$

13 $y = 3x - 14$
$x - 2y = 13$

14 $4x = 13 + 7y$
$6x = 8y + 17$

15 $4x + 3y = 3$
$8x - 9y - 1 = 0$

Challenges

1 Choose any two values for x and y, and make up a pair of simultaneous equations which can be solved to give your chosen values of x and y.
Check the solution.
Then make up another pair of equations with the same solution, and check again.

2 Solve the simultaneous equations $y = 5 - x$ and $y = 2x + 14$ by all three methods – graphical, substitution and elimination.

8 Using simultaneous equations to find formulae

Example   The cost ($£C$) of hiring a Mad Mountain Bike is related to the number of days hire (n days) by a formula of the form $C = an + b$.
Dave hired a bike for 6 days at a total cost of £54.
Davina paid £38 for 4 days.
Find the values of a and b and write down the equation expressing C in terms of n.

Clue 1 gives: $54 = 6a + b$ ... A
Clue 2 gives: $38 = 4a + b$ ... B

A − B: $16 = 2a$
$\Rightarrow a = 8$

Substituting $a = 8$ in equation A
$\Rightarrow 54 = 6 \times 8 + b$
$\Rightarrow b = 6$
$\Rightarrow C = 8n + 6$

Exercise 8.1

1 Two variables are connected by a formula of the form $Q = aP + b$.
When $P = 2$, $Q = 11$.
When $P = 3$, $Q = 14$.
The first clue leads to the equation $11 = 2a + b$.
a Write down the equation that can be formed using clue 2.
b Solve the pair of equations for a and b.
c Express Q in terms of P.

2 G is related to T by a formula of the form $G = aT + b$.
When $T = 2$, $G = 10$. When $T = 4$, $G = 14$.
a Form a pair of simultaneous equations in a and b.
b Solve the equations for a and b.
c Express G in terms of T.

3 K is related to M by a formula of the form $K = aM + b$.
When $M = -1$, $K = 5$.
When $M = 4$, $K = -5$.
Express K in terms of M.

4 It is known that x is related to y by the equation $y = ax + b$ where a and b are constants.
An experiment has shown that when $x = 11$, $y = 9$ and when $x = 3$, $y = 1$.
Find the equation connecting y and x.

5 Lovely Lakes issue fishing permits by the hour.
The equation for the cost (£C) of a permit for n hours is of the form

$C = an + b$.

It costs Rod £12 to fish for 6 hours. Sally pays £9 for 4 hours.
a Form a pair of simultaneous equations.
b Solve the equations.
c Write down the equation connecting C and n.

6 Perfect Plumbers have a call-out charge plus an hourly rate.
The formula $C = an + b$ is used to calculate the bill.
£C is the total bill and n is the number of hours.
A 9 hour job costs £160. A 6 hour job costs £115.
a Form a pair of simultaneous equations.
b Solve the equations.
c Write down the equation connecting C and n.
d What would the charge be for work which takes 5 hours?

7 The pressure, P, at depth x in the ocean is of the form $P = ax + b$.
At the surface (depth = 0) $P = 15$, and when $x = 60$, $P = 45$.
a Calculate a and b, and write down the equation connecting P and x.
b Estimate the pressure when $x = 80$.
c Why is $P = 15$ at the surface?

Challenge

On its first day of flowering, a Christmas cactus plant had three flowers.
Two more flowers opened the next day.
The total number of flowers, f, after n days is given by the
formula $f = an + b$, where a and b are numbers.

a i Check that for $n = 1$ and $f = 3$, $a + b = 3$.

ii Make another equation involving a and b.

iii Solve the two equations for a and b.

iv Complete the formula $f = \dots n + \dots$.

b If the plant first flowered on 23 December, how many
flowers did it have on 1 January (assuming that none
had withered)?

9 Using simultaneous equations to solve problems

Example 1   3 bags of sand and 2 bags of cement weigh 91 kg.
4 bags of sand and 3 bags of cement weigh 124 kg.
Find the weight of one bag of **i** sand **ii** cement.

Let x = the weight of a bag of sand and y = the weight of a bag of cement.

Clue 1 lets us form the equation: $3x + 2y = 91$ ... A
Clue 2 lets us form the equation: $4x + 3y = 124$ ... B

$$
\begin{array}{lll}
\text{A} \times 3: & 9x + 6y = 273 & \dots \text{C} \\
\text{B} \times 2: & 8x + 6y = 248 & \dots \text{D} \\
\hline
\text{C} - \text{D}: & x \quad\quad = 25 &
\end{array}
$$

Substituting $x = 25$ in equation A, $3x + 2y = 91$,
$\Rightarrow 3 \times 25 + 2y = 91$
$\Rightarrow 2y = 91 - 75$
$\Rightarrow y = 8$

Explain the solution: the weights of the bags are sand 25 kg, cement 8 kg.

Exercise 9.1

1 Two posts laid end to end measure 12 metres.
One is 6 metres longer than the other.
Find the length of each post.

2 3 chews and 2 mints cost 15p.
5 chews and 1 mint cost 11p.
How much does: **a** a chew   **b** a mint cost?

3 Sally is 48 cm taller than her little sister.
The total of their heights is 242 cm.
How tall are the two girls?

4 Robert is 5 times Richard's age. The sum of their ages is 42. How old is:
  a Richard
  b Robert?

5 Two adult theatre tickets and three children's tickets cost £33. Three adult theatre tickets and four children's tickets cost £47. How much does
  a a child's
  b an adult's ticket cost?

6 One CD and three DVDs cost £41.
  Four CDs and two DVDs cost £54.
  Calculate the cost of:
  a a CD   **b** a DVD.

7 To make a bit of money Martin hires out his rowing boat and his motor boat.
  On one day when the rowing boat is hired for 6 hours and the motor boat for 5 hours he earns £59.
  On another day when the rowing boat is hired for 8 hours and the motor boat for 3 hours he earns £53.
  What is the hourly rate for hiring:
  a the rowing boat   **b** the motor boat?

Example 2   In a quiz, points are awarded for correct answers and deducted for incorrect answers.
The Red team score 60 points with 7 correct and 2 incorrect answers.
The Blue team score 65 points with 8 correct and 3 incorrect answers.
How are points awarded?

Let points for correct answers $= x$.
Let points deducted for incorrect answers $= y$.

Red team clue: $7x - 2y = 60$ ... A
Blue team clue: $8x - 3y = 65$ ... B

$$\begin{aligned} \text{A} \times 3:\ & 21x - 6y = 180 \\ \text{B} \times 2:\ & 16x - 6y = 130 \\ \hline \text{A} - \text{B}:\ & 5x\quad\ \ = 50 \end{aligned}$$

$\Rightarrow x = 10$

Substituting $x = 10$ in equation A, $7x - 2y = 60$,

$\Rightarrow 70 - 2y = 60$
$\Rightarrow 2y = 10$
$\Rightarrow y = 5$

Correct answers score 10 points; incorrect answers have 5 points deducted.

Exercise 9.2

Form pairs of equations and solve them to answer the following questions.

1 Finest Flours sell two sizes of bags of flour.
   The difference in their weights is 1 kg.
   Flora buys 4 large bags and 2 small bags of flour, total weight 13 kg.
   Calculate the weight of each type of bag.

2 Harbour High School hockey team have won three times
   more matches than they have drawn.
   Their points total is 40 (3 points for a win, 1 point for
   a draw).
   How many matches have they:
   a drawn   **b** won?

3 The difference between the length and breadth of a rectangular play area is 50 m.
   The perimeter is 200 m. Calculate the length and breadth.

4 In an Australian Rules football game, West scored 2 goals below the bar and 5 goals
   above the bar. East scored 3 below and 2 above.
   The final score was West 17, East 20.
   How many points are awarded for goals: **a** below **b** above the bar?

5 Three gym sessions with two discount vouchers cost £28.
   Five gym sessions with three discount vouchers cost £48.
   Find the cost of **a** one gym session **b** a discount voucher.
   (Remember: discount means subtract.)

6 Ken works in a chemist's shop.
   He notices that five small shampoo bottles contain exactly
   the same volume as two large bottles.
   On one morning he sells three large bottles and two small ones
   with a total volume of 760 ml of shampoo.
   What are the volumes of the two sizes of bottles?

7 In a quiz a fixed number of points are scored for correct answers and a fixed number
   of points are deducted for wrong answers.
   Debbie gets 9 questions right and 3 wrong. She scores a total of 30 points.
   Dennis gets 8 questions right and 5 wrong. He scores a total of 22 points.
   How many points are:
   a awarded for a correct answer
   b deducted for an incorrect answer?

8 Phil is a professional photographer. He makes a fixed profit when customers buy a
   photograph of themselves. However, he makes a certain loss when customers reject
   his work.
   On a day when he makes 8 successful sales and suffers 3 rejections he makes a total
   profit of £134. On another day when he has 10 successful sales and 6 rejections he
   makes a profit of £136. How much does he:
   a get paid for a photo   **b** lose when a photo is rejected?

Brainstormer

Tariq is training for a triathlon. In one session when he runs for 2 hours and cycles for 2 hours he covers a total of 64 km. In another session when he runs for 1·5 hours and cycles for 2·5 hours he covers 71 km.

Assuming he runs and cycles at constant speeds, calculate these speeds.

Investigations

1 **a** Investigate the solution of this system of equations:

$x + 2y = 8$, $3x + y = 9$, $2x - y = 1$ and $x - y = -1$.

Include graphs of the equations on the same diagram in your answer.

b Investigate the possible number of different points in which four straight lines can meet. Illustrate in diagrams.

2 Investigate the solutions of these pairs of equations. Try different methods, for example 'trial and error', tables of values, graphs, substitution.

a $y = x$

$y = x^2$

b $y = x$

$y = x^3$

c $y = x$

$y = \dfrac{16}{x}$

d $y = x$

$x^2 + y^2 = 8$

◄◄ RECAP

You should be able to solve simultaneous equations by:

- drawing graphs (this may involve finding points that lie on straight lines)
- substitution
- elimination.

With algebraic methods it may be necessary to rearrange the order of the terms.

You should also be able to use simultaneous equations to solve problems.

1 a Copy and complete the tables for these equations:

i $y = 2x + 1$

x	0	1	2
y			

ii $y = 4 - x$

x	0	1	2	3	4
y					

b On the same axes draw the graphs of the two equations. (Use scales from 0 to 5.)
c Write down the solutions to the simultaneous equations $y = 2x + 1$ and $y = 4 - x$.
d Check that the solution fits each of the equations.

2 a Use the graph to solve this pair of simultaneous equations:

$y = x - 3$ and $y = -x - 6$

b Check that the solution fits each of the equations.

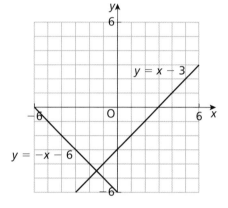

3 Solve the pair of equations $2x + y = 6$ and $2x - y = 4$ by graphical methods.

4 Solve these simultaneous equations by substitution.

a $y = 4x$
$y = 2x + 4$

b $y = 2x + 1$
$x + y = 10$

c $x - 2y = 10$
$y = 2 - 3x$

d $x = 4 - y$
$2x + 3y = 7$

5 Solve these simultaneous equations by elimination.

a $2x + y = 9$
$x - y = 3$

b $3x - 4y = 17$
$x - y = 5$

c $2x + 3y = -8$
$5x + 2y = -9$

d $5y = 7x + 9$
$3y + 5x + 13 = 0$

6 Two variables are related by the formula $y = ax + b$ where a and b are constants.
When $x = 2$, $y = 1$. When $x = -1$, $y = -8$. Express y in terms of x.

7 Solve these simultaneous equations by the most suitable method.

a $x - 3y = 14$
$4x + y = 4$

b $3x + 4y = 17$
$y = x + 6$

c $5x - 4y = -5$
$2y = 13 - x$

d $2x + 3y - 2 = 0$
$5y - 3x + 22 = 0$

8 William is 19 kg heavier than Wendy. The sum of their weights is 111 kg.
What is: **a** Wendy's **b** William's weight?

9 Jan's Saturday earnings are three times greater than Friday's.
Altogether she earns £150 for the two days.
How much does she earn on: **a** Friday **b** Saturday?

10 In a quiz, points are awarded for correct answers and deducted for incorrect
answers. Harry's team score a total of 52 points with 12 correct and 5 incorrect
answers. Harriet's team's total score is -4 points with 4 correct and 7 incorrect
answers. Find how many points are awarded for a correct answer and how many
are deducted for a wrong answer.

14 Chapter revision

Revising Chapter 1   Calculations and the calculator

1 Calculate, to 3 significant figures, the value of:

a $\dfrac{56 \cdot 2}{13 \cdot 9 \times 1 \cdot 4}$ **b** $3 \cdot 5^2 + 2 \cdot 6^2$ **c** $\dfrac{3 + \sqrt{(-3)^2 - 4 \times 6 \times (-2)}}{2 \times 6}$ **d** $\sqrt[4]{463 \cdot 2}$

2 An engineering company made a profit last year of £14.95 million.
  a The factory was in production for 342 days of the year.
    What was the average daily profit rounded to the nearest thousand?
  b The company employed 23 754 people.
    Calculate the profit per employee, to 4 significant figures.

3 Express each of the following as a decimal fraction of an hour, correct to 4 decimal places:
  a 1 minute   **b** 1 second

4 Which of these numbers do you think could equal $79 \times 8 \cdot 2$?
  a i 6·478   **ii** 64·78   **iii** 647·8   **iv** 6478   **v** 64 780
  b Check your answer on the calculator.

5 a Write these numbers in scientific notation:
  i 78 000   **ii** 13·4   **iii** 0·0057   **iv** 0·000 000 000 009
  b Write these numbers in normal form:
  i $2 \cdot 6 \times 10^5$ **ii** 7×10^{-3} **iii** $9 \cdot 01 \times 10^4$ **iv** $1 \cdot 1 \times 10^{-2}$

6 The frequency of a light wave is given by the formula $f = c \div \lambda$, where c is the speed of light, 3×10^{10} cm/s. Calculate the frequency of each light colour in the table. (Remember to use the constant facility or memory in your calculator.)

Colour	Wavelength (λ)
Red	$6 \cdot 5 \times 10^{-5}$
Yellow	$5 \cdot 8 \times 10^{-5}$
Green	$5 \cdot 4 \times 10^{-5}$
Blue	$4 \cdot 7 \times 10^{-5}$

7 Calculate, in their simplest form:
  a $\frac{5}{6} - \frac{2}{5}$ **b** $4\frac{1}{3} \times 2\frac{3}{4}$
  c $1\frac{3}{5} \div \frac{4}{7}$ **d** $\frac{3}{8} + 1\frac{2}{3}$

8 In a local election, $\frac{3}{8}$ of the electorate voted Conservative, $\frac{2}{5}$ Labour and $\frac{1}{10}$ Liberal Democrat. The remainder, 125 people, did not vote.
  a Which candidate was elected?
  b How many people were eligible to vote?

9 A wall contained $4 \cdot 2 \times 10^7$ mosaic tiles. $\frac{2}{5}$ of the tiles were square and $\frac{3}{8}$ of the remainder were blue rhombuses. How many, in scientific notation and to 2 significant figures, are:
  a blue rhombuses   **b** not blue rhombuses?

Revising Chapter 2 Integers

1 Write down the number that is:

   a 1 greater than -7 **b** 1 less than -2

2 Which of these are true and which are false?

   a $-1 < -2$ **b** $0 > -10$ **c** $-6 > -2$ **d** $-5 < -3$

3 Write down the number that is:

   a 7 greater than -3 **b** 6 less than -2

4 Calculate the following:

   a $8 + (-2)$ **b** $5 - (-4)$ **c** $-3 + (-1)$ **d** $-12 - 2$ **e** $-5 + (-6)$

   f $-1 - (-8)$ **g** $7 + (-11)$ **h** $-9 - (-2)$ **i** $6 \times (-7)$ **j** $-8 \div (-2)$

   k -2×10 **l** $36 \div (-4)$ **m** -1×0 **n** $-14 \div 7$ **o** $-6 \times (-12)$

5 Calculate the value of each expression for $a = -3$, $b = 4$ and $c = -2$:

   a $a + b + c$ **b** $a - b - c$ **c** $c - b - a$ **d** $b - a - c$

   e abc **f** $bc - ac$ **g** $2a^2$ **h** ac^2

   i $\dfrac{ab}{c}$ **j** $\dfrac{5b - 2c}{a}$ **k** $\dfrac{(bc)^2}{2a + c}$ **l** $\dfrac{c - 5ab}{ac - b}$

6 Simplify:

   a $2a - 5a - a$ **b** $m - 3n - 4m + 7n$ **c** $a^2 - 2a - 3a - 6a^2$

   d $4x \times (-3y)$ **e** $3p \times (-2p)$ **f** $(-a)^4$

7 A straight line has the equation $x + 2y + 16 = 0$.

   Calculate the y coordinate of a point on the line with x coordinate equal to:

   a -4 **b** 0 **c** 2 **d** -30

8 Solve these equations:

   a $x + 6 = 0$ **b** $x + 4 = 2$ **c** $y - 3 = -8$

   d $y + 5 = -1$ **e** $2a + 7 = 5$ **f** $6 - 2a = 10$

9 Over a 24-hour period, from midday until midday, the temperature of parts of Alaska changed according to the formula $T = \frac{1}{4}t^2 - 6t + 20$, where T is the temperature in degrees Celsius and t is the number of hours past midday.

   a What was the temperature at the start of the 24-hour period, i.e. at $t = 0$?

   b What was the temperature at:

      i $t = 4$ **ii** $t = 6$ **iii** $t = 10$ **iv** $t = 12$ **v** $t = 16$ **vi** $t = 19$?

Revising Chapter 3 Brackets and equations

1 Remove the brackets:

   a $2(r - 6)$ **b** $9(b + 2)$ **c** $5(8 + x)$

   d $9(f - 3)$ **e** $3(a - b)$ **f** $11(w + x)$

   g $23(d + e)$ **h** $2(3y + 2)$ **i** $c(c + 2)$

   j $q(r - s)$ **k** $d(d - 5)$ **l** $w(w + 2y)$

   m $g(g - 7)$ **n** $h(4 - h)$ **o** $n(3n - 7)$

   p $a(6b - 5a)$ **q** $k(3k - 5)$ **r** $b(31 - 4b)$

2 Multiply out, then simplify:

a $4 + 2(x - 8)$ **b** $7 - 2(m + 4)$ **c** $6x - (x - 2)$

d $13 - 3(8 - k)$ **e** $7 + 5(8 + r)$ **f** $8d - 3(d - 1)$

g $3w + 3(6 + 5w)$ **h** $9 + (6 - n)$ **i** $3 - 3(4 - m)$

j $4y - (3 + y)$ **k** $8k - (5 + k)$ **l** $12 - (n + 12)$

m $14 + 6(d - 2)$ **n** $3 - 5(8 - m)$ **o** $12 + 3(t - 7)$

p $2 - 8(7 - 3h)$ **q** $5a + 7(2a + 1)$ **r** $8 - (5b - 3)$

s $2k - 2(6k - 5)$ **t** $5 + 2(8y - 7)$ **u** $-2(b + 4) - b$

v $-(7 + a) + 2a$ **w** $-3(9 - c) - 3c$ **x** $-5(3 - 6v) + 13$

3 Make an equation for each picture and solve it to find the weight of one object:

a

$m - 6$ kg

7 objects weigh 28 kg

b

$y + 5$ kg

5 objects weigh 40 kg

c

$k - 6$ kg

9 objects weigh 63 kg

d

$d - 12$ kg

21 objects weigh 63 kg

4 Solve:

a $7(a - 3) = 56$ **b** $4(y + 1) = 27$ **c** $55 = 5(a + 12)$

d $6(b - 1) = 35$ **e** $9(x + 5) = 63$ **f** $14(n - 3) = 0$

g $3(n - 7) = 3$ **h** $5(y + 1) = 60$ **i** $7(d + 3) = 49$

j $3(w - 2) = -6$ **k** $6(a + 1) = -18$ **l** $5(k + 2) = 35$

m $9(c - 1) = -27$ **n** $4(k + 3) = 0$ **o** $7(y + 3) = -63$

p $-8 = 2(x + 5)$ **q** $-15 = -5(t - 2)$ **r** $-18 = -6(u - 1)$

5 Multiply out:

a $(x + 1)(x + 7)$ **b** $(u - 4)(u - 1)$ **c** $(n - 6)(n + 4)$

d $(w - 10)(w - 3)$ **e** $(9 + e)(9 - e)$ **f** $(g + 3)(g - 7)$

g $(n - 4)(n + 4)$ **h** $(b - 11)(b + 7)$ **i** $(a + 4)(a - 4)$

j $(x + 10)(x - 3))$ **k** $(y - 2)(y + 2)$ **l** $(u - 7)(u + 8)$

m $(a + 7)^2$ **n** $(2 + n)^2$ **o** $(8 + d)^2$

p $(4 - x)^2$ **q** $(10 - k)^2$ **r** $(4 - a)^2$

s $(7 + 2h)^2$ **t** $(5 - 2g)^2$ **u** $(9 + 7x)^2$

v $(5 - 3x)^2$ **w** $(9 + 4y)^2$ **x** $(12b - 1)^2$

6 Solve:

a $x(x + 3) = x^2 + 15$ **b** $a(a - 5) = a^2 - 50$

c $3n(2n + 3) = 3(2n^2 - 9)$ **d** $(y + 2)(y - 4) = y(y - 3)$

e $(u + 4)(u - 1) = u(u + 2)$ **f** $w(w + 3) = (w + 1)^2$

g $x(x + 4) = (x - 2)^2$ **h** $(f + 1)^2 = (f + 4)(f - 1)$

i $(n - 9)^2 = n^2 - 117$ **j** $(d + 2)(2d - 1) = (d + 2)(2d + 5)$

k $(k + 11)(k - 3) = (k + 9)(k - 5)$ **l** $(2x - 5)^2 = (2x - 1)^2$

REVISE

Revising Chapter 4   Money

1 a Super Sports buy a pair of skis for £150. They make a profit of 16%.
Calculate the selling price.

   b The store buys ski boots for £95 and sells them for £124·99. Calculate the profit as
a percentage of the cost price, correct to 1 decimal place.

   c They sell pairs of ski poles for £31·35. This makes them a profit of 14%.
Calculate the cost price, correct to the nearest penny.

2 a The pre-VAT cost of a computer desk at Optimum Office Furniture is £59·99.
Calculate the total cost including VAT at 17·5%.

   b The cost of a computer chair, including VAT at 17·5%, is £27·99.
Calculate the cost, to the nearest penny, before VAT is added.

3 An Atlas computer can be bought for £899·99 cash or on hire purchase.
HP terms are: 12% deposit + 12 monthly instalments of £69·99.

   a Calculate the total cost of buying the computer on HP.

   b What is the difference between the HP price and the cash price?

   c Calculate the extra amount paid on HP as a percentage of the cash price, to 1 d.p.

4 Malcolm changes £650 into euro for a trip to Belgium.

   a At £1 = €1·38 calculate the amount he receives.

   b His hotel bill comes to €286. How much is this in pounds,
correct to the nearest penny?

   c On returning to the UK he changes his remaining €95 into pounds and gets
£70·37. Calculate the exchange rate in terms of £1 = €? to the nearest cent.

5 a Pat's annual car insurance premium is £572·40 before her 65% no-claims discount
is deducted.

     i   Calculate the discount.

     ii How much does she pay for her insurance?

   b James pays £389·16 for his annual car insurance premium. This includes a 40%
no-claims discount. Calculate the premium before the no-claims discount.

6 The Safe As Houses Insurance Company's annual charges are:

   Buildings £0·68 per £1000; Contents £4·38 per £1000.

   a The Jacksons' house is valued at £180 000, and its contents at £30 000.
Calculate their annual premium for their

     i   buildings   **ii** contents insurance.

   b The Patels pay £98·60 for their buildings insurance and £100·74 for their contents
insurance. Calculate the value of their

     i   house   **ii** contents.

7 The table shows some of Tragic
Travel's insurance charges (in £).

   a Harriet flies to Boston for 4 weeks.
How much does her insurance cost?

   b What is the maximum number
of days' insurance cover for the
UK that £54·65 will buy?

No. of days	UK	Europe	Worldwide
10–17	14·83	24·85	42·50
18–25	18·56	26·90	45·37
26–35	22·85	30·25	48·52
Each extra week	5·30	8·25	15·78

REVISE

Revising Chapter 5 Factors

1 List all the factors of:

   a 30   **b** gh **c** $8y$ **d** $3c^2$ **e** p^3

2 Write down the highest common factor of:

   a 24 and 16   **b** $2de$ and $4d^2$ **c** $6xy$ and $8y$ **d** $9x^2$ and $12y^2$

   e $2a^2$ and a **f** r^2t and $2rt$ **g** g^2h and gh^2 **h** $12k^2$ and $8k^3$

3 Factorise:

   a $9r - 12$ **b** $8x + 24$ **c** $ax - 2at$ **d** $2x^2 + x$

   e $5h - h^2$ **f** $6ab - 10a$ **g** $5a + 10b - 15c$ **h** $d^3 - 6d^2$

4 Factorise:

   a $m^2 - q^2$ **b** $t^2 - r^2$ **c** $16 - x^2$ **d** $k^2 - 25$

   e $81 - n^2$ **f** $9w^2 - 1$ **g** $49 - 9y^2$ **h** $64a^2 - 4b^2$

   i $q^2 - 25r^2$ **j** $100m^2 - 121n^2$ **k** $25d^2 - 144e^2$ **l** $400x^2 - 225$

5 Without using a calculator, use factors to calculate:

   a $17 \times 48 + 17 \times 52$ **b** $97 \cdot 5^2 - 2 \cdot 5^2$

   c $222^2 - 22^2$ **d** $0 \cdot 6 \times 8 + 0 \cdot 6 \times 7$

6 Factorise:

   a $d^2 - 6d + 5$ **b** $c^2 + c - 6$ **c** $m^2 - 4m - 21$ **d** $y^2 + 4y + 4$

   e $r^2 - r - 20$ **f** $e^2 + 7e + 12$ **g** $3u^2 - 4u + 1$ **h** $2f^2 + 9f + 7$

   i $2b^2 - 3b + 1$ **j** $7z^2 - 11z - 6$ **k** $1 - w - 2w^2$ **l** $1 + 4y + 3y^2$

   m $1 - 3w - 18w^2$ **n** $6 - 5e - 6e^2$ **o** $6c^2 + 7c - 3$ **p** $9g^2 + 6gh - 8h^2$

7 Factorise fully:

   a $3x^2 + 15x + 12$ **b** $2m^2 - 12m + 16$ **c** $7 - 28d^2$ **d** $3d^2e + de^2$

   e $k - k^3$ **f** $24n^2 - 14n - 24$

8 Factorise fully:

   a $ab + ac$ **b** $10x + 30y$ **c** $3r^2 - 6r^3$ **d** $2h^2 - 200$

   e $b^2 - 3b - 10$ **f** $x^2 + 16x + 64$ **g** $14gu + 8gv$ **h** $7d - 14d^2$

   i $ka - a^2$ **j** $2w - 8wa^3$ **k** $18x^2 - 32y^2$ **l** $pa^2 + 2pa$

   m $3 - 27x^2$ **n** $1 - b^4$ **o** $ax^2 + 10ax + 25a$ **p** $(mn)^2 + 6mn + 9$

   q $7w^2 + 14w - 56$ **r** $bx^2 - 2bx - 8b$ **s** $(x + y)^2 - y^2$ **t** $(u - v)^2 - u^2$

Revising Chapter 6 Statistics – charts and tables

1 Sales appear to be increasing steadily.

   a Comment on the graph.

   b Draw a corrected version.

   c Are sales increasing as healthily as it seems?

Steady increase in sales

REVISE

2 The table shows the results of sampling a collection of containers to see what they are made of.

card	plastic	glass	card	card
card	plastic	plastic	card	plastic
glass	card	card	card	glass
card	plastic	card	card	card
glass	card	plastic	glass	plastic
plastic	card	glass	glass	plastic

a i Make a frequency table of the findings.
  ii Which material was most commonly used?
b i Add a relative frequency column.
  ii What fraction of the containers were made of glass?
  iii Draw a pie chart to illustrate the findings.

3 The number of visitors to a school during the last few weeks of an exhibition was as shown.

```
46   42   60   41   35
43   47   37   53   65
30   70   33   61   47
60   70   54   49   55
```

a Arrange the data in ascending order with the aid of a stem-and-leaf diagram.
b Illustrate the data using a dot plot (using 30s, 40s, 50s, 60s, 70s as categories).
c Give a 5-figure summary of the data.
d Draw a box plot to illustrate the distribution of numbers of visitors.

4 Children collecting football stickers were each asked two questions:
- For how many weeks have you been collecting?
- How many stickers do you have (to the nearest 10)?

Number of weeks	1	6	3	8	4	10	7	9	6	2	3	10	4	9	2
Number of stickers	20	30	20	50	30	50	40	50	40	20	30	60	40	60	30

a Make a scatter diagram to illustrate the data.
b Describe the relationship between 'No. of weeks' and 'No. of stickers'.
c Add a line of best fit to the diagram
d Estimate the number of stickers that might be collected after 5 weeks.

Revising Chapter 7   Proportion and variation

1 Write these relationships in words:

  a $Q \propto r^2$ **b** $U \propto xy$ **c** $J \propto \dfrac{rh^2}{p}$

2 Write these relationships using the proportional symbol $\propto$:
  a A varies directly as m and as the square root of s.
  b Z varies inversely as the cube of d.
  c J varies directly as the square of x and inversely as the square of y.

REVISE

3 a Make a new table of y against $\dfrac{1}{x}$.

x	1	2	4	5	10
y	40	20	10	8	4

  b Draw a graph to illustrate the table.
  c Explain the relationship between x and y.
  d Write down a formula connecting x and y.

4 a Given that $y \propto x$, copy and complete the table.

x	5	10	15	20	25
y					150

  b Given that $y \propto \dfrac{1}{x}$, copy and complete the table.

x	5	10	15	20	25
y					150

5 The surface area (A cm²) of a sphere varies directly as the square of the radius (r cm).
  a Write down a formula for A in terms of r and a constant k.
  b A sphere with a radius of 4 cm has a surface area of 201 cm².
    What is the value of k?
  c Calculate the surface area of a sphere with a radius of 7 cm.

6 F varies inversely as the cube of d. When $d = 6$, $F = 8$.
  a Find a formula for F.
  b Calculate F when $d = 4$.
  c What is the value of d when $F = 64$?

7 The number of tufts (N) in a home-made rectangular rug varies directly as the length (L cm) and the breadth (B cm). When $L = 120$ and $B = 70$, $N = 18\,900$.
  a Find a formula for N in terms of L and B.
  b Calculate the number of tufts in a rug when $L = 90$ and $B = 50$.

8 The force (F units) needed to stop a lorry varies directly as the square of the speed (S km/h) and inversely as the stopping distance (D metres).
  a Write down a formula for F in terms of S, D and a constant k.
  b A force of 40 units stops a lorry travelling at 50 km/h in 200 m.
    Find a formula for F.
  c What force is needed to stop a lorry going at 40 km/h in 160 m?
  d A force of 64 units is applied to a lorry travelling at 80 km/h.
    Calculate the stopping distance.

Revising Chapter 8   Pythagoras

1 Colin finds himself in a traffic jam on Jackdaw Road.
He thinks that if he goes down Abbey Hill and then
Anniesfield Drive he will avoid the jam.
How much further will he have to travel?

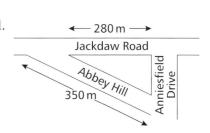

2 The label on the front of a box is in the shape of an isosceles triangle.
It is 15 cm tall and has a base of 16 cm.
What is the length of the two sloping edges?

3 Three gorillas, A, B and C, are being monitored using
tracking devices and their position is then marked on a
coordinate grid.
Which two gorillas are closest together?

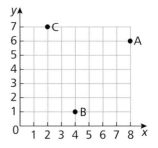

4 Calculate the length of the space diagonal, AG, of this cuboid.

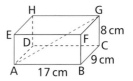

5 In ΔLMN, LM = 35 cm, MN = 83 cm and LN = 91 cm.
Is ΔLMN right-angled?

Revising Chapter 9   Time, distance and speed

1 Calculate the speed of a train that travels 575 km in 5 hours.

2 How far would a cyclist travel in two and a half hours at 16 mph?

3 How fast would a man be running if he ran 135 metres in 18 seconds?

4 Pattie set off from home at 10 47 to drive the 112 km to her friend Jan's house.
She drove at an average speed of 64 km/h. When did she arrive at Jan's house?

5 At full speed a tortoise can move at 80 centimetres per minute.
How long does it take to cross a road 5 metres wide?

6 In the 100 metre race at the Junior Championships, the winner had a time of
14·32 seconds.
He beat the second runner by three hundredths of a second and the third runner
was a further seven hundredths of a second behind.
a Calculate, to 3 significant figures, the speed of each runner.
b When the winner crossed the line how far behind him was the second runner?

7 Zak walks for 25 minutes and covers 3·1 km, then he runs 3·4 km in 17 minutes.
a Calculate the total
  i   time taken
  ii   distance travelled.
b Calculate Zak's average speed over the whole journey
  (correct to 2 decimal places).

REVISE

8 The map shows a motorist's journey from Eveton to Ruthven. Calculate:
   a the time it took to travel each leg of the journey
   b the overall average speed (correct to 1 decimal place).

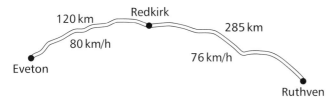

9 In 2002, during the Queen's Golden Jubilee celebrations, a baton was carried by runners over a distance of 63 000 miles. The journey took 137 days.
Calculate the average speed that the baton travelled, correct to 1 decimal place.

10 A lorry leaves its garage to travel to Ayr.
   a How long does the lorry take to travel to Ayr?
   b Calculate the lorry's average speed.
   c A bus leaves Ayr at the same time as the lorry leaves the garage.
      For how long does the bus stop?
   d How far from Ayr do the lorry and bus pass each other?
   e Calculate the average speeds of the bus on the fastest and slowest parts of its journey.

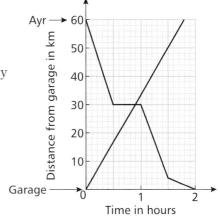

11 A spaceship bound for Mars, 72 million km away, will average a speed of 16 000 km/h. The launch was at 00 00 h on Wednesday 21 June. Find the day and date of its arrival.

Revising Chapter 10   Angles and circles

1 In each of these diagrams, O is the centre of the circle and A and B are points on the circumference. Calculate x.

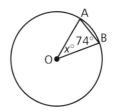
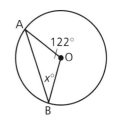

2 In this diagram O is the centre of the circle, AB is the diameter and C is a point on the circumference.
All measurements are in centimetres.
Find the diameter of the circle to 3 significant figures.

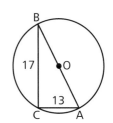

3 O is the centre of the circle and ED is a tangent which touches the circle at E.

Calculate the radius of the circle to 3 significant figures.

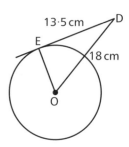

4 a What size is ∠ADC? Give reasons.
  b The radius of the circle is 13 cm. The chord AB is 10 cm long. Calculate the distance DE.
  c Calculate the area of the circle.
  d Calculate its circumference.

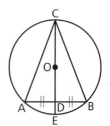

5 A wedge of cheese is a sector of a circle of radius 7 cm. The angle at the centre is 30°.
  a Calculate the area of a label that would cover the top of the cheese.
  b Calculate the length of arc of the wedge, correct to 1 decimal place.

Revising Chapter 11   Angles and triangles

1 A lighthouse, L, is 850 m from a small harbour, H, on a bearing of 155°.
A boat, B, is in distress 680 m from the lighthouse on a bearing of 218°.
  a Choosing a suitable scale, make a scale drawing showing the relative positions of H, L and B.
  b Use your scale drawing to find the distance and bearing of the boat from the harbour.

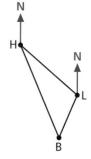

2 Port Ross is 86 km due south of Port Alice.
Port Penny is on a bearing of 240° from Port Alice and 305° from Port Ross.
  a Use a scale drawing to find the sailing distance from Port Penny to **i** Port Alice **ii** Port Ross.
  b Also find the bearing from Port Penny of
    i   Port Alice   **ii**   Port Ross.

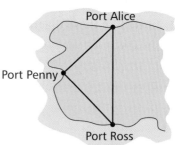

3 Calculate *x* in each right-angled triangle to 1 decimal place. All lengths are in centimetres.

a   **b**   **c**   **d** 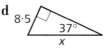 **e**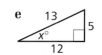

4 A mine shaft CD is 1600 m long.
It slopes at an angle of 28° to the horizontal.
a Calculate the depth, *d* metres, of the mine shaft.
b A ventilation shaft AB is such that the horizontal
distance AC is 1200 m.
Calculate the depth of the ventilation shaft.

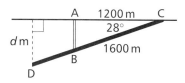

5 The diagonals of a rhombus are 18 cm and 12 cm. Calculate:
a the angles of the rhombus
b the length of side of the rhombus.

6 The diagram shows the cross-section of a tent.
It is symmetrical about XY.
a Calculate the height of the tent.
b Calculate the width of the tent, AB.
Give your answers to 1 decimal place.

7 There is a traffic jam on a straight stretch
of motorway.
The angle of depression from a
helicopter directly above the motorway
to end P of the traffic jam is 36°.
The angle of elevation from Q to the
helicopter is 62°.
The distance from the helicopter to P is 940 m. Calculate:
a the height of the helicopter
b the length of the traffic jam, PQ.

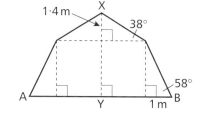

Revising Chapter 12 More statistics

1 The table shows the findings when the numbers of pages in
different books are counted.
a Calculate the mean number of pages to 1 d.p.
b State the modal number of pages.

Pages	Frequency
8	2
16	3
32	8
64	12

2 James measured the lengths (in centimetres) of worms caught in a bucket.

12·8   6·7   5·8   7·5   12·8   15   10·4   10·8   13   7·3
9·6   11   13·4   12·1   8·8   6·4   7·5   8·1   8·3   9·3

a Calculate   i the mean length   ii the modal length.
b What is the range of lengths?
c Calculate the median and quartiles.
d Calculate the semi-interquartile range.
e Any length which is more than 3 SIQRs from the median is considered
exceptional. Are there any worms of exceptional length?

3 Some students in first year have their heights measured. The table shows the results.

Height (cm)	Frequency
140	1
142	5
144	8
146	8
148	6
150	2

  a Copy the table and add a cumulative frequency column.
  b Draw a cumulative frequency diagram and use it to estimate the median and quartiles of the distribution.
  c Estimate the semi-interquartile range.

4 Complaints were made that pupils were having to carry too many books. A quick sampling of the contents of some schoolbags produced the following numbers of books: 1, 1, 4, 8, 3, 3, 4, 2, 1, 7.
  a Calculate the mean number of books in a schoolbag.
  b Calculate the standard deviation.
  c Two standard deviations above the mean is considered a lot of books. Is anyone in the sample carrying a lot of books?

5 Calculate the probability that a card chosen at random from a standard pack of 52 cards:
  a is an ace
  b is a red 4
  c has a face value less than 6.

6 The frequency table shows the length of the queue at the fast till in the supermarket, noted at regular intervals.

Queue length	3	4	5	6	7	8
Frequency	7	6	3	1	1	2

Estimate the probability that when you join the queue there will be fewer than 6 people in it.

Revising Chapter 13　Simultaneous equations

1 a Copy and complete the tables for these equations:
    i $y = x - 1$ **ii** $y = 4 - x$

x	1	2	3	4	5
y					

x	0	1	2	3	4
y					

  b On the same grid, draw graphs of the solutions of the two equations.
  c Write down the solution to the simultaneous equations $y = x - 1$ and $y = 4 - x$.
  d Check that the solution fits each equation.

2 Solve the equations $x + 2y = 4$ and $x - 2y = 0$ simultaneously by graphical means.

3 Solve these simultaneous equations by substitution.
  a $y = 5x$ **b** $y = x + 3$ **c** $x + 2y = -13$ **d** $x = 3 - y$
    $y = 3x + 4$ $x + y = 9$ $y = 2x - 4$ $3x - y = 9$

REVISE

4 Solve these simultaneous equations by elimination.

   a $2x + y = 13$ **b** $2x + 5y = 13$ **c** $3x - 2y = 12$ **d** $4y = 3x + 5$

       $x - y = 5$ $3x + y = 0$ $5x - 3y = 19$ $5y + 2x + 11 = 0$

5 P is related to Q by the formula $Q = aP + b$.

   When $P = 3$, $Q = -1$. When $P = -4$, $Q = 13$.

   a Find the values of a and b.

   b Find a formula for Q in terms of P.

6 Solve these simultaneous equations by the most suitable method.

   a $x - 4y = -5$ **b** $2x + y = 16$ **c** $3x - 2y = -22$ **d** $4y = 3x - 2$

       $3x + y = 11$ $y = 6x$ $y = -3 - 2x$ $4x + 2 - 3y = 0$

7 The difference of two numbers is 18. The mean of the two numbers is 26. Find the two numbers.

8 Two gym sessions with two discount vouchers cost £18.

   Three gym sessions with four discount vouchers cost £21.

   Find the cost of:

   a one gym session   **b** a discount voucher.

9 Carol works 7 days in a week before Christmas. She earns three times as much for weekend days as for weekdays. Altogether she earns £715 in the week.

   How much does she earn on:

   a Friday   **b** Sunday?

10 Five nuts and six bolts weigh 98 g. Seven nuts and three bolts weigh 94 g.

   What is the weight of:

   a a nut   **b** a bolt?

REVISE

Answers

1 Calculations and the calculator

Page 1 Exercise 1·1

1 a 19·27　**b** 2·59　**c** 222·6　**d** 6·8
　e 16·07　**f** 27·46　**g** 42·48　**h** 7·4
　i 103·4　**j** 4·09

2 a 7800　**b** 20 800　**c** 495 000　**d** 20
　e 40　**f** 20 000　**g** 800　**h** 20
　i 108 900　**j** 41

3 a 85·4　**b** 468　**c** 30　**d** 0·2351
　e 0·002　**f** 77·2　**g** 485　**h** 11 840
　i 363 000　**j** 3·43　**k** 0·016　**l** 0·016
　m 0·0425　**n** 0·005　**o** 0·245

4 a 34　**b** 4　**c** 20　**d** 33
　e 48　**f** 144　**g** 11　**h** 8
　i 15　**j** 7

5 a 81　**b** 1　**c** 169　**d** 1600
　e 4　**f** 11　**g** $\frac{1}{2}$　**h** 30

6 a 3·142　**b** 3·14　**c** 3·1

7 a $15·96　**b** $159·64　**c** $1596·40

8 a 57 218 000　**b** 234

9 a 159·25　**b** 14·06　**c** 2212·67　**d** 10·5

Page 2 Investigations

1 a add even digits, multiply by odd digits
　b 4545

2 a i 1, 4, 9, 16, … square numbers　**ii** 10 000
　b i 1, 4, 9, … square numbers
　　ii 250 000
　　iii $2 + 4 + 6 + 8 … =$
　　　$1 + 1 + 1 + 3 + 1 + 5 … =$
　　　$1 + 1 + 1 … + 1 + 3 + 5 + … =$
　　　$500 + 250 000 = 250 500$
　c i −100　**ii** −50

Page 3 Exercise 2·1

1 a 2000　**b** 5000　**c** 100　**d** 40 000
　e 50　**f** 3　**g** 40　**h** 0·6
　i 0·009　**j** 0·1

2 a 5300　**b** 190　**c** 480　**d** 22 000
　e 3·1　**f** 0·83　**g** 0·0018　**h** 7·0
　i 0·90　**j** 0·054

3 a 3·4　**b** 1·5　**c** 0·22　**d** 21

4 a 10·1　**b** 97·3　**c** 190　**d** 3740

5 a 3　　**b** 3　　**c** 423 cm^2

6 a 3·10 cm^2　**b** 160 cm^2　**c** 35 cm^2

7 a 960　**b** 273　**c** £8·25　**d** 18·8 kg

Page 5 Exercise 3·1

1 a 0·714　**b** 3·67　**c** 5·25

2 a 4·6　**b** 6·25　**c** 11·9

3 a 1·22　**b** 1·42　**c** 2·07

4 a 21·7　**b** 3·26　**c** 10·3

5 a 5·9　**b** 11·2　**c** 99·4

6 a 45　**b** 14　**c** 18

7 a 2·27　**b** 1·63　**c** 0·761

8 a 4·83　**b** 0·006 32　**c** 0·830

9 a 64　**b** 182　**c** 183 000

10 a 10·8　**b** 20·2　**c** 13·4

Page 6 Exercise 4·1

1 a 32　**b** 64　**c** 1
　d 10 000　**e** 144　**f** $\frac{1}{4}$

2 a 2　**b** 2　**c** 10
　d 3　**e** 1　**f** 7

3 a 1296　**b** 161 051　**c** 2·744
　d 0·1296　**e** 571·787

4 a 2·22　**b** 2·94　**c** 2·82
　d 3·15　**e** 1·20

5 a 376　**b** 1440　**c** 2030　**d** 52
　e 5　**f** 1·12　**g** 4·20　**h** 1·57

6 42·9 m^3, 4·10 cm^3, 12 200 mm^3, 7300 m^3

7 a 9 cm　**b** 4·4 m　**c** 13 mm　**d** 1·2 m

Page 7 Exercise 5·1

1 a 504·80　**b** 4322·35　**c** 13·50
　d 31·70　**e** 112·45　**f** 58·55

2 a 54　**b** 74　**c** 45　**d** 96　**e** 18

3 a i 22·224　**ii** 103·712　**iii** 351·88
　b i 7·02　**ii** 41·3　**iii** 229

4 a £105·75　**b** £59·34　**c** £176·25
　d £1022·25　**e** £1257·25

5 a i $84·35　**ii** $997·87
　　iii $14 371·25　**iv** $1 591 500
　b i £18·85　**ii** £110·27
　　iii £2792·61　**iv** £628 338·05

Page 8 Challenge

1 3·17

2 a 6·63 cm　**b** 3·91 cm
　c 2·37 or −3·37　**d** 2·37

Page 9 Exercise 6·1

1 a 5×10^2　**b** 6×10^1　**c** $1·7 \times 10^3$
　d $2·3 \times 10^4$　**e** $5·6 \times 10^7$　**f** $9·87 \times 10^4$
　g $1·75 \times 10^6$　**h** $8·3 \times 10^1$

2 a 7×10^{-1} **b** 7×10^{-2}
   c 7×10^{-3} **d** $8 \cdot 1 \times 10^{-2}$
   e $4 \cdot 2 \times 10^{-1}$ **f** $3 \cdot 9 \times 10^{-5}$
   g $1 \cdot 52 \times 10^{-1}$ **h** 6×10^{-4}

3 a $6 \cdot 7 \times 10^{2}$ **b** 5×10^{-2}
   c $2 \cdot 06 \times 10^{4}$ **d** $8 \cdot 8 \times 10^{-4}$
   e $1 \cdot 8 \times 10^{7}$ **f** 2×10^{-1}
   g $2 \cdot 13 \times 10^{-2}$ **h** $1 \cdot 9 \times 10^{0}$

4 a 3×10^{8} **b** $5 \cdot 5 \times 10^{7}$
   c $4 \cdot 046 \times 10^{3}$ **d** $4 \cdot 497 \times 10^{9}$
   e 5×10^{-8} **f** $1 \cdot 82 \times 10^{7}$
   g 6×10^{-4}

5 a $6 \cdot 6 \times 10^{21}$ **b** $1 \cdot 2 \times 10^{-6}$

6 a 70 000   **b** 3200
   c 0·06   **d** 0·0015
   e 74 000 000   **f** 0·000 28
   g 0·009 66   **h** 0·7215
   i 0·001 14   **j** 2·35
   k 70·3   **l** 0·000 000 000 8

7 a 320 000   **b** 8 600 000
   c 0·0025   **d** 8 370 000
   e 0·000 000 000 000 000 000 000 001 675

8 a 600   **b** 52

Page 10 Exercise 7·1

1 a 2×10^{8}, 200 000 000
   b $1 \cdot 23 \times 10^{7}$, 12 300 000
   c $1 \cdot 337 \times 10^{-2}$, 0·013 37
   d $1 \cdot 8 \times 10^{4}$, 18 000
   e 8×10^{-4}, 0·0008
   f 8×10^{3}, 8000
   g 4×10^{10}, 40 000 000 000
   h $7 \cdot 35 \times 10^{3}$, 7350
   i $2 \cdot 88 \times 10^{-1}$, 0·288
   j 3×10^{3}, 3000
   k $2 \cdot 4 \times 10^{3}$, 2400
   l 7×10^{4}, 70 000

2 a R **b** S **c** P and T

3 a $7 \cdot 98 \times 10^{9}$ **b** $9 \cdot 5 \times 10^{2}$
   c $4 \cdot 52 \times 10^{2}$ **d** $8 \cdot 4 \times 10^{6}$

4 795·6 m/s

5 $1 \cdot 1352 \times 10^{16}$ km

6 a 5×10^{12} **b** $3 \cdot 125 \times 10^{13}$

7 $5 \cdot 96 \times 10^{24}$ kg

8 a $1 \cdot 03 \times 10^{26}$ kg   **b** $6 \cdot 56 \times 10^{23}$ kg
   c $5 \cdot 66 \times 10^{26}$ kg   **d** $4 \cdot 77 \times 10^{24}$ kg

9 a $9 \cdot 5 \times 10^{17}$ km   **b** $2 \cdot 85 \times 10^{18}$ km

10 a $4 \cdot 39 \times 10^{9}$ km   **b** $42 : 1$

Page 11 Exercise 7·2

1 a $9 \cdot 36 \times 10^{11}$ **b** $1 \cdot 034 \times 10^{-11}$ **c** $5 \cdot 7 \times 10^{4}$
   d 3×10^{17} **e** $1 \cdot 5 \times 10^{-5}$

2 a $6 \cdot 73 \times 10^{4}$
   b i $6 \cdot 12 \times 10^{8}$
     ii $3 \cdot 89 \times 10^{5}$
     iii $7 \cdot 32 \times 10^{-16}$

3 a $1 \cdot 4 \times 10^{-2}$ **b** $4 \cdot 3 \times 10^{-20}$
   c $7 \cdot 4 \times 10^{3}$ **d** $2 \cdot 2 \times 10^{-6}$

4 $7 \cdot 25 \times 10^{14}$ m^2

5 a $1 \cdot 41 \times 10^{6}$ **b** £$(3 \cdot 80 \times 10^{7})$

Page 12 Investigation

a i 19 998   **ii** 29 997   **iii** 39 996

b 49 995, 59 994, 69 993, 79 992, 89 991

Page 13 Exercise 8.1

1 a $\frac{1}{2}$ **b** $\frac{3}{5}$ **c** $\frac{1}{4}$ **d** $\frac{3}{7}$ **e** 3

2 a $1\frac{1}{4}$ **b** $3\frac{2}{3}$ **c** $3\frac{3}{7}$ **d** $5\frac{2}{9}$ **e** $4\frac{1}{3}$

3 a $\frac{7}{2}$ **b** $\frac{14}{3}$ **c** $\frac{19}{10}$ **d** $\frac{79}{7}$ **e** $\frac{177}{8}$

4 $\frac{100}{3}$

5 a $\frac{3}{7}$ **b** $\frac{3}{10}$ **c** $\frac{13}{18}$ **d** $\frac{1}{10}$
   e $5\frac{5}{9}$ **f** $\frac{5}{8}$ **g** $\frac{3}{20}$ **h** $\frac{6}{7}$
   i $\frac{1}{12}$ **j** $4\frac{3}{8}$ **k** $\frac{2}{5}$ **l** $3\frac{1}{2}$

Page 13 Exercise 8.2

1 a = **d**, **b** = **e**, **c** = **g**, **f** = **h**

2 a $2\frac{1}{3}$ **b** $2\frac{1}{7}$ **c** $5\frac{1}{6}$ **d** $9\frac{5}{11}$

3 a $\frac{23}{5}$ **b** $\frac{20}{11}$ **c** $\frac{127}{8}$ **d** $\frac{400}{3}$

4 a $21\frac{3}{4}$ km   **b** $20\frac{1}{4}$ km   **c** $4\frac{1}{4}$ km   **d** $5\frac{3}{4}$ km

5 4

6 a $\frac{7}{8}$ **b** $\frac{1}{8}$

7 248

8 $1\frac{13}{16}$ inches, $\frac{11}{16}$ inch

9 a i $41\frac{1}{2}$ cm   **ii** 39 cm
   b i $103\frac{1}{8}$ cm^2 **ii** $95\frac{1}{16}$ cm^2
   c $8\frac{1}{16}$ cm^2

10 a 4   **b** $5\frac{3}{4}$ tonnes

11 a i $13\frac{1}{3}$ inches
     ii $39\frac{1}{16}$ inches
   b i $83\frac{1}{3}$ inches^2
     ii $520\frac{5}{6}$ inches^2

12 a $15\frac{3}{4}$ lb   **b** $10\frac{2}{9}$ kg   **c** $13\frac{1}{2}$ litres
   d 25 miles   **e** 80 inches   **f** $7\frac{1}{5}$ inches

Page 15 Challenge

A (table 1, 4 cakes); B (table 2, 3 cakes);
C (table 3, 2 cakes); D (table 1, 2 cakes);
E (table 2, $\frac{3}{2}$ cakes); F (table 1, $\frac{4}{3}$ cakes);
G (table 3, 1 cake); H (table 2, 1 cake);
I (table 1, 1 cake); J (table 1, $\frac{4}{5}$ cake);
19th gets $\frac{4}{9}$ at table 1

Page 16 Exercise 9·1

1 a $3 : 4$ **b** $1 : 3$ **c** $9 : 8$
   d $5 : 7$ **e** $11 : 20$ **f** $1 : 4$
   g $5 : 7$ **h** $2 : 3$ **i** $7 : 5$

2 a $25 : 275 = 1 : 11$ **b** $450 : 1500 = 3 : 10$
   c $650 : 2000 = 13 : 40$ **d** $12 : 30 = 2 : 5$
   e $100\,000 : 50 = 2000 : 1$ **f** $3000 : 750 = 4 : 1$
   g $280 : 56 = 5 : 1$ **h** $220 : 77 = 20 : 7$

3 a $24 : 29$ **b** $3 : 5$ **c** $7 : 19$

Page 16 Exercise 9·2

1 a £150, £350   **b** £11, £66
  c £600, £400   **d** 150 g, 90 g
  e 32 m, 24 m   **f** 170 ml, 680 ml
  g 320 mm, 512 mm   **h** 3·5 kg, 2·5 kg
  i 2 km, 2·5 km
2 a i £350, £200   **ii** £220, £330
   iii £165, £385
  b i 7 : 4   **ii** £185 more
3 red 46 litres, yellow 115 litres
4 flour 80 g, butter 40 g, sugar 20 g
5 cement 25 kg, sand 50 kg, gravel 75 kg
6 a 3 : 4   **b** Eric £27, Doug £36
7 blonde 561, brunette 459, auburn 102
8 a 88 litres   **b i** blue   **ii** 9 litres
9 £1 460 000, £2 555 000, £730 000, £365 000
10 a tea 4·4 kg, herbs 600 g   **b** £11·50
11 a 70 kg, 105 kg, 70 kg   **b** £411·25

Page 19 Revision

1 a 3·67   **b** 61·5   **c** 6640
  d 157   **e** 105 000   **f** 0·0135
2 a 141   **b** 1·55   **c** 10 400   **d** 2·46
3 c
4 a £2607   **b** £601·62
5 a $1·56 \times 10^6$ **b** 1×10^{-6}
6 a $£1·2 \times 10^9$ **b** $£4·38 \times 10^{11}$
7 a $1·66 \times 10^{16}$ **b** $3·67 \times 10^{-6}$
  c $5·94 \times 10^{-13}$
8 $2·2 \times 10^{-6}$ t
9 a $\frac{3}{10}$ **b** $1\frac{1}{8}$ **c** $\frac{1}{6}$ **d** $1\frac{1}{4}$
  e $4\frac{5}{8}$ **f** $2\frac{5}{8}$ **g** $1\frac{1}{2}$ **h** $\frac{36}{49}$
10 $\frac{13}{16}$ inch
11 a $\frac{1}{5}$ **b** 120
12 a £20, £15   **b** 15, 10, 5

2 Integers

Page 21 Exercise 1.1

1 a Anchorage −17 °C, Helsinki −12 °C, Toronto
  −9 °C, Moscow −7 °C, Edinburgh −2 °C,
  New York −1 °C, Belfast 0 °C, London 1 °C,
  Lanzarote 18 °C, Sydney 36 °C
  b i 2 degrees   **ii** 7 degrees
  c i 27 degrees   **ii** 5 degrees
  d 53 degrees
2 a −7 °C   **b** −10 °C   **c** −9 °C   **d** −7 °C
  e −3 °C   **f** −2 °C   **g** −5 °C   **h** −7 °C
3 a Bren (0, 0), Tor (5, 1), Haven (1, 2),
  Cliffton (−2, 3), Bosun (−4, 2), Lee (−7, 0),
  Shell (−6, −3), Dove (2, −2), Pelt (6, −1)
  b Bren (2, −3), Tor (7, −2), Haven (3, −1),
  Cliffton (0, 0), Bosun (−2, −1), Lee (−5, −3),
  Shell (−4, −6), Dove (4, −5), Pelt (8, −4)
  c (−4, −1·5)

4 a 1900 m   **b** 2900 m   **c** 1950 m
  d 12 650 m   **e** 5950 m   **f** 2550 m
  g 6655 m
5 a i 7   **ii** 5
  b £90 000
  c £15 000
  d £105 000

Page 23 Exercise 2.1

1 a $2 < 7$ **b** $3 > 0$
  c $-2 < 0$ **d** $-5 < 4$
  e $-1 > -7$ **f** $-4 < -3$
  g $9 > -12$ **h** $-14 < 11$
  i $-99 > -101$ **j** $-2·4 < -2$
2 a −7, −6, −1, 4   **b** −8, −3, −1, 1
  c −3, −2, 0, 1   **d** −5, −4, 2, 6
3 a −1   **b** −5
  c −13   **d** −13
  e −17   **f** 2
  g −1   **h** −4
4 a 4   **b** 6   **c** −2   **d** −2   **e** −8   **f** −12
5 a 6   **b** 3   **c** −2   **d** −5   **e** −3   **f** −22
6 35·00, 15·00, 25·00, −5·00, −12·00, −2·00
7 a D(1, −5)
  b A(1, −2), B(−2, −2), C(0, −8), D(3, −8)
  c A(−1, −1), B(−4, −1), C(−2, 5), D(1, 5)

Page 24 Challenge
−5

Page 25 Exercise 3.1

1 a 1   **b** 3   **c** −2   **d** −3   **e** −4   **f** 4
  g −5   **h** −3   **i** −3   **j** −5   **k** −5   **l** 0
  m −10 **n** 0   **0** −4
2 a 5   **b** −3   **c** 3   **d** 27   **e** 8
  f −36   **g** −37   **h** 0   **i** −13   **j** −74
3

+	−5	−2	4	−3
−5	−10	−7	−1	−8
−2	−7	−4	2	−5
4	−1	2	8	1
−3	−8	−5	1	−6

4 a −8
  b −12
5 a i 35, 43, 51   **ii** 8
  b i 38, 35, 32   **ii** −3
  c i −2, 0, 2   **ii** 2
  d i −5, −1, 3   **ii** 4
  e i −33, −40, −47   **ii** −7
  f i −2, −11, −20   **ii** −9
6 a i 3   **ii** 3
  b i 6   **ii** 6
  c i 7   **ii** 7
  d i 0   **ii** 0;
  each pair of answers is equal

Page 26 Exercise 4.1

1 a/b

−	−5	−4	−3	−2	−1	0	1	2	3	4	5
5	10	9	8	7	6	5	4	3	2	1	0
4	9	8	7	6	5	4	3	2	1	0	−1
3	8	7	6	5	4	3	2	1	0	−1	−2
2	7	6	5	4	3	2	1	0	−1	−2	−3
1	6	5	4	3	2	1	0	−1	−2	−3	−4
0	5	4	3	2	1	0	−1	−2	−3	−4	−5
−1	4	3	2	1	0	−1	−2	−3	−4	−5	−6
−2	3	2	1	0	−1	−2	−3	−4	−5	−6	−7
−3	2	1	0	−1	−2	−3	−4	−5	−6	−7	−8
−4	1	0	−1	−2	−3	−4	−5	−6	−7	−8	−9
−5	0	−1	−2	−3	−4	−5	−6	−7	−8	−9	−10

2 a 9   **b** 7   **c** 4   **d** 6   **e** 2
   f 2   **g** 2   **h** −4   **i** −3   **j** 1
3 a i 7   **ii** 7   **b i** −3   **ii** −3
   c i −3   **ii** −3   **d i** −1   **ii** −1
   e i −3   **ii** −3   **f i** −7   **ii** −7
   g i 1   **ii** 1   **h i** −2   **ii** −2

Page 27 Exercise 4.2

1 a −1   **b** −6   **c** −8   **d** −4   **e** −9
   f −13   **g** 3   **h** −3   **i** 5   **j** 0
2 a −64   **b** 91   **c** −45   **d** −11   **e** 9
   f 25   **g** −11   **h** 17
3 a 16   **b** −1   **c** −17   **d** −8
   e 6   **f** 3   **g** 0   **h** 0
   i −28   **j** 9   **k** −26   **l** −1
4 A profit of £9000
5 a i Venus is 274 degrees warmer
   ii the Earth is 161 degrees warmer
   iii Saturn is 51 degrees warmer
   b i 332 degrees
   ii 193 degrees
   iii 72 degrees
   c 519 degrees
   d −18 °C
6 a 19 883 m   **b** 4600 m   **c** 2187 m

Page 28 Exercise 5.1

1 a 3   **b** −2   **c** 7   **d** −5   **e** −7
   f 13   **g** −3   **h** 6   **i** 3   **j** −12
   k −5   **l** −4   **m** −1   **n** −2   **o** 1
   p −1   **q** 3   **r** 7
2 a i 10 m
   ii 0 m
   iii −15 m
   b i The glider is 10 m above the cliff edge
   ii the glider is level with the cliff edge
   iii the glider is 15 m below the cliff edge
3 a i −£7000   **ii** −£2000
   iii £3000   **iv** £8000
   b 120 passengers

4 a

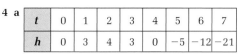

t	0	1	2	3	4	5	6	7
h	0	3	4	3	0	−5	−12	−21

b

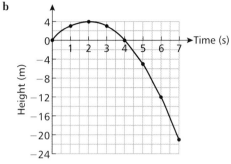

c 6 seconds
5 a $5x$ **b** y **c** $-7a$ **d** $-4t$
   e $3m$ **f** $-6d$ **g** $-9x$ **h** $2c$
   i $2x^2$ **j** $-y^2$ **k** 0   **l** $-5p^2$
6 a $5m$ **b** 0   **c** a **d** 0   **e** $2x$
   f $7p$ **g** $5y^2$ **h** $-5b^3$ **i** $-5x^2$
7 a $3a - 2b$ **b** $4m - 4n$ **c** $8x - y$
   d $3p - 4q$ **e** $-4c$ **f** $-3a - 5b$
   g $-2a^2 + 2b^2$ **h** $x^2 - xy$ **i** $-2bc - 2ac$

Page 30 Investigation

Set 1: 1, −1; 2 different values.
Set 2: 1, −1, 2, −2; 4 different values.
Set 3: 1, −1, 2, −2, 3, −3; 6 different values.
For Set n there are $2n$ different values

Page 30 Challenges 1

1 a

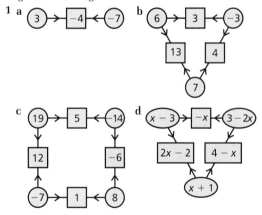

2

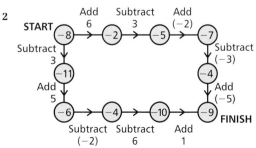

Page 31 Exercise 6.1

1 a–d

Second number

First number

×	−5	−4	−3	−2	−1	0	1	2	3	4	5
5	−25	−20	−15	−10	−5	0	5	10	15	20	25
4	−20	−16	−12	−8	−4	0	4	8	12	16	20
3	−15	−12	−9	−6	−3	0	3	6	9	12	15
2	−10	−8	−6	−4	−2	0	2	4	6	8	10
1	−5	−4	−3	−2	−1	0	1	2	3	4	5
0	0	0	0	0	0	0	0	0	0	0	0
−1	5	4	3	2	1	0	−1	−2	−3	−4	−5
−2	10	8	6	4	2	0	−2	−4	−6	−8	−10
−3	15	12	9	6	3	0	−3	−6	−9	−12	−15
−4	20	16	12	8	4	0	−4	−8	−12	−16	−20
−5	25	20	15	10	5	0	−5	−10	−15	−20	−25

2 a −8 **b** −3 **c** −10 **d** −2 **e** −15 **f** −16

3 a 12 **b** 5 **c** 8 **d** 6 **e** 3 **f** 16

4 a i 18 **ii** −18 **iii** −18 **iv** 18
b i 72 **ii** −72 **iii** −72 **iv** 72
c i −21 **ii** 21 **iii** 21 **iv** −21
d i 10 **ii** −10 **iii** −10 **iv** 10

5 a −24 **b** −7 **c** −30 **d** 18 **e** −40
f 72 **g** −9 **h** −17 **i** 0 **j** 49
k −1 **l** 0 **m** 26 **n** 9 **o** 100
p 1 **q** −75 **r** −12 **s** 48 **t** −1000

6 a 2 × (−3) = −6, 2 × (−6) = −12, −3 × (−6) = 18
b −4 × (−1) = 4, −4 × 3 = −12, −1 × 3 = −3
c −7 × 2 = −14, −7 × 6 = −42, 2 × 6 = 12
d −2 × (−5) = 10, −2 × (−8) = 16, −5 × (−8) = 40
e −3 × 10 = −30, −3 × (−9) = 27, 10 × (−9) = −90

Page 32 Exercise 6.2

1 a 6 **b** 120 **c** −42 **d** 80
e 28 **f** 0 **g** −54 **h** −48
i −144 **j** −1 **k** −125 **l** −1000
m −24 **n** 9 **o** −108 **p** −49
q −192 **r** −6000 **s** 24 **t** −72

2 a 21 **b** 18 **c** −7 **d** −10
e 20 **f** −5 **g** −9 **h** 11
i −2 **j** 0 **k** 7 **l** 33

3 a −2 **b** 6 **c** −25 **d** 3
e 9 **f** 49 **g** 30 **h** 26

Page 33 Challenge

a i 0 × 5 − (−7) or −1 × 0 − (−7) or 0 × 4 + 7
ii −2 × 1 + (−7) or −1 × 5 −4 or 2 × (−7) − (−5) or 1 × (−6) + (−3)
iii 1 × (−7) − (−4) or 1 × (−6) − (−3)
iv −4 × (−6) − 5 or −3 × (−6) + 1

b i 46 from −7 × (−6) + 4
ii −42 from 7 × (−5) + (−7)

Page 33 Exercise 7.1

1 a 0 **b** −11 **c** 0 **d** 3 **e** 24 **f** −20
2 a 6 **b** 20 **c** −7 **d** 9 **e** −31 **f** 75
3 a 8 **b** 0 **c** −8 **d** 11 **e** 4 **f** 245
4 a 24 **b** 2 **c** −16 **d** 9 **e** 11 **f** 56

5 a ab **b** $-ab$ **c** $-ab$ **d** ab
e $-12x$ **f** $-20x$ **g** $6y^2$ **h** $-5m^2$
i x^2 **j** $-18a^2$ **k** $36pq$ **l** $-14xy$
m t^2 **n** $25k^2$ **o** $-x^3$ **p** x^4
q m^2n^2 **r** $-a^2b^2$

6 a i 10 m **ii** −30 m **iii** 40 m **iv** 90 m.
Joint 6 is 30 m below sea level
b i 30 m **ii** 30 m **iii** 110 m

7 a i 20 m/s **ii** 10 m/s
b 6 s
c i 3 seconds before the train passes Ron
ii 45 m/s
d 65 m/s

8 a i 95 °F **ii** suitable
b i 14 °F **ii** suitable
c i −28·48 °F **ii** suitable
d i −28·3 °F **ii** suitable
e i −108·76 °F **ii** unsuitable
f i −126·22 °F **ii** unsuitable

Page 35 Challenge

Numerous possibilities including: 0 = 3 − 2 −1; −1 = 2 − 3 × 1; −2 = 2 −3 −1; −3 = 3 × (1 −2); −4 = (1 −3) × 2; −5 = 1 −2 × 3; −6 = 2 × (−3) × 1; −7 = −3 × 2 − 1; −8 = (1 + 3) × (−2)

Page 35 Investigations

1 a i true **ii** true
b only **iii** is true

2 a if n is odd, $x = 1$ is the only real solution; if n is even, $x = 1$ and $x = -1$ are the two real solutions
b if n is odd, $x = -1$ is the only real solution; if n is even, there are no real solutions

3 a if n is odd, the value is −1; if n is even, the value is 1
b for positive a, a^n is positive for all positive whole numbers n; for negative a, a^n is positive for even values of n and negative for odd values of n

Page 36 Exercise 8.1

1 a Negative **b** positive **c** positive
d negative **e** negative **f** positive

2 a −4 **b** 7 **c** −4 **d** 3 **e** −4
f −20 **g** 0 **h** −10 **i** 2 **j** −1

3 a −4 **b** 5 **c** −9
d $-\frac{1}{16}$ **e** −100 **f** $\frac{1}{27}$

4 −2

5 −3 °C

6 a i 10 °C **ii** −10 °C **iii** −25 °C **iv** −40 °C
b i 23 °F **ii** −4 °F **iii** −85 °F **iv** −328 °F

7 a -3 **b** 3 **c** -6 **d** 1 **e** -3
  f -6 **g** -6 **h** 0 **i** -1 **j** -3
8 a M$(1, -2)$ **b** M$(0, -1)$
  c M$(-3, -5)$ **d** M$(-0.5, -0.5)$
9 a i 9 am **ii** 7 am **iii** 6 am **iv** 4 am
  v 2 pm **vi** 7 pm **vii** 5 pm **viii** 10 pm
  b i 8 hours **ii** 14 hours
10 a $x = -3$ **b** $x = -9$ **c** $x = -2$ **d** $x = -7$
  e $x = -3$ **f** $x = -1$ **g** $x = -6$ **h** $x = -9$
  i $x = -3$ **j** $x = -5$ **k** $x = -3$ **l** $x = -4$

Page 38 Exercise 9.1

1 a -15 **b** -15 **c** 16 **d** 32 **e** 30
  f 5 **g** -22 **h** -13 **i** -17 **j** -2
  k 9 **l** -75 **m** -45 **n** -98 **o** 72
  p 240 **q** -77 **r** 25 **s** 12 **t** -4
  u -25 **v** -16 **w** -10 **x** 14
2 a -10 **b** -4 **c** 2
  d 105 **e** -240 **f** 48
3 a 2 **b** 3 **c** -26
  d -80 **e** -82 **f** -200
4 a 16 **b** -72 **c** 2 **d** -6 **e** 36
5 a i -55
  ii -55 m or 55 m below sea level
  b i $h = 275 - 35n$
  ii 11 steps
6 a 2.5×10^5 **b** 1.65×10^7
  c 2.45×10^{-4} **d** 8×10^{-6}
  e 8.4×10^{-10}

Page 40 Revision

1 a true **b** false **c** true
2 $-7, -5, -3, 0, 1, 2, 4$
3 a -13 **b** 8 **c** -5 **d** -56
  e -75 **f** -12 **g** 32 **h** 1
  i -20 **j** -55
4 a 15 degrees **b** $-1\,°C$
5 P$(-2, -8)$, Q$(11, -12)$, R$(2, -3)$
6 a 626 degrees **b** oxygen
  c i 86 degrees **ii** 328 degrees
7 a 24 **b** 6 **c** 2 **d** 2 **e** -1
8 a $-15x^2$ **b** $24a^2$ **c** $-7p^3$ **d** $-4y$
9 a $x = -7$ **b** $x = -4$ **c** $x = -4$
10 a i $5\,°F$ **ii** $-49\,°F$
  b i $-5\,°C$ **ii** $-30\,°C$

3 Brackets and equations

Page 41 Exercise 1.1

1 a -1 **b** 5 **c** 2 **d** -2
  e 0 **f** -6 **g** -15 **h** 6
  i 36 **j** -3 **k** -3 **l** 3
2 a $3a$ **b** $-6x$ **c** $9e$ **d** $2m^2$
  e $18c^2$ **f** $3x + 3y$ **g** $-3w$
3 a 10 **b** 4 **c** 3 **d** $-12\frac{1}{2}$

4 a $3y - 3$ **b** $9k - 18n$ **c** $15z + 12$
  d $3a - ab$ **e** $f^2 + 5f$ **f** $3x^2 + 5x$
  g $2a^2 - 3ab$ **h** $5x^2 - 20x$
5 a $n = 8$ **b** $x = -3$ **c** $y = -9$
  d $t = 8$ **e** $y = -1$ **f** $e = 5$
  g $x = 6$ **h** $h = -5$
6 a $y = -5$ **b** $a = -3$ **c** $y = 1$
7 a $x = 2$; 12 cm **b** $y = 6$; 3 kg
8 a $4(x + 12)$ cm^2 **b** $x = 2$
9 a $y - 2$ cm **b** $y + 3$ cm

Page 43 Exercise 2.1

1 a $3y - 21$ **b** $2m + 6$ **c** $5n - 20$
  d $9x + 9$ **e** $7a + 21$ **f** $7b - 28$
  g $4z - 24$ **h** $10t - 20$ **i** $2k - 2$
  j $11c - 44$ **k** $42 + 6y$ **l** $8 + 8u$
  m $25 - 5h$ **n** $24 - 12a$ **o** $21 - 7e$
  p $6x + 6y$ **q** $8x - 8y$ **r** $26 - 13f$
  s $80 + 20x$ **t** $7a - 7b$ **u** $15k + 15a$
  v $16y - 48$ **w** $38 - 19a$ **x** $23m + 23n$
2 a $4(x - 5)$; $4x - 20$ **b** $3(10 - y)$; $30 - 3y$
  c $6(a + b)$; $6a + 6b$ **d** $5(n + 2)$; $5n + 10$
  e $2(m - n)$; $2m - 2n$ **f** $7(13 + y)$; $91 + 7y$
3 a $3(h - 4)$; $3h - 12$ **b** $4(10 - x)$; $40 - 4x$
  c $2(n + 7)$; $2n + 14$
4 a $4(v - 3)$; $4v - 12$ **b** $3(13 + y)$; $39 + 3y$

Page 44 Exercise 2.2

1 a $12x + 15$ **b** $10y - 5$ **c** $4 + 6m$
  d $3 - 9k$ **e** $56w - 16$ **f** $cy + 2c$
  g $ax + a$ **h** $ef - 3e$ **i** $rk - 3r$
  j $xy + 4x$ **k** $xy + xz$ **l** $bc + bd$
  m $ex - ey$ **n** $k^2 + 3k$ **o** $a^2 - 5a$
  p $r^2 - rs$ **q** $4e - e^2$ **r** $x^2 - 8x$
  s $a^2 + 2ab$ **t** $4x^2 - 5x$ **u** $6xy - 5y^2$
  v $2x^2 - 3xy$ **w** $5m^2 - 6m$ **x** $25x - 2x^2$
2 a $3a + 3b - 9$ **b** $4x + 4y + 4$
  c $2m - 2n - 14$ **d** $8x + 16y + 8z$
  e $12a - 6b + 3c$ **f** $50x - 60y + 30$
  g $y^3 - 4y$ **h** $a^3 + 3a$
  i $h^3 - h^2$ **j** $a^2 + a^3$
  k $w^4 - w^2$ **l** $2k^4 - 10k^3$
3 a i $x(4x - 5)$
  ii $4x^2 - 5x$
  b i $2x(4x - 5)$
  ii $8x^2 - 10x$
  c i $2x^2(4x - 5)$
  ii $8x^3 - 10x^2$

Page 44 Exercise 3.1

1 a $-3a - 6$ **b** $-2k + 2$ **c** $-7c - 21$
  d $-5x + 20$ **e** $-40 - 8x$ **f** $-2 + n$
  g $-14 - x$ **h** $-8 + 4h$ **i** $-2a - 2b$
  j $-4m + 4n$ **k** $-x - y$ **l** $-w - w^2$
  m $-6x + 6x^2$ **n** $-4y^2 - 4y^3$ **o** $-2a + a^2$
  p $-x^2 - 5x$ **q** $-m^2 - mn$ **r** $-ah + bh$
  s $-7k + k^3$ **t** $-x^3 - 3x^2$

2 a $3a + 10$ **b** $11 - 2x$ **c** $7w - 3$
d $2 - 2w$ **e** $3y + 26$ **f** $14 - 3x$
g $3x - 3$ **h** $7 - x$ **i** $-3r$
j $-5 - 4y$ **k** $3 - k$ **l** $-1 - z$
m $6 + m$ **n** $3f - 6$ **o** $3t$
p $-4 - 8x$ **q** $7a + 19$ **r** $26 - 9b$
s $3 - h$ **t** $7y - 16$ **u** $-4x - 6$
v $y - 8$ **w** $x - 28$

3 a $12x$ **b** $10(x - 2)$
c difference of areas   **d** $2x + 20$
4 i a $12y$ **b** $9(y - 3)$
    c $12y - 9(y - 3)$ **d** $3y + 27$
ii a $9a$ **b** $5(a - 4)$
    c $9a - 5(a - 4)$ **d** $4a + 20$
5 a $15k - 13(k - 2)$ **b** $2k + 26$

Page 46 Exercise 3.2

1 a i $7(y - 4) - 4(y - 5)$ **ii** $3y - 8$ **iii** 34 cm^2
  b i $9(x + 3) - 7(x + 1)$ **ii** $2x + 20$ **iii** 28 cm^2
  c i $5(m + 2) - 7(m - 1)$ **ii** $17 - 2m$ **iii** 1 cm^2
  d i $11(n - 1) - 12(n - 3)$ **ii** $25 - n$ **iii** 10 cm^2
2 a $3m - 14$ **b** $2x + 28$ **c** $12k - 36$
  d $x + 4$ **e** $-3w - 12$ **f** $4n - 50$
  g $x + 4$ **h** $45 - 9r$ **i** x
3 a i $5(x - 4); 3(x - 6)$ **ii** $2x - 2$ **iii** £16
  b i $4(2n + 2); 6(n + 3)$ **ii** $2n - 10$ **iii** £4
  c i $20(20 - 2x); 15(13 - x)$ **ii** $205 - 25x$ **iii** £5

Page 47 Exercise 4.1

1 a $m = 4$ **b** $y = 9$ **c** $x = 1$
  d $x = 9$ **e** $n = 3$ **f** $k = 10$
  g $r = 7$ **h** $w = 0$ **i** $k = 0$
  j $x = 3$ **k** $x = 0$ **l** $n = 2$
2 a $x = 0$ **b** $n = -2$ **c** $k = -3$
  d $w = -1$ **e** $k = -2$ **f** $y = -5$
  g $x = -1$ **h** $x = -1$ **i** $r = -2$
  j $y = -9$ **k** $t = -2$ **l** $k = 6$
3 a i $5(y - 5) = 10$ **ii** $y = 7$; 2 kg
  b i $8(x + 3) = 64$ **ii** $x = 5$; 8 kg
  c i $7(x - 10) = 42$ **ii** $x = 16$; 6 kg
  d i $9(m - 12) = 27$ **ii** $m = 15$; 3 kg
4 a $x = -1$ **b** $k = 0$ **c** $m = -6$
  d $x = 4$ **e** $w = -3$ **f** $x = -9$
  g $r = -10$ **h** $x = -3$ **i** $y = 6$

Page 48 Exercise 4.2

1 a $x = 5$ **b** $w = 1$ **c** $x = 7$
  d $r = 3$ **e** $x = 0$ **f** $w = 5$
2 a i $8(m - 3) = 4(m + 1); m = 7$ **ii** £4, £8
  b i $9(f - 7) = 4(f + 3); f = 15$ **ii** £8, £18
  c i $4(x + 2) = 6(x - 2); x = 10$ **ii** £12, £8
3 a $8(2x + 3)$
  b $x = 4$
  c 8 cm $\times$ 11 cm
4 a $12y + 8(2y + 1)$
  b $y = 5$
  c 4 cm $\times$ 15 cm; 8 cm $\times$ 11 cm

5 a $x = 4$ **b** $x = 4$ **c** $x = 2$
  d $x = 5$ **e** $x = -5$ **f** $x = 4$
  g $x = 5$ **h** $x = 5$ **i** $x = -1$
  j $x = 3$ **k** $x = 11$ **l** $x = -1$

Page 49 Challenge

(from left to right, top to bottom) 12, 25; 38, 13, 16;
31, 32, 10; 16, 24

Page 50 Exercise 5.1

1 a $m^2 + 5m + 6$ **b** $m^2 + m - 6$
  c $m^2 - m - 6$ **d** $m^2 - 5m + 6$
  e $a^2 + 3a + 2$ **f** $a^2 + a - 2$
  g $a^2 - a - 2$ **h** $a^2 - 3a + 2$
  i $w^2 + 12w + 35$ **j** $w^2 + 2w - 35$
  k $w^2 - 2w - 35$ **l** $w^2 - 12w + 35$
2 a $x^2 - 10x + 24$ **b** $x^2 - 2x - 24$
  c $x^2 + 10x + 24$ **d** $x^2 + 2x - 24$
  e $y^2 - 8y - 9$ **f** $y^2 - 10y + 9$
  g $y^2 + 8y - 9$ **h** $y^2 + 10y + 9$
  i $t^2 - 13t + 30$ **j** $t^2 + 13t + 30$
  k $t^2 + 7t - 30$ **l** $t^2 - 7t - 30$
  m $n^2 - 4$ **n** $n^2 - 4n + 4$
  o $n^2 - 4$ **p** $n^2 + 4n + 4$
3 a $m^2 - 4m - 21$ **b** $n^2 - n - 6$
  c $p^2 - 5p - 6$ **d** $r^2 + r - 56$
  e $t^2 - 4$ **f** $w^2 - 16$
  g $x^2 + 3x - 28$ **h** $y^2 - y - 6$
  i $a^2 + 11a + 10$ **j** $c^2 - 16$
  k $d^2 - 7d - 60$ **l** $f^2 - 13f + 42$
  m $h^2 + 2h + 1$ **n** $x^2 - 36$
  o $y^2 + 5y - 24$ **p** $a^2 - 9$
  q $b^2 + 8b + 16$ **r** $w^2 - 7w + 12$
  s $y^2 + 20y + 99$ **t** $e^2 + 2e - 99$
  u $m^2 + 3m - 180$ **v** $n^2 - 22n - 23$
  w $x^2 - 7x - 260$ **x** $y^2 - 15y - 450$

Page 50 Exercise 5.2

1 a $6m^2 - 4m - 2$ **b** $2y^2 + 3y - 9$
  c $6k^2 + 10k - 4$ **d** $12x^2 - 19x + 5$
  e $10h^2 - 23h + 12$ **f** $2y^2 - y - 21$
  g $4x^2 - 2x - 2$ **h** $3m^2 - 11m - 42$
  i $4y^2 - 8y - 5$ **j** $14c^2 + 25c + 6$
  k $24n^2 - 58n + 35$ **l** $14n^2 - 46n - 40$
  m $6 - 5y + y^2$
  o $24 - 52a + 20a^2$ **n** $4 + 10x - 6x^2$
2 a $(6y^2 - y - 2)$ cm^2
  b $(10x^2 - 19x - 15)$ cm^2
  c $(6m^2 - 29m + 28)$ cm^2
  d $(24w^2 - w - 3)$ cm^2
3 1st row: $64 - 48w + 9w^2$; $16 + 2w - 3w^2$;
            $24 - 17w + 3w^2$;
            $24 - w - 3w^2$; $72 - 43w + 6w^2$
    2nd row: $16 + 2w - 3w^2$; $4 + 4w + w^2$;
            $6 + w - w^2$; $6 + 5w + w^2$;
            $18 + 5w - 2w^2$

3rd row: $24 - 17w + 3w^2$; $6 + w - w^2$;
$9 - 6w + w^2$; $9 - w^2$; $27 - 15w + 2w^2$

4th row: $24 - w - 3w^2$; $6 + 5w + w^2$; $9 - w^2$;
$9 + 6w + w^2$; $27 + 3w - 2w^2$

5th row: $72 - 43w + 6w^2$; $18 + 5w - 2w^2$;
$27 - 15w + 2w^2$; $27 + 3w - 2w^2$;
$81 - 36w + 4w^2$

4 $x^3 + x^2 - 3x + 9$

5 a $x^3 - x^2 - 5x + 2$ **b** $x^3 - 2x^2 - 6x + 9$
  c $x^3 - 3x^2 - 2x + 4$ **d** $2x^2 - 4x - 23$
  e $-9y + 29$ **f** $7m^2 - 3m + 2$
  g $7w^2 - 16w + 18$

6 a $(x - 2)(x + 3)$ **b** $(x - 3)(x + 2)$
  c difference of areas   **d** $2x$

7 i a $(2k + 3)(k + 7)$
    b $(2k + 1)(k + 5)$
    c $(2k + 3)(k + 7) - (2k + 1)(k + 5)$
    d $6k + 16$
  ii a $(12 - x)(8 - 2x)$
    b $(11 - x)(7 - 2x)$
    c $(12 - x)(8 - 2x) - (11 - x)(7 - 2x)$
    d $19 - 3x$

8 a $5x - 2 - (2 \times 2)$ for path
  b $(2x + 1)$ m
  c $(2x + 5)(5x - 2)$, $(2x + 1)(5x - 6)$
  d $28x - 4$
  e $x = 5$, 136 m^2

Page 52 Challenge

1 91   **2** checking
3 checking   **4** expressions are equal

Page 53 Exercise 6.1

1 a $t^2 + 2tm + m^2$ **b** $a^2 - 2ab + b^2$
  c $k^2 + 2ks + s^2$ **d** $u^2 - 2uv + v^2$
  e $m^2 - 2mn + n^2$ **f** $c + 2cd + d^2$
  g $x^2 - 2xy + y^2$ **h** $f^2 - 2fg + g^2$
  i $c^2 - 2cw + w^2$ **j** $w^2 + 2wx + x^2$
  k $e^2 - 2ef + f^2$ **l** $x^2 + 2xy + y^2$
  m $a^2 + 6a + 9$ **n** $x^2 + 2x + 1$
  o $y^2 - 2y + 1$ **p** $e^2 + 16e + 64$
  q $w^2 + 10w + 25$ **r** $x^2 - 4x + 4$
  s $f^2 - 14f + 49$ **t** $a^2 + 18a + 81$
  u $e^2 - 18e + 81$ **v** $x^2 - 6x + 9$
  w $y^2 + 20y + 100$ **x** $w^2 - 16w + 64$

2 a i $(y + 5)^2$ **ii** $y^2 + 10y + 25$
  b i $(x - 4)^2$ **ii** $x^2 - 8x + 16$
  c i $(m + 7)^2$ **ii** $m^2 + 14m + 49$
  d i $(k - 6)^2$ **ii** $k^2 - 12k + 36$
  e i $(w - 1)^2$ **ii** $w^2 - 2w + 1$

3 a $64 + 16x + x^2$ **b** $16 - 8a + a^2$
  c $81 + 18k + k^2$ **d** $1 - 2y + y^2$
  e $1 + 2m + m^2$ **f** $49 + 14f + f^2$
  g $4 - 4x + x^2$ **h** $9 - 6c + c^2$
  i $100 - 20d + d^2$ **j** $25 + 10h + h^2$
  k $36 - 12g + g^2$ **l** $144 + 24x + x^2$

Page 53 Exercise 6.2

1 a $9y^2 + 12y + 4$ **b** $25x^2 + 10x + 1$
  c $9c^2 - 42c + 49$ **d** $16w^2 + 24w + 9$
  e $4f^2 - 4f + 1$ **f** $9d^2 - 36d + 36$
  g $4 + 16y + 16y^2$ **h** $25 - 30x + 9x^2$
  i $49 + 42k + 9k^2$ **j** $100 - 140h + 49h^2$
  k $25a^2 + 20ab + 4b^2$ **l** $16a^2 - 40ab + 25b^2$
  m $4c^2 - 12cd + 9d^2$ **n** $64d^2 - 48de + 9e^2$
  o $4x^2 + 16xy + 16y^2$ **p** $25e^2 - 30ef + 9f^2$
  q $81x^2 + 36xg + 4g^2$ **r** $100y^2 - 140xy + 49x^2$
  s $16a^2 + 16ad + 4d^2$ **t** $16b^2 - 24ab + 9a^2$

2 a Pond area $= (x - 4)^2$, difference of areas
  b $12x - 12$
  c 84 m^2

3 a $x^2 + 2 + \dfrac{1}{x^2}$ **b** $y^2 - 2 + \dfrac{1}{y^2}$

  c $25 + \dfrac{10}{n} + \dfrac{1}{n^2}$ **d** $9 - \dfrac{6}{w} + \dfrac{1}{w^2}$

  e $a^2 + 4 + \dfrac{4}{a^2}$ **f** $64 - \dfrac{48}{k} + \dfrac{9}{k^2}$

  g $m^2 + 8 + \dfrac{16}{m^2}$ **h** $4x^2 - 4 + \dfrac{1}{x^2}$

  i $\dfrac{1}{a^2} + \dfrac{2}{ab} + \dfrac{1}{b^2}$ **j** $\dfrac{4}{x^2} - \dfrac{12}{xy} + \dfrac{9}{y^2}$

  k $16m^2 + 16 + \dfrac{4}{m^2}$ **l** $49x^2 - 42 + \dfrac{9}{x^2}$

  m $\dfrac{1}{a^2} + \dfrac{4}{a} + 4$ **n** $\dfrac{9}{y^2} - \dfrac{42}{y} + 49$

  o $\dfrac{4}{m^2} + 4 + m^2$ **p** $\dfrac{9}{h^2} - 24 + 16h^2$

4 a $2y^2 + 14y + 25$ **b** $6x + 21$
  c $8t^2 - 14t - 15$ **d** $37y^2 + 2y + 26$
  e $5x^2 - 26x + 24$ **f** $8w^2 - 48w + 40$

5 a $(15 + x)^2 - 15^2 = 30x + x^2$
  b $47{\cdot}25$ cm^2
  c 21%

Page 54 Challenge

1 checking
2 $a^4 + 4a^3b + 6a^2b^2 + 4ab^3 + b^4$
3 Sum of two 'reds' above gives 'red' below.

Page 55 Exercise 7.1

1 a $m = 5$ **b** $y = -3$ **c** $a = -3$
  d $x = 3$ **e** $k = 4$ **f** $n = 1$
  g $b = \frac{1}{2}$ **h** $a = -2$ **i** $y = 0$
  j $w = \frac{1}{2}$ **k** $y = -1$ **l** $d = \frac{1}{2}$

Page 56 Exercise 7.2

1 a $x = 20$; 20 cm $\times$ 35 cm and 10 cm $\times$ 70 cm
2 b $x = 24$; 12 cm $\times$ 40 cm and 20 cm $\times$ 24 cm
  c $x = 25$; 20 cm $\times$ 27 cm and 18 cm $\times$ 30 cm
  d $x = 11$; 20 cm $\times$ 30 cm and 24 cm $\times$ 25 cm

2 a $m = 1$ **b** $x = -1$ **c** $y = 5$
  d $n = -3$ **e** $k = -2$ **f** $a = \frac{1}{2}$
  g $w = 5$ **h** $x = 2$ **i** $d = 2$
  j $n = 1$ **k** $a = 2$ **l** $h = -4$

Page 57 Revision

1 a $11w + 33$ **b** $7k - 14$ **c** $6h + 2$
   d $16 - 8d$ **e** $pq + pr$ **f** $a^2 - 2ab$
   g $-4h - 12$ **h** $-5y + 20$ **i** $-48 + 40x$
   j $8x - 8y + 32$ **k** $m^3 - 3m$ **l** $3n^4 - 6n^3$

2 a $1 + 3n$ **b** $-12 - 5y$ **c** $6x + 3$
   d $-10 + 2m$ **e** $-w - 8$ **f** $27 - 26y$

3 a $7a$ **b** $5(a - 2)$
   c $7a - 5(a - 2)$ **d** $2a + 10$

4 a $a = 8$ **b** $y = 3$ **c** $p = -11$

5 a $7(5x - 1) = 21(x + 1)$; $x = 2$
   b £9 and £3

6 a $y = -5$ **b** $a = -3$ **c** $w = -9$

7 a $y^2 + 7y + 10$ **b** $t^2 - 4t + 3$
   c $m^2 - 4m - 21$ **d** $8x^2 + 10x + 3$
   e $9 - d^2$ **f** $x^2 + 10x + 25$
   g $4c^2 - 20c + 25$ **h** $81y^2 - 144xy + 64x^2$

8 a $x = 6$ **b** $y = 8$ **c** $r = 7$ **d** $m = 1$

4 Money

Page 58 Exercise 1.1

1 a £12·49   **b** £8·71   **c** £72·20
   d £12·36   **e** £17·75   **f** £17·86
   g £34

2 a £57·39   **b** £2·61

3 a £6·10   **b** £53·70   **c** £80·40
   d £66·70   **e** £9·90

4 a 38p   **b** 8p   **c** 84p
   d £2·84   **e** £8·00   **f** £19·08

5 a £18   **b** £63   **c** £280   **d** £7

6 a £42·80   **b** £63   **c** £840
   d £0·90   **e** £3·05   **f** £7·38

7 a £2·92   **b** £114·75   **c** £239·94
   d £1·74   **e** £6·46   **f** £34·05
   g £1868·80   **h** £2·45

8 a i £1·20   **ii** £3   **iii** £3·60   **iv** £1·80
   b i £70   **ii** £175   **iii** £210   **iv** £105
   c i £0·56   **ii** £1·40   **iii** £1·68   **iv** £0·84
   d i £840   **ii** £2100   **iii** £2520   **iv** £1260
   e i £1·72   **ii** £4·30   **iii** £5·16   **iv** £2·58

9 a £2·90   **b** £1·34
   c £43·95   **d** £483·20

10 a 25%   **b** 40%
   c 70%   **d** 8%

11 a $\frac{1}{10}$ **b** $\frac{3}{20}$ **c** $\frac{3}{4}$ **d** $\frac{1}{3}$

12 a £17 972·24   **b** £13·82

13 £156·25

Page 59 Exercise 2.1

1 a £12   **b** £60   **c** £0·56   **d** £21·25
   e £6·75   **f** £540   **g** £340   **h** 2p

2 a i £4   **ii** 50%
   b i £2   **ii** 20%
   c i £6   **ii** 30%

3 a i £7·20   **ii** £43·20
   b i £1·30   **ii** £7·80
   c i £10·72   **ii** £64·32
   d i £22·40   **ii** £134·40

4 a £2580   **b** £83 420

5 28%

6 a 42·9%; 53·8%
   b necklace by 10·9%

7 39·6%

8 a 37·5% profit, 16·7% profit, 12·5% loss
   b 13·9%

9 a Cosmic Cars £56·50 dearer
   b Cosmic Cars make 0·4% more profit

10 16·7%

Page 61 Exercise 2.2

1 50% profit, 25% loss

2 a 75%
   b £91

3 Selling price = 300%, £600 ÷ 300 × 100 = £200

4 £4

5 8p

6 £650 000

7 £67·50

8 a £13   **b** £32·50   **c** £64·24

9 Echo Electrics by 27p

10 £120 000

Page 62 Brainstormers

1 $1·25 \times 0·8 = 1$, so price is same as the original price.

2 £11 648

Page 63 Exercise 3.1

1 a £2   **b** 35p   **c** £11·50
   d 4p   **e** 88p

2 a £5·20, £2·60, £1·30, £9·10
   b £27, £13·50, £6·75, £47·25
   c £9·38, £4·69, £2·35, £16·42

3 a £3·50   **b** £1·05   **c** £147
   d £1102·50   **e** £0·28

4 a i £5·50   **ii** £115·50
   b i £4·37   **ii** £91·77
   c i £2·96   **ii** £62·16
   d i £6·28   **ii** £131·88

5 a i £22·75   **ii** £152·75
   b i £16·87   **ii** £113·27
   c i £27·51   **ii** £184·71

6 a £423   **b** £559·30   **c** £41·83

7 £151·16, £12·75, £8·99, £57·00, £229·90, £40·23, £270·13

8 £11·90

9 a £205·03   **b** £305·21
   c £1486·38   **d** £2044·49

10 a Florida Fun   **b** £49·69

11 £270·98

Page 65 Exercise 3.2

1 a £85, £42·50, £21·25, £148·75
 b £520, £260, £130, £910
 c £23·48, £11·74, £5·87, £41·09
2 a £21·15   **b** £66·27   **c** £156·04
3 a i £82·08   **ii** £89·30   **iii** £79·80
 b i £242·78   **ii** £264·14   **iii** £236·04
4 £84
5 a £13·61   **b** £340·38   **c** £2127·23
6 89p
7 a 0·05   **b** 1·05   **c** £63
 d £73·50 ÷ 1·05 **e** £70
8 £100·61, £91·88, £102·75 total amount required
 = 295·24
9 £16·80   **10** £13 738

Page 66 Brainstormers

1 a £681·50, £1614·45   **b** $\frac{47}{7}$
2 £3·63 × 10^{10}

Page 67 Exercise 4.1

1 a £2688   **b** £188
2 a £7920   **b** £1420
3 a i £59·94   **ii** £9·95
 b i £84·50   **ii** £5·45
 c i £288·40   **ii** £28·91
 d i £679·30   **ii** £79·40
 e i £244·70   **ii** £14·70
 f i £156·40   **ii** £16·40
4 a i £845·00   **ii** £9964·76   **iii** £1514·81
 b i £2399·88   **ii** £23 854·08   **iii** £3855·08
5 £46·55, £71·18, £124·25

Page 69 Exercise 4.2

1 a £2340   **b** £810
2 a i £594·40   **ii** £44·41
 b i £386·32   **ii** £10·87
3 a £74·50   **b** £34·99
4 a i £1689·74   **ii** £100·49   **iii** 6·3%
 b i £1793·48   **ii** £204·23   **iii** 12·9%
5 £66
6 £2460·30
7 £19·69
8 £720
9 £2499

Page 71 Exercise 5.1

1 a €1400   **b** $1600
 c 2250 francs   **d** 10 000 kroner
 e 12 500 rand   **f** 75 000 rupees
 g 191 500 yen
2 a €7   **b** £20
3 a 100 rand   **b** £40
4 a i €63   **ii** €102   **iii** €31
 b i £78   **ii** £15   **iii** £63
5 a $6·40   **b** $48   **c** $320
 d $51·20   **e** $7·20

6 a £200   **b** £500   **c** £4000
 d £4500   **e** £6400   **f** £2666·67
 g £5221·93
7 £0·63, £0·44, £0·08
8 a €665   **b** £62·10
9 a Japan   **b** 2p
10 £122

Page 72 Exercise 5.2

1 a 13·1 dollars   **b** 104 800 dollars
2 a £48·30   **b** £31·83
3 a €0·88   **b** $1·14
4 a £200   **b** £197·53
5 1·7 yen
6 a €140·38   **b** £101·72
7 7·84%
8 €10 185
9 £2141·11
10 a £269·98   **b** £105·02

Page 75 Exercise 6.1

1 a £584   **b** £683   **c** £625
2 a £245   **b** £245
3 a £252·80   **b** £1011·20
4 £194·80
5 £1331·10
6 £196 per year
7 a £490   **b** £49
8 £211·20
9 3 years
10 Jane, £109·10
11 £548

Page 77 Exercise 7.1

1 a £16·80   **b** £11·52   **c** £85   **d** £64·30
2 £99·40
3 a £48·52   **b** £1·73
4 £2·87
5 £25·80
6 £145·18
7 6 days
8 9 days

Page 78 Exercise 8.1

1 a £64·24   **b** £76·65   **c** £137·97
2 a £32·13   **b** £53·55   **c** £117·81
3 a £28·50   **b** £40·38   **c** £190
4 a i £29·20   **ii** £42·84   **b** £72·04
5 £430·35
6 a £144 000   **b** £27 000
7 a i £81·47   **ii** £80·33   **b** £161·80
8 £190 000
9 £25 000
10 a £36 000   **b** £97·27

Page 80 Exercise 9.1

1 a £1·25   **b** £0·86   **c** £1·20
2 a £17·20   **b** £4128

3 a i £2·85   **ii** £34·20
  b i £3·30   **ii** £39·60
  c i £3·75   **ii** £45
  d i £4·20   **ii** £50·40
4 a £10·40   **b** £2496
5 £180 000
6 a £1344   **b** £3878·40
7 a £180 000   **b** £28·80
8 a i £8880   **ii** £6660
  b i £3120   **ii** £2700

Page 82 Revision

1 a £55·68   **b** 31·9%   **c** £15·80
2 a £3779·71   **b** £180·71
3 17·5%, £141·41, £76·32
4 a i $62·32   **ii** £457·32
  b i £1 = 2·27 francs   **ii** £44·05
5 a Le Bleu is cheaper by £3·26
  b Blue Racer cheaper by £1·87
6 a £79·20   **b** £117·15   **c** £136·50
7 a £843·20   **b** £872
8 a £16·85   **b** £125·30
9 a £6·84   **b** £1641·60

5 Factors

Page 84 Exercise 1.1

1 a $1 \times 6, 2 \times 3$ **b** $1 \times 4, 2 \times 2$
  c $1 \times 10, 2 \times 5$ **d** $1 \times 18, 2 \times 9, 3 \times 6$
  e $1 \times 20, 2 \times 10, 4 \times 5$
2 a 1, 7   **b** 1, 2, 4, 8
  c 1, 2, 3, 4, 6, 12   **d** 1, 2, 4, 8, 16
  e 1, 5, 25
3 2, 3, 5, 7, 11, 13, 17, 19, 23, 29, 31, 37, 41, 43, 47
4 a $1, 5, a, 5a$ **b** $1, x, x^2$
  c $1, a, b, ab$ **d** $1, 2, 4, y, 2y, 4y$
  e $1, 3, m, 3m, n, 3n, mn, 3mn$
5 a b **b** m **c** $2k$ **d** 3   **e** $4xy$
6 a 2, 7, 12, 17, 22
  b 11, 15, 19, 23
  c 1, 4, 9, 16, 25, 36; square numbers
  d 1, 3, 6, 10, 15, 21; triangular numbers
7 a $5(x + 4)$ **b** $5x + 20$
8 a $5y - 15$ **b** $7x + 28$ **c** $30k + 20$
  d $16 - 8n$ **e** $x^2 + 3x$ **f** $a^2 - ab$
  g $2m^2 + 3m$ **h** $14y - 28y^2$
9 a $5m - 5$ **b** $3x - 6$ **c** $x + 14y$ **d** $2x^2$
10 a $uv + v + 2u + 2$ **b** $x^2 + x - 12$
  c $y^2 + 5y - 14$ **d** $w^2 - 8w + 15$
  e $6x^2 + x - 1$ **f** $9x^2 - 25$
  g $35 + 9t - 2t^2$ **h** $x^2 - 6x + 9$
  i $9 - 12y + 4y^2$ **j** $a^2 - 4ab + 4b^2$
  k $16c^2 + 40cd + 25d^2$ **l** $x^2 + 2 + \dfrac{1}{x^2}$
11 a i $2n + 1$ **ii** $5n - 4$ **iii** n^2
  b 21, 46, 100

Page 85 Challenge 1

From top clockwise: A − F − I − E − B − J − H − G − C − D

Page 86 Challenge 2

a 8   **b** 16
c doubling each time or expression with n letters has 2^n factors; 32
d a^n has $n + 1$ factors

Page 86 Exercise 2.1

1 a $1 \times 4, 2 \times 2$
  b 1×13
  c $1 \times 9, 3 \times 3$
  d $1 \times 6, 2 \times 3$
  e $1 \times 20, 2 \times 10, 4 \times 5$
  f $1 \times 12, 2 \times 6, 3 \times 4$
  g $1 \times 24, 2 \times 12, 3 \times 8, 4 \times 6$
  h $1 \times 27, 3 \times 9$
  i $1 \times 30, 2 \times 15, 3 \times 10, 5 \times 6$
  j $1 \times 45, 3 \times 15, 5 \times 9$
  k 1×17
  l $1 \times 81, 3 \times 27, 9 \times 9$
  m $1 \times 50, 2 \times 25, 5 \times 10$
  n $1 \times 100, 2 \times 50, 4 \times 25, 5 \times 20, 10 \times 10$
2 a 3   **b** b **c** a **d** ab
  e 2   **f** x **g** n **h** n^2
  i $2cd$ **j** $6d$ **k** $3cd$ **l** $2cd$
  m $3cd$ **n** $3c$ **o** $2c$ **p** $2a$
  q a **r** 2   **s** $4a$ **t** $2a$
  u 6   **v** $2n$ **w** $2x$ **x** a
3 a $1 \times 3a, 3 \times a$
  b $1 \times 11x, 11 \times x$
  c $1 \times cd, c \times d$
  d $1 \times 4r, 2 \times 2r, 4 \times r$
  e $1 \times 14k, 2 \times 7k, 7 \times 2k, 14 \times k$
  f $1 \times 6n, 2 \times 3n, 3 \times 2n, 6 \times n$
  g $1 \times 2xy, 2 \times xy, x \times 2y, y \times 2x$
  h $1 \times 3kw, 3 \times kw, k \times 3w, w \times 3k$
  i $1 \times d^2, d \times d$
  j $1 \times 2x^2, 2 \times x^2, x \times 2x$
  k $1 \times 3d^2, 3 \times d^2, d \times 3d$
  l $1 \times 6ef, 2 \times 3ef, 3 \times 2ef, 6 \times ef, e \times 6f,$
     $2e \times 3f, 3e \times 2f, 6e \times f$
4 a $1, 2, 4, x, 2x, 4x$
  b $1, 2, 3, 6, b, 2b, 3b, 6b$
  c $1, m, n, mn$
  d $1, h, h^2$
  e $1, 3, 9, y, 3y, 9y$
  f $1, 3, w, 3w, w^2, 3w^2$
  g $1, 17, h, 17h$
  h $1, 2, w, 2w, x, 2x, wx, 2wx$
  i $1, 5, d, 5d, d^2, 5d^2$
  j $1, 2, 4, n, 2n, 4n, n^2, 2n^2, 4n^2$
  k $1, a, a^2, b, ab, a^2b$
  l $1, a, b, b^2, ab, ab^2$
5 $1 - e, 2 - a, 3 - d, 4 - f, 5 - b, 6 - c$

Page 87 Exercise 3.1

1 a 2 is still a common factor in the partners
b partner factors have no common factor other than 1
c y is still a common factor in the partners
d partner factors have no common factor other than 1
e 2 is still a common factor in the partners
f partner factors have no common factor other than 1
g c is still a common factor in the partners
h partner factors have no common factor other than 1

2 a i $3x, 2$ **ii** $2x$
b i $3w, 2x$ **ii** $3x$
c i $2a, 2a$ **ii** $2a$
d i $2x, 2x$ **ii** $2x$

3 a 2 **b** a **c** 4 **d** w
e 5 **f** y **g** 7 **h** m
i x **j** a **k** $2y$ **l** h
m 2 **n** $2x$ **o** $2xy$ **p** $2a$
q $2g$ **r** $2k$ **s** $5h$ **t** xy
u $5a$ **v** $6x$ **w** $4h$ **x** $4ab$

Page 88 Challenge

a i a^4
ii a^5
b take the smallest of n and m and HCF is a to this power

Page 88 Exercise 4.1

1 a $4(a + 2)$ **b** $3(2y - 5)$ **c** $2(5e + 4)$
d $4(3h + 2)$ **e** $8(2 - x)$ **f** $5(1 - 3y)$
g $2(3a + 4b)$ **h** $7(m - 2n)$ **i** $2(8 - 3c)$
j $11(2h + 1)$ **k** $7(4x - 1)$ **l** $4(2w - 5)$
m $6(4x - 3)$ **n** $4(5y + 3)$ **o** $23(1 - 2t)$
p $4(3 + 2y)$

2 a $2(2y + 4)$ **b** $2(2x + 3)$ **c** $5(2a + 5)$
d $5(t - 3)$ **e** $2(3n - 4)$ **f** $2(2b + 3)$
g $3(1 + 3r)$ **h** $4(2 - 3a)$ **i** $x(x + 1)$
j $a(1 - a)$ **k** $n(2 + n)$ **l** $y(y - 3)$
m $2(ef - 2)$ **n** $3(2 - kh)$ **o** $4(2t + 3k)$
p $2a(b - 2)$ **q** $3k(m + 4)$ **r** $2x(x - 2)$
s $y(7 - y)$ **t** $3d(1 + 2d)$

3 a $a(a + 1)$ **b** $y(1 - y)$ **c** $m(m + 7)$
d $y(y - 3)$ **e** $3k(k + 2)$ **f** $2t(3t - 4)$
g $2a(4 - 3a)$ **h** $d(5d - 3)$ **i** $2d(1 + 4d)$
j $4k(3k + 5)$ **k** $2z(3z - 4)$ **l** $12f(1 + 4f)$
m $2g(13 - 14g)$ **n** $8w(2w - 3)$ **o** $2x(23 + 9x)$
p $2a(a + 3b)$ **q** $2n(3n - 1)$ **r** $4(3m + 2n)$
s $2a(b - 2c)$ **t** $2b(3x - 2y)$ **u** $3x(3y - 4z)$
v $2h(3h + 2)$ **w** $3w(5w - 2x)$ **x** $\frac{1}{2}a(b - c)$

4 a 12 is the common factor; 1200
b i 3200 **ii** 92
iii 1900 **iv** 15
v 1 **vi** 2005

Page 89 Exercise 4.2

1 a £34
2 £26
3 a i $2m + 6 + 5m - 55$ **ii** $7m - 49$
iii $7(m - 7)$
b i $4y + 4 - 2y - 16$ **ii** $2y - 12$
iii $2(y - 6)$
c i $6x - 36 + 2x + 28$ **ii** $8x - 8$
iii $8(x - 1)$
d i $7y + 14 - 3y + 18$ **ii** $4y + 32$
iii $4(y + 8)$
e i $5k - 5 - 2k - 10$ **ii** $3k - 15$
iii $3(k - 5)$
f i $10d - 50 + 2d + 2$ **ii** $12d - 48$
iii $12(d - 4)$

Page 89 Challenge

(from top to bottom, left to right) $3ab$, $2a^2b$, $4a^2b^3$, $3b^3$; ab, $2a^2b$, b^3; ab, b; b

Page 90 Exercise 5.1

1 a $(c - d)(c + d)$ **b** $(e - f)(e + f)$
c $(a - b)(a + b)$ **d** $(y - 2)(y + 2)$
e $(x - 7)(x + 7)$ **f** $(8 - a)(8 + a)$
g $(3 - w)(3 + w)$ **h** $(9 - x)(9 + x)$
i $(1 - y)(1 + y)$ **j** $(m - 1)(m + 1)$
k $(h - 3)(h + 3)$ **l** $(n - 1)(n + 1)$
m $(w - 4)(w + 4)$ **n** $(9 - e)(9 + e)$
o $(y - x)(y + x)$ **p** $(b - 4)(b + 4)$
q $(7 - k)(7 + k)$ **r** $(x - 5)(x + 5)$
s $(a - 10)(a + 10)$ **t** $(6 - b)(6 + b)$
u $(1 - k)(1 + k)$ **v** $(11 - x)(11 + x)$
w $(2 - h)(2 + h)$ **x** $(7 - n)(7 + n)$

2 a $(2y - 5)(2y + 5)$ **b** $(3x - 8)(3x + 8)$
c $(2a - 1)(2a + 1)$ **d** $(7a - 2)(7a + 2)$
e $(3y - 4)(3y + 4)$ **f** $(4k - 3)(4k + 3)$
g $(9x - a)(9x + a)$ **h** $(a - 3b)(a + 3b)$
i $(7a - 3b)(7a + 3b)$ **j** $(10h - 3d)(10h + 3d)$
k $(m - 4n)(m + 4n)$ **l** $(d - 6z)(d + 6z)$
m $(2w - 3x)(2w + 3x)$ **n** $(3y - 4x)(3y + 4x)$
o $(10e - 9f)(10e + 9f)$ **p** $(1 - 11k)(1 + 11k)$
q $(6x - 1)(6x + 1)$ **r** $(10x - 13y)(10x + 13y)$
s $(8u - 3v)(8u + 3v)$ **t** $(12x - 15y)(12x + 15y)$

3 a 9600 **b** 600 **c** 170
d 401 **e** $\frac{1}{3}$ **f** 3·96

4 A–i $(a - 5b)(a + 5b)$ A–ii $(a - 6b)(a + 6b)$
A–iii $(a - 7b)(a + 7b)$ A–iv $(a - 8b)(a + 8b)$
B–i $(2a - 5b)(2a + 5b)$ B–ii $(2a - 6b)(2a + 6b)$
B–iii $(2a - 7b)(2a + 7b)$ B–iv $(2a - 8b)(2a + 8b)$
C–i $(3a - 5b)(3a + 5b)$ C–ii $(3a - 6b)(3a + 6b)$
C–iii $(3a - 7b)(3a + 7b)$ C–iv $(3a - 8b)(3a + 8b)$
D–i $(4a - 5b)(4a + 5b)$ D–ii $(4a - 6b)(4a + 6b)$
D–iii $(4a - 7b)(4a + 7b)$ D–iv $(4a - 8b)(4a + 8b)$

Page 91 Exercise 5.2

1 a $3(a - 2)(a + 2)$ **b** $5(x - 1)(x + 1)$
c $7(d - 2)(d + 2)$ **d** $6(y - 2)(y + 2)$

e $2(3 - x)(3 + x)$ **f** $2(5 - y)(5 + y)$

g $8(1 - x)(1 + x)$ **h** $5(1 - 2a)(1 + 2a)$

i $3(a - b)(a + b)$ **j** $10(c - 2d)(c + 2d)$

k $2(k - 2m)(k + 2m)$ **l** $3(c - 3d)(c + 3d)$

m $12(a - b)(a + b)$ **n** $9(m - 2n)(m + 2n)$

o $10(x - 3y)(x + 3y)$ **p** $17(d - e)(d + e)$

q $2(e - 7f)(e + 7f)$ **r** $2(x - 9y)(x + 9y)$

s $5(4x - y)(4x + y)$ **t** $8(4u - v)(4u + v)$

u $4(2y - 3t)(2y + 3t)$ **v** $5(3a - 4b)(3a + 4b)$

w $3(4c - 3d)(4c + 3d)$ **x** $2(2a - 5w)(2a + 5w)$

2 a $a(x - y)(x + y)$ **b** $p(a - b)(a + b)$

c $a(x - 2y)(x + 2y)$ **d** $x(w - 3z)(w + 3z)$

e $2d(e - f)(e + f)$ **f** $3a(x - 2y)(x + 2y)$

g $2m(k - 2)(k + 2)$ **h** $5a(m - 3)(m + 3)$

i $y(2x - 3)(2x + 3)$ **j** $2b(2a - 5)(2a + 5)$

k $3k(2x - y)(2x + y)$ **l** $2e(3c - d)(3c + d)$

3 a large square minus small square

b $4(2x - y)(2x + y)$

c 600 mm^2

Page 91 Challenge

1 $a^8 - 1 = (a - 1)(a + 1)(a^2 + 1)(a^4 + 1)$;

$a^{16} - 1 = (a - 1)(a + 1)(a^2 + 1)(a^4 + 1)(a^8 + 1)$;

$a^{32} - 1 = (a - 1)(a + 1)(a^2 + 1)(a^4 + 1)(a^8 + 1)$
$\qquad (a^{16} + 1)$

2 a $a^2 - 1 = (a - 1)(a + 1)$;

$a^4 - a^2 = a^2(a - 1)(a + 1)$;

$a^6 - a^4 = a^4(a - 1)(a + 1)$;

$a^8 - a^6 = a^6(a - 1)(a + 1)$; identical except first factor where power goes up 2 each time

b $a^{2n}(a - 1)(a + 1)$

Page 93 Exercise 6.1

1 a $(a + 2)(a - 1)$ **b** $(a - 2)(a - 1)$

c $(a + 2)(a + 1)$ **d** $(a - 2)(a + 1)$

e $(x + 2)(x + 3)$ **f** $(x - 3)(x + 2)$

g $(x - 2)(x - 3)$ **h** $(x + 3)(x - 2)$

i $(m - 5)(m - 1)$ **j** $(m - 5)(m + 1)$

k $(m + 5)(m - 1)$ **l** $(m + 5)(m + 1)$

2 a $(t + 4)(t + 2)$ **b** $(q - 2)(q - 2)$

c $(y + 4)(y + 5)$ **d** $(n + 3)(n - 2)$

e $(k - 4)(k - 4)$ **f** $(x + 1)(x + 1)$

g $(w - 1)(w - 1)$ **h** $(y - 4)(y - 5)$

i $(u - 5)(u - 7)$ **j** $(x + 2)(x + 1)$

k $(p - 2)(p - 1)$ **l** $(x - 7)(x + 1)$

m $(y + 3)(y + 5)$ **n** $(v - 2)(v - 8)$

o $(x + 5)(x + 1)$ **p** $(k - 3)(k - 3)$

q $(x + 2)(x + 5)$ **r** $(c + 10)(c + 1)$

s $(d + 2)(d + 3)$ **t** $(r - 3)(r - 7)$

u $(t + 8)(t + 1)$ **v** $(u - 3)(u - 7)$

w $(a - 6)(a - 1)$ **x** $(w - 5)(w - 1)$

3 a $(w - 3)(w - 3)$ **b** $(x + 3)(x + 3)$

c $(t - 8)(t + 7)$ **d** $(m + 2)(m + 8)$

e $(b + 5)(b + 5)$ **f** $(a - 5)(a - 5)$

g $(n - 3)(n + 1)$ **h** $(t + 16)(t + 1)$

i $(c + 4)(c + 4)$ **j** $(t - 2)(t - 8)$

k $(b - 16)(b - 1)$ **l** $(p - 10)(p - 10)$

m $(x + 6)(x + 6)$ **n** $(y + 3)(y - 2)$

o $(w + 9)(w - 8)$ **p** $(x + 2)(x + 2)$

q $(e - 2)(e + 1)$ **r** $(a + 5)(a - 1)$

s $(b - 7)(b + 3)$ **t** $(r - 5)(r + 2)$

u $(x - 2)(x - 2)$ **v** $(d - 2)(d - 8)$

w $(t + 2)(t + 4)$ **x** $(u + 5)(u - 4)$

4 a i $x + 5$ **ii** $12 \text{ cm} \times 12 \text{ cm}$

b i $x + 7$ **ii** $11 \text{ cm} \times 11 \text{ cm}$

c i $x + 2$ **ii** $8 \text{ cm} \times 8 \text{ cm}$

d i $x + 1$ **ii** $6 \text{ cm} \times 6 \text{ cm}$

5 a $(y - 3)(y + 2)$ **b** $(w + 5)(w + 13)$

c $(x + 3)(x + 4)$ **d** $(n + 2)(n - 1)$

e $(k - 5)(k + 4)$ **f** $(n + 6)(n - 5)$

g $(x - 3)(x - 4)$ **h** $(y + 4)(y - 3)$

i $(p + 5)(p - 2)$ **j** $(n - 4)(n + 3)$

k $(b - 2)(b - 6)$ **l** $(w - 6)(w + 4)$

m $(c + 12)(c - 1)$ **n** $(v + 6)(v - 2)$

o $(q + 5)(q - 3)$ **p** $(d - 12)(d - 1)$

q $(c - 5)(c + 3)$ **r** $(k + 5)(k - 4)$

s $(a - 6)(a + 2)$ **t** $(r - 9)(r + 4)$

u $(b + 10)(b - 2)$ **v** $(u - 9)(u - 2)$

w $(y - 11)(y + 1)$ **x** $(c + 6)(c + 3)$

y $(g + 7)(g + 7)$ **z** $(w + 24)(w - 3)$

Page 94 Challenge

a 2, 6, 12, 20, 30, 42; product of two consecutive whole numbers

b 3, 8, 15, 24, 35, 48

c $x^2 - 3x - c$: 4, 10, 18, 28, 40; $x^2 - 4x - d$: 5, 12, 21, 32, 45

d pupil's own results

Page 95 Exercise 7.1

1 a $(2w + 1)(w + 1)$ **b** $(3y - 1)(y - 1)$

c $(3b + 1)(b - 1)$ **d** $(2m - 1)(m + 1)$

e $(3k + 1)(k + 1)$ **f** $(3d + 2)(d - 1)$

g $(3a + 1)(a + 2)$ **h** $(3f + 2)(f + 1)$

i $(5e - 1)(e - 1)$ **j** $(5x + 1)(x + 2)$

k $(2p + 7)(p + 1)$ **l** $(2x - 1)(x - 3)$

m $(2c - 1)(c - 2)$ **n** $(2x + 1)(x + 2)$

o $(3v - 2)(v - 1)$ **p** $(5k - 1)(k - 3)$

q $(5n + 2)(n + 1)$ **r** $(11u + 2)(u + 1)$

s $(2x - 1)(x - 1)$ **t** $(3r - 2)(r + 1)$

u $(5b - 1)(b + 1)$ **v** $(13u - 6)(u + 1)$

w $(17a - 8)(a + 1)$ **x** $(7w + 3)(w - 2)$

2 a $(2x - 3)(2x + 1)$; $7 \text{ cm} \times 11 \text{ cm}$

b $(9x - 2)(x + 1)$; $7 \text{ cm} \times 2 \text{ cm}$

c $(4x - 1)(2x + 3)$; $11 \text{ cm} \times 9 \text{ cm}$

3 a $(4d + 1)(d + 1)$ **b** $(3x - 1)(2x - 1)$

c $(4d - 1)(2d + 3)$ **d** $(4y - 3)(y - 1)$

e $(3w - 1)(3w - 1)$ **f** $(4t - 1)(t + 1)$

g $(3n + 2)(4n - 1)$ **h** $(4b - 3)(2b + 1)$

i $(6a - 1)(a + 3)$ **j** $(2c - 1)(6c - 1)$

k $(3x + 1)(3x - 2)$ **l** $(2m + 1)(2m + 1)$

m $(6w + 1)(w + 1)$ **n** $(2x - 1)(2x - 3)$

o $(3h - 1)(2h + 3)$ **p** $(9b - 1)(b - 1)$
q $(3t + 1)(2t + 1)$ **r** $(3v + 1)(4v + 1)$
s $(8r - 1)(3r + 1)$ **t** $(6a - 1)(4a + 1)$
4 a $(5y - 1)(5y - 1)$ **b** $(3a + 2)(2a - 3)$
c $(9e - 1)(e - 2)$ **d** $(1 + 3d)(1 + d)$
e $(1 - 2c)(1 + c)$ **f** $(4r - 3)(r - 2)$
g $(1 - 6w)(1 + 3w)$ **h** $(5 - 4b)(1 + 3b)$
i $(2x - 1)(5x + 4)$ **j** $(3 - 2d)(5 + d)$
k $(1 - 4n)(1 - 4n)$ **l** $(2 - 3w)(3 + 2w)$
m $(2a + 1)(9a - 4)$ **n** $(3m - 4)(4m + 3)$
o $(p - 2q)(p + q)$ **p** $(a - b)(a - b)$
q $(2x + y)(x + 5y)$ **r** $(3a + 4d)(3a - 2d)$
s $(3m + 2n)(2m - 3n)$ **t** $(3e + 4f)(4e - f)$

Page 96 Challenge
(from top, clockwise) A – H – E – C – D – J – L – I – F – G – B – K

Page 97 Exercise 8.1
1 a $4(m + 2)$ **b** $w(1 - 2w)$
c $2(a - b)(a + b)$ **d** $3(k + 3)^2$
e $t(t - u)$ **f** $2d(2 - d)$
g $2(m + 3)(m - 2)$ **h** $3y(3y + 2)$
i $5(g - 2)(g + 2)$ **j** $a(b + ac)$
k $4(x - 2)(x - 1)$ **l** $2(4 - xy)$
m $x(x - 1)(x + 1)$ **n** $2(6 - m)(6 + m)$
o $2(p + 4)(p + 2)$ **p** $2b(2b + c)$
q $3(2p^2 - q^2)$ **r** $7(q - 2)^2$
s $2(u - v)(u + v)$ **t** $3(k - 4)^2$
u $9(c - 10)(c + 10)$ **v** $6(x + 5)(x - 3)$
w $2(x - 3)(x + 3)$ **x** $x^2(x - 2)$
2 a $8(w + 3)(w - 1)$ **b** $2x(3x - 1)(3x + 1)$
c $2b(2a - 3c)$ **d** $2y(1 + y + y^2)$
e $r(r - 2)(r + 2)$ **f** $3x(x - 3)(x + 3)$
g $11(x + 1)^2$ **h** $2ab(3a - 4b)$
i $8(p - 3)(p + 3)$ **j** $2(n - 9)(n + 8)$
k $3y(x + 2b^2)$ **l** $3b(b - 4)$
m $3f(f - 3)(f + 3)$ **n** $2(2w + 5)(w - 1)$
o $3(u - 5)(u - 7)$ **p** $30a(a - 1)$

Page 97 Exercise 8.2
1 a $5(6 - d)(6 + d)$ **b** $3(4n - 3)(n - 2)$
c $2yz(x - 4w)$ **d** $2v(3 + 8v^2)$
e $14(2q + 1)(q - 1)$ **f** $16(1 - 5a)(1 + 5a)$
g $17(1 - x)^2$ **h** $m(m - 3n)(m + 3n)$
i $(3x - 4)(2x - 3)$ **j** $w^2(u - 2)(u + 2)$
k $28(x + 3)(x - 2)$ **l** $2(7x + 3)(x + 1)$
m $y(3 - 4y)(3 + 4y)$ **n** $36(1 + 3a)(1 - a)$
o $abc(c + a)$ **p** $x^2y^2(y - x)(y + x)$
2 a $(p + q - r)(p + q + r)$ **b** $y(2x - y)$
c $a(a + 2b)$ **d** $4xy$
e $2(e^2 + f^2)$ **f** $(x + y)(a + b)$
g $(x + y)(a + b)$ **h** $(p + q)(3 + a)$
i $(e - g)(e + 2f + g)$
j $w^2(1 - w)(1 + w)(1 + w^2)$
k $3(x + 3y)(x - 2y)$
l $-(q + p)(3p - q)$ or $(q + p)(q - 3p)$

m $(x - 1)(x + 1)(x^2 + 1)$
n $(x - y)(1 - x + y)$
o $(a + 1)(a - 1)(a + 3)$
p $2(x - y)(1 - 3x + 3y)(1 + 3x - 3y)$

Page 98 Challenge
1 a $3n + 5$ **b** $5n - 2$
c $9n - 8$ **d** $13n - 8$
2 a $n + 1$ **b** $5n - 2$
c $(n + 1)(5n - 2)$; product of two nth terms
3 a i $3, 15, 35, 63$
    ii $(2n - 1)(2n + 1)$
    iii $1 \times 3, 3 \times 5, 5 \times 7, 7 \times 9$
b i $3, 20, 49, 90$
    ii $(3n - 2)(2n + 1)$
    iii $1 \times 3, 4 \times 5, 7 \times 7, 10 \times 9$
c i $5, 42, 135, 308$
    ii $n(2n - 1)(2n + 3)$
    iii $1 \times 1 \times 5, 2 \times 3 \times 7, 3 \times 5 \times 9, 4 \times 7 \times 11$
4 a $63, 99$
b $3 \times 5, 5 \times 7, 7 \times 9, 9 \times 11$
c $(2n + 1)(2n + 3) = 4n^2 + 8n + 3$
d no since the nth term formula factorises

Page 100 Revision
1 a 9 **b** q **c** $3xy$ **d** $3y$
e $2m$ **f** $4w$ **g** $2p$ **h** c
2 a $1, 2, 3, 4, 6, 8, 12, 24$ **b** $1, d, e, de$
c $1, w, w^2$ **d** $1, 2, g, g^2, 2g, 2g^2$
e $1, 2, 4, a, 2a, 4a, b, 2b, 4b, a^2, 2a^2, 4a^2, ab, 2ab,$
    $4ab, a^2b, 2a^2b, 4a^2b$
3 a 6 **b** 2 **c** $3a$ **d** $2nm$
4 a $5(a - 5)$ **b** $7(1 - a)$ **c** $b(b + 2)$
d $4c(3c + 5)$ **e** $ap(R - r)$ **f** $2x(y - 2z)$
g $7(8 - x^2)$ **h** $gh(g + h)$
5 a $(k - h)(k + h)$ **b** $(n - 1)(n + 1)$
c $(a - 3b)(a + 3b)$ **d** $(2b - 7c)(2b + 7c)$
6 a $(d + 3)(d + 7)$ **b** $(u + 7)(u - 3)$
c $(y - 3)(y - 9)$ **d** $(k - 8)(k + 1)$
e $(3m + 2)(m - 1)$ **f** $(13x - 6)(x + 1)$
g $(3n - 1)(2n - 1)$ **h** $(3u + 2)(2u - 3)$
7 a $(3n + 1)(2n - 7)$ **b** 16 cm $\times$ 3 cm
8 a $a(a - b)$ **b** $4(w - 2)(w - 1)$
c $8(d - e)(d + e)$ **d** $y(y - 1)(y + 1)$
e $4(a - 10)(a + 10)$ **f** $8(b + 3)(b - 1)$
g $3e(e - 3)(e + 3)$ **h** $4(7 - d)(7 + d)$

6 Statistics – charts and tables

Page 101 Exercise 1.1
1 a summer   **b** £250
c £150   **d** pictograph
e £25
f i easy to read at a glance
    ii can't be very precise

2 a green   **b** 210   **c** $\frac{60}{210} = \frac{2}{7}$

  d 2 : 1   **e** no

  f i easy to read at a glance

    ii can't be very precise

3 a yes

  b winter (65), spring (180), summer (285), autumn (140)

  c 45   **d** 2 : 1   **e** no

  f i easy to read trends

    ii can't read meaning into points on line between data points

4 a i 180°   **ii** 72°

  b i 5   **ii** 4

  c $\frac{9}{30} = \frac{3}{10}$

  d i easy to read proportion

    ii requires calculation to get actual frequencies

5 a

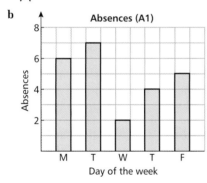

Absences (whole school)

represents 5 pupils

b

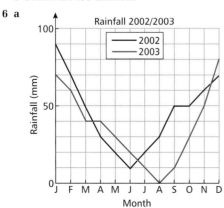

c Scales are too different

6 a

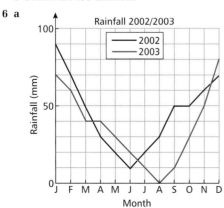

b easier to compare profiles

c 4

d September

7 a 92   **b**

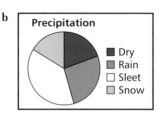

Precipitation
- Dry
- Rain
- Sleet
- Snow

Page 104 Exercise 2.1

1 a apparently doubled

  b i £1·01   **ii** £1·03   **iii** $\frac{2}{101}$

  c scales not uniform; origin is not (0, 0)

2 a cinema

  b i 50%   **ii** 8%

  c i 5   **ii** 3

  d

	Ci	Di	Ce	Do
S1 (%)	50	30	10	10
S2 (%)	8	18	34	40
Totals (%)	**58**	**48**	**44**	**50**
S1 Actual	5	3	1	1
S2 Actual	3	7	14	16
Totals (actual)	**8**	**10**	**15**	**17**

  e don't mind, ceilidh, disco, cinema (almost reversed)

  f icons do not represent the same frequency

3 a 4

  b unspecified

  c units on y axis not meaningful

4 a first impressions suggest climbing

  b i £25 000   **ii** £15 000   **iii** £10 000

  c decreasing

  d origin not (0, 0); x axis reversed

  e student's own drawing

5 a decline seems to be reduced

  b i £10 000   **ii** £10 000   **iii** £15 000

  c scale on x axis is not uniform

6 a steadily increasing improvement

  b student's own drawing

  c rate of increase

7 a 1, 2, 3, 4

  b 70°, 80°, 90°, 120°

  c outlet 1: 194 444; outlet 2: 222 222; outlet 3: 250 000; outlet 4: 333 333

  d order is reversed

  e area is not proportional to frequency

8 a i 100 million   **ii** 200 million

  b 2

  c 4

  d implied area is proportional to frequency

Page 107 Exercise 3.1

1 a 25 (4), 26 (3), 27 (9), 28 (3), 29 (6)

  b left (6), right (10), ahead (8), return (1)

  c ♥ (8), ♣ (11), ♦ (4), ♠ (2)

2 a 30 (2), 35 (4), 40 (4), 45 (8), 50 (11), 55 (1)

  b 30

  c 30 (0·07), 35 (0·13), 40 (0·13), 45 (0·27), 50 (0·37), 55 (0·03)

  d

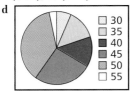

☐	30
▨	35
▨	40
▨	45
▨	50
☐	55

  e 6

  f 23

3 a 3 (3), 4 (7), 5 (14), 6 (22), 7 (8), 8 (6)

  b 60

  c 50

  d 51

  e 3 $(\frac{1}{20})$, 4 $(\frac{7}{60})$, 5 $(\frac{7}{30})$, 6 $(\frac{11}{30})$, 7 $(\frac{2}{15})$, 8 $(\frac{1}{10})$

  f $\frac{7}{30}$

  g $\frac{2}{15}$

4 a i 8   **ii** 5   **iii** 18

  b 35

  c i $\frac{1}{5}$ **ii** $\frac{1}{7}$

  d 38 mm

  e 38 mm

Page 109 Exercise 3.2

1 a 8, 13, 15, 27, 28, 31

  b 14, 26, 35, 41, 44, 46

  c 11, 37, 68, 116, 130, 138

2 1, 3, 8, 10, 7, 6, 5

3 a 15, 36, 67, 90, 98, 100

  b i c.f.(3) − c.f.(2) = 90 − 67 = 23

   ii c.f.(5) − c.f.(3)= 100 − 90 = 10

   iii c.f.(3) − c.f.(1) = 90 − 36 = 64

  c 2

Page 112 Exercise 4.1

1 a 5·7 mm   **b** 20

  c 2·3, 2·3, 2·4, 2·6, 2·7

  d 1·3, 1·3, 1·5, 2·3, 2·3, 2·4, 2·6, 2·7, 3·1, 3·3, 3·4, 3·5, 3·5, 3·8, 4·2, 4·2, 4·5, 4·6, 5·0, 5·7

  e 3·3, 3·4

  f

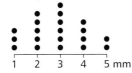

Depth of tread

2 a i 20·1 s   **ii** 25·7 s

  b 24·4 s

  c i 21·1 s   **ii** 22·3 s   **iii** 23·0 s   **iv** 24·2 s

3 a

Scores											
5	1	2	2	3	3	5	6	7	9	9	9
6	5	7	7	8							
7	1	3	4	5	8	8	9	9			
8	1	3	6								
9	1	2	2	3	5	5	6	9			

$n = 35$ 5 | 1 = 5·1

  b 7·3

  c i 5·1   **ii** 9·9

  d student's own diagram

4 a

Number of pages						
24	0	1	2	2	6	7	8
25	1	5	6	7	8	8
26	0	5	9			
27	1	3	3	4	9	
28	0	1	3	7		

$n = 25$ 24 | 0 = 240

  b 25

  c i 240   **ii** 287   **iii** 258

Page 113 Exercise 4.2

1 a

Friday		Wednesday
9 8 8 8 5 5 5 3 2	3	0 1 1 4 6
8 4 3 1 0 0	4	1 5
9 6 5 3 1	5	2 2 9 9
0	6	0 1 1 1 4 5 7
	7	0 1 1

$n = 21$ $n = 21$

3 | 0 = 30 years old

  b i lowest is Wednesday with 30 years

   ii highest is Wednesday with 71 years

   iii mid scores are F(40) and W(59)

  c Friday group is typically younger

2 a 0·21 s

  b i 1   **ii** 4

  c i 0·6 s   **ii** 0·5 s

  d difficult as there is no one middle score

3

2003	Satellite dish	2002
9 7 7 3 2 1 1	1	2 3 3 4 4 4 5 5 5 6
8 8 8 8 7 7 6 5 5 5 4 4 4 3 2 2 0	2	0 1 4 5 6 6 7 7 7 8 8 9
	3	0 0

$n = 24$ 1 | 2 = 12 sales $n = 24$

  b unclear if any improvement; although 2002 has higher maximum, it has a lot more lower figures

Page 115 Exercise 5.1

1 a 6, 8, 12, 16, 28   **b** 12, 13·5, 16, 25, 29

  c 22, 25, 35, 44, 63   **d** 46, 55, 72, 80, 85

2 a 1, 4, 10, 10, 12, 15, 16, 18, 20, 23, 25, 27, 27, 29, 30, 34, 35, 38, 40, 40, 41, 44, 46, 47, 48, 50, 55, 55, 57, 58

  b 1, 18, 32, 46, 58

3 a 2,3,4, 8, 8, 9, 9, 14, 14, 15, 16, 16, 17, 17, 18, 19, 21, 22, 23, 23, 25, 26, 27, 27, 28, 29, 31, 32, 32, 32, 35, 35, 39, 39, 40

  b 2, 14, 22, 31, 40

4 a i 25 **ii** 35 **iii** 48

  b 20, 25, 35, 48, 61

5 a i £1·20, £3·05, £3·95, £4·40, £5·70

  ii £1·30, £1·70, £2·70, £3·65, £4·30

  b Kirsty uses it less often

Page 117 Exercise 6.1

1 a

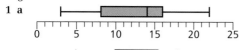

  b

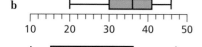

  c

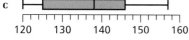

  d

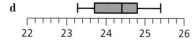

  e

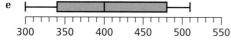

2 a

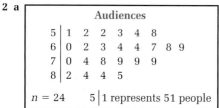

  b 51, 59, 67·5, 79, 85

  c

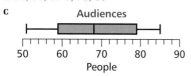

3 a 53, 20 **b** $Q_1 = 25$, $Q_2 = 32$, $Q_3 = 46$

  c

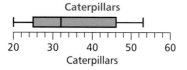

4 a 193, 199·5, 206, 215·5, 221

  b

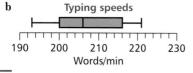

Page 118 Exercise 6.2

1 a i 24·3 °C **ii** 24·3 °C

  b i 23·7 °C **ii** 24·0 °C

  c The median temperatures are the same. July is more consistent.

2 a Mega: 96, 104, 108, 116, 120;
    Supa: 96, 122, 128, 134, 140

  b The typical amount of time you get is far longer at Supa Shop with more than 75% of the times better than the best time for Mega Stores.

Page 119 Investigation

The student's own research

Page 120 Exercise 7.1

1 a i

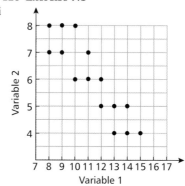

  ii negative correlation

  b i

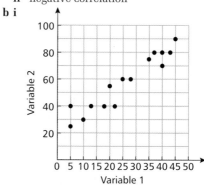

  ii positive correlation

  c i

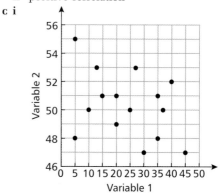

  ii no correlation

d i

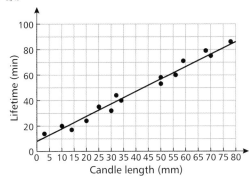

ii no correlation

2 a negative (until antique)

b none

c negative

3 a/b

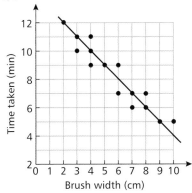

c positive correlation **d** 48 min

4 a/c

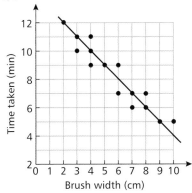

b negative **d** 8 min

5 a positive **b** student's own diagram

c 24 hours

Page 124 Revision

1 Time axis is not uniform, giving false impression of significant increase in 2004

1 a i 1(10), 2(6), 3(4), 4(2), 5(2), 6(1)

ii 6

b i $\frac{2}{5}, \frac{6}{25}, \frac{4}{25}, \frac{2}{25}, \frac{2}{25}, \frac{1}{25}$

b ii **Dice results**

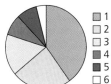

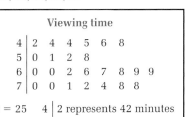

c 10, 16, 20, 22, 24, 25

3 a

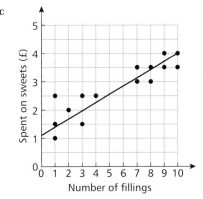

	Viewing time					
4	2	4	4	5	6	8
5	0	1	2	8		
6	0	0	2	6	7	8 9 9
7	0	0	1	2	4	8 8

$n = 25$ 4 | 2 represents 42 minutes

b

c 42, 49, 62, 70, 78

d

4 a/c

b positive

d £2·50

7 Proportion and variation

Page 125 Exercise 1.1

1 a 20 days

b 5 days

2 a and **c**

3 a, c and **d**

4 a 90 g

b 180 cm³

5 a

b yes   **c** straight line through (0,0)

d 125 mm

6 1, 16, 256, 625, 10 000; 1, 2 , 4, 5, 10;
    1, 0·25, 0·0625, 0·04, 0·01

7 a $a = 7$ **b** $b = 36$ **c** $c = 28$ **d** $d = 0.0625$
    e $e = 0.1$ **f** $f = 3.2$ **g** $g = 8$ **h** $h = 6$

8 a 1·25   **b** 9   **c** 4·5

9 a 6   **b** 24   **c** 3   **d** 48

10 Only **b** shows y is directly proportional to x

Page 127 Exercise 2.1

1 a, b and **d**

2 a 25%   **b** 20%   **c** 12·5%   **d** 10%

3 24

4 75

5 3 hours

6 a 64 s   **b** 12·8 m/s

7 a £2400   **b** 6 days (total 30 days)

8 a £13 500   **b** 5

9 a 18   **b** 45 days   **c** 4 litres

10 a 3750 ml   **b** 7·5 m²

Page 129 Exercise 3.1

1 a

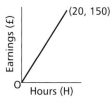

b yes, straight line through (0, 0)

c = 7·5

2 a 16, 32, 48, 64, 80   **b** 1·6   **c** $D = 1.6P$

3 a

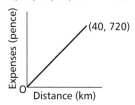

b Straight line through (0, 0); $\dfrac{e}{d} = 18$ **c** $e = 18d$

4 a

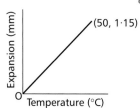

b Straight line through (0, 0)

c 0·023

d $E = 0.023t$

5 a

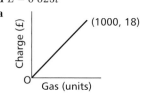

b yes, 0·018

c $C = 0.018G$

Page 131 Exercise 3.2

1 a

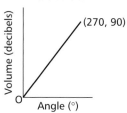

b Straight line through (0, 0); $\dfrac{v}{a} = \dfrac{1}{3}$

c $V = \dfrac{a}{3}$

d 42 decibels

2 a R: 100, 225, 400, 625; S: 20, 30, 40, 50

    b $S = 2\sqrt{R}$

    c 44 m/s

3 a $\dfrac{D}{S}$ = varies; no

    b S^2, 0, 100, 400, 900, 1600

    c $\dfrac{D}{S^2} = 0.05$ in each case

    d

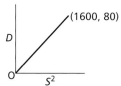

    Straight line through (0, 0)

    e $D = 0.05S^2$

    f 245 feet

4 a $T \propto \sqrt{L}$

    b $\sqrt{L}$: 0, 3, 4, 5, 6; T: 0, 0·6, 0·8, 1·0, 1·2

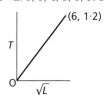

    c $T = 0.2\sqrt{L}$ **d** 1·6 s

Page 132 Investigation

a 365^2

b 684 days

Page 133 Exercise 4.1

1 a

N	1	2	3	4	5	6
V£	1800	900	600	450	360	300

b

c

$\dfrac{1}{N}$	1	0·5	0·33	0·25	0·2	0·17
V	1800	900	600	450	360	300

d

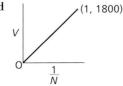

e $V \times N = 1800$ so $k = 1800$ **f** £225

2 b $\dfrac{1}{n}$ 0·50, 0·33, 0·25, 0·2, 0·17, 0·13, 0·11, 0·1, 0·08

c

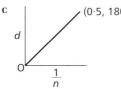

d yes, d is inversely proportional to n **e** 24°

3 a $\dfrac{1}{t}$: 1, 0·5, 0·33, 0·25, 0·2, 0·17;
n: 60, 30, 20, 15, 12, 10

b

c Straight line through (0, 0)

d $n \times t = 60$ so $n = \dfrac{60}{t}$ **e** 24

4 a $\dfrac{1}{R}$: 2·5, 1·25, 0·833, 0·625, 0·5;
I: 30, 15, 10, 7·5, 6

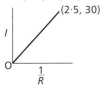

b $I = \dfrac{12}{R}$

5 a 130 **b** $H = \dfrac{130}{D^2}$ **c** 0·9 cm

Page 135 Exercise 5.1

1 a $C = 8\cdot5m$ **b** 204
2 a $y = 4\cdot6x$ **b** 73·6
3 a $R = 0\cdot4L$ **b** 12 ohms
4 a $N = 0\cdot25M$ **b** 7 g **c** 48 min
5 a $d = 0\cdot375\,n$ **b** 3·75 mm **c** 28
6 a $t = 0\cdot003h$ **b** 10·8 °C **c** 8000 m

Page 136 Exercise 5.2

1 a $C \propto A;\ C = kA$ **b** $d \propto t^2;\ d = kt^2$
   c $V \propto r^3;\ V = kr^3$ **d** $h \propto \sqrt{d};\ h = k\sqrt{d}$
2 a $d = 2\cdot5t^2$ **b** 90 m
3 a $V = 2\sqrt{r}$ **b** 18 m/s
4 a $W = 0\cdot0473r^3$ **b** 194 kg
5 a $D = 5t^2$ **b** 180 m **c** 5 s

Page 137 Brainstormer

$\dfrac{5}{9}$

Page 138 Exercise 6.1

1 a $M = \dfrac{k}{N}$ **b** 36 **c** 0·75

2 a $H = \dfrac{102}{w}$ **b** 1·7

3 a $P = \dfrac{6}{A}$ **b** 12 kg/m²

4 a $I = \dfrac{500}{R}$ **b** 2·5 amps **c** 125 ohms

5 a $P = \dfrac{1200}{V}$ **b** 400 **c** 1·5

6 a $H = \dfrac{6000}{R}$ **b** 15 cm **c** 600 m

Page 139 Exercise 6.2

1 a $V = \dfrac{540}{P}$ **b** 1·8

2 a $Q = \dfrac{1350}{E^3}$ **b** 10·8

3 a $y = \dfrac{15}{\sqrt{x}}$ **b** 1·5 **c** 16

4 a $I = \dfrac{80}{D^2}$ **b** 1·25 lumens/m² **c** 5 m

5 a $P = \dfrac{48}{\sqrt{t}}$ **b** 16 units **c** 16 s

6 a $R = \dfrac{0\cdot008}{r^2}$ **b** 0·2 ohm **c** 0·4 mm

Page 139 Brainstormers

1 48 kg
2 a i ×2 **ii** ÷2
   b i ÷2 **ii** ×2
   c i ×4 **ii** ÷4
   d i ×8 **ii** ÷8

Page 140 Investigation

a x; 120, 90, 72, 60

b $x = \dfrac{360}{n}$

Page 141 Exercise 7.1

1 a $P \propto \dfrac{T}{V}$ **b** $A \propto LW$

  c $V \propto hr^2$ **d** $W \propto \dfrac{\sqrt{A}}{B}$

2 a E varies directly as a and as b
  b S varies directly as D and inversely as T
  c T varies directly as W and as the square root of L
  d h varies directly as V and inversely as the square of R

3 a $J = 2MN$ **b** 120

4 a $y = \dfrac{56x}{z}$ **b** 64

5 a $W = kDS$ **b** 0·45 **c** 27 g

6 a $V = \dfrac{kT}{P}$ **b** 240 **c** 54 cm³

7 a $P = kYS$ **b** $\dfrac{1}{80}$ **c** £12 000

Page 142 Exercise 7.2

1 a $B \propto \sqrt{C}\,D$ **b** $y \propto \dfrac{x^2}{z^2}$ **c** $F \propto \dfrac{M_1 M_2}{d^2}$

2 a W varies directly as D and as the cube of r
  b V varies jointly as L, W and H
  c y varies directly as the square of x and inversely as the square root of z

3 a $V = kAT^3$ **b** 0·1875 **c** 486

4 a $y = \dfrac{k\sqrt{x}}{z^3}$ **b** 216 **c** 20·25

5 a $L = 0·0125d\sqrt{s}$ **b** 20 litres

6 a $T = 1·5\, dt^2$ **b** 18 min **c** 27 min

7 a $I = 0·01PTR$ **b** £600

8 a $F = \dfrac{S^2 M}{75R}$ **b** 36 newtons

Page 143 Brainstormer

a $F = \dfrac{kQ_1 Q_2}{d^2}$

b 9×10^9

c $7·91 \times 10^{-5}$ newtons

d i attract **ii** repel

Page 144 Revision

1 a 100 s **b** 10·5 h

2 a H varies directly as n
  b D varies directly as m and as the square of t
  c B varies directly as the square root of R and inversely as S

3a $C \propto u^2$ **b** $P \propto \dfrac{1}{\sqrt{r}}$ **c** $V \propto \dfrac{mg}{e^2}$

4 a **b**

5 a

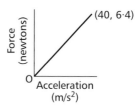

b Straight line through (0, 0)
  c $F = 0·16a$

6 a $W = 6·5h$ **b** 71·5 tonnes **c** 6 hectares

7 a $W = \dfrac{300\,000}{f}$ **b** 750 kHz **c** 200 m

8 a $R = k\sqrt{S}$ **b** 180 **c** 1800 newtons

9 a $L = \dfrac{0·4M}{BH}$ **b** 10

8 Pythagoras

Page 145 Exercise 1.1

1 a 9 **b** 49 **c** 25 **d** 6·25 **e** 0·09

2 a 9 **b** 6 **c** 1·5 **d** 27

3 a 53·29 cm² **b** 20·25 cm² **c** 0·49 cm²

4 a 11 cm **b** 12 cm **c** 14·5 cm

5 a 81 **b** 64 **c** 145 **d** 12·0

6 a △PQR, △SQR, △SRP **b** △ABC, △ADC, △ACG

7 a 49 cm² **b** 25 cm² **c** 5 cm

Page 147 Exercise 2.1

1 a $p^2 = q^2 + r^2$ **b** $x^2 = v^2 + w^2$ **c** $a^2 = 6^2 + 3^2$

2 a $a = 75$ **b** $x = 34$ **c** $y = 13$ cm

3 a 8·1 **b** 2·2 **c** 7·6

Page 148 Exercise 2.2

1 a 19·3 cm **b** 37·0 cm **c** 122·6 cm

2 a 7·5 m **b** 3·8 m

3 6·7

Page 149 Exercise 3.1

1 a 15 mm **b** 6 mm **c** 20 mm

2 a 30 cm **b** 75 cm **c** 4·0 cm

3 a 12·8 mm **b** 15·2 mm

4 a 0·76 m **b** 1·73 m

Page 150 Exercise 3.2

1 a i AC **ii** 10·9 mm
  b i AB **ii** 10·6 cm

2 a 6·65 cm **b** 178 cm **c** 72·1 cm
  d 0·752 cm **e** 223 cm

3 a 7·81 **b** 7·62

4 7·14 m

Page 151 Exercise 4.1

1 4·2 m **2** 29·2 m **3** 57·0 cm

4 30·2 cm **5** 4·0 km

Page 152 Exercise 4.2

1 46 cm **2** 1·97 m **3** 3·32 m **4** 53 cm

5 a 5 cm **b** 20 cm

6 875 cm **7** 36·8 cm **8** 519 m **9** 161 cm

Page 154 Exercise 5.1

1 a $x = 12$ cm, $y = 13\cdot4$ cm

b $x = 8$ cm, $y = 20\cdot6$ cm

c $x = 30$ cm, $y = 13\cdot7$ cm

d $x = 21\cdot9$ cm, $y = 15$ cm

2 12·1 cm

3 a 9·7 cm **b** 21·2 cm

4 No, space diagonal is only 3·9 m

Page 156 Exercise 6.1

1 a, **b** and **e** are right-angled

2 a i 40 cm **ii** 30 cm **iii** 50 cm **b** yes

3 a Not exactly since $118\cdot79^2 \neq 98^2 + 67^2$.

b No, diagonal is only 8 cm longer. This is insignificant over such a length.

4 Yes, $35^2 = 1225$ and $28^2 + 21^2 = 1225$

5 a PS = 58 m, SR = 60·9 m

b $PR^2 = 7072\cdot81$, $PS^2 + SR^2 = 7072\cdot81$

Page 157 Exercise 6.2

1 Yes

2 $AB^2 = 20$, $BC^2 = 45$,

$AC^2 = 65$ so $AC^2 = AB^2 + BC^2$ so $\triangle ABC$ is right-angled at B

3 $EF^2 = 5^2 + 12^2 = 169$,

$FC^2 = 5\cdot25^2 + 12\cdot6^2 = 186\cdot3225$,

$EC^2 = 7\cdot6^2 + 17\cdot5^2 = 355\cdot3225$,

so $EF^2 + FC^2 = EC^2$ so $\angle EFC$ is right-angled

4 $QP^2 + QR^2 = 49 + 49 = 98$, $PR^2 = 11^2 = 121$,

so $QP^2 + QR^2 \neq PR^2$ so $\angle PQR \neq 90°$

so $\angle QPR + \angle QRP \neq 90°$,

so since $\angle QPR = \angle QRP$, $\angle QRP \neq 45°$

5 $BC^2 = 9^2 + 12^2 = 225$, $CD^2 = 64$, $BD^2 = 17^2 = 289$,

$BC^2 + CD^2 = BD^2$ so $\triangle BCD$ is right-angled at C

Page 159 Revision

1 a 2·2 cm **b** 16 cm **c** 100 cm

d 1·1 cm **e** 85 cm

2 82 cm

3 a **b** 79·7 km

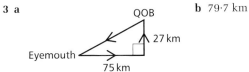

QOB

27 km

Eyemouth

75 km

4 1108 m

5 6·3

6 b is right-angled

9 Time, distance and speed

Page 160 Exercise 1.1

1 a 63 km **b** Edmonton and Fairholm

2 a 2 h 15 min **b** 30 min **c** 4 h 33 min

3 a 07 57 **b** Dungarven **c** 1 h 47 min

d i 10 45 **ii** 3 h 30 min

4 a 4 h 25 min **b** 09 18 (next day)

5 a i 40 m **ii** 90 m **b i** 8 s **ii** 11 s

6 a i 180 **ii** 270 **iii** 5

b i 48 **ii** 7·5 **iii** 8760

c i 6 **ii** 30 **iii** 92

7 a 0·5 **b** 0·25 **c** 1·75 **d** 3·1 **e** 0·3

8 a 30 mph **b** 50 mph

9 a 61 **b** 29·3 **c** 89

Page 162 Exercise 2.1

1 50 mph

2 a 20 km/h **b** 17 km/h

c 60 km/h **d** 69 km/h

3 a 8 m/s **b** 6·67 m/s

c 5·71 m/s **d** 4·69 m/s

4 6·3 m/s

5 1840 km/h

6 a 10 mph **b** 6·9 m/s **c** 5·3 km/h

d 68·8 km/h **e** 494·7 mph

7 40 mph

8 a 2 h 30 min **b** 60 km/h **c** 66·7 km/h

9 a 93·75 miles/day **b** 3·9 mph

Page 164 Exercise 2.2

1 a 0·5 **b** 0·75 **c** 0·25 **d** 0·3

e 0·9 **f** 0·45 **g** 0·1 **h** 0·65

2 a 3·2 **b** 1·95 **c** 10·15

3 a 0·87 **b** 6·47 **c** 2·77

4 a 3h 12 min **b** 5 h 9 min **c** 1 h 18 min

d 3 h 15 min **e** 6 h 39 min

5 a 2·6 h **b** 50 km/h

6 a 72 km/h **b** 55 km/h

c 50 km/h **d** 30 km/h

7 a 57·1 mph **b** 47·8 mph **c** 51·5 mph

d 51·7 mph **e** 49·5 mph

8 a 3750 km, 2·25 h

b 1666·7 km/h

9 a 20 km/h **b** 4·6 km/h **c** 0·3 km/h

10 a 13 m/s **b** 80 km/h

Page 165 Brainstormer

a $365 \times 24 = 8760$ hours $= 8\cdot8 \times 10^3$ hours (2 s.f.)

b $S = D/T = (3 \times 2 \times 9\cdot3 \times 10^7) \div (8\cdot8 \times 10^3)$

$= 634\,00$ miles per hour

Page 165 Exercise 3.1

1 a

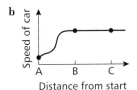

b

c

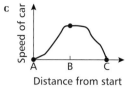

d

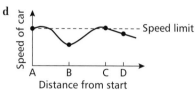

e

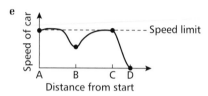

2 Stopped at A, speeds up to steady speed of just below the speed limit at B, slows down and stops at C, reaches a steady speed of just below the speed limit at D

3 a going past B

b

Page 167 Exercise 4.1

1 4 h

2 a 7 h   **b** 50 s   **c** 3·5 h   **d** 25 s

3 a 3 h 6 min   **b** 6 h 37 min   **c** 3 h 9 min

4 a 2 h 30 min   **b** 1 h 42 min   **c** 18 min

5 a 42 s   **b** 30 s

6 20 min

7 a 19 34   **b** 56 min

8 13 56   **9** 0·9 s   **10** 5 × 10⁷ s

Page 168 Exercise 5.1

1 a 208 miles   **b** 315 m   **c** 864 miles   **d** 100 feet

2 210·8 miles   **3** 252 m   **4** 79·2 km

5 60 km   **6** 900 miles   **7** 1·2 km

8 407 km   **9** 6·3 km   **10** 2·4 miles

Page 170 Exercise 6.1

1 a 150 m   **b** 5 m/s   **c** 300 m

d 225 m   **e** 75 s

2 a 50 miles   **b** half an hour

c 50 miles   **d** 110 miles

e i 50 mph   **ii** 27·5 mph

f 13 13

3 a

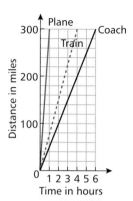

b plane, fastest speed gives steepest line

c i 50 mph   **ii** 75 mph   **iii** 300 mph

4 a 1 h   **b** 40 miles

c 45 min   **d** 1 h 30 min

5 a two and a half minutes   **b** going

c after 2·5 min and (approx.) 6·2 min

6

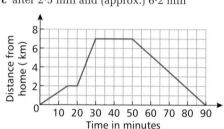

Page 172 Exercise 6.2

1 a 4 h   **b** 20 miles   **c** half an hour

d 36 miles   **e** first   **f** 20 mph

2 a 100 km   **b** 48 min

c i 50 km/h   **ii** 62·5 km/h

d 15 59

3 a 90 km   **b** 1 h 48 min, 2 h 42 min, 3 h 24 min

c 90 km, 130 km, 170 km   **d** 24 min

4 a 12 24   **b** 90 miles   **c** 2 h

d i 38·5 mph **ii** 87·5 mph

5 Amir and Ny set off at the same time with Ny running faster at first. Amir speeds up and passes Ny after 9 seconds at around 40 metres from the start. Amir goes on to win the 100 metre race in 14 seconds. Ny finished half a second later, i.e. 14·5 seconds

6 a

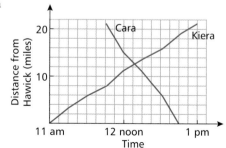

b approx. 13 miles   **c** approx. 12·08

d Keira 10·5 mph, Cara 21 mph

Page 174 Exercise 7.1

1 a 19 s   **b** 108 km   **c** 16 mph

2 $3·35 \times 10^6$ m

3 a 4 h 12 min

  b 21 32

4 16·7 m/s

5 a 47 km/h, 55 km/h, 95 km, 1 h 45 min

  b 339 km

  c 7 h 27 min

6 a 1·7 s   **b** 0·7 s   **c** 0·5 s

7 a 51 min   **b** 14 21   **c** 50 mph

8 a 84 km   **b** 16 km/h

Page 175 Exercise 7.2

1 a 3 h   **b** 12·5 m/s

  c 52·5 km   **d** 24 min

2 36·5 km/h, 37·0 km/h

3 $2·6 \times 10^3$ s

4 a 2350 km/h   **b** 2·24

5 27·8 m

6 0·3 m

Page 176 Challenge

Stagger Tom from scratch; Ian $7\frac{9}{13}$ m start; Bill 4 m start; Angus $1\frac{39}{61}$ start

Page 178 Revision

1 a 25 km/h   **b** 212·5 m

  c 3·5 h   **d** 3×10^5 km/h

2 1296 m

3 8·23 m/s

4 2 h 42 min

5 a 50 mph   **b** 1 h 20 min   **c** 44·5 mph

6 a 1 h 32 min   **b** 15 03

  c i 47 min   **ii** 28·1 mph

7 33·8 km

8 a 14 00   **b** approx. 170 km

  c 60 km/h   **d** 30 min

  e i 70 km/h

   ii 64 km/h

10 Angles and circles

Page 180 Exercise 1.1

1 a 38°   **b** 68°, 44°   **c** 90°, 62°

2 a 45°   **b** 72°   **c** 246°

3 Fold the circle in half twice.

  The centre is where the two folds cross.

4 a 12·5   **b** 15 cm

Page 181 Exercise 2.1

1 $a° = 59°$, $b° = 77°$, $c° = 136°$

2 $x° = 65°$, $y° = 19°$, $z° = 16°$

3 $a° = 72°$, $b° = 54°$

4 a i
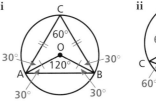
 ii
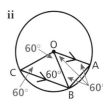

iii
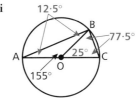

  b 90°

Page 182 Exercise 3.1

1 a 32°   **b** 67°   **c** 44°

2 $a° = 67°$, $b° = 51°$, $c° = 29°$, $d° = 61°$, $e° = 67°$,

  $f° = 67°$

3 $x° = 45°$, $y° = 24°$

4 a ∠ACB is an angle in a semicircle so ΔABC is a

  right-angled triangle.

  b 8·1 cm

5 a 10·7 cm   **b** 3·4 cm   **6 b**

7 a ΔAOC is isosceles   **b** ΔOCB is isosceles

  c $2x + 2y$ is the sum of the angles of ΔABC

  d $x° + y° = 180° \div 2 = 90°$

Page 185 Exercise 4.1

1 a 73°   **b** 57°   **c** 33°

2 a
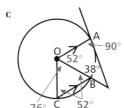
 b
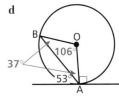

  c

 d
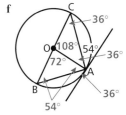

  e
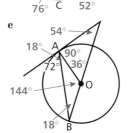
 f

3 a 4 cm   **b** 19·5 cm   **c** 13·5 cm   **4** 22·4 mm

Page 187 Exercise 5.1

1 a bisects   **b** right angles
  c bisects, right angles

2 a   **b**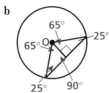

  c

3 a 15   **b** 16   **c** 58·7
4 a 34·9   **b** 30·0
5 a 12·5   **b** 15
6 a 30   **b** 24
7 16 m   **8** 6·3 cm   **9** 6 m

Page 188 Exercise 5.2

1 No, distance between shelves is 70 cm.
2 Positions 1 and 5 AB = 44·7 cm, positions 2 and
  4 AB = 56·6 cm, position 3 AB = 60 cm
3 0·8 cm
4 a AB is longer by 1·32 cm
  b RS by 0·86 cm

Page 190 Exercise 6.1

1 and 2 Show your teacher

Page 191 Exercise 7.1

1 a 37·7 cm   **b** 57·8 m
  c 392·5 mm   **d** 81·6 km
2 a i 28 cm   **ii** 88·0 cm
  b i 45·2 m   **ii** 142·0 m
  c i 288 mm   **ii** 904·8 mm
  d i 90 km   **ii** 282·7 km
3 a 8000 miles   **b** 25 000 miles
4 a 264 mm   **b** 8 cm by 26·4 cm
5 a 8·80 m   **b** 1·26 m
6 a 12·7 cm   **b** 31·8 mm
  c 7·5 m   **d** 236·2 km
7 a 0·8 cm **b** 1·3 cm **c** 8·6 mm **d** 0·6 cm
8 a 80 m   **b** 40 m
9 a 6 cm
  b i 12·6 m   **ii** 6·28 cm
  c i 628 m   **ii** 6·28 cm
  d 6·28 cm
10 a 2765 cm   **b** 391 cm

Page 193 Exercise 8.1

1 a 15·7 cm   **b** 2·4 cm   **c** 11·0 cm
  d 2·1 cm   **e** 66·0 cm

2 78·5 cm
3 269 cm
4 21 plants
5 2·83 m
6 a 75 cm   **b** $\frac{10}{75} = \frac{2}{15}$ **c** 48°   **d** 216°
7 a 69 cm   **b** 113°

Page 194 Exercise 9.1

1 a 2827·4 cm²   **b** 6361·7 mm²
  c 162·9 m²   **d** 22 698·0 km²
2 a 201·1 cm²   **b** 6082·1 mm²
  c 295·6 m²   **d** 6361·7 km²
3 1667·4 m²
4 45·3 cm²
5 a 19·6 m²   **b** 12·6 m²
6 a 6358·5 mm²   **b** 1256 mm²
  c 5102·5 mm²   **d** 5868·7 mm²
  e 2826 mm²
7 a 19·6 m²   **b** 140·8 m²
8 a i 5·6 cm **ii** 2·9 mm **iii** 35·7 m
  b i 6·2 cm **ii** 11·2 mm **iii** 9·8 m
9 301·6 mm²
10 a 15·9 cm   **b** 795·8 cm²
11 79 577·5 m²

Page 196 Exercise 10.1

1 a 43·6 cm² **b** 12·8 m² **c** 942·5 mm²
  d 9·0 m²   **e** 25·1 m²
2 1·2 m²
3 5989·8 cm²
4 a 3487 cm² **b** 280 cm² **c** 3207 cm²
5 a i 28·3 cm² **ii** $\frac{16}{28·3}$ **iii** 203·5° **iv** 10·6 cm
  b i 3·14 m² **ii** $\frac{0·26}{3·14}$ **iii** 29·8° **iv** 52·0 cm
  c i 153·9 m² **ii** $\frac{130}{153·9}$ **iii** 304·1° **iv** 37·1 m
  d i 132·7 m² **ii** $\frac{42}{132·7}$ **iii** 113·9° **iv** 12·9 m
  e i 314·2 m² **ii** $\frac{280}{314·2}$ **iii** 321° **iv** 56·0 m
6 a 321·7°   **b** 474·5 cm²   **c** 11·6 cm

Page 199 Revision

1 $a = 75°$, $b = 130°$
2 a 28°   **b** 75°
3 a 39 cm   **b** 10·5 cm   **c** 6·2 cm
4 a 14   **b** 25
5 a 356·9 cm   **b** 254·5 m
6 a 1390 cm²   **b** 13·9 m²
7 a 1718 cm²   **b** 5 m   **c** 120°
  d 88 m²   **e** 15 m

11 Angles and triangles

Page 200 Exercise 1.1

1 a 090° **b** 180° **c** 270° **d** 000° **e** 225°
2 530 m, 255°
3 a 63°   **b** 39°
4 a AC   **b** OP
5 ST = 7·3 m

6 a 0·36   **b** 5·36   **c** 70·59

7 a $x = 72$

  b i $x = 6·66$ **ii** $x = 17·5$

8

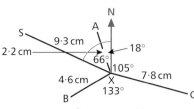

Scale: 1 cm to 100 m

9 a Using a scale of 1 cm to 2 m gives the height of
the school as 10·5 m + 1·8 m = 12 m to nearest
metre

  b They take a considerable amount of time; they
involve measurement which causes error
depending on the scale used and the accuracy
of the drawing and measuring instruments.

Page 201 Exercise 2.1

1 b 145°, 67 km

2 b

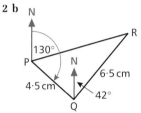

Scale: 1 cm to 10 km

  c i 076°

    ii 80 km

3 b

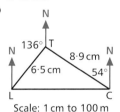

Scale: 1 cm to 100 m

  c 1·17 km, 093°

4 55 km from ship A; 46 km from ship B

5 b

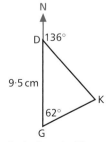

Scale: 1 cm to 2 km

  i 13·8 km

  ii 17·4 km

6 b

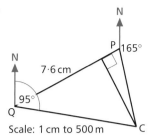

Scale: 1 cm to 500 m

  c 2700 m

7 a 65°; the acute angles are alternate angles for
the parallel north lines

  b 245°

8 a 220°   **b** 250°   **c** 262°   **d** 280°

  e 300°   **f** 338°   **g** 000°   **h** 010°

  i 025°   **j** 060°   **k** 110°   **l** 140°

9 $(x + 180)°$ if $x < 180$;
$(x - 180)°$ if $180 \leqslant x < 360$

10 359°

Page 203 Exercise 3.1

1 a PQ, LN, ST, DE

  b PR, MN, RT, DF

  c QR, LM, RS, EF

  d QR, LM, RS, EF

  e PR, MN, RT, DF

2 a 0·923   **b** 0·417

3 a 0·8   **b** 1·333   **c** 1·333   **d** 0·8

Page 204 Exercise 4.1

1 a–c students' own answers

  d all entries in the last column of the table
should be close to 0·65

Page 205 Exercise 4.2

1 a i $\frac{8}{6}$ **ii** 1·333

  b i $\frac{20}{21}$ **ii** 0·952

  c i $\frac{5}{12}$ **ii** 0·417

  d i $\frac{15}{20}$ **ii** 0·75

2 a 3·429   **b** 0·952

  c 2·4   **d** 0·292

3

Angle A	0°	10	20°	30°	40°	50°	60°	70°	80°
tan A	0·000	0·176	0·364	0·577	0·839	1·192	1·732	2·747	5·671

4 a 0·087   **b** 0·754   **c** 1·111

  d 1·963   **e** 3·172   **f** 22·904

5 a 0·488   **b** 1·280

  c 2·500   **d** 0·065

6 a $\angle A = 31°$ **b** $\angle H = 37°$ **c** $\angle P = 45°$

  d $\angle K = 51°$ **e** $\angle T = 64°$ **f** $\angle W = 90°$

7 a i 0·292   **ii** 16°

  b i 1·05   **ii** 46°

  c i 0·417   **ii** 23°

  d i 3·429   **ii** 74°

Page 206 Challenge

1 c In each right-angled triangle, the ratio $\dfrac{\text{opposite side}}{\text{adjacent side}}$ for each 45° angle is 1 as the opposite side and the adjacent side are always equal in length (sides of a square). Hence tan 45° is always equal to 1.

2 a by giving the answer 'error'.

 b tan 89·999 999 = 57 295 780

 c as the angle approaches 90°, the length of the opposite side is increasing. In theory, when the angle is 90°, the opposite side is infinitely long. Tan 90° is undefined.

Page 207 Exercise 5.1

1 $\tan 52° = \dfrac{h}{18} \Rightarrow h = 18 \times \tan 52° \Rightarrow$ height of chimney = 23 m (to the nearest metre)

2 a 19·5 cm   b 20·6 cm   c 4·4 cm

3 a 13·9 m   b 14·1 m   c 14·9 m

4 a 8·0 m   b 4·7 m

5 a 13·3 m   b 13·1 m   c 12·7 m
 river a is widest; 0·2 m wider than river b and 0·6 m wider than river c.

6 a 288·7 m   b 350·1 m   c 419·5 m

7 113 m

8 3·9 m

9 a Alternate angles are equal and the small triangle is an isosceles triangle.

 b 296·5 m

10 a 137 m   b 149 m   c 300 m

11 a 125·0 m   b 101·9 m   c 76·8 m

12 95·5 m

13 46·1 m

Page 210 Exercise 5.2

1 a 9·6 cm   b 16·2 cm
 c 3·8 cm   d 24·5 cm

2 a 13·8 cm
 b 9·6 cm

3 36 932·2 feet

4 1·4 m

5 291 m

6 16 km

Page 211 Exercise 6.1

1 a 52·1°   b 29·4°
 c 57·0°   d 49·4°

2 a 39°   b 11°   c 52°

3 20°

4 a ∠BAD = 99°, ∠ABD = ∠ADB = 41°,
 ∠DBC = ∠BDC = 66°, ∠BCD = 47°

 b ∠QSR = ∠PQS = ∠PRS = ∠QPR = 27°,
 ∠PSQ = ∠SQR = ∠PRQ = ∠SPR = 63°,
 ∠PTQ = ∠STR = 126°,
 ∠PTS = ∠QTR = 54°

Page 212 Exercise 7.1

1

Angle A	0	10	20	30	40	50	60	70	80	90
sin A	0·000	0·174	0·342	0·500	0·643	0·766	0·866	0·940	0·985	1·000

2

Angle A	30	64	6	14	50	28	73
sin A	0·5	0·9	0·1	0·25	0·77	0·469	0·956

3 No, the angle it makes with the ground is 48·6° which is greater than 40°.

4 a $\sin A = \dfrac{\text{EC}}{\text{AE}} = \dfrac{6}{11}$ b $\sin A = \dfrac{\text{FH}}{\text{AH}} = \dfrac{12}{15}$

 c $\sin A = \dfrac{\text{DG}}{\text{AD}} = \dfrac{8}{10}$ d $\sin A = \dfrac{\text{KT}}{\text{AK}} = \dfrac{12}{13}$

5 a i $\frac{5}{13}$ ii 23°
 b i $\frac{24}{30}$ ii 53°
 c i $\frac{30}{34}$ ii 62°
 d i $\frac{1\cdot5}{3\cdot9}$ ii 23°

6 a 17°   b 74°

7 KM = 37·8(2) + 55·5(4) = 93·3(6) cm

8 a EH = 25·7 cm
 b 30·7 cm, using EH = 25·7 cm; 30·6 cm, using full calculator display for EH.

Page 214 Exercise 7.2

1 a 4·1   b 24·7   c 8·6   d 61·1

2 a 10·1 cm   b 2·5 m   c 2·9 m   d 10·0 cm

3 a 394·5 m   b 808·9 m

4 a 43·1 m   b 30·8 m

5 55°

6 6·4°

7 a 90°   b 501·8 m

Page 215 Exercise 8.1

1 a 6·6 cm   b 6·9 cm   c 3·2 cm   d 78·1 m

2 a 50 cm   b 7·8 m
 c 8·5 m   d 13·9 cm, 13·9 cm

3 a 7·0 m   b 3·6 m + 3·5 m = 7·1 m

4 a 61·3 km   b 86·7 km   c 112·7 km

Page 216 Exercise 9.1

1

Angle A	0	10	20	30	40	50	60	70	80	90
cos A	1·000	0·985	0·940	0·866	0·766	0·643	0·500	0·342	0·174	0·000

2

Angle A	60	46	78	70	35	74	19
cos A	0·5	0·7	0·2	0·35	0·82	0·276	0·943

3 a i $\frac{9}{14}$ ii 50°
 b i $\frac{7\cdot5}{15}$ ii 60°
 c i $\frac{1\cdot6}{2\cdot0}$ ii 37°
 d i $\frac{16}{34}$ ii 62°

4 a 11·4   **b** 2·3   **c** 16·0   **d** 37°

5 52°

6 No, the angle to the ground is 17·8°, greater than the maximum angle of 16°

7 a 11·5 km   **b** 9·6 km

8 BC = 8·9 m

Page 218 Exercise 10.1

1 a sin, 6·3   **b** cos, 7·0
  c tan, 11·3   **d** sin, 7·5

2 a 47°   **b** 43°
  c 66°   **d** 54°

3 i Television **a**. It is 79·5 cm wide; television **b** is only 72·1 cm wide
  ii Television **a** is 42·3 cm high; television **b** is 45·0 cm high

4 17°

5 585 m

6 The angle at A is 37°; the angle at B is 32°. There is a wider shooting angle in football, but the penalty spot is nearer the goal in hockey. The width of the goal and the height of the crossbar are other things that need to be considered. How good the goalkeepers are and how good the players are at taking penalties are also important!

7 a 426·5 m   **b** 3473·9 m

8 a 23°   **b** 180 m
  c 180 m   **d** 13 500 m²

9 a 335 m
  b 65°
  c RS = 409 m

Page 219 Exercise 10.2

1 a i 179 m   **ii** 689 m
  b 6°

2 a The tangent of the angle is $\frac{1\cdot5}{3} = 0\cdot5 \Rightarrow$ the angle is 27°, to the nearest degree
  b i 3·4 m   **ii** 3·4 m

3 8 km

4 a 6 cm
  b 8·7 cm

5 b i 26·5 cm
    ii 371 cm²
    iii ∠E = ∠F = 62°, ∠D = 56°

6 a 34° and 56°
  b 68° and 112°

7 125 m

8 a Gradient of AB = $\frac{2}{3}$, ∠BAC = 34°
  b i $\frac{3}{8}$ **ii** $\frac{2}{5}$ **iii** $\frac{3}{8}$

9 a In right-angled triangle ADC, $\sin C = \dfrac{AD}{b}$;
    hence AD = $b\sin C$
  b $\frac{1}{2}ab \sin C$
  c 12·2 cm²

10 a 18 cm
  b 48°

Page 221 Investigations

1 sin A and tan A both increase; cos A decreases

2 a

Angle A	0	10	20	30	40	50	60	70	80	90
sin A	0·00	0·17	0·34	0·50	0·64	0·77	0·87	0·94	0·98	1·00
cos A	1·00	0·98	0·94	0·87	0·77	0·64	0·50	0·34	0·17	0·00

  b The cosine is the 'complement' of the sine, i.e. sin x° = cos (90 − x)°, e.g. sin 10° = cos 80°
  c 45°
  d i sin 15° = cos 75°   **ii** cos 25° = sin 65°
    iii cos 1° = sin 89°   **iv** sin 37° = cos 53°
  e

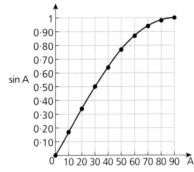

  f

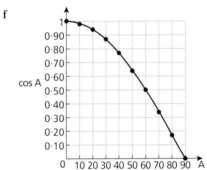

Page 223 Revision

1 a

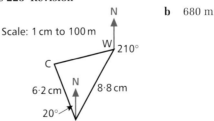

Scale: 1 cm to 100 m

  b 680 m

2 a Scale: 1 cm to 1 km

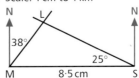

  b *Mona Mae* 3·7 km; *Sea Spray* 6·9 km

3 315°

4 a $\frac{3}{5}$ **b** $\frac{3}{5}$ **c** $\frac{5}{12}$

  d $\frac{5}{13}$ **e** $\frac{15}{8}$ **f** $\frac{8}{17}$

5 a 7·1   **b** 45·6°   **c** 34·7°   **d** 10·5

6 AC = 15·4, RS = 16·3

7 a 67·4° and 112·6°   **b** 14·4 cm

8 a 53·1°   **b** 150 cm

9 a 66·6 m   **b** 134·0 m

10 a 96·2 m

  b 15 390 m²

  c i 525 m   **ii** 525 m

12 More statistics

Page 225 Exercise 1.1

1 a 2(5), 3(3), 4(3), 5(4), 6(1), 7(1), 8(2), 9(1)

  b 2 letters

  c i 9 letters   **ii** 2 letters

2 a i 26   **ii** 40

  b 35

  c i 31   **ii** 38

3 a 15   **b** 25

  c 17, 30   **d** between 30 and 35

4 a 12

  b 0·3

  c 0·1, 0·2, 0·3, 0·25, 0·15; 4, 12, 24, 34, 40

  d 1

5 a 24

  b i 1·2 cm   **ii** 6·1 cm

  c 3·25 cm

  d 2·25 cm, 4·5 cm

6 a 4 min   **b** 4 min   **c** 4·3 min

Page 227 Exercise 2.1

1 a 5   **b** 149   **c** 3·5   **d** 2·8

2 a 11·7 years   **b** no   **c** 6 years

3 a 14   **b** 12·6 min   **c** 11·4 min   **d** more

4 a i 26·2   **ii** 32·3

  b yes

Page 229 Exercise 2.2

1 a i 15, 36, 49, 8

   ii 17, 108

   iii 6·4

  b i 45, 100, 220, 300

   ii 12, 665

   iii 55·4

  c i 2, 8, 30, 24, 10

   ii 12, 74

   iii 6·2

  d i 168, 66, 23, 24, 175

   ii 20, 456

   iii 22·8

  e i 3·6, 7·4, 30·4, 27·3, 8

   ii 20, 76·7

   iii 3·8

2 a 29   **b** 7233 ml

  c 249·4 ml   **d** it would seem OK

3 a 12, 24, 16, 10, 6   **b** 3·2   **c** yes

4 a No. of cars: 3, 4, 5, 6, 7;

   Frequency: 4, 9, 6, 4, 5

  b 4·9 cars

  c no

5 a i 7·7   **ii** 7·8

  b no real significant difference

Page 231 Exercise 3.1

1 a 6   **b** 4

  c amber   **d** 1·2 and 2·4

2 a A(4), B(3), C(10), D(8), E(5)

  b C

  c can't be calculated

3 a 3·3 min   **b** 4 min

  c i 11   **ii** 3

  d mean

4 a both equal at 70·8

  b 60, 100

  c mode

Page 232 Exercise 4.1

1 a 32   **b** 181   **c** 14·8

2 a 32·05, 46·4   **b** 49, 46

  c yes   **d** no

3 a 460 g, 450 g and 451 g

  b 458·4 g, 450·8 g

  c 4 g, 2 g

  d with bigger range, machine 1

4 a 124·7, 132·6; after course improved mean

  b 6, 3; after course less variable

  c yes

5 a −1·5, −4·1

  b 3, 7

  c Prima is, on average, closer to the right time
    and is also less variable

6 Could pick Philip for best mean score; could
  pick Mairi for most consistent player; could pick
  Philip as he has only got less than the target
  score 3 times out of 12 (compare Mairi's 7 times)

7 a 17·3 years

  b 40 years

  c i 16

   ii 0

  d small change in data pool can make a big
    difference in range

Page 235 Exercise 5.1

1 a $Q_1 = 2$; $Q_2 = 3$; $Q_3 = 7$

  b 5·7, 5·95, 10·2

  c 129·5, 139, 145

  d 735, 768·5, 841·5

  e 8, 12, 27

2 a 9·25 kg   **b** 10·5 m   **c** 0·20255 s   **d** £12·50

3 a

```
1 | 1
2 | 1 2 8 8 9
3 | 0 1 3 4 4 4 5 5 7 8 8 9 9
4 | 6
5 | 1 6 7 8 8

n = 25        1 | 1 represents £11
```

b £29·50, £35, £42·50
c i £47   **ii** £6·50   **d i** £54, £8   **ii** range
4 a 40, 52, 60   **b** 10
  c i 84, 90   **ii** 20, 18
5 a 48, 50, 58   **b** 5
  c 2, 2, 3, 3, 3, 3, 3, 3, 4, 4, 4, 4, 5, 5

Page 238 Exercise 5.2
1 a i 6, 14, 20, 30, 37, 40
  ii
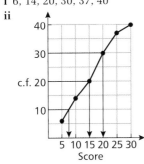
  iii $Q_1 = 8$; $Q_2 = 15$; $Q_3 = 20$
b i 1, 6, 13, 19, 23, 24
  ii
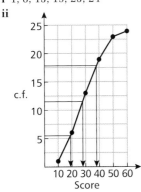
  iii $Q_1 = 19$; $Q_2 = 28$; $Q_3 = 38$
c i 5, 13, 27, 39, 49, 56
  ii
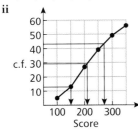
  iii $Q_1 = 150$; $Q_2 = 210$; $Q_3 = 270$

2 a/b
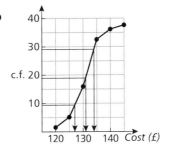

$Q_1 = £127$; $Q_2 = £131$; $Q_3 = £134$
  c £3·50   **d** £145   **e** £120
3 a 100 g   **b** 96 g   **c** 106 g
  d 10 g   **e** 5 g
  f this apple is typical of the bunch
4 a i 15   **ii** 11 km
  b 8 km, 15 km   **c** 7 km   **d** 3·5 km
  e
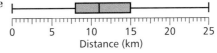
  f this is one of his best 25% efforts
5 a this year: 80; last year: 84
  b this year: 79, 82, 3, 1·5;
     last year: 82, 89, 7, 3·5;
  c
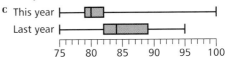
  d This year's exam would seem harder as the median was lower and the exam 'stretched' the pupils

6
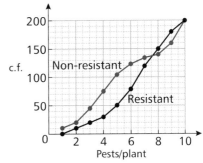

  b non-resistant 5; resistant 6·5
  c non-resistant 5·5; resistant 3
  d no, higher median

Page 240 Exercise 6.1
1 a/b deviations: −15, 0, 3, 5, 7;
     dev^2: 225, 0, 9, 25, 49;
     total 308
  c 61·6   **d** 7·85 g
2 a i 94 absences   **ii** 4·9 absences
  b i 92 absences   **ii** 8·3 absences
    iii first week   **iv** second week

Page 243 Exercise 7.1

1 a 154·6 ml   **b** 2·2 ml

2 a i 6·5   **ii** 2·9

  b i 6·5, 0·9   **ii** no   **iii** yes

3 12 hours; 8·9 hours

4 a i 57   **ii** 11   **iii** 19·0

  b i 63   **ii** 26   **iii** 21·1

  c SIQR

5 a i 71·8   **ii** 21·5   **b i** 63·9   **ii** 19·1

  c i 7·9 down

    ii mean changed by about half a deviation;
      effect noticeable

Page 245 Exercise 7.2

1 a 4·9   **b** 1·6   **c** no change required

2 a i 3·04 amp   **ii** 0·18 amp   **b** all is OK

3 a i 198·4 hours   **ii** 5·5 hours

  b another sample will be taken

4 a Glen Flow: 19·3 mm, 4·3 mm;
    Bendhui: 16·9 mm, 7·0 mm

  b Glen Flow

Page 246 Exercise 8.1

1 a $\frac{1}{2}$ **b** $\frac{1}{4}$ **c** $\frac{1}{52}$ **d** $\frac{3}{13}$ **e** $\frac{2}{13}$

2 a 50   **b** 4   **c** $\frac{2}{25}$

3 a i $\frac{3}{7}$ **ii** $\frac{2}{3}$ **b** $\frac{5}{17}$

4 a row 1: 2, 3, 4, 5, 6, 7;
    row 2: 3, 4, 5, 6, 7, 8;
    row 3: 4, 5, 6, 7, 8, 9;
    row 4: 5, 6, 7, 8, 9, 10;
    row 5: 6, 7, 8, 9, 10, 11;
    row 6: 7, 8, 9, 10, 11, 12

  b i 2   **ii** $\frac{2}{36} = \frac{1}{18}$

  c i $\frac{4}{36} = \frac{1}{9}$ **ii** $\frac{5}{36}$ **iii** 0

  d i $\frac{1}{6}$ **ii** $\frac{11}{12}$ **iii** 1

5 a i 12   **ii** 18

  b i $\frac{2}{5}$ **ii** $\frac{3}{5}$ **c** $\frac{5}{6}$

Page 248 Exercise 8.2

1 a $\frac{1}{5}, \frac{1}{6}, \frac{2}{5}, \frac{1}{5}, \frac{1}{30}$

  b i $\frac{1}{5}$ **ii** $\frac{2}{5}$ **iii** $\frac{19}{30}$

2 a $\frac{1}{8}$

  b i $\frac{3}{10}$ **ii** $\frac{7}{40}$ **iii** $\frac{27}{40}$

    iv $\frac{33}{40}$ **v** $\frac{23}{40}$ **vi** 1

3 a 30

  b i 0·2   **ii** 0·48

  c i 0·3   **ii** 0·68   **iii** 0·3

4 a 1(10), 2(10), 3(11), 4(10), 5(10), 6(5)

  b i $\frac{1}{6}$ **ii** $\frac{1}{3}$

  c i $\frac{5}{56}$ **ii** $\frac{15}{56}$

  d It would seem to be biased against 6

Page 250 Revision

1 a 15·45   **b** 16

2 a i 0·605 cm   **ii** 1 cm

  b 0·9 cm   **c** 0·65 cm, 0·35 cm, 0·9 cm

  d 0·275 cm   **e** no

3 a 1, 5, 15, 23, 29, 30

  b

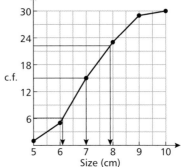

  $Q_1 = 6·2$ cm, $Q_2 = 7$ cm, $Q_3 = 8$ cm

  c 0·9 cm

4 a 4·3   **b** 1·7   **c** no

5 a row 1: H1, H2, H3, H4, H5, H6;
    row 2: T1, T2, T3, T4, T5, T6

  b i $\frac{1}{12}$ **ii** $\frac{1}{4}$

6 0·48

13 Simultaneous equations

Page 251 Exercise 1.1

1 a 2   **b** −2   **c** −8

  d −2   **e** 2

2 −9, −6, −3, 0, 3, 6, 9;
  −4, −3, −2, −1, 0, 1, 2;
  7, 6, 5, 4, 3, 2, 1;
  −2, 0, 2, 4, 6, 8, 10

3 a–c

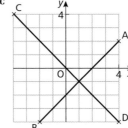

  d (1, −1)

4 a 5x   **b** x   **c** x   **d** −7x

5 a x   **b** −2x   **c** −5x   **d** 2x

6 a 5   **b** −1   **c** 0   **d** −8

7 a −6   **b** 6   **c** −1   **d** 2

8 a 3x + 12   **b** 2x − 6   **c** 12x − 4

  d 8 − 6x   **e** −6 + 15x

9 a x = 2   **b** x = −6   **c** x = 2   **d** x = 3

  e y = 3   **f** y = 4   **g** y = 0·5   **h** y = 4

10 a 3x   **b** 2x

11 4x + 6y kg

Page 253 Exercise 2.1

1 a x = 2, y = 3

2 a x = 4·5, y = 1·5

3 a i 0, 1, 2, 3, 4, 5, 6   **ii** 4, 3, 2, 1, 0

b

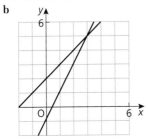

c $x = 2, y = 2$

4 a i 2, 3, 4, 5, 6   **ii** 1, 3, 5

b

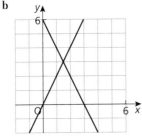

c $x = 3, y = 5$

5 a 0, 2, 4, 6; 6, 4, 2, 0

b

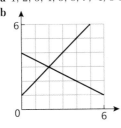

c $x = 1\cdot5, y = 3$

6 a 1, 2, 3, 4, 5, 6, 7; 4, 3·5, 3, 2·5, 2, 1·5, 1

b

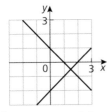

c $x = 2, y = 3$

Page 255 Exercise 2.2

1 a i $-5, -4, -3, -2, -1, 0, 1; 4, 3, 2, 1, 0, -1, -2$

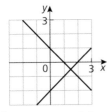

ii $x = 1\cdot5, y = -0\cdot5$

b i $-9, -8, -7, -6, -5, -4, -3, -2, -1, 0, 1,$
2, 3; $-18, -15, -12, -9, -6, -3, 0, 3, 6, 9,$
12, 15, 18;
student's own graph lines intersecting at
$(-1\cdot5, -4\cdot5)$

ii $x = -1\cdot5, y = -4\cdot5$

c i 0, 1, 2, 3, 4, 5, 6; 1, 0, $-1, -2, -3, -4, -5;$
student's own graph lines intersecting at
$(-2\cdot5, 0\cdot5)$

ii $x = -2\cdot5, y = 0\cdot5$

d i $-16, -14, -12, -10, -8, -6, -4, -2, 0, 2,$
4, 6, 8; 2, 1, 0, $-1, -2, -3, -4, -5, -6, -7,$
$-8, -9, -10;$
student's own graph lines intersecting at
$(0, -4)$

ii $x = 0, y = -4$

e i $-3, -1, 1, 3, 5, 7, 9; 3, 2, 1, 0, -1, -2, -3;$
student's own graph lines intersecting at
$(-1, 1)$

ii $x = -1, y = 1$

f i 18, 15, 12, 9, 6, 3, 0, $-3, -6, -9, -12, -15,$
$-18; 9, 8, 7, 6, 5, 4, 3, 2, 1, 0, -1, -2, -3;$
student's own graph lines intersecting at
$(-1\cdot5, 4\cdot5)$

ii $x = -1\cdot5, y = 4\cdot5$

Page 256 Exercise 3.1

1 a $x = 2, y = 4$ **b** $x = 1\cdot5, y = 3$
c $x = 5, y = 1$ **d** $x = -2, y = -2$
e $x = 2, y = 3$ **f** $x = -1, y = -3$
g $x = 4, y = 5$ **h** $x = 2, y = 1\cdot5$
i $x = -2, y = 3\cdot5$ **j** $x = -2, y = 0$
k $x = 2, y = 2$ **l** $x = -0\cdot5, y = -4$

Page 256 Brainstormers

1 Lines are parallel so there is no solution.

2 $x = 1\cdot5, y = 2\cdot5$

Page 257 Exercise 4.1

1 a $x = 2, y = 4$ **b** $x = 2, y = 6$
c $x = 2, y = 5$ **d** $x = 1, y = 6$
e $x = 6, y = 12$ **f** $x = 5, y = 20$
g $x = -4, y = -12$ **h** $x = 4, y = 11$
i $x = 13, y = 34$ **j** $x = 2, y = 7$
k $x = -3, y = -19$ **l** $x = 6, y = -1$
m $x = 0\cdot5, y = -3\cdot5$ **n** $x = -2\cdot5, y = 9$

2 a $y = 2x$ and $y = x + 78$
b i 78 cm   **ii** 156 cm

3 a $y = 100 - x$ and $y = x + 12$
b i 44 kg   **ii** 56 kg

Page 258 Exercise 4.2

1 a $x = 4, y = 8$ **b** $x = -1, y = -5$
c $x = 5, y = 6$ **d** $x = 10, y = 9$
e $x = -2, y = -6$ **f** $x = 4, y = 6$
g $x = 2, y = 1$ **h** $x = 3, y = 7$
i $x = 4, y = -1$ **j** $x = 5, y = -2$
k $x = -2, y = 4$ **l** $x = -1\cdot5, y = -3\cdot5$

2 a $x = 5, y = 4$ **b** $x = -4, y = -12$
c $x = 0.5, y = -0.5$
3 a 15 min **b** 60 min

Page 259 Brainstormers
1 $y = 3x, x + y = 100$; 75% correct
2 $y = 7x, x + y = 100$; 87.5% correct

Page 260 Exercise 5.1
1 a $x = 5, y = 4$ **b** $x = 5, y = 2$
c $a = 4, b = -2$ **d** $c = 2, d = 3$
2 a $x = 4, y = 1$ **b** $x = 3, y = 6$
c $e = 2, f = 1$ **d** $g = 7, h = 4$
3 a $x = -1, y = 4$ **b** $x = 5, y = 2$
c $x = 0, y = -6$ **d** $p = 3, q = -1$
e $m = -5, n = -7$ **f** $u = -3, v = -1$
g $s = 3, t = -1$ **h** $w = -1, z = -2$
i $i = -3, j = -2$

Page 261 Exercise 5.2
1 a $x = 6, y = 4$ **b** $x = 4, y = 7$
c $x = 4, y = 2$ **d** $x = 2, y = 1$
e $x = 4, y = 1$ **f** $x = 3, y = 2$
g $a = 5, b = 2$ **h** $c = 4, d = -5$
i $e = 3, f = 1$ **j** $g = 4, h = 1$
k $j = 2, k = -5$ **l** $m = -4, n = -3$
m $p = 3, q = 8$ **n** $s = 3, t = -4$
o $u = 2, v = 3$
2 a $w = 1, z = 3$ **b** $x = 0.5, y = -2$
c $x = -\frac{3}{2}, y = -\frac{1}{3}$

Page 262 Exercise 6.1
1 $x = 1, y = 2$ **2** $x = 4, y = 2$
3 $x = 2, y = 3$ **4** $x = 1, y = 2$
5 $x = 3, y = 1$ **6** $x = 5, y = 2$
7 $a = 3, b = 1$ **8** $m = 1, n = -1$
9 $p = -2, q = 1$ **10** $r = 2, s = 1$
11 $u = 3, v = 1$ **12** $c = 2, d = 4$
13 $g = 2, h = -3$ **14** $i = 3, j = -2$
15 $s = -2, t = -3$

Page 262 Exercise 6.2
1 $a = -2, b = 3$ **2** $c = 2, d = 0.5$
3 $e = -2, f = -4$ **4** $g = -2, h = -4$
5 $m = 2, n = -1$ **6** $i = -3, j = 2$
7 $p = 0, q = -3$ **8** $r = 2, s = 1$
9 $t = 4, u = -3$ **10** $x = -0.5, y = 0.5$
11 $k = 3, z = 0.5$ **12** $v = -\frac{2}{3}, w = -\frac{1}{2}$

Page 264 Exercise 7.1
1 $x = 6, y = 5$ **2** $x = 3, y = 6$
3 $x = 4, y = 2$ **4** $x = -1, y = -3$
5 $x = -5, y = 4$ **6** $x = 7, y = 9$
7 $x = 2, y = -2$ **8** $x = 6, y = 1$
9 $x = -3, y = 2$ **10** $x = -2, y = -1$
11 $x = -3, y = 2$ **12** $x = -2, y = -5$
13 $x = 3, y = -5$ **14** $x = 1.5, y = -1$
15 $x = \frac{1}{2}, y = \frac{1}{3}$

Page 264 Challenges
2 $x = -3, y = 8$

Page 265 Exercise 8.1
1 a $14 = 3a + b$
b $a = 3, b = 5$
c $Q = 3P + 5$
2 a $10 = 2a + b$; $14 = 4a + b$
b $a = 2, b = 6$
c $G = 2T + 6$
3 $5 = -a + b$; $-5 = 4a + b$; $a = -2, b = 3$;
$K = -2M + 3$
4 $9 = 11a + b$; $1 = 3a + b$; $a = 1, b = -2$; $y = x - 2$
5 a $12 = 6a + b$; $9 = 4a + b$
b $a = 1.5, b = 3$
c $C = 1.5n + 3$
6 a $160 = 9a + b$; $115 = 6a + b$
b $a = 15, b = 25$
c $C = 15n + 25$
d £100
7 a $a = 0.5, b = 15$; $P = 0.5x + 15$
b 55
c air pressure = 15 units

Page 266 Challenge
a ii $2a + b = 5$ **iii** $a = 2, b = 1$ **iv** $f = 2n + 1$
b 21

Page 266 Exercise 9.1
1 3 m, 9 m
2 a 1p **b** 6p
3 97 cm, 145 cm
4 a 7 years **b** 35 years
5 a £5 **b** £9
6 a £8 **b** £11
7 a £4 **b** £7

Page 268 Exercise 9.2
1 1.5 kg, 2.5 kg
2 a 4 **b** 12
3 75 m, 25 m
4 a 6 **b** 1
5 a £12 **b** £4
6 80 ml, 200 ml
7 a 4 **b** 2
8 a £22 **b** £14

Page 269 Brainstormer
Runs at 9 km/h, cycles at 23 km/h

Page 269 Investigations
1 a $x = 2, y = 3$
b student's own diagrams
2 a $x = 0, y = 0$ and $x = 1, y = 1$
b $x = 0, y = 0$, $x = 1, y = 1$ and $x = -1, y = -1$
c $x = 4, y = 4$ and $x = -4, y = -4$
d $x = 2, y = 2$ and $x = -2, y = -2$

Page 270 Revision

1 **a** 1, 3, 5; 4, 3, 2, 1, 0
  b two straight lines intesecting at (1, 3)
  c $x = 1, y = 3$
2 **a** $x = -1.5, y = -4.5$
3 $x = 2.5, y = 1$
4 **a** $x = 2, y = 8$ **b** $x = 3, y = 7$
  c $x = 2, y = -4$ **d** $x = 5, y = -1$
5 **a** $x = 4, y = 1$ **b** $x = 3, y = -2$
  c $x = -1, y = -2$ **d** $x = -2, y = -1$
6 $a = 3, b = -5; y = 3x - 5$
7 **a** $x = 2, y = -4$ **b** $x = -1, y = 5$
  c $x = 3, y = 5$ **d** $x = 4, y = -2$
8 **a** 46 kg   **b** 65 kg
9 **a** £37·50   **b** £112·50
10 **a** 6   **b** 4

14 Chapter revision

Page 271 Revising Chapter 1

1 **a** 2·89   **b** 19·0   **c** 0·879
2 **a** £44 000   **b** £629·40
3 **a** 0·0167   **b** 0·0003
4 **a** iii   **b** student's own work
5 **a i** 7.8×10^4 **ii** 1.34×10^1
  iii 5.7×10^{-3} **iv** 9.0×10^{-12}
  b i 260 000   **ii** 0·007
  iii 90 100   **iv** 0·011
6 red: 4.6×10^{14};   yellow: 5.2×10^{14};
  green: 5.6×10^{14};   blue: 6.4×10^{14}
7 **a** $\frac{13}{30}$ **b** $11\frac{11}{12}$ **c** $2\frac{4}{5}$ **d** $2\frac{1}{24}$
8 **a** Labour   **b** 1000
9 **a** 9.5×10^6 **b** 3.3×10^7

Page 272 Revising Chapter 2

1 **a** -6 **b** -3
2 **a** False   **b** True   **c** False   **d** True
3 **a** 4   **b** -8
4 **a** 6   **b** 9   **c** -4
  d -14 **e** -11 **f** 7
  g -4 **h** -7 **i** -42
  j 4   **k** -20 **l** -9
  m 0   **n** -2 **o** 72
5 **a** -1 **b** -5 **c** -3 **d** 9
  e 24   **f** -14 **g** 18   **h** -12
  i 6   **j** -8 **k** -8 **l** 29
6 **a** $-4a$ **b** $-3m + 4n$ or $4n - 3m$
  c $-5a^2 - 5a$ **d** $-12xy$
  e $-6p^2$ **f** a^4
7 **a** -6 **b** -8 **c** -9 **d** 7
8 **a** $x = -6$ **b** $x = -2$ **c** $y = -5$
  d $y = -6$ **e** $a = -1$ **f** $a = -2$
9 **a** 20 °C
  b i 0 °C   **ii** -7 °C   **iii** -15 °C
    iv -16 °C   **v** -12 °C   **vi** -3.75 °C

Page 272 Revising Chapter 3

1 **a** $2r - 12$ **b** $9b + 18$ **c** $40 + 5x$
  d $9f - 27$ **e** $3a - 3b$ **f** $11w + 11x$
  g $23d + 23e$ **h** $6y + 4$ **i** $c^2 + 2c$
  j $qr - qs$ **k** $d^2 - 5d$ **l** $w^2 + 2wy$
  m $g^2 - 7g$ **n** $4h - h^2$ **o** $3n^2 - 7n$
  p $6ab - 5a^2$ **q** $3k^2 - 5k$ **r** $31b - 4b^2$
2 **a** $2x - 12$ **b** $-2m - 1$ **c** $5x + 2$
  d $3k - 11$ **e** $5r + 47$ **f** $5d + 3$
  g $18w + 18$ **h** $15 - n$ **i** $3m - 9$
  j $3y - 3$ **k** $7k - 5$ **l** $-n$
  m $2 + 6d$ **n** $5m - 37$ **o** $3t - 9$
  p $24h - 54$ **q** $19a + 7$ **r** $11 - 5b$
  s $10 - 10k$ **t** $16y - 9$ **u** $-3b - 8$
  v $a - 7$ **w** -27 **x** $30v - 2$
3 **a** $7(m - 6) = 28; m = 10; 4$ kg
  b $5(y + 5) = 40; y = 3; 8$ kg
  c $9(k - 6) = 63; k = 13; 7$ kg
  d $21(d - 12) = 63; d = 15; 3$ kg
4 **a** $a = 11$ **b** $y = 5.75$ **c** $a = -1$
  d $b = 6\frac{5}{6}$ **e** $x = 2$ **f** $n = 3$
  g $n = 8$ **h** $y = 11$ **i** $d = 4$
  j $w = 0$ **k** $a = -4$ **l** $k = 5$
  m $c = -2$ **n** $k = -3$ **o** $y = -12$
  p $x = -9$ **q** $t = 5$ **r** $u = 4$
5 **a** $x^2 + 8x + 7$ **b** $u^2 - 5u + 4$
  c $n^2 - 2n - 24$ **d** $w^2 - 13w + 30$
  e $81 - e^2$ **f** $g^2 - 4g - 21$
  g $n^2 - 16$ **h** $b^2 - 4b - 77$
  i $a^2 - 16$ **j** $x^2 + 7x - 30$
  k $y^2 - 4$ **l** $u^2 + u - 56$
  m $a^2 + 14a + 49$ **n** $4 + 4n + n^2$
  o $64 + 16d + d^2$ **p** $16 - 8x + x^2$
  q $100 - 20k + k^2$ **r** $16 - 8a + a^2$
  s $49 + 28h + 4h^2$ **t** $25 - 20g + 4g^2$
  u $81 + 126x + 49x^2$ **v** $25 - 30x + 9x^2$
  w $81 + 72y + 16y^2$ **x** $144b^2 - 24b + 1$
6 **a** $x = 5$ **b** $a = 10$ **c** $n = -3$ **d** $y = 8$
  e $u = 4$ **f** $w = 1$ **g** $x = \frac{1}{2}$ **h** $f = 5$
  i $n = 11$ **j** $d = -2$ **k** $k = -3$ **l** $x = 1\frac{1}{2}$

Page 274 Revising Chapter 4

1 **a** £174   **b** 31·6%   **c** £27·50
2 **a** £70·49   **b** £23·82
3 **a** £947·88   **b** £47·89   **c** 5·3%
4 **a** €897   **b** £207·25   **c** €1·35
5 **a i** £372·06   **ii** £200·34
  b £648·60
6 **a i** £122·40   **ii** £131·40
  b i £145 000   **ii** £23 000
7 **a** £48·52   **b** 77 days

Page 275 Revising Chapter 5

1 **a** 1, 2, 3, 5, 6, 10, 15, 30   **b** 1, g, h, gh
  c 1, 2, 4, 8, y, $2y$, $4y$, $8y$ **d** 1, 3, c, $3c$, c^2, $3c^2$
  e 1, p, p^2, p^3

2 a 8   **b** $2d$ **c** $2y$ **d** 3
e a **f** rt **g** gh **h** $4k^2$

3 a $3(3r-4)$ **b** $8(x+3)$
c $a(x-2t)$ **d** $x(2x+1)$
e $h(5-h)$ **f** $2a(3b-5)$
g $5(a+2b-3c)$ **h** $d^2(d-6)$

4 a $(m-q)(m+q)$
b $(t-r)(t+r)$
c $(4-x)(4+x)$
d $(k-5)(k+5)$
e $(9-n)(9+n)$
f $(3w-1)(3w+1)$
g $(7-3y)(7+3y)$
h $(8a-2b)(8a+2b)$
i $(q-5r)(q+5r)$
j $(10m-11n)(10m+11n)$
k $(5d-12e)(5d+12e)$
l $25(4x-3)(4x+3)$

5 a 1700   **b** 9500
c 48 800   **d** 9

6 a $(d-5)(d-1)$ **b** $(c+3)(c-2)$
c $(m-7)(m+3)$ **d** $(y+2)^2$
e $(r-5)(r+4)$ **f** $(e+3)(e+4)$
g $(3u-1)(u-1)$ **h** $(2f+7)(f+1)$
i $(2b-1)(b-1)$ **j** $(7z+3)(z-2)$
k $(1-2w)(1+w)$ **l** $(1+3y)(1+y)$
m $(1-6w)(1+3w)$ **n** $(2-3e)(3+2e)$
o $(2c+3)(3c-1)$ **p** $(3g-2h)(3g+4h)$

7 a $3(x+4)(x+1)$ **b** $2(m-2)(m-4)$
c $7(1-2d)(1+2d)$ **d** $de(3d+e)$
e $k(1-k)(1+k)$ **f** $2(3n-4)(4n+3)$

8 a $a(b+c)$ **b** $10(x+3y)$
c $3r^2(1-2r)$ **d** $2(h-10)(h+10)$
e $(b-5)(b+2)$ **f** $(x+8)^2$
g $2g(7u+4v)$ **h** $7d(1-2d)$
i $a(k-a)$ **j** $2w(1-4a^3)$
k $2(3x-4y)(3x+4y)$ **l** $pa(a+2)$
m $3(1-3x)(1+3x)$ **n** $(1-b)(1+b)(1+b^2)$
o $a(x+5)^2$ **p** $(mn+3)^2$
q $7(w+4)(w-2)$ **r** $b(x-4)(x+2)$
s $x(x+2y)$ **t** $-v(2u-v)$ or $v(v-2u)$

Page 275 Revising Chapter 6

1 a vertical scale is not linear
b

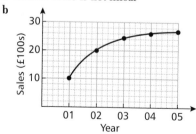

Sales (£100s) vs Year

c no

2 a i card (14), glass (7), plastic (9)
ii card

b i card $(\frac{7}{15})$, glass $(\frac{7}{30})$, plastic $(\frac{3}{10})$
ii $\frac{7}{30}$
iii

Containers

3 a

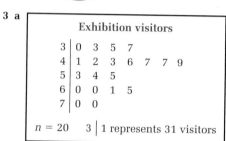

Exhibition visitors

3	0 3 5 7
4	1 2 3 6 7 7 9
5	3 4 5
6	0 0 1 5
7	0 0

$n = 20$ 3 | 1 represents 31 visitors

b

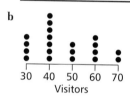

Visitors

c 30, 41·5, 48, 60, 70
d

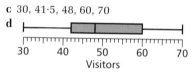

Visitors

4 a/c

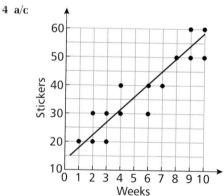

Stickers vs Weeks

b positive correlation
d 35

Page 276 Revising Chapter 7

1 a Q varies directly as the square of r
b U varies directly as x and y
c J varies directly as r and as the square of h and inversely as p

2 a $A \propto m\sqrt{s}$ **b** $Z \propto \dfrac{1}{d^3}$
c $J \propto \dfrac{x^2}{y^2}$

3 a 1, 0·5, 0·25, 0·2, 0·1

b

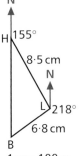

(1, 40)

c y varies inversely as x **d** $y = \dfrac{40}{x}$

4 a 30, 60, 90, 120, 150

b 750, 375, 250, 187·5, 150

5 a $A = kr^2$ **b** 12·5625 **c** 616 cm²

6 a $F = \dfrac{1728}{d^3}$ **b** 27 **c** 3

7 a $N = 2·25LB$ **b** 10 125

8 a $F = \dfrac{kS^2}{D}$ **b** $F = \dfrac{3·2S^2}{D}$

c 32 units **d** 320 m

Page 277 Revising Chapter 8

1 280 m

2 17 cm

3 AB = 6·4, AC = 6·1, BC = 6·3, so A and C are closest

4 20·8 cm

5 no

Page 278 Revising Chapter 9

1 115 km/h

2 40 miles

3 7·5 m/s

4 12 32

5 6·25 minutes

6 a 6·98 m/s, 6·97 m/s, 6·93 m/s

b 0·209 m

7 a i 42 min **ii** 6·5 km

b 9·29 km/h

8 a 1·5 h, 3·75 h **b** 77·1 km/h

9 19·2 mph

10 a 1·8 hours **b** $33\frac{1}{3}$ km/h

c 30 min **d** 30 km

e 60 km/h, 8 km/h (not counting the period when it is stopped)

11 noon 25th December

Page 279 Revising Chapter 10

1 $x = 32°$, $x = 29°$

2 21·4 cm

3 11·9 cm

4 a 90° (a radius bisecting a chord is always at right angles to that chord)

b DE = 1 cm

c 531 cm²

d 81·7 cm

5 a 12·8 cm² **b** 3·7 cm

Page 280 Revising Chapter 11

1 a **b** 1310 m, 28° + 155° = 183°

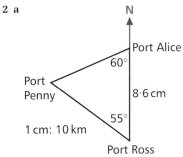

1 cm: 100 m

2 a

Port Alice, 60°, 8·6 cm, Port Penny, 55°, Port Ross

1 cm: 10 km

i 78 km **ii** 82 km

b i 060° **ii** 125°

3 a 10·1 cm **b** 6·0 cm **c** 8·0 cm

d 14·1 cm **e** 22·6°

4 a 751 m **b** 638 m

5 a 67° and 113° (or 68° and 112°)

b 10·7 to 10·9 cm

6 a 3·0 m **b** 5·6 m

7 a 553 m **b** 1054 m

Page 281 Revising Chapter 12

1 a 43·5 **b** 64

2 a i 9·83 cm **ii** 7·5 cm and 12·8 cm

b 9·2 cm **c** 9·45 cm, 7·5 cm, 12·45 cm

d 2·48 cm **e** no

3 a 1, 6, 14, 22, 28, 30

b

$Q_1 = 143$ cm; $Q_2 = 145$ cm; $Q_3 = 147$ cm **c** 2 cm

4 a 3·4 books   **b** 2·46 books
  c No, (no more than 8 needed)
5 a $\frac{1}{13}$ **b** $\frac{1}{26}$ **c** $\frac{5}{13}$
6 $\frac{4}{5}$

Page 282 Revising Chapter 13
1 a i   0, 1, 2, 3, 4   **ii** 4, 3, 2, 1, 0
  b   **c** $x = 2·5, y = 1·5$

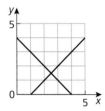

2 $x = 2, y = 1$

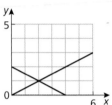

3 a $x = 2, y = 10$
  b $x = 3, y = 6$
  c $x = -1, y = -6$
  d $x = 3, y = 0$
4 a $x = 6, y = 1$
  b $x = -1, y = 3$
  c $x = 2, y = -3$
  d $x = -3, y = -1$
5 a $a = -2, b = 5$
  b $Q = -2P + 5$
6 a $x = 3, y = 2$
  b $x = 2, y = 12$
  c $x = -4, y = 5$
  d $x = -2, y = -2$
7 17 and 35
8 a £15
  b £6
9 a £65
  b £195
10 a 10 g
  b 8 g